THE VOYEUR'S GUIDE

TO EN

IN THE MOVIES

THE VOYEUR'S GUIDE

TO 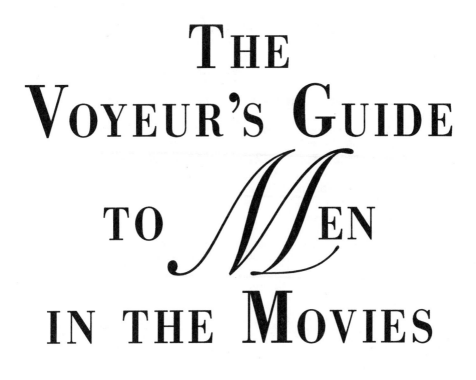EN

IN THE MOVIES

MART MARTIN

CONTEMPORARY
BOOKS

CHICAGO

Library of Congress Cataloging-in-Publication Data

Martin, Mart.
    The voyeur's guide to men in the movies / Mart Martin.
       p.   cm.
    Title on added t.p., inverted: The voyeur's guide to women in the
movies.
    Includes bibliographical references.
    ISBN 0-8092-3642-7
    1. Motion pictures—Anecdotes.   2. Motion pictures—Humor.
3. Motion pictures—Miscellanea.   4. Men in motion pictures.
5. Women in motion pictures.   I. Title.   II. Title: Voyeur's guide
to women in the movies.
PN1994.9.M36   1994
791.43—dc20   94-35121
                                                  CIP

Published by Contemporary Books, Inc.
Two Prudential Plaza, Chicago, Illinois 60601-6790
Manufactured in the United States of America
International Standard Book Number: 0-8092-3642-7

10   9   8   7   6   5   4   3   2   1

Dedicated to
Phillip T. Tran,
the bravest man I know,
who sailed in a small, crowded boat
filled with refugees across the shark-filled South China Sea
to become my dearest friend and guardian angel

CONTENTS

"The only way to approach the truth about Hollywood
is with a sense of humor."
— George Cukor

PREFACE

In assembling this book, I have purposely made no distinction between *cinema* films and *telefilms*, or those productions made for TV.
Each year sees more and more of the latter appearing, with many of
them also receiving a theatrical release overseas after appearing on
American television.

Some avid cinemaphiles may be offended by my lack of distinction. So be it. Besides, John McCarty preceded me in doing this,
when he pierced this now almost-artificial barrier in his 1985 book,
Psychos. Keeping one of the many film review collections handily
available while perusing this guide might provide some comfort to
those readers so offended. Plus, those publications contain valuable
information about ratings, running times, and release dates, which I
have chosen to omit.

This book also makes little if no comment—except in a humorous vein—about the quality of the films mentioned. In truth, the
quality varies considerably. The films noted here range from Excellent to Absolutely Excruciating for a viewer to watch. I leave such
"reviews" to the capable likes of Leonard Maltin and the others,
whose guides serve that purpose most admirably. But a cautionary
note must be added. In many instances, there is a wide variance
between their opinions. Astute cinema voyeurs soon learn to form
their own personal opinions, naturally after having actually viewed
a film.

One of the real pleasures in assembling information of this type
is the friends who help with the endeavor. My sincere thanks to Joe
Campbell, Scott Lee, Bob Stoll, Chuck Thompson, and Frank Wright.
I appreciate the support and enthusiasm you've shown me, and hope
this book meets your expectations.

The final words of thanks are for my agent and my editor. My

literary agent Mitch Rose personifies competence. That, combined
with his always encouraging voice, makes any contact with him most
pleasurable. As for Gene Brissie, my editor, I was fortunate in being
able to work with him—for he is one of the recognized masters of
his trade.

INTRODUCTION

Once upon a time I reviewed films—a perfectly respectable undertaking. Then, my attention got distracted by, shall we say, all the *nasty stuff* happening in those films. Naked butts scampered across the screen, causing me to promptly forget the plot. The most horrid creatures imaginable suddenly erupted from unsuspecting stomachs, as I slid lower in my seat, squealing over the special effects. Leading ladies vomited, and my mind drifted while I remembered how someone else devoured a cockroach with relish in another film.

Suddenly, it became impossible for me to concentrate on any particular film. All at once, I had ceased being a reviewer. I had become something else: a *voyeur*. When I watched a film, I wiggled in anticipation of what titillating thing I was going to see next. And Hollywood didn't disappoint me. Wondering if I'd missed anything important, I started viewing some of the older films again. This time what I saw in those films was enlightening. All of these *nasty* things had always been present in films. These more recent films weren't doing anything new. I merely hadn't paid close enough attention to the older films the first time around. Now, I was absolutely hooked. I truly had become a genuine cinema voyeur.

Film noir, new wave, avant-garde, psychodramas, made-for-TVers. If I wanted to read a study of the genre, or pore through a comprehensive listing of casting credits, or even peruse a critical collection of film essays, all I had to do was reach for one of the informative guides on the market. But my addiction, you see, was for something far, far different. And no guide existed that would tell me what I wanted to know.

Ever seen a naked butt scamper across the screen of a film you were watching and wonder where else you'd seen it? Or watched an actor gobble a cockroach and been curious about which other actors had been brave enough to perform the same stunt? Want to see your favorite actor prance around in his black briefs? Well, if so, welcome to *The Voyeur's Guide to Men in the Movies*. Forget film plots, ignore technical and performance artistry, and don't even give a thought to technique. Don't try to look for critical ratings, cast credits, or scholarly treatises in here. If that's the type of information you seek, then there are plenty of other excellent, informative references available. Exactly what will you find in this guide? Frankly put, the cheap thrills. The naughty shenanigans. The unsavory things the other guides overlooked (and your mother warned you that polite people ignored). Let's just say that this guide is full of things a true cinema voyeur looks for and relishes.

If I've made mistakes and omissions, don't curse me. Send them in, and I'll try and include them in the next edition.

One final comment about this guide. Because a voyeur's thrill comes from peeking, don't try and "read" this guide from cover to cover. It's not that kind of book. Instead, *peek at it*. Flip it open anywhere, any page, and take a peek. Go ahead; it's *gratifying*.

THE ACADEMY AWARDS: THIRTEEN DISTINCTIVE CATEGORIES

"Gentlemen of the Academy and fellow suckers,
I got one of these once for a best performance.
They don't mean a thing. People get 'em every year.
What I want's a special award—something nobody else can get.
I want a statue for the worst performance of the year."
—Fredric March, *A Star Is Born*

Presented each April, those little golden statues are meant to represent a unique achievement: the best performance by a film actor in a given year. Even so, the list of winners still can be divided into distinctive categories.

Blatantly Biographical

George Arliss	*Disraeli* ('29-30)
Charles Laughton	*Private Life of Henry VIII* ('32-33)
Paul Muni	*The Story of Louis Pasteur* ('36)
Spencer Tracy	*Boys Town* ('38)
Gary Cooper	*Sergeant York* ('41)
James Cagney	*Yankee Doodle Dandy* ('42)
Yul Brynner	*The King and I* ('56)
Paul Scofield	*A Man for All Seasons* ('66)
Ben Kingsley	*Gandhi* ('82)
F. Murray Abraham	*Amadeus* ('84)
Daniel Day-Lewis	*My Left Foot* ('89)
Jeremy Irons	*Reversal of Fortune* ('90)

Blue-Collar Busters

Marlon Brando	*On the Waterfront* ('54)
Ernest Borgnine	*Marty* ('55)
Sidney Poitier	*Lilies of the Field* ('63)
Robert Duvall	*Tender Mercies* ('83)

Boozers and Mental Cases

Ray Milland	*The Lost Weekend* ('45)
Ronald Colman	*A Double Life* ('47)
Cliff Robertson	*Charly* ('68)
Jack Nicholson	*One Flew over the Cuckoo's Nest* ('75)
Dustin Hoffman	*Rain Man* ('88)

Campy Classics

Fredric March	*Dr. Jekyll and Mr. Hyde* ('31-32)
Spencer Tracy	*Captains Courageous* ('37)
Laurence Olivier	*Hamlet* ('48)
Broderick Crawford	*All the King's Men* ('49)
Jose Ferrer	*Cyrano de Bergerac* ('50)
Charlton Heston	*Ben-Hur* ('59)

Courtroom Capers

Lionel Barrymore	*A Free Soul* ('30-31)
Maximilian Schell	*Judgment at Nuremburg* ('61)
Gregory Peck	*To Kill a Mockingbird* ('62)
Dustin Hoffman	*Kramer vs. Kramer* ('79)
Tom Hanks	*Philadelphia* ('93)

Cowboys

Warner Baxter	*In Old Arizona* ('28-29)
Gary Cooper	*High Noon* ('52)
Lee Marvin	*Cat Ballou* ('65)
John Wayne	*True Grit* ('69)

Crotchety Codgers

Art Carney	*Harry and Tonto* ('74)
Henry Fonda	*On Golden Pond* ('81)
Al Pacino	*Scent of a Woman* ('92)

Fourth Estaters

Clark Gable	*It Happened One Night* ('34)
James Stewart	*The Philadelphia Story* ('40)
Peter Finch	*Network* ('76)

Heroes and Heels

Paul Lukas	*Watch on the Rhine* ('43)
Humphrey Bogart	*The African Queen* ('51)
David Niven	*Separate Tables* ('58)
Jack Lemmon	*Save the Tiger* ('73)
Richard Dreyfuss	*The Goodbye Girl* ('77)
Paul Newman	*The Color of Money* ('86)
Michael Douglas	*Wall Street* ('87)

Inside/Outside the Law

Victor McLaglen	*The Informer* ('35)
Rod Steiger	*In the Heat of the Night* ('67)
Gene Hackman	*The French Connection* ('71)
Marlon Brando	*The Godfather* ('72)
William Hurt	*Kiss of the Spider Woman* ('85)
Anthony Hopkins	*The Silence of the Lambs* ('91)

Macho Militarists

Emil Jannings	*The Last Command* ('27-28)
Fredric March	*The Best Years of Our Lives* ('46)
William Holden	*Stalag 17* ('53)
Alec Guinness	*The Bridge on the River Kwai* ('57)
George C. Scott	*Patton* ('70)
Bruce Dern	*Coming Home* ('78)

Pudgy Pugilists

Wallace Beery	*The Champ* ('31-32)
Robert De Niro	*Raging Bull* ('80)

Religionists and Intelligentsia

Robert Donat	*Goodbye, Mr. Chips* ('39)
Bing Crosby	*Going My Way* ('44)
Burt Lancaster	*Elmer Gantry* ('60)
Rex Harrison	*My Fair Lady* ('64)

THE BLACK OSCARS

The Academy of Motion Picture Arts and Sciences certainly hasn't shown a propensity for awarding its Oscars to Black actors. Since the awards began, there have been only three Black male winners and a grand total of only fourteen nominations for Black actors, with most of those in the Best Supporting Actor category. Beginning with the 1980s however, Black actors have been more likely to be nominated than in the past. (BA = Best Actor, BSA = Best Supporting Actor)

Sidney Poitier	*The Defiant Ones* ('58), BA
	Lilies of the Field ('63), BA—winner
Rupert Crosse	*The Reivers* ('69), BSA
James Earl Jones	*The Great White Hope* ('70), BA
Paul Winfield	*Sounder* ('72), BA
Howard E. Rollins	*Ragtime* ('81), BSA
Louis Gossett Jr.	*An Officer and a Gentleman* ('82), BSA—winner
Adolph Caesar	*A Soldier's Story* ('84), BSA
Dexter Gordon	*Round Midnight* ('86), BA
Morgan Freeman	*Street Smart* ('87), BSA
Denzel Washington	*Cry Freedom* ('87), BSA
Morgan Freeman	*Driving Miss Daisy* ('89), BA
Denzel Washington	*Glory* ('89), BSA—winner
Denzel Washington	*Malcolm X* ('92), BA
Laurence Fishburne	*What's Love Got to Do with It* ('93), BA

Quick Quiz

Who was the only white actor ever to receive a Best Actor nomination for portraying a Black? **Sir Laurence Olivier**, for the title role in *Othello* ('65).

What Best Actor winner is buried in Arlington National Cemetery, next to boxer Joe Louis? **Lee Marvin**, who won for *Cat Ballou* ('65).

GOING FOR THE GOLD, MISSING THE GLITTER

These guys went for the gold—Olympic gold, or silver—and won it. But their attempts to translate that gold into screen glitter was only marginal at best.

Bruce Bennett	*Mildred Pierce* ('45)
Larry (Buster) Crabbe	*King of the Jungle* ('33)
Bruce Jenner	*Can't Stop the Music* ('80)
Rafer Johnson	*The Lion* ('63)
Jean-Claude Killy	*Snow Job* ('72)
Greg Louganis	*Dirty Laundry* ('87)
Bob Mathias	*The Minotaur* ('61)
Glenn Morris	*Tarzan's Revenge* ('38)
Harold ("Oddjob") Sakata	*Goldfinger* ('64)
Johnny Weissmuller	*Swamp Fire* ('46)

ADDICTS

THE LUSH LIFE

"I've had hangovers before, but this time even my hair hurts."
—Rock Hudson, *Pillow Talk*

Give them a Scotch and soda or maybe an extra large jigger of gin. But once they begin drinking, one isn't enough, because they can't stop. Let's bend an elbow in salute to the lushes and the alcoholics.

Albert Finney	*Under the Volcano* ('84)
Van Heflin	*Johnny Eager* ('41)
David Janssen	*A Sensitive, Passionate Man* ('77)
Jack Lemmon	*The Days of Wine and Roses* ('62)
Lee Marvin	*Cat Ballou* ('65)
Ray Milland	*The Lost Weekend* ('45)
Dudley Moore	*Arthur* ('81)
Paul Newman	*The Verdict* ('82)
Jack Nicholson	*Ironweed* ('87)
Mickey Rourke	*Barfly* ('87)

DRUGGED UP

"You know, since I started taking lithium, I feel more sensible than this month's *Good Housekeeping*."
—Kelly Bishop, *An Unmarried Woman*

Cocaine, heroin, marijuana—even an addictive imaginary drug produced by a monster—these guys are hooked on the hard stuff.

Michael Chiklis	*Wired* ('89)
Tommy Chong	*Up in Smoke* ('78)
Chuck Connors	*Death in Small Doses* ('57)
Matt Dillon	*Drugstore Cowboy* ('89)
Robert Downey Jr.	*Less than Zero* ('87)
Michael J. Fox	*Bright Lights, Big City* ('88)
Rick Herbst	*Brain Damage* ('88)
Dustin Hoffman	*Lenny* ('74)
Stacy Keach	*Watched!* ('72)
Michael Keaton	*Clean and Sober* ('88)
Harvey Keitel	*The Bad Lieutenant* ('92)

Cheech Marin	*Cheech & Chong's Nice Dreams* ('81)
James Mason	*Bigger than Life* ('56)
Sal Mineo	*The Gene Krupa Story* ('59)
Cameron Mitchell	*Monkey on My Back* ('57)
Don Murray	*A Hatful of Rain* ('57)
Al Pacino	*Panic in Needle Park* ('71)
Jason Patric	*Rush* ('91)
Anthony Perkins	*Edge of Sanity* ('89)
Richard Pryor	*Lady Sings the Blues* ('72)
John Putch	*Angel Dusted* ('81)
Steve Railsback	*Torchlight* ('84)
Frank Sinatra	*The Man with the Golden Arm* ('55)
Philip-Michael Thomas	*Death Drug* ('78)
Dennis Weaver	*Cocaine: One Man's Seduction* ('83)
James Woods	*The Boost* ('88)

ANIMAL LOVERS

"Yankee dog! Prepare to die! You come to my village, steal my wife,
rape my goat. Prepare to die!"
—Tommy Chong, *Far Out Man*

Zoophilia—sexual contact with animals—remains the strongest taboo
for the cinema. While barriers against incest, homosexuality, and
pedophilia have all fallen, those against depicting animal lovers in
films remain, except for rare screen treatments.

Animal Lovers ('72)—A truly repulsive film, which actually was shown in some
American theaters, although they usually were quickly raided by local police.
The film featured both males and females having sex with animals, including
scenes of a pig being fellated and a horse being masturbated.

End of the Road ('70)—A man has sex with a chicken.

Everything You Always Wanted to Know About Sex ('72)—In one of the episodes in Woody Allen's comedy, Gene Wilder discusses his love for a female sheep with a psychiatrist, who later conducts his own affair with the animal.

Futz ('69)—The cinematic version of Tom Horgan's late '60s mild off-Broadway hit seemed to have no plot, except a man is in love with his pig.

Night on Earth ('91)—In one segment, Roman cab driver Robert Benigni describes his sexual exploits with a sheep, among other "things" he's made love with, to his passenger, a conservative and shocked priest.

Padre Padrone ('77)—This Italian film traces the difficult lives of young Sardinian shepherds. As part of portraying their loneliness, sexual intercourse with a sheep, a donkey, and some geese is shown.

Walker ('88)—After a group of William Walker's mercenaries has entered a small Nicaraguan village, they rush up to a sheep pen. While they clamor up the fence into the pen, the sex-starved men begin pulling at their clothes and identifying the particular sheep each one wants.

Honorable Mentions

Rex Harrison—*Doctor Dolittle* ('67)—Because he only *talked* to the animals!

Unknown Actor—*The Great Muppet Caper* ('81)—Because he made love to Miss Piggy.

EMU-LATED SEX

In 1992, the *New York Post* reported that **Tony Huston**, son of director **John Huston**, had been making some unusual movies. According to the *Post*, Tony had shown his friends a five-minute video of himself having simulated sex with an emu. Huston's plot was simple: He takes a swim in a pool, falls asleep on a lawn, then is attacked by a horny bird. When he suddenly wakes up, this emu is on top of him. One source was reported as saying, "It is actually quite tasteful and amusing. It plays on your imagination."

FULL OF BULL

"I could dance with you until the cows come home. On second thought, I'd rather dance with the cows."

—Groucho Marx, *Duck Soup*

Olé . . . the matador, the toreador. Hot-blooded, impulsive, yet calm and calculating enough to withstand the fury of a charging bull.

Carlos Arruza	*Arruza* ('71)
Cantinflas	*Around the World in 80 Days* ('56)
Eddie Cantor	*The Kid from Spain* ('32)
Patrick Catalifo	*Sand and Blood* ('87)
Arturo de Cordova	*Masquerade in Mexico* ('45)
Robert Evans	*The Sun Also Rises* ('57)
Mel Ferrer	*The Brave Bulls* ('51)
Stan Laurel	*The Bullfighters* ('45)
Miguel Mateo Miguelin	*The Moment of Truth* ('64)
Tyrone Power	*Blood and Sand* ('41)
Anthony Quinn	*The Magnificent Matador* ('55)
Gustavo Rojo	*The Miracle* ('59)
Gilbert Roland	*The Bullfighter and the Lady* ('51)
Peter Sellers	*The Bobo* ('67)
Robert Stack	*The Bullfighter and the Lady* ('51)
Tommy Steele	*Tommy the Toreador* ('60)
Rudolph Valentino	*Blood and Sand* ('22)

AVANT-GARDE: TWO PIECES FOR CONNOISSEURS

"Of course, as far as I'm concerned, art is just a guy's name."
—Rock Hudson, *Magnificent Obsession*

Avant-garde, "off the beaten track," but well worth viewing to the connoisseur of male flesh in the cinema.

Dinah East

An independently made film released in the early '70s, *Dinah East* has now almost disappeared from circulation. It's a well-made film with an interesting story and credible performances, and even sports a catchy theme song, "I Want to Thank You, Alexander Graham Bell."

Dinah East begins with the discovery—at her death—that one of filmdom's greatest sex symbols was not a woman, but a man. Told in flashback from that point, the film traces the efforts of a young man to break into motion pictures by working as an extra. One particular day, he discovers that the studio is hiring only women. Desperate for work, he rushes home to disguise himself as a woman and returns to the studio where he is admitted by a friendly studio guard, who suspects the ruse but admires his tenacity.

Events happen fast—as they always do in films about people trying to break into the movies—and soon the young man, still disguised as a woman, has moved to second leads, then on to starring parts, but now as a woman named Dinah East.

Forced to lead a life as a "real" woman to preserve the career he has created, Dinah East is trapped in a web of lies. East is victimized by a trusted lawyer, even adopts a child, and eventually finds true love with a heterosexual former boxer, who doesn't care when he discovers that Dinah is a man. Their relationship endures until Dinah dies suddenly of a heart attack.

The film ends with Dinah's funeral. By that time, the story of the "real" Dinah has been splashed across the papers as another Hollywood scandal. One by one, the few attendees at the funeral—the studio guard, the adopted son, the lover—meet and reveal to each other how knowing Dinah East, and the truth about the person behind the legend of the sex symbol, changed their lives.

The Fourth Man

The Fourth Man, by Paul Verhoeven and released in 1979, is an unusual—and highly erotic—love story and thriller. It's full of religious symbolism, even featuring a scene in a church of fantasized sex with a man on a cross posed like Christ.

The plot revolves around a bisexual, alcoholic writer who meets a mysterious woman who keeps taking pictures of him. She also has a sexy boyfriend, whom the writer has briefly glimpsed on a train and sexually desires. Convinced by the writer to go fetch her boyfriend to her house for some sexual instruction by him, the woman leaves the writer alone in her house. While she's gone, he discovers she's a woman with three past dark secrets.

When she returns with the boyfriend, the writer is torn between his desire for the younger man and trying to convince him of the woman's past. It's apparent to the writer that one of the two of them will be the fourth man, but which one?

THESE GUYS HAVE BALLS

"Oh, this is the happiest day of my life!
I think my testicles are dropping."
—Steve Martin, *Dirty Rotten Scoundrels*

Baseballs, that is. Pitching, slugging, or sliding into home plate to tie up the score in the big game, these guys sure look good in—or out— of their team's baseball uniform.

Eddie Albert	*Ladies Day* ('43)
William Bendix	*The Babe Ruth Story* ('48)
Tom Berenger	*Major League* ('89)
Joe E. Brown	*Elmer the Great* ('33)
Gary Cooper	*Pride of the Yankees* ('42)
Kevin Costner	*Bull Durham* ('88)
Dan Dailey	*The Pride of St. Louis* ('52)
Robert De Niro	*Bang the Drum Slowly* ('73)
Michael Douglas	*It's My Turn* ('80)
John Goodman	*The Babe* ('92)
Mark Harmon	*Stealing Home* ('88)
Tab Hunter	*Damn Yankees* ('58)
Tommy Lee Jones	*Cobb* ('94)
Ray Liotta	*Field of Dreams* ('89)

Mickey Mantle	*Safe at Home!* ('62)
Roger Maris	*Safe at Home!* ('62)
Ray Milland	*It Happens Every Spring* ('49)
Michael Moriarty	*Bang the Drum Slowly* ('73)
Michael O'Keefe	*The Slugger's Wife* ('85)
Anthony Perkins	*Fear Strikes Out* ('57)
William Petersen	*Long Gone* ('87)
Ronald Reagan	*The Winning Team* ('52)
Robert Redford	*The Natural* ('84)
Tim Robbins	*Bull Durham* ('88)
Jackie Robinson	*The Jackie Robinson Story* ('50)
Tom Selleck	*Mr. Baseball* ('92)
Charlie Sheen	*Major League* ('89); *Eight Men Out* ('88)
Frank Sinatra	*Take Me Out to the Ball Game* ('49)
James Stewart	*The Stratton Story* ('49)
Billy Dee Williams	*The Bingo Long Traveling All-Stars and Motor Kings* ('76)

THE FOOTBALL HEROES

"Was it the Rose Bowl he made his famous run?" "It was the
Punch Bowl, honey. The cut-glass Punch Bowl."
—Jack Carson and Madeleine Sherwood,
Cat on a Hot Tin Roof

They call him Mr. Touchdown, the great big football hero. He runs, he
passes, he catches the ball, he scores . . . on the field and off.

Alan Alda	*Paper Lion* ('68)
Sean Austin	*Rudy* ('93)
Scott Bakula	*Necessary Roughness* ('91)
Warren Beatty	*Heaven Can Wait* ('78)
Joe E. Brown	*Maybe It's Love* ('30)
Johnny Mack Brown	*70,000 Witnesses* ('32)

Gary Busey	*Bloodsport* ('73); *Bear* ('84)
Tony Curtis	*The All-American Boy* ('53)
Mac Davis	*Semi-Tough* ('77)
John Derek	*Saturday's Hero* ('51)
Douglas Fairbanks Jr.	*Forward Pass* ('29)
Charlie Farrell	*Fighting Youth* ('35)
Van Heflin	*Saturday's Heroes* ('37)
Charlton Heston	*Number One* ('69)
Rock Hudson	*Peggy* ('50)
Sam Jones	*Flash Gordon* ('80)
Burt Lancaster	*Jim Thorpe—All American* ('51)
Peter Lawford	*Good News* ('47)
Jerry Lewis	*That's My Boy* ('51)
Victor Mature	*Easy Living* ('49)
Kevin McCarthy	*Death of a Salesman* ('51)
Nick Nolte	*North Dallas Forty* ('79)
Jack Oakie	*Rise and Shine* ('41)
Hugh O'Brien	*A Punt, a Pass and a Prayer* ('53)
Pat O'Brien	*Knute Rockne, All American* ('40)
Ronald Reagan	*Knute Rockne, All American* ('40)
Burt Reynolds	*Semi-Tough* ('77); *The Longest Yard* ('74)
Craig Sheffer	*The Program* ('93)
Marshall Thompson	*The Rose Bowl Story* ('52)
Ken Wahl	*The Taking of Beverly Hills* ('91)
Damon Wayans	*The Last Boy Scout* ('91)
Henry Winkler	*The One and Only* ('78)

BALLS . . . BUT NO ASS

Check out **Frank Sinatra**'s sailor suit in *Take Me Out to the Ball Game* ('49). Rumor was it had to be padded in the butt to give him a more shapely ass.

NO BALLS

The Last Imperial Eunuch, a 1990 China-Hong Kong production, tells the tale of the long reign of Xu Ci (Tz'u-hsi), the dowager empress of China, as seen through the eyes of her chief eunuch, a castrated male.

BATHING BEAUTIES

"I ain't dirty. I washed my face and hands before I came. I did."
—Wendy Hiller, *Pygmalion*

It's not often that the boys lower their bodies into a bathtub, but when they do, the bubbles fly! If one of them needed his back scrubbed, would you oblige?

Marlon Brando	*The Missouri Breaks* ('76)
Keith Carradine	*An Almost Perfect Affair* ('79)
James Coburn	*Pat Garrett and Billy the Kid* ('73)
Clint Eastwood	*High Plains Drifter* ('73)
Emilio Estevez	*Wisdom* ('86)
Richard Harris	*Camelot* ('67)
Wings Hauser	*Deadly Force* ('83)
Dustin Hoffman	*Little Big Man* ('70)
Dennis Hopper	*The American Dreamer* ('71)
Rock Hudson	*Pillow Talk* ('59)
Mick Jagger	*Performance* ('70)
Paul Newman	*The Secret War of Harry Frigg* ('68)
Peter O'Toole	*Becket* ('64)
Michael Paré	*The Women's Club* ('87)
Burt Reynolds	*Rent-a-Cop* ('88)

George Segal	*The Owl and the Pussycat* ('70)
Donald Sutherland	*Start the Revolution Without Me* ('70)
Michael Woods	*Lady Beware* ('87)

COME ON GUYS! LET'S HIT THE SHOWERS!

"I hate cold showers. They stimulate me,
then I don't know what to do."
—Oscar Levant, *Humoresque*

All right! This is where those hunky, hot guys hit the showers. Each of the following films contains shower scenes well worth watching, either for the male views presented or for what happens while they're showering.

The Doubly Bubbly Big Winner

Gimme an F ('84)—**Stephen Shellen**, a handsome summer camp counselor, does a long combination strip-tease, disco-dance, and gymnastic routine in a steamy shower. As the stud struts his stuff, he's being watched by a group of girls. They've gathered around outside and peep through cracks in the walls trying to see him naked.

The Soapy Bubbles of Honorable Mention

The Best Little Whorehouse in Texas ('82)	*Number One* ('69)
Breathless ('83)	*The Odd Angry Shot* ('79)
Can't Stop the Music ('80)	*Once Bitten* ('85)
The Class of '63 ('73)	*The Onion Field* ('79)
Drive, He Said ('72)	*Pixote* ('81)
Fear No Evil ('81)	*Running Brave* ('83)
Fortune and Men's Eyes ('71)	*Semi-Tough* ('77)
Hollywood Hot Tubs ('84)	*Slapshot* ('77)
if. . . . ('68)	*Spring Break* ('83)
The Lords of Discipline ('83)	*Tomboy* ('85)
Midnight Express ('78)	*Zapped!* ('82)
Not for Publication ('84)	

BEAT ME, WHIP ME

"When you're slapped you'll take it and like it."
—Humphrey Bogart, *The Maltese Falcon*

Hardly a male star with a shred of sex appeal has escaped the cinematic whip. Tied up seminaked, taut muscles glistening, his bold
body now passive—indeed, spread-eagled—our hero has his very
manhood threatened. Being *muy macho*, he cringes and bears his
fate. Finally, his ordeal's over, but bloody whelps cover his sweaty
back. As the camera gazes into his eyes, we see his determination
for revenge.

Marlon Brando	*One-Eyed Jacks* ('61)
Brad Davis	*Midnight Express* ('78)
Errol Flynn	*Captain Blood* ('35)
Richard Harris	*Mutiny on the Bounty* ('62)
Louis Jourdan	*Anne of the Indies* ('51)
Alan Ladd	*Two Years Before the Mast* ('46)
Victor Mature	*Samson and Delilah* ('49)
Elvis Presley	*Jailhouse Rock* ('57)
Rudolph Valentino	*Son of the Sheik* ('26)
Robert Wagner	*The True Story of Jesse James* ('57)
Patrick Warburton	*Dragonard* ('88)

SLAVE TRADERS

Nobody can really wield a whip or mete out punishment like a good
old-fashioned slave trader or a white slave trader.

Walter Huston	*Kongo* ('32)
Ray Milland	*Slavers* ('78)
Vincent Price	*House of 1,000 Dolls* ('67)
Peter Ustinov	*Ashanti* ('79)
Edward Woodward	*Uncle Tom's Cabin* ('87)

In *My Wicked, Wicked Ways*, his autobiography, **Errol Flynn** claimed that he once actually had worked as a slave trader.

THE WHIPPING EXPERT AWARD

Awarded to **Al "Lash" LaRue**, for his expertise on the bullwhip in *Mark of the Lash* ('48).

IT'S DELIGHTFUL, IT'S DELOVELY—IT'S A DE SADE

"When I was in Catholic school, I'd have visions of a guy dressed as a priest, wearing a Chicago Bears helmet, spanking me."
—Kyra Sedgwick, *Pyrates*

Keir Dullea	*De Sade* ('69)
Klaus Kinski	*Marquis de Sade: Justine* ('68)
Patrick Magee	*The Assassination and Persecution of Jean-Paul Marat as Performed by the Inmates of the Asylum at Charenton under the Direction of the Marquis de Sade* ('66)
Jack Palance	*Justine* ('69)
Michel Piccoli	*The Milky Way* ('70)

TORTURED, BUT STILL HUNKY

In one of the more brutal torture scenes enacted by a star, **Mel Gibson** in *Lethal Weapon* ('87) is trussed up, arms above his head, and severely beaten. Then his shirt is stripped off and he's hosed down with water, before electrodes from an electric battery are attached to his nipples for a shocking finale. Mel may be truly tortured, but he's still hunky enough to whip the bad guy by the film's end!

OUCH! THAT HURTS!

La Maîtresse (French, '78), a sadomasochistic cult film with **Gerard Depardieu** and **Bulle Ogier**, includes a truly painful scene in which a real-life dominatrix actually nails a man's penis to a wooden board, drawing blood.

BIG DADDIES

"Big Daddy! Now what makes him so big? His big heart? His big
belly? Or, his big money?"
                                —Paul Newman, *Cat on a Hot Tin Roof*

Big daddies . . . jelly-roll honeybuns . . . tons of fun . . . lard-ass
loverboys. Call them flabby, call them tubby; they have their admirers.
For the chubby chasers, here's some oversized big boys to chew the
fat over.

Joe Don Baker	*The Killing Time* ('87)
John Belushi	*Continental Divide* ('81)
Robert Blake	*Second-Hand Hearts* ('80)
Ernest Borgnine	*Marty* ('55)
Peter Boyle	*Joe* ('70)
Marlon Brando	*Apocalypse Now* ('79)
John Candy	*Uncle Buck* ('89)
James Coco	*Only When I Laugh* ('81)
Broderick Crawford	*Born Yesterday* ('50)
Dom DeLuise	*Fatso* ('80)
Jackie Gleason	*The Hustler* ('61)
Gene Hackman	*Twice in a Lifetime* ('85)
Burl Ives	*Cat on a Hot Tin Roof* ('58)
James Earl Jones	*Claudine* ('74)
George Kennedy	*Cool Hand Luke* ('67)
Walter Matthau	*House Calls* ('78)
Zero Mostel	*The Producers* ('68)
Rod Steiger	*In the Heat of the Night* ('67)
Topol	*Fiddler on the Roof* ('71)
Peter Ustinov	*Hot Millions* ('68)
M. Emmett Walsh	*Blood Simple* ('84)

Jack Warden	*Shampoo* ('75)
Orson Welles	*The Lady from Shanghai* ('48)
Jack Weston	*The Ritz* ('76)

BIG SCREEN BODY PARTS

"Young man, let's see your legs. . . . No. No. No. No. New rule
tonight: Every man here has got to show his legs. . . . Come on,
come on. The other one, too."
—Rosalind Russell, *Picnic*

The advent of the big screen presented us with the opportunity to examine close up the bodies of our favorite male stars. Too often, the result was ridiculous, especially when spread across a huge Technicolor screen.

The Beastmaster ('82) —During one scene, Marc Singer, as the Beastmaster garbed in a tight loincloth, squats down. As he does, the camera moves in for a close-up—which fills the entire screen with Singer's crotch, with his pubic hairs curling from beneath the skimpy, bulging loincloth.

Fandango ('85)—To alert a friend not to jump from an airplane, Kevin Costner and two buddies strip to their underpants and arrange their clothes on the ground in a message. In one of the camera angles used in the scene, the camera is positioned between Kevin's knees, angled upward toward his body. The only purpose of the shot appears to be to present Kevin's basket on a full screen for his hungry fans. The length at which the camera remains in the crotch shot only makes the whole situation more bizarre.

King of Kings ('61)—When Jeffrey Hunter, as Jesus, is hung on the cross, the camera pans in close for a wide-screen view of the Savior's suffering face. As part of the close-up, the viewer is treated to Hunter's armpits splayed across the big screen. It is disconcerting to note that they have been shaven.

The Prize ('63)—As the camera focuses on Paul Newman's chest, a doctor gives Paul, who's just had a heart attack, an injection. Newman's nipple, with a few hairs circling it, encompasses the whole screen and peers out at the viewer like a gigantic, misshapen pizza.

DID JOHN RISE TO THE OCCASION?

Alfred Hitchcock claimed **John Gavin** played the opening bed scene in *Psycho* ('60) with an erection. According to the director, it seemed that initially Gavin was acting wooden over being bare-chested. Then, Hitch discussed the matter quietly with costar Janet Leigh. When shooting on the scene resumed, Leigh supposedly used some finger touching in the right places to help Gavin overcome his shyness and to help get his libido—and acting—up to Hitchcock's expectations.

BIOS

"As an actor, no one could touch him. As a human being,
no one wanted to touch him."
—Walter Matthau, *The Sunshine Boys*

Hollywood films the biographies of its own. Sometimes they're accurate; sometimes the end product is overembellished for dramatic appeal.

Maurice Bernard	*Lucy and Desi: Before the Laughter* ('91)
Keefe Brasselle	*The Eddie Cantor Story* ('53)
James Brolin	*Gable and Lombard* ('76)
James Cagney	*Man of a Thousand Faces* ('57)
Michael Chiklis	*Wired* ('89)
Charles Dance	*Good Morning, Babylon* ('87)
Ray Danton	*The George Raft Story* ('61)
Anthony Dexter	*Valentino* ('51)
Robert Downey Jr.	*Chaplin* ('92)
Errol Flynn	*Too Much, Too Soon* ('58)
Buddy Hackett	*Bud and Lou* ('78)

Anthony Higgins	*Darlings of the Gods* ('90)
Harvey Korman	*Bud and Lou* ('78)
Jason Scott Lee	*Dragon: The Bruce Lee Story* ('93)
Hsiao Lung	*The Bruce Lee Story* ('74)
Rudolph Nureyev	*Valentino* ('77)
Donald O'Connor	*The Buster Keaton Story* ('57)
Kevin O'Connor	*Bogie* ('80)
Larry Parks	*The Jolson Story* ('46); *Jolson Sings Again* ('49)
Will Rogers Jr.	*The Story of Will Rogers* ('52)
Rod Steiger	*W. C. Fields and Me* ('76)

STAR TRASH

The untold "story" behind the headlines . . . star trash or stars trashed? Tinseltown rubs off the glitter to take a peep at what's underneath.

Victor Garber	*Liberace: Behind the Music* ('88)
Thomas Ian Griffith	*Rock Hudson* ('90)
Duncan Regehr	*My Wicked, Wicked Ways* ('85)
Andrew Robinson	*Liberace* ('88)

BLACK LEATHER KNIGHTS

"My, what unusual leather pants. They look like cowboy chaps. Oh, they are cowboy chaps. Well . . . I was just thinking . . . they look like cowboy chaps."

—Jack Weston, *The Ritz*

The men of black leather, those dark knights of brooding and mystery, are sensuous, intriguing, and frightening.

Hart Bochner	*Apartment Zero* ('88)
Marlon Brando	*The Wild One* ('54)
Colin Campbell	*The Leather Boys* ('63)
Pierre Clementi	*Belle de Jour* ('67)
James Dean	*Rebel Without a Cause* ('55)
Michael Douglas	*Black Rain* ('89)
Peter Fonda	*The Wild Angels* ('66)
Mel Gibson	*The Road Warrior* ('81)
Steve Guttenberg	*Don't Tell Her It's Me* ('90)
Rutger Hauer	*Spetters* ('80); *Dandelions* ('74)
Michael Keaton	*Batman* ('89)
Perry King	*The Lords of Flatbush* ('74)
Christopher Lee	*Serial* ('80)
Paul Le Mat	*Easy Wheels* ('89)
Steve Martin	*Little Shop of Horrors* ('86)
Ryan O'Neal	*Partners* ('82)
Al Pacino	*Cruising* ('80)
Sylvester Stallone	*The Lords of Flatbush* ('74)
Henry Winkler	*The Lords of Flatbush* ('74)

BONDMANIA

"Bond . . . James Bond."
—Sean Connery, *Dr. No*

With those memorable words, Connery first introduced himself to moviegoers as Ian Fleming's super secret agent and launched the most successful series in motion picture history. The appeal of these movies transcends the sex barrier: males envied Bond's curvaceous women, his multitude of "toys," and his fast cars, while women appreciated his debonair manner and ultrasophisticated lifestyle.

Six actors brought Bond to life on the screen, yet viewers never were treated to a nude view, not even from the rear. Connery frequently bared his hairy chest, yet Roger Moore—who began to show his age in the role—rarely followed Connery's lead. And the latest, Timothy Dalton, didn't even bare his chest in his first outing as Bond.

Sean Connery	*Dr. No* ('62)
	From Russia with Love ('63)
	Goldfinger ('64)
	Thunderball ('65)
	You Only Live Twice ('67)
David Niven	*Casino Royale* ('67)
Woody Allen	*Casino Royale* ('67)
George Lazenby	*On Her Majesty's Secret Service* ('69)
Sean Connery	*Diamonds Are Forever* ('71)
Roger Moore	*Live and Let Die* ('73)
	The Man with the Golden Gun ('74)
	The Spy Who Loved Me ('77)
	Moonraker ('79)
	For Your Eyes Only ('81)
	Octopussy ('83)
Sean Connery	*Never Say Never Again* ('83)
Roger Moore	*A View to a Kill* ('85)
Timothy Dalton	*The Living Daylights* ('87)
	License to Kill ('89)

THE FIRST JAMES BOND

Barry Nelson played Bond in a one-hour presentation of *Casino Royale*, on "Climax Mystery Theatre," CBS-TV, in 1954.

BROTHERS

"Your brother is an old-fashioned man. He believes in your sister's honor. Me? I'm a modern man. The twentieth-century type. I run."
—John Ireland, *All the King's Men*

Brothers, real-life brothers. Some bear a physical resemblance, while others carry the same family name. Each one, however, has brought his own particular acting style to the movies.

Dana Andrews	*Laura* ('44)
Steve Forrest	*The Bad and the Beautiful* ('52)
James Arness	*Them!* ('54)
Peter Graves	*Night of the Hunter* ('55)
Alec Baldwin	*Beetlejuice* ('88)
Daniel Baldwin	*Harley Davidson & the Marlboro Man* ('91)
Stephen Baldwin	*Born on the Fourth of July* ('89)
William Baldwin	*Three of Hearts* ('93)
John Barrymore	*Don Juan* ('26)
Lionel Barrymore	*A Family Affair* ('37)
James Belushi	*Red Heat* ('88)
John Belushi	*National Lampoon's Animal House* ('78)
Collin Bernsen	*Puppet Master II* ('90)
Corbin Bernsen	*Major League* ('89)
Scott Brady	*The Model and the Marriage Broker* ('51)
Lawrence Tierney	*Dillinger* ('45)

Beau Bridges	*Norma Rae* ('79)
Jeff Bridges	*Tucker: The Man and His Dream* ('88)
Benjamin Bottoms	*Island Sons* ('87)
Joseph Bottoms	*Surfacing* ('84)
Sam Bottoms	*The Last Picture Show* ('71)
Timothy Bottoms	*The Paper Chase* ('73)
David Carradine	*Bound for Glory* ('76)
Keith Carradine	*An Almost Perfect Affair* ('79)
Robert Carradine	*Number One with a Bullet* ('87)
Neil Connery	*Operation Kid Brother* ('67)
Sean Connery	*The Name of the Rose* ('86)
Tom Conway	*I Walked with a Zombie* ('43)
George Sanders	*Hangover Square* ('45)
Brad Davis	*Cold Steel* ('87)
Gene Davis	*Night Games* ('80)
Brian Deacon	*A Zed & Two Noughts* ('85)
Eric Deacon	*A Zed & Two Noughts* ('85)
Kevin Dillon	*Immediate Family* ('89)
Matt Dillon	*Drugstore Cowboy* ('89)
Eric Douglas	*Student Confidential* ('87)
Michael Douglas	*Romancing the Stone* ('84)
Emilio Estevez	*Wisdom* ('86)
Joe Estevez	*Soultaker* ('90)
Charlie Sheen	*Wall Street* ('87)
Martin Sheen	*Da* ('88)
Ramon Sheen	*Turn Around* ('89)

Edward Fox	*Day of the Jackal* ('73)
James Fox	*A Passage to India* ('84)
Christopher Guest	*Girlfriends* ('78)
Nicholas Guest	*Appointment with Death* ('88)
Clint Howard	*Evilspeak* ('82)
Ron Howard	*American Graffiti* ('73)
Marlon Jackson	*Student Confidential* ('87)
Michael Jackson	*The Wiz* ('78)
James Keach	*Stand Alone* ('85)
Stacy Keach	*The Ninth Configuration* ('80)
Chad Lowe	*Apprentice to Murder* ('88)
Rob Lowe	*The Outsiders* ('83)
Carlos Montalban	*Bananas* ('71)
Ricardo Montalban	*Star Trek II: The Wrath of Khan* ('82)
Charlie Murphy	*CB4* ('93)
Eddie Murphy	*The Golden Child* ('86)
Bill Murray	*What About Bob?* ('91)
John Murray	*Moving Violations* ('85)
Christopher Penn	*Made in USA* ('88)
Matthew Penn	*Delta Force 3* ('90)
Sean Penn	*Colors* ('88)
Dennis Quaid	*Great Balls of Fire!* ('89)
Randy Quaid	*Parents* ('89)

Dick Smothers	*Terror at Alcatraz* ('78)
Tom Smothers	*Get to Know Your Rabbit* ('72)
Frank Stallone	*The Pink Chiquitas* ('86)
Sylvester Stallone	*F.I.S.T.* ('78)
Dean Stockwell	*Married to the Mob* ('88)
Guy Stockwell	*Beau Geste* ('66)
Don Swayze	*Edge of Honor* ('91)
Patrick Swayze	*Ghost* ('90)
Joey Travolta	*Sunnyside* ('79)
John Travolta	*Blow Out* ('81)
Jimmy Van Patten	*Lunch Wagon* ('80)
Nels Van Patten	*Grotesque* ('88)
Timothy Van Patten	*Class of 1984* ('82)
Vincent Van Patten	*Hell Night* ('81)
Alan Vint	*Macon County Line* ('74)
Jesse Vint	*Forbidden World* ('82)
John Ethan Wayne	*The Manhunt* ('86)
Patrick Wayne	*Beyond Atlantis* ('73)
James Woods	*The Onion Field* ('79)
Michael Woods	*Lady Beware* ('87)

THE BROTHERS AS BROTHERS

In *The Long Riders* ('80), real-life brothers David and Keith Carradine, James and Stacy Keach, Randy and Dennis Quaid, and Nicholas and Christopher Guest appear as the gunslinging Younger, James, Miller, and Ford brothers, respectively.

BUDDIES

"Louis, I think this is the start of a beautiful friendship."
—Humphrey Bogart, *Casablanca*

Buddies don't always have to be two males; buddies can be a two-some, a threesome, a group—just as long as they're buddies. Presented below are some of the strangest combinations of buddies ever seen in films.

A Boy and His Dog ('75)—**Don Johnson** and his faithful dog roam around a postapocalyptic world. The dog can talk (yes, in English) and philosophizes about sex a lot. Don meets a girl and has sex, but she ends up being cooked and eaten for dinner. The dog and Don walk happily into the sunset at the conclusion.

The Boys in the Band ('70)—Definitely not a musical, as the ad campaign proclaimed when the film was released originally, but plenty of truly odd buddies do abound in the film.

Brideshead Revisited ('81)—**Jeremy Irons** and **Anthony Edwards** poof it up as two very queenly, upper-class British gents.

Deathtrap ('82)—**Michael Caine** and **Christopher Reeve** as a scheming playwright and his "friend."

A Different Story ('78)—**Perry King** and **Meg Foster** are a gay and lesbian couple who fall in love and decide to straighten their lives out together by marrying.

The Empty Canvas ('64)—**Horst Buchholz** (the Teutonic James Dean) and **Bette Davis** appear as son and mother in an adaption of an Alberto Moravia novel. As *Time* commented when this '60s cinema nouvelle piece was released, it's amusing to watch La Davis breast the French new wave of cinema with bitchy authority.

Female Trouble ('74)—**Divine** rapes **Divine**? Yes, through trick photography, Divine (as a man) rapes the film's heroine (Divine, again, as a woman). Sound gross? Look for the "skid marks" in the male Divine's underpants during the rape scene.

The Gay Deceivers ('69)—**Kevin Couglin** and **Larry Casey** pretend to be gay lovers in a bid to avoid the draft in this now-dated '60s period piece.

Little Fauss and Big Halsy ('70)—**Robert Redford** (Halsy) and **Michael J. Pollard** (Fauss) never exactly define what male attribute makes one of them "big" and the other "little."

Making Love ('82)—**Michael Ontkean** and **Harry Hamlin** as a less than dynamic duo. Both are handsome men, but they're sort of dull as far as any real action is concerned.

The Man Who Would Be King ('75)—**Sean Connery** and **Michael Caine** in an adventure film about nineteenth-century rogues.

Midnight Cowboy ('69)—**Jon Voight** and **Dustin Hoffman** try to fulfill their dreams in New York City. Voight's character keeps referring to all the "tutti-fruttis" in the city.

Midnight Express ('78)—**Brad Davis** and **Norbert Weisser** exercise together and then have a showertime buddy soap-up. It gets hot and steamy, but Brad doesn't consummate their relationship in the film. Truly a cinematic cop-out! In the book, author Billy Hays revealed that he really did lather some hot suds with his buddy.

Myra Breckenridge ('70)—**Rex Reed** and **Raquel Welch** as Myron and Myra Breckenridge: the before, after, and furthermore of hilarious sex changes.

Nijinsky ('80)—**Alan Bates** and **George de la Peña** appear as Diaghliev and Nijinsky—the talented, the tormented, and sadly terrible.

Partners ('82)—**Ryan O'Neal** and **John Hurt** as policeman partners, one straight and one gay, who pretend to be lovers to catch a murderer.

Prick Up Your Ears ('87)—**Gary Oldman** and **Alfred Molina** as Joe Orton and his murderous, untalented lover, proving you always slay the one you love. (The title is an Orton joke: "ears" is an anagram for *arse*.)

Querelle ('82)—**Franco Nero** and **Brad Davis** as ship's captain and horny, handsome sailor, while Jeanne Moreau stands around, looking pouty as usual.

Reflections in a Golden Eye ('67)—**Marlon Brando** as a career Army officer obsessed with enlisted man **Robert Forster**, who spends his off-hours riding a horse bare-assed in the woods.

The Sergeant ('68)—**Rod Steiger** as a sergeant possessed with desire for soldier **John Phillip Law.**

The Servant ('63)—**James Fox** and **Dirk Bogarde** as master and servant in modern-day Britain. Bogarde insidiously turns the tables on Fox, assuming the master's role.

Something for Everyone ('70)—**Michael York** and the whole cast, whom he diddles. First, he seduces the Countess (Angela Lansbury), who's accompanied everywhere by Despo, a strange Greek woman who always clutches worry beads. Then, York moves on to Lansbury's son and finally ends up having to marry Lansbury's chubby unattractive daughter, who's more of a schemer than York's character.

Staircase ('69)—**Richard Burton** and **Rex Harrison** as a pair of bickering, middle-aged lovers.

Sunday, Bloody Sunday ('71)—**Peter Finch** and **Murray Head** as lovers, with Glenda Jackson as the third.

Thunderbolt and Lightfoot ('74)—**Clint Eastwood** and **Jeff Bridges** as a strange duo of bank robbers, with sweet-pie Jeff even having to get dressed up as a woman to pull off their heist.

Women in Love ('69)—**Alan Bates** and **Oliver Reed** strip to the buff and wrestle before a roaring fire to exhibit their manly affection toward one another.

BUT THEY DIDN'T SHOW THEM HUMPIN'

Midnight Cowboy was the first mainstream, general-release film to feature an onscreen sexual encounter between two men. Other films had alluded to such, but *Midnight Cowboy* showed it, although the camera focused on Jon Voight's face rather than his crotch, the location of the climactic scene.

BUMPIN' AND GRINDIN'

"I'm a desperate man, Doctor. I've got to change the way I live . . .
and I'm gonna change the way I strut my stuff."
—John Ritter, *Skin Deep*

Bump those buns! Grind those hips! Push that pelvis to and fro! Shake your booty, baby! Ooooooh! Go, hunk, go! Watch these guys bump and grind their way through a striptease right down to a jockstrap, a G-string . . . or maybe less?

Christopher Atkins	*A Night in Heaven* ('83)
Blake Bahner	*Sensations* ('88)
Thomas Calabro	*Ladykillers* ('88)
Gregory Harrison	*For Ladies Only* ('81)
Laurence Harvey	*The Magic Christian* ('69)
James Horan	*Image of Passion* ('82)
Ken Olandt	*Summer School* ('87)
Michael Ontkean	*Slap Shot* ('77)
Marc Singer	*For Ladies Only* ('81)

LIVE SEX-SHOW PERFORMERS

"I didn't stuff my pants. God did that."
—David Keith, *Heartbreak Hotel*

The acts these studs perform go a lot further than mere bumps and grinds . . . they go all the way. Nothing prudish or held back with them. They get up on a stage in front of an audience and perform in live sex-act shows.

Mircha Carven	*A Man for Sale* ('82)
Christopher Lambert	*Rendez-vous* ('85)

THE GO-GO BOYS ON WHEELS

"Hey, boy, what you doin' with my Momma's car?"
—Faye Dunaway, *Bonnie and Clyde*

The go-go boys: big men on wheels . . . the fast-track auto racers. Roaring around the tarmac as the frantic crowd screams its delight at their driving skills, pushing themselves to go faster and faster, that's how they strive to prove their masculinity. Speed demons . . . hell on wheels . . . go boys go!

Richard Arlen	*Danger on Wheels* ('40)
John Ashley	*Hot Rod Gang* ('58)
Frankie Avalon	*Fireball 500* ('66)
Joe Don Baker	*Checkered Flag or Crash* ('77)
Robert Blake	*Corky* ('72)
Jeff Bridges	*The Last American Hero* ('73)
James Caan	*Red Line 7000* ('65)
James Cagney	*The Crowd Roars* ('32)
Rory Calhoun	*Thunder in Carolina* ('60)
William Campbell	*The Young Racers* ('63)
David Carradine	*Death Race 2000* ('75)
Richard Conte	*Race for Life* ('54)
Tom Cruise	*Days of Thunder* ('90)
Tony Curtis	*Johnny Dark* ('54)

Mark Damon	*The Young Racers* ('63)
James Darren	*The Lively Set* ('64)
Kirk Douglas	*The Racers* ('55)
Howard Duff	*Roar of the Crowd* ('53)
Emilio Estevez	*Freejack* ('92)
Peter Fonda	*Dirty Mary and Crazy Larry* ('74)
Fabian Forte	*The Wild Racers* ('68)
Clark Gable	*To Please a Lady* ('50)
James Garner	*Grand Prix* ('66)
Brett Halsey	*Speed Crazy* ('59)
Ron Howard	*Eat My Dust!* ('76)
Dean Jones	*The Love Bug* ('69)
Edward Judd	*Stolen Hours* ('63)
Raul Julia	*Gumball Rally* ('76)
Tommy Kirk	*Track of Thunder* ('68)
Steve McQueen	*Le Mans* ('71)
Yves Montand	*Grand Prix* ('66)
Paul Newman	*Winning* ('69)
Al Pacino	*Bobby Deerfield* ('77)
John Payne	*Indianapolis Speedway* ('39)
Richard Pryor	*Greased Lightning* ('77)
Elvis Presley	*Spinout* ('66)
Mickey Rooney	*Drive a Crooked Road* ('54)
Massimo Serrato	*The Widow* ('55)
Anthony Steele	*Checkpoint* ('56)
Donald Sutherland	*Steelyard Blues* ('73)
Jean-Louis Trintignant	*A Man and a Woman* ('66)
Robert Wagner	*Winning* ('69)
Cornel Wilde	*The Devil's Hairpin* ('57)

SPREAD LEGS AND A THROBBIN' ROD

These dudes love to spread their legs across a throbbin' rod—their hot, revving motorcycles.

Robert Blake	*Electra Glide in Blue* ('73)
Marlon Brando	*The Wild One* ('54)
Alex Cord	*Sidewinder I* ('77)
Peter Fonda	*Easy Rider* ('69)
Dennis Hopper	*Easy Rider* ('69)
Joe Namath	*C.C. and Company* ('70)
Michael Parks	*Sidewinder I* ('77); *Bus Riley's Back in Town* ('65)
Robert Redford	*Little Fauss and Big Halsy* ('70)

DEATH ON WHEELS

Early in his career, **Clark Gable**, driving while intoxicated, supposedly struck a female pedestrian and killed her. No word of the potential scandal ever reached the public, however. Rumor has it that Louis Mayer, head of MGM, Gable's studio, helped arrange to cover up the crime, thus protecting his valuable property.

CASTING:
THE CREATIVE APPROACH

"Oh, we're both fakes. Isn't faking the essence of acting?"
—Katharine Hepburn, *Stage Door*

Sometimes Hollywood gets the casting exactly right. Other times, it messes it up miserably. And then there are the times when it's innovative, unusual . . . or truly creative.

Aria ('88)—*Character*: King Zog of Albania, who survives an assassination attempt by firing back and killing his assailants. *Played by*: Theresa Russell.

Come Back to the Five and Dime, Jimmy Dean, Jimmy Dean ('82)—*Character*: Joe, the only male member in the group of James Dean fans who work in a dimestore in a small Texas town. One night, he was raped on a tombstone in the local cemetery by several local rowdies and vanished from the town shortly thereafter. He reappears, years later, after having undergone a sex change. *Played by*: Karen Black.

Everything You Always Wanted to Know About Sex ('72)—*Characters*: Two of the many sperm awaiting ejaculation in a penis. *Played by*: Burt Reynolds and Woody Allen.

Stars and Stripes Forever ('52)—*Character*: John Philip Sousa, a sergeant-major of the U.S. Marine Corps. *Played by*: Clifton Webb, Hollywood's notoriously effeminate mama's boy.

The World According to Garp ('82)—*Character*: Roberta Muldoon, an over-six-foot-tall, ex-football player who's had a sex change. *Played by*: John Lithgow.

The Year of Living Dangerously ('83)—*Character*: Billy Kwan, a half-Asian, half-European dwarf photographer, who appears to have a crush on Mel Gibson's character. *Played by*: Linda Hunt (who won the only Oscar awarded for playing a member of the opposite sex).

THE OFFBEAT APPROACH

Sometimes Hollywood's casting is completely hard to fathom, as these examples prove:

A Mafia kingpin named "God"	**Groucho Marx** in *Skidoo* ('68)
Notorious outlaw Jesse James	**Roy Rogers** in *The Days of Jesse James* ('39)
Napoleon	**Dennis Hopper** in *The Story of Mankind* ('57)
A transvestite nightclub entertainer	**George Sanders** in *The Kremlin Letter* ('70)

MULTIPLE ROLES

And then there's the "multiple" role, where the actor likes to prove his versatility:

Both male and female roles	**Alec Guinness** in *Kind Hearts and Coronets* ('49)

	Kazuo Hasegawa in *An Actor's Revenge* ('63)
	Peter Sellers in *The Mouse That Roared* ('59)
	Alistair Sim in *The Belles of St. Trinians* ('55)
Both black and white roles	**Eddie Murphy** in *Coming to America* ('88)
An American, a German, and a Briton	**Peter Sellers** in *Dr. Strangelove* ('64)

HOW TO CAST A FLOP!

Good casting often can save a bad film, but miscasting leads only to the misery of a flop, as these leading men can attest:

Tom Cruise	*Legend* ('85)
Clint Eastwood	*Paint Your Wagon* ('69)
Clark Gable	*Parnell* ('37)
Richard Gere	*King David* ('85)
Steve McQueen	*An Enemy of the People* ('77)
Paul Newman	*The Silver Chalice* ('54)
Al Pacino	*Revolution* ('85)
Sylvester Stallone	*Rhinestone* ('84)
John Travolta	*Moment by Moment* ('78)
John Wayne	*The Conqueror* ('56)

CLASSICAL INTERLUDES

"Making love to the piano—one of my more attractive
minor accomplishments."

—Van Heflin, *Possessed*

Periodically, some studio mogul or producer decides to go on a culture "kick" and pulls all the stops out to fling a musician across the screen—accompanied by a musical score blasting out familiar classical music.

Beethoven	Karl Boehm	*The Magnificent Rebel* ('62)
Brahms	Robert Walker	*Song of Love* ('47)
Chopin	Hugh Grant	*Impromptu* ('91)
	Cornel Wilde	*A Song to Remember* ('45)
Grieg	Toralv Maurstad	*Song of Norway* ('70)
Handel	Wilfred Lawson	*The Great Mr. Handel* ('42)
Herbert	Allan Jones	*The Great Victor Herbert* ('39)
Liszt	Dirk Bogarde	*Song Without End* ('60)
	Roger Daltrey	*Lisztomania* ('75)
	Julian Sands	*Impromptu* ('91)
Mahler	Dirk Bogarde	*Death in Venice* ('71)
	Robert Powell	*Mahler* ('74)
Mozart	Tom Hulce	*Amadeus* ('84)
Paganinni	Stewart Granger	*The Magic Bow* ('47)
Puccini	Robert Stephens	*Puccini* ('67)
Rimsky-Korsakov	Jean-Pierre Aumont	*Song of Scheherazade* ('47)
Romberg	Jose Ferrer	*Deep in My Heart* ('54)
Salieri	F. Murray Abraham	*Amadeus* ('84)
Schubert	Nils Asther	*Love Time* ('34)
Shostakovich	Ben Kingsley	*Testimony* ('87)
Shumann	Paul Henreid	*Song of Love* ('47)
Strauss	Horst Buchholz	*The Great Waltz* ('72)
Tchaikovsky	Richard Chamberlain	*The Music Lovers* ('71)

| Wagner | Richard Burton | *Wagner* ('83) |
| | Carlos Thompson | *Magic Fire* ('56) |

ARTISTIC AFFAIRS

"You know, whenever you put about fifty artists together in one room, you get a really pleasant combination of gossip, paranoia, envy, fear, trembling, hatred, lust, and pretense. It's wonderful."
—Alan Bates, *An Unmarried Woman*

Painting, painting, painting. And when they're not painting, they're emoting, emoting, emoting about their unappreciated artistic talents.

Cellini	Fredric March	*The Affairs of Cellini* ('34)
Delacroix	Ralph Brown	*Impromptu* ('91)
El Greco	Mel Ferrer	*El Greco* ('65)
Gainsborough	Cecil Kellaway	*Kitty* ('45)
Gauguin	Anthony Quinn	*Lust for Life* ('56)
	George Sanders	*The Moon and Sixpence* ('42)
Goya	Anthony Franciosa	*The Naked Maja* ('59)
Michelangelo	Charlton Heston	*The Agony and the Ecstasy* ('65)
Modigliani	Gerard Philipe	*The Lovers of Montparnasse* ('57)
Rembrandt	Charles Laughton	*Rembrandt* ('36)
Rublev	Anatoli Solonitzine	*Andrei Rublev* ('66)
Toulouse-Lautrec	Jose Ferrer	*Moulin Rouge* ('52)
van Gogh	Kirk Douglas	*Lust for Life* ('56)
	Tim Roth	*Vincent & Theo* ('90)

CANTATA FOR PECTORAL AND THIGH

"And so, with deep pride and gratitude, I dedicate this music to my brother, known to most of you as Young Sampson."
—Arthur Kennedy, *City for Conquest*

Grand Prize Winner

"(Ain't There) Anybody Here for Love?" from *Gentlemen Prefer Blondes* ('52)—Features the 1952 vintage, awesomely constructed Jane Russell cavorting amid dozens of scantily clad superathletic types. Jane, who's sailing to Europe with a blond friend (guess who?), discovers the guys, members of an athletic team, in the ship's gym. Her number, a lament about the nonchalance with which the guys view her, features America's Dairyland Sweetheart spinning, twirling, and even doing chin-ups on the boys' biceps. Russell's romp with the boys is probably the most hunky beefcake musical number ever featured in a film, with close-up following close-up of the guys' physical attributes.

Honorable Mentions

"Armide" from *Aria* ('88).

"Black Boys, White Boys" from *Hair* ('79).

"Dancing Dildoes" from *The First Nudie Musical* ('76).

"Everything's Coming Up Roses" from *The Ritz* ('76).

"75 Miles to Heaven" from *Best Little Whorehouse in Texas* ('82).

"There Is Nothing Like a Dame" from *South Pacific* ('58).

"YMCA" from *Can't Stop the Music* ('80).

COLD BODIES, HOT PASSION

"You're dead, I killed you. Care for a little necrophilia?"
—Jonathan Pryce, *Brazil*

Dead bodies get some men soooo hot—because they're cold to the touch, smelling of rot. And the sight of a hearse only makes their passionate desires worse.

Bad Timing: A Sensual Obsession ('80)—Art Garfunkel makes love to the dead body of his girlfriend, in an attempt to inject her with life and bring her back from the dead. He fails.

Children Shouldn't Play with Dead Things ('72)—A male corpse is exhumed from a cemetery by a group of people and taken to the bedroom of a nearby cabin, where it is placed on a bed. The obviously gay leader of the group gently strokes the corpse, gives it a name, and while talking to it, makes it very plain that he's going to have sex with the corpse as soon as the others have gone to bed.

Dinah East ('70)—The corpse of actress Dinah East is delivered to a mortuary for preparation. The mortician, ecstatic at having a famous actress—albeit, a dead one—caresses Dinah's body and begins to undress it for sex. As he strips her panties away, the hitherto-unrevealed transvestite Dinah's penis flops out, which provides the lustful mortician with a most unwelcome surprise.

Lune Froide (Cold Moon) ('91)—In director Patrick Bouchitey's film, two beer-swilling louts stumble on the body of a beautiful dead girl and they both have sex with it. When the film premiered at the 1991 Cannes Film Festival, one critic commented, "There are some scenes in that film I find simply intolerable."

The Offspring ('86)—Mild-mannered Stanley (Clu Gulager) avidly pursues the younger Grace, a coworker who's not interested in return. After she spurns his advances, Stanley strangles Grace and dumps her body. Full of remorse that he killed her before sex, he breaks into the mortuary where he toasts Grace with champagne, before climbing into her coffin to have sex with her body.

GREAT DEAD MOMENTS

The Loved One ('65)—Set in the Whispering Glades Mortuary and Cemetery—a takeoff on Los Angeles' Forest Lawn—this Tony Richardson-directed film was released as "the film with something to offend everyone." Featuring Jonathan Winters in dual roles as the Blessed Reverend, the shyster owner of Whispering Glades, and his twin brother, who owns a pet cemetery next door, the cast also includes Robert Morse, Anjanette Comer, Rod Steiger, and lots of cameos—such as Liberace, who's a casket salesman. It's a rather ribald, often hilarious look at the truly American way of death.

Return of the Living Dead: Part II ('88)—Those dead bodies, released by a toxic gas and turned into ghouls, are back for a second time crying "Brains, brains." Yes, they're carnivorous and they attack everyone in sight, to feast on their brains. The love scene to end all love scenes occurs when one of the ghouls catches his girlfriend in a church. He explains that he wants to be the one to eat her brains, because he simply can't bear the thought that some other man would have the first opportunity at her. She finally consents and dies with her true love munching into her head.

BEST DEAD PERFORMANCE BY AN ACTOR

Treat Williams—*Dead Heat* ('88)—As a detective who returns from the dead, and decomposing rapidly, he helps his partner (Joe Piscopo) pursue the criminals who killed him.

Jonathan Winters—*Oh Dad, Poor Dad, Mama's Hung You in the Closet and I'm Feeling So Sad* ('67)—In a rare nonspeaking, nonmoving role, Winters is the corpse of Rosalind Russell's late husband. The overly possessive widow and her son (Robert Morse) play a peripatetic duo who always travel with the deceased husband's coffin, hanging his body in the closet each time they reach their destination.

Elliott Gould—*Dead Men Don't Die* ('91)—As a television newscaster who's murdered, Gould is brought back to the microphone by voodoo. His role provided much fodder for those wits who have long insisted that *all* TV news anchors are a deadly dull lot.

Terry Kiser—*Weekend at Bernie's* ('89)—Playing Bernie, the boss who's invited some coworkers over for the weekend at his beach house, Kiser ends up spending the weekend dead after being murdered. His visitors try to pretend nothing has happened, to keep from spoiling the fun for everyone.

Andrew Lowery—*My Boyfriend's Back* ('92)—Lowery is a young teen whose desire for his girlfriend is so strong that the grave can't hold him. Only problem is that some of his "body parts" keep falling off. Such are the hazards of being a lovesick zombie.

Death Scenes

205 West 57th Street, Apartment 1BB, New York City—Where **Gig Young** killed his fifth wife, Kim Schmidt, and then committed suicide on Thursday, October 19, 1978, at approximately 2:30 P.M.

916 North Genesee, West Hollywood—Where **Russ Columbo** accidentally committed suicide when he fired a supposedly unloaded antique dueling pistol into his eye on September 2, 1934.

1579 Benedict Canyon Road, Beverly Hills—Where **George Reeves** committed suicide on June 16, 1959.

1731 North Normandie, Los Angeles—Where **Albert Dekker** scribbled obscenities on his body, dressed bizarrely, put on handcuffs, and hung himself from the shower pipe in the bathroom on May 5, 1968.

8221 Sunset Boulevard, Chateau Marmont (Bungalow 3), Los Angeles—Where **John Belushi** died of a drug overdose in 1982.

8563 Holloway Drive, West Hollywood—Where **Sal Mineo** was stabbed to death during an aborted robbery a few yards to the right of the driveway on February 12, 1976.

10400 Columbus Avenue, Mission Hills—Where **Carl "Alfalfa" Switzer** was shot to death during an argument over $50 on January 21, 1959.

12900 Mulholland Drive, Los Angeles—Where **Christian Brando**, Marlon's son, shot and killed Dag Drollet, his sister's lover.

Intersection of Yucca Street and Cherokee Avenue, Hollywood—Where **Percy Kilbride** was struck by a car on December 11, 1964, during an early evening stroll; he died of his injuries eight days later.

THEY KEEP CHANGING COLORS

"White. I'll tell you what kind of white. You know that little piece of white that's on top of chicken shit? That's the kind of white."
—P. J. Johnson, *Paper Moon*

Black. White. Blacks passing as white. White pretending to be black.

Black Like Me ('64)—**James Whitmore** in the real-life story of a white journalist who takes chemicals to alter his skin to black for an exposé he's writing on being a Black male in America.

Coming to America ('88)—In a cameo, **Eddie Murphy** portrays Morris, an elderly Jewish patron of a Black barbershop.

Dr. Black, Mr. Hyde ('76)—**Bernie Casey**, a Black scientist, tries an experimental serum on himself, which turns him into a *white* monster.

Lost Boundaries ('49)—**Mel Ferrer**'s whole light-skinned Black family passes for white in a small New England town until their secret is discovered.

Shadows ('60)—**Ben Carruthers**, a Black man, passes as white, along with his attractive sister, to the disgust of their older brother, who's blacker and unable to pass.

Soul Man ('86)—**C. Thomas Howell**, a white college student, pretends to be Black to attend college on a special scholarship for minority students.

True Identity ('91)—**Lenny Henry**, a Black policeman, goes undercover as a white man.

Watermelon Man ('70)—**Godfrey Cambridge**, as a white bigot, awakes one morning to discover that he's turned into a Black man overnight.

BEST RACIAL TRANSFORMATION

The Zebra Force ('77)—A group of Vietnam vets forms a commando squad to battle drug dealers. When the soldiers (Caucasians) attack one Los Angeles drug lord, they turn into Blacks. As soon as the attack is over, they revert back to Caucasians—without an explanation given for either transformation!

ALBINOS

"I don't mean no conjurer. Why, I'm talking about an albino.
They can see right through the ground like it was a glass of water.
It's strictly scientific."
—Buddy Hackett, *God's Little Acre*

Pinkish skin, white hair, almost red eyes . . . the albinos. They make a lasting visual impression on anyone who sees them.

Robert Duvall	*To Kill a Mockingbird* ('62)
Brion James	*Nightmare at Noon* ('87)
Stacy Keach	*The Life and Times of Judge Roy Bean* ('72)
Stacy Keach	*Class of 1999* ('90)
Michael Landon	*God's Little Acre* ('58)
Dar Robinson	*Stick* ('85)
John Saxon	*Final Alliance* ('90)
Anthony Zerbe	*The Omega Man* ('71)

COMPARE THE DIFFERENCE

"The only difference in men is the color of their ties."
—Helen Broderick, *Top Hat*

Hollywood has a long history of "remakes," or redoing a film years after the original. This often has conflicted with the effort of the actor to make each role "his own." Compare these selections of actors who have given performances in the same roles, noting the differences in their styles.

Brian Donlevy	*Beau Geste* ('39)
Telly Savalas	*Beau Geste* ('66)
Emil Jannings	*The Blue Angel* ('30)
Curt Jurgens	*The Blue Angel* ('59)
William Holden	*Born Yesterday* ('50)
Don Johnson	*Born Yesterday* ('93)
Robert Mitchum	*Cape Fear* ('62)
Robert De Niro	*Cape Fear* ('91)
Jack Benny	*Charley's Aunt* ('41)
Ray Bolger	*Where's Charley?* ('52)
Richard Dix	*Cimarron* ('31)
Glenn Ford	*Cimarron* ('60)
Bing Crosby	*A Connecticut Yankee in King Arthur's Court* ('49)
Dennis Dugan	*Unidentified Flying Oddball* ('79)
Sidney Poitier	*Cry, the Beloved Country* ('51)
Clifton Davis	*Lost in the Stars* ('74)
Edmond O'Brien	*D.O.A.* ('49)
Tom Tryon	*Color Me Dead* ('69)
Dennis Quaid	*D.O.A.* ('88)
Gary Cooper	*A Farewell to Arms* ('32)
Rock Hudson	*A Farewell to Arms* ('57)

David Hedison	*The Fly* ('58)
Jeff Goldblum	*The Fly* ('86)
Adolphe Menjou, Pat O'Brien	*The Front Page* ('31)
Cary Grant, Rosalind Russell	*His Girl Friday* ('40)
Jack Lemmon, Walter Matthau	*The Front Page* ('74)
Burt Reynolds, Kathleen Turner	*Switching Channels* ('88)
Steve McQueen	*The Getaway* ('72)
Alec Baldwin	*The Getaway* ('94)
Robert Donat	*Goodbye, Mr. Chips* ('39)
Peter O'Toole	*Goodbye, Mr. Chips* ('69)
Alan Ladd	*The Great Gatsby* ('49)
Robert Redford	*The Great Gatsby* ('74)
Lon Chaney	*The Hunchback of Notre Dame* ('23)
Charles Laughton	*The Hunchback of Notre Dame* ('39)
Anthony Quinn	*The Hunchback of Notre Dame* ('57)
Anthony Hopkins	*The Hunchback of Notre Dame* ('82)
Victor McLaglen	*The Informer* ('35)
Raymond St. Jacques	*Up Tight* ('68)
Kevin McCarthy	*Invasion of the Body Snatchers* ('56)
Donald Sutherland	*Invasion of the Body Snatchers* ('78)
Charles Laughton	*Island of Lost Souls* ('33)
Burt Lancaster	*The Island of Dr. Moreau* ('77)

Al Jolson	*The Jazz Singer* ('27)
Danny Thomas	*The Jazz Singer* ('53)
Neil Diamond	*The Jazz Singer* ('80)
Wayne Morris	*Kid Galahad* ('37)
Elvis Presley	*Kid Galahad* ('62)
Henry Fonda	*The Lady Eve* ('41)
George Gobel	*The Birds and the Bees* ('56)
Warren William	*Lady for a Day* ('33)
Glenn Ford	*Pocketful of Miracles* ('61)
Vincent Price	*The Last Man on Earth* ('64)
Charlton Heston	*The Omega Man* ('71)
Pierre Richard	*Le Jouet* ('75)
Richard Pryor	*The Toy* ('82)
Adolphe Menjou	*Little Miss Marker* ('34)
Walter Matthau	*Little Miss Marker* ('80)
Jack Nicholson	*Little Shop of Horrors* ('60)
Bill Murray	*Little Shop of Horrors* ('86)
Ronald Colman	*Lost Horizon* ('37)
Peter Finch	*Lost Horizon* ('73)
Paul Ford	*The Matchmaker* ('58)
Walter Matthau	*Hello, Dolly!* ('69)
Eddie Bracken	*The Miracle of Morgan's Creek* ('44)
Jerry Lewis	*Rock-a-Bye Baby* ('58)

John Barrymore	*Moby Dick* ('30)
Gregory Peck	*Moby Dick* ('56)
Charles Coburn	*The More the Merrier* ('43)
Cary Grant	*Walk, Don't Run* ('66)
Adolphe Menjou	*Morning Glory* ('33)
Henry Fonda	*Stagestruck* ('58)
Dick Powell	*Murder, My Sweet* ('44)
Robert Mitchum	*Farewell, My Lovely* ('75)
Clark Gable	*Mutiny on the Bounty* ('35)
Marlon Brando	*Mutiny on the Bounty* ('62)
Mel Gibson	*The Bounty* ('85)
Charles Laughton	*Mutiny on the Bounty* ('35)
Trevor Howard	*Mutiny on the Bounty* ('62)
Anthony Hopkins	*The Bounty* ('85)
William Powell	*My Man Godfrey* ('36)
David Niven	*My Man Godfrey* ('57)
Leslie Howard	*Of Human Bondage* ('34)
Laurence Harvey	*Of Human Bondage* ('64)
Lon Chaney	*Oliver Twist* ('22)
Alec Guinness	*Oliver Twist* ('48)
Ron Moody	*Oliver!* ('68)
George C. Scott	*Oliver Twist* ('82)
Lon Chaney	*Phantom of the Opera* ('25)
Claude Rains	*Phantom of the Opera* ('43)
Herbert Lom	*Phantom of the Opera* ('62)

William Finley	*Phantom of the Paradise* ('74)
Maximilian Schell	*Phantom of the Opera* ('83)
Charles Dance	*Phantom of the Opera* ('90)
Robert Englund	*Phantom of the Opera* ('90)
Cary Grant, James Stewart	*The Philadelphia Story* ('40)
Bing Crosby, Frank Sinatra	*High Society* ('56)
John Garfield	*The Postman Always Rings Twice* ('46)
Jack Nicholson	*The Postman Always Rings Twice* ('81)
Toshiro Mifune	*Rashomon* ('51)
Paul Newman	*The Outrage* ('64)
Tyrone Power	*The Razor's Edge* ('46)
Bill Murray	*The Razor's Edge* ('84)
Clark Gable	*Red Dust* ('32)
Clark Gable	*Mogambo* ('53)
Randolph Scott	*Roberta* ('35)
Red Skelton	*Lovely to Look At* ('52)
Giancarlo Gianinni	*The Seduction of Mimi* ('74)
Richard Pryor	*Which Way Is Up?* ('77)
John Wayne	*Stagecoach* ('39)
Alex Cord	*Stagecoach* ('66)
Kris Kristofferson	*Stagecoach* ('86)
Fredric March	*A Star Is Born* ('37)
James Mason	*A Star Is Born* ('54)
Kris Kristofferson	*A Star Is Born* ('76)

Pierre Richard	*The Tall Blond Man with One Black Shoe* ('72)
Tom Hanks	*The Man with One Red Shoe* ('85)
Jack Benny	*To Be or Not to Be* ('42)
Mel Brooks	*To Be or Not to Be* ('83)
Bernard-Pierre Donnadieu	*The Vanishing* ('88)
Jeff Bridges	*The Vanishing* ('92)
Gene Bervoets	*The Vanishing* ('88)
Kiefer Sutherland	*The Vanishing* ('92)
Frank Morgan	*The Wizard of Oz* ('39)
Richard Pryor	*The Wiz* ('78)
Laurence Olivier	*Wuthering Heights* ('39)
Timothy Dalton	*Wuthering Heights* ('70)
Robert Taylor	*A Yank at Oxford* ('38)
Rob Lowe	*Oxford Blues* ('84)

I SPY, YOU SPY, HE SPIED

In 1992, a KGB colonel revealed that a noted French actor had been a spy for Soviet intelligence agencies during the '30s and '40s. According to Colonel Igor Prelin, **Michel Simon**, who died in 1975 and starred in Jean Renoir's *Bondu Saved from Drowning* ('32), was recruited by the Soviets after he helped establish the Swiss Communist Party in the '20s. Simon's role as the "bum" in the film was played by Nick Nolte when the film was remade as *Down and Out in Beverly Hills* ('86).

DARLING! WHAT AN ADORABLE DRESS YOU HAVE ON!

"Oh, my God! Someone's been sleeping in my dress."
—Bea Arthur, *Mame*

Drag: the dubious—but often humorous—gimmick of having a male star dress in female attire. Ever wonder how many of the men secretly enjoy it?

Frankie Avalon	*Ski Party* ('65)
Kevin Bacon	*JFK* ('91)
Jim Bailey	*The Surrogate* ('84)
Lionel Barrymore	*The Devil-Doll* ('36)
Jim Belushi	*Taking Care of Business* ('90)
Jack Benny	*Charley's Aunt* ('41)
Helmut Berger	*The Damned* ('69)
Ray Bolger	*Where's Charley?* ('52)
Marlon Brando	*The Missouri Breaks* ('76)
Jeff Bridges	*Thunderbolt and Lightfoot* ('74)
Yul Brynner	*The Magic Christian* ('69)
Gary Busey	*Under Siege* ('92)
Michael Caine	*Dressed to Kill* ('80)
John Candy	*Armed and Dangerous* ('86); *Who's Harry Crumb?* ('89)
David Carradine	*Sonny Boy* ('90)
T. K. Carter	*He's My Girl* ('87)
Lon Chaney	*The Unholy Three* ('25)
Charlie Chaplin	*A Woman* ('15)
Lee J. Cobb	*In Like Flint* ('67)
Dabney Coleman	*Meet the Applegates* ('91)

Quentin Crisp	*Orlando* ('93)
Bing Crosby	*High Time* ('60)
Tim Curry	*The Rocky Horror Picture Show* ('75)
Tony Curtis	*Some Like It Hot* ('59)
Jaye Davidson	*The Crying Game* ('92)
Dom DeLuise	*Haunted Honeymoon* ('86)
Gerard Depardieu	*Menage* ('86)
Jimmy Durante	*Hollywood Party* ('34)
Peter Falk	*Happy New Year* ('73)
James Fox	*Thoroughly Modern Millie* ('67)
Michael J. Fox	*Back to the Future Part II* ('89)
Cary Grant	*I Was a Male War Bride* ('49)
Michael Greer	*Fortune and Men's Eyes* ('71)
Joel Grey	*Cabaret* ('72)
Jack Guilford	*A Funny Thing Happened on the Way to the Forum* ('66)
Alec Guinness	*Kind Hearts and Coronets* ('49)
Arsenio Hall	*Coming to America* ('88)
George Hamilton	*Zorro, the Gay Blade* ('81)
Rutger Hauer	*Chanel Solitaire* ('81)
Hugh Herbert	*La Conga Nights* ('35)
Christopher Hewett	*The Producers* ('68)
Dwayne Hickman	*Ski Party* ('61)
Dustin Hoffman	*Tootsie* ('82)
Bob Hope	*The Lemon Drop Kid* ('51)
John Hurt	*Romeo-Juliet* ('88)
Eric Idle	*Monty Python's The Meaning of Life* ('83)
Paul Jabara	*Day of the Locust* ('75)
Lou Jacobi	*Everything You Always Wanted to Know About Sex* ('72)
Terry Jones	*Monty Python's The Meaning of Life* ('83)

Danny Kaye	*On the Double* ('61)
Burt Lancaster	*The Crimson Pirate* ('52); *The List of Adrian Messenger* ('63)
Jack Lemmon	*Some Like It Hot* ('59)
John Lithgow	*The World According to Garp* ('82)
Paul Lynde	*The Glass Bottom Boat* ('66)
Steve Martin	*Dead Men Don't Wear Plaid* ('82)
Walter Matthau	*House Calls* ('78)
Roddy McDowall	*Rabbit Test* ('78)
Ted McGinley	*Revenge of the Nerds* ('84)
Matthew Modine	*Private School* ('83)
Dudley Moore	*Bedazzled* ('67)
Michael Palin	*Monty Python's The Meaning of Life* ('83)
Anthony Perkins	*Psycho* ('60)
Roman Polanski	*The Tenant* ('76)
Robert Preston	*Victor/Victoria* ('82)
Richard Pryor	*Jo Jo Dancer, Your Life Is Calling* ('86)
Mickey Rooney	*Babes on Broadway* ('41)
Craig Russell	*Outrageous* ('77)
Kurt Russell	*Tango & Cash* ('89)
George Sanders	*The Kremlin Letter* ('70)
Michael Sarrazin	*Mascara* ('87)
Arnold Schwarzenegger	*Total Recall* ('90)
Peter Sellers	*The Mouse That Roared* ('59)
Michel Serrault	*La Cage aux Folles* ('78), *II* ('80), *III* ('85)
Dick Shawn	*Angel* ('84)
Phil Silvers	*A Funny Thing Happened on the Way to the Forum* ('66)
Gene Simmons	*Never Too Young to Die* ('86)
Red Skelton	*Bathing Beauty* ('44)

Sylvester Stallone	*Nighthawks* ('81)
Rod Steiger	*No Way to Treat a Lady* ('68)
Jerry Stiller	*The Ritz* ('76)
Terence Stamp	*Priscilla, Queen of the Desert* ('94)
Robert Vaughn	*S.O.B.* ('81)
Jack Weston	*Fuzz* ('72)
Robin Williams	*Mrs. Doubtfire* ('93)

FUNNIEST, MOST BELIEVABLE DRAG

Alistair Sim, as Miss Millicent, plays the headmistress at the girl's school in *The Belles of St. Trinians* ('55).

GEE, DIDYA SEE THE MUSTACHE ON THAT NUN!

One "Attaboy" award to *Burt Reynolds* in *Fuzz* ('72), who dressed up as a nun for a stakeout on a park bench. Burt didn't even shave off his mustache, and that was *some* nun he made!

SONGBIRDS IN DRAG

". . . Allow me, in conclusion, to congratulate you on your sexual
intercourse as well as your singing."
—Celia Johnson, *The Prime of Miss Jean Brodie*

Whenever one of the guys has to get dressed up like a woman, it seems less likely to compromise his masculinity if the purpose of the drag is to sing a song.

The Kick Up Your High Heels Grand Prize

Yul Brynner—*The Magic Christian* ('69)—Brynner does a rendition of Noel Coward's "Mad About the Boy" in full drag. In fact, Brynner is so unrecognizable that when he snatches off his wig at the end of the number revealing his well-known bald pate, a male patron in the cabaret watching Brynner's performance shrieks, "Oh, no!" The ex-King of Siam leans forward and hisses to both the patron and the screen audience, "Oh, yes!"

The Shake Your Falsies Honorable Mentions

Helmut Berger as Marlene Dietrich in *The Damned* ('69).

Bob Hope as Carmen Miranda in *The Road to Rio* ('47).

Danny Kaye as Marlene Dietrich in *On the Double* ('61).

Jerry Lewis as Carmen Miranda in *Scared Stiff* ('53).

Dennis Quilley as Carmen Miranda in *Privates on Parade* ('82).

Mickey Rooney as Carmen Miranda in *Babes on Broadway* ('41).

Craig Russell as Barbra Streisand in *Outrageous* ('77).

HE WAS A WHOLE LOTTA WOMAN

Divine (real name: Glenn Milstead).

Poor Divine! Did any other man ever depict so much female suffering, trauma, and stress on the screen? He took acid and jumped out of a window as a tormented Diane Linkletter in *The Diane Link-letter Story* ('68).

Joan Crawford and Bette Davis certainly never had the misfortunes befall them that Divine endured in *Multiple Maniacs* ('70). First, he was raped by a man wearing a dress; then, he was seduced in a church by a woman who gave him an "anal rosary job" while reciting the Stations of the Cross. If those humiliations weren't enough to bear, near the film's end he was raped by a giant lobster.

Scarlett O'Hara may have eaten turnips in *Gone with the Wind* ('39), but in *Pink Flamingos* ('72), Divine really showed his stuff by eating dog feces.

In *Female Trouble* ('74), playing a truly troubled character named Dawn Davenport, Divine ran away from home only to be raped by a degenerate (Divine playing a male role), by whom he later gave birth. As his child grew older, Divine fell in with an unsavory crowd and was soon leading a life of dissolution and crime, fostered by his drug dependence on mainlining eye shadow. After one crime too many, he ended up sentenced to fry in the electric chair. As the film concluded, Divine, sitting in the electric chair, put on a performance that eclipsed Susan Hayward's in *I Want to Live!* ('58).

After all these feminine roles, what could be more suited to Divine than to be a typical suburban housewife, Francine Fishpaw, in *Polyester* ('81). Plagued by rebellious children, nosy neighbors, a dog that crapped on her carpet, and a philandering husband, Divine somehow still managed to find happiness in the arms of her dreamboat beau, Todd Tomorrow. Donna Reed and June Cleaver's versions of suburbia certainly were never like this.

With big breasts bouncing to rival Jane Russell's in *The Outlaw* ('43) and thighs hotter than Jennifer Jones's thighs in *Duel in the Sun* ('46), Divine next established himself as one of the definitive rugged—but sexy—women of the Old West in *Lust in the Dust* ('85). Cursed with a tattoo on his buttock and raped by a dwarf, Divine's character showed he still had enough spunk to indulge in a barroom brawl to match the fury of any female. The audience knew this was not a woman to be trifled with when he sang "These Lips Were Made for Kissing."

For his last feminine role, Divine returned to his roots in Baltimore and director John Waters in *Hairspray* ('88), to tackle social issues such as integration, rock-and-roll music, and teenage peer competition. Sadly, this was to be Divine's last contribution to helping define the mystique of the American woman.

The Tearful Hanky Award for Other Suffering Pseudofemales

Candy Darling (James Slattery), starring in *Andy Warhol's Heat* ('72) and *Andy Warhol's Trash* ('70).

Holly Woodlawn (Harold Rodrigues), starring in *Andy Warhol's Heat* ('72), *Andy Warhol's Trash* ('70); and *Is There Sex After Death?* ('71).

WAS THAT A MAN OR A WOMAN?

> "There aren't any hard women, only soft men."
> —Raquel Welch, *Hannie Caulder*

Jean Arless in *Homicidal* ('61), directed by William Castle. *Homicidal*, a William Castle production, has a plot laced with intricacies and a killer's disguise that is both sophisticated and elaborate. Even the overall low budget and production quality of the film cannot squelch an excellent performance that leaves the audience wondering, "Was that a man or a woman?"

During the film's opening sequence, Emily, a very beautiful blond, marries a perfect stranger and then, without apparent reason or provocation, stabs the county clerk who has just married the couple.

Next, the film introduces Warren Webster, an attractive young man who has brought Emily back from Sweden to meet Miriam

Webster, Warren's stepsister from another mother. Warren soon will inherit all his family's property on his twenty-first birthday, with Miriam in line for the legacy should anything happen to Warren.

Miriam's suspicions of Emily's intentions are heightened when she learns that Warren and Emily are married. Meanwhile, the police have begun to suspect that Emily was the one who murdered the county clerk.

Emily has, during this interval, threatened to kill Helga, once Warren and Miriam's nursemaid, who's now a mute paralytic. Miriam, trying to warn her stepbrother that his wife may be a murderer, goes to Warren's house. Emily, already in the house, has killed Helga and when Miriam arrives, tries to kill her as well. When Miriam screams for Warren to help her, Emily rips off her wig to reveal that she's really Warren. The speedy arrival of the police saves Miriam, and Warren falls down a staircase, stabbing himself with the knife he had attempted to use on Miriam.

The film closes at the police station, where the audience learns that Warren was actually born a girl. Helga had been present at the birth and the county clerk had registered it. Warren's mother raised him as a boy, to ensure that he/she would receive the inheritance, for it was stipulated that it would go to her child only if she bore a son.

To collect the inheritance, Warren had to dispose of Helga and the county clerk, the only people who knew he really was not a male and not the rightful heir.

A concluding sequence to the film uses a split-screen appearance of both Warren and Emily, where it is revealed that both roles were played by a Jean Arless, an androgynous name. No explanation was provided about whether Jean Arless was male or female.

In his autobiography, director William Castle revealed that Jean Arless was an actress named Joan Marshall. According to Castle, his first choice to play both roles had been a male, but after countless interviews, mostly with transvestites, he was unable to find anyone he felt was suitable for the film.

The Eva Gabor Dynel Wig Award for Other Transvestite Killers

Lionel Barrymore	*The Devil-Doll* ('36)
Michael Caine	*Dressed to Kill* ('80)
Stephen Joyce	*The Red Spider* ('84)
Marion Marshall	*Gunn* ('67)

Christopher Morley	*Freebie and the Bean* ('74)
Ray Walston	*Caprice* ('67)
Jim Williams	*The Newlydeads* ('75)

DINNERTIME TREATS

"You're the kind of man who would end the world famine problem
by having them all eat out, preferably at a good
Chinese restaurant."
—Jane Fonda, *California Suite*

Candlelight, romantic music, and excellent cuisine—the perfect items
to complement any of these ideal dinner companions.

Albert Finney	*Tom Jones* ('63)
Andre Gregory	*My Dinner with Andre* ('81)
Ryan O'Neal	*The Thief Who Came to Dinner* ('73)
Sidney Poitier	*Guess Who's Coming to Dinner* ('67)
Mickey Rourke	*Diner* ('82)
Monty Woolley	*The Man Who Came to Dinner* ('41)

The Wipe Your Face When You're Finished Eating Award
Awarded to **Gunter Hanse**, as Leatherface, in *The Texas Chainsaw
Massacre* ('74), who not only consumes human flesh, but scampers
around wearing masks made from his victims' faces.

The Eat Until You Pop Award
Awarded to **Michel Piccoli** in *La Grande Bouffe* ('73), who eats so
much he perishes in his own excrement.

The Bon Appétit Award

Awarded to **Anthony Hopkins,** as the ultracarnivorous Dr. Hannibal (the Cannibal) Lector, in *The Silence of the Lambs* ('91), who boasts that he once ate the liver of a U.S. Census taker with some fava beans and a nice Chianti.

BEEF A LA ORIENTAL

"We've got to get these guys ashore. They're going Asiatic."
—Ward Bond, *Mister Roberts*

Beginning in the late 1950s, Hollywood discovered a new kind of Asian male—more exciting, more macho, altogether more realistic. Gone suddenly were the old cinematic stereotypes, who had always been portrayed—bizarre as it seems—by Caucasian actors.

Marc Hayashi	*Chan Is Missing* ('82)
Evan Kim	*The Dead Pool* ('88)
Bruce Lee	*Enter the Dragon* ('73)
Jason Scott Lee	*Dragon: The Bruce Lee Story* ('93)
John Lone	*The Last Emperor* ('87)
Mako	*The Sand Pebbles* ('66)
Yusaku Matsuda	*Black Rain* ('89)
Haing S. Ngor	*The Killing Fields* ('84)
Dustin Nguyen	*Heaven and Earth* ('93)
Ho Nguyen	*Alamo Bay* ('85)
Soon Teck Oh	*Steele Justice* ('87)
Yuji Okumoto	*Aloha Summer* ('88)
Keanu Reeves	*Little Buddha* ('94)
Ryuichi Sakamoto	*Merry Christmas, Mr. Lawrence* ('83)
Koichi Sato	*Shadow of China* ('91)
James Shigeta	*Walk Like a Dragon* ('60)
Robin Shou	*Forbidden Nights* ('90)
George Takei	*Star Trek* ('79), *II* ('82), *III* ('84), *IV* ('86), *V* ('89), *VI* ('91)

Liem Whatley	*The Iron Triangle* ('89)
B. D. Wong	*Chan* ('95)
Russell Wong	*China Girl* ('87)
Kelvin Han Yee	*A Great Wall* ('86)
David Yip	*Ping Pong* ('88)

Royalties: Royal Thais

For an excellent example of Caucasians as Asians, contrast these performances: **Rex Harrison** in *Anna and the King of Siam* ('48) and **Yul Brynner** in *The King and I* ('56). Both essay the same polygamous—but forward-oriented—King of Thailand. Rex was at the height of his Hollywood fame as "Sexy Rexy," while Brynner (who was actually half-Asian) gave baldness a new sexuality. Curiously, neither film has ever been shown in Thailand, because of the extreme reverence attached to the Thai monarchy.

Charlie Chan's Number-One Son

Keye Luke, who played Charlie Chan's Number-One Son in such films as *Charlie Chan at the Opera* ('36) was also an accomplished artist who specialized in murals. Look closely in *The Shanghai Gesture* ('41) and *Macao* ('52) and you'll see some examples of his artistry.

HOT AND SPICY SALSA

"I'd like to take you south of my border, and north of my garter."
—Lainie Kazan, *Lust in the Dust*

Hispanics . . . Latinos . . . it doesn't matter what you call them . . . *aiee caramba* are these chili peppers hot or what?

Joaquim de Almeida	*The Sun and the Moon* ('89)
Robert Beltran	*Eating Raoul* ('82)
Ruben Blades	*Crossover Dreams* ('85)
Raul Julia	*Kiss of the Spider Woman* ('85)
Edward James Olmos	*The Ballad of Gregorio Cortez* ('82)
A Martinez	*She-Devil* ('89)

Lou Diamond Phillips	*La Bamba* ('87)
Robby Rosa	*Salsa* ('88)
Pepe Serna	*The Day of the Locust* ('75)
Jimmy Smits	*Old Gringo* ('89)

SOUL FOOD

"Black guys are so yummy, chocolate-covered love."
—Nell Carter, *Hair*

From singers to farmers, from detectives to lovers . . . a tasty sampling of bros.

Harry Belafonte	*Island in the Sun* ('57)
Jim Brown	*100 Rifles* ('69)
Nat "King" Cole	*St. Louis Blues* ('58)
Clifton Davis	*Lost in the Stars* ('74)
Al Freeman	*Finian's Rainbow* ('68)
Danny Glover	*The Color Purple* ('85)
Dennis Haysbert	*Love Field* ('92)
Cleavon Little	*Blazing Saddles* ('73)
Eddie Murphy	*Beverly Hills Cop* ('84)
Ron O'Neal	*Superfly* ('72)
Sidney Poitier	*For Love of Ivy* ('68)
Richard Pryor	*Blue Collar* ('78)
Howard E. Rollins	*Ragtime* ('81)
Richard Roundtree	*Shaft* ('71)
Wesley Snipes	*White Men Can't Jump* ('92)
Philip-Michael Thomas	*Death Drug* ('78)
Robert Townsend	*Hollywood Shuffle* ('87)
Mario Van Peebles	*Jaws the Revenge* ('87)
Melvin Van Peebles	*Sweet Sweetback's Baadasssss Song* ('71)
Denzel Washington	*Cry Freedom* ('87)

Keenen Ivory Wayans	*I'm Gonna Git You Sucka* ('88)
Carl Weathers	*Action Jackson* ('88)
Billy Dee Williams	*Lady Sings the Blues* ('72)
Fred Williamson	*The Messenger* ('87)
Paul Winfield	*Sounder* ('72)

MATZO BALLS

"I gave Moses the tablets because he had a bad memory."
—George Burns, *Oh, God!*

Putz, nebbish, schlemiel, mensch, meshuggeneh. Portrayals of Jewish males range from put-upon sons and henpecked husbands to historical heroes and gangsters. A selection of matzo balls for your sampling:

Woody Allen	*Annie Hall* ('77)
Alan Arkin	*Simon* ('80)
George Arliss	*Disraeli* ('29)
Alan Bates	*The Fixer* ('68)
Richard Benjamin	*Portnoy's Complaint* ('72)
Robby Benson	*The Chosen* ('81)
James Caan	*Funny Lady* ('75)
Godfrey Cambridge	*Bye Bye Braverman* ('68)
Montgomery Clift	*Judgment at Nuremburg* ('61); *Freud* ('62)
Ben Cross	*Chariots of Fire* ('81)
Tony Curtis	*Lepke* ('75)
Richard Dreyfuss	*The Apprenticeship of Duddy Kravitz* ('74)
Elliott Gould	*The Night They Raided Minsky's* ('68)
Charles Grodin	*The Heartbreak Kid* ('72)
Charlton Heston	*Ben-Hur* ('59)
Dustin Hoffman	*The Marathon Man* ('76); *Lenny* ('74)
Brendan Hughes	*School Ties* ('92)

Steven Keats	*Hester Street* ('75)
Alan King	*Just Tell Me What You Want* ('80)
Ron Leibman	*Norma Rae* ('79)
Zero Mostel	*The Producers* ('68); *The Angel Levine* ('70)
Paul Newman	*Exodus* ('60)
Laurence Olivier	*The Boys from Brazil* ('78); *The Jazz Singer* ('80)
Michael Ontkean	*Willie and Phil* ('80)
Gregory Peck	*Gentleman's Agreement* ('47)
Saul Rubinek	*Soup for One* ('82)
Reni Santoni	*Enter Laughing* ('67)
Maximilian Schell	*The Man in the Glass Booth* ('75)
George Segal	*Where's Poppa?* ('70)
Peter Sellers	*I Love You, Alice B. Toklas* ('68)
Topol	*Fiddler on the Roof* ('71)
Gene Wilder	*The Frisco Kid* ('79)

SEAFOOD

"There's a magic in water that draws all men away from the land,
that leads them over the hills, down the creeks and streams
and rivers to the sea—the sea where each man,
as in a mirror, finds himself."

—Richard Basehart, *Moby Dick*

Oh, sing a sea chantey of sailorboys, sailorboys in pants of white, stretched across delectable backsides so tight.

James Caan	*Cinderella Liberty* ('73)
Brad Davis	*Querelle* ('82)
Errol Flynn	*The Sea Hawk* ('40)
John Garfield	*The Sea Wolf* ('41)
Jeffrey Hunter	*Sailor of the King* ('53)
Gene Kelly	*On the Town* ('49)

Kris Kristofferson	*The Sailor Who Fell from Grace with the Sea* ('76)
Burt Lancaster	*The Crimson Pirate* ('52)
Jack Nicholson	*The Last Detail* ('73)
Gregory Peck	*The World in His Arms* ('52)
Jurgen Prochnow	*Das Boot* ('81)
Frank Sinatra	*On the Town* ('49)
Terence Stamp	*Billy Budd* ('62)
John Wayne	*In Harm's Way* ('65)

ASSORTED PASTA DISHES

"You say to me, 'Caesar, there are rumblings in the Senate.' Well, I say to you nonsense, it's just all that damn spaghetti they eat."
—Kenneth Williams, *Carry on Cleo*

The Italian male—a selection of tasty pasta dishes for your pleasure. Some hot, some cold, some *al dente*, some tender.

Joseph Bologna	*Made for Each Other* ('71)
Marlon Brando	*The Godfather* ('72)
Nicolas Cage	*Moonstruck* ('87)
Vittorio De Sica	*General Della Rovere* ('59)
Peter Falk	*Cookie* ('89)
Vittorio Gassman	*A Wedding* ('78)
Gene Kelly	*The Black Hand* ('50)
Christopher Lambert	*The Sicilian* ('87)
Burt Lancaster	*The Leopard* ('63)
Marcello Mastroianni	*Marriage Italian-Style* ('64)
Franco Nero	*Salamander* ('81)
Jerry Orbach	*The Gang That Couldn't Shoot Straight* ('71)
Al Pacino	*The Godfather, Part II* ('74)
Peter Sellers	*After the Fox* ('66)

Vincent Spano	*Good Morning, Babylon* ('87)
Dean Stockwell	*Married to the Mob* ('88)
Raf Vallone	*A View from the Bridge* ('62)

Oooooh! How I Love Italian Food

Murray Creature plays a hungry, humanoid alien in *Eat and Run* ('86), who's addicted to Italian food—Italian men and women, that is.

FROGS' LEGS

"Married, divorced, married, divorced. Oh, *l'amour, l'amour.*
That's French for love."
—Mary Boland, *The Women*

La cuisine français—the French male. Romantic, debonair, full of *joie de vivre* and effervescent like the finest champagne. The truly "Continental" male—the male by whom all other romantic males are judged.

Armand Assante	*Belizaire the Cajun* ('86)
Charles Aznavour	*Shoot the Piano Player* ('60)
Jean-Paul Belmondo	*That Man from Rio* ('64)
Charles Boyer	*Algiers* ('38)
Maurice Chevalier	*Can-Can* ('60)
Pierre Clementi	*Benjamin* ('68)
Alain Delon	*Joy House* ('64)
Gerard Depardieu	*Bye Bye Monkey* ('78)
Patrick Dewaere	*Get Out Your Handkerchiefs* ('78)
Jean Gabin	*Pepe Le Moko* ('37)
Johnny Hallyday	*Family Business* ('86)
Louis Jourdan	*Gigi* ('58)
John Malkovich	*Dangerous Liaisons* ('88)
Jean Marais	*Beauty and the Beast* ('46)
Yves Montand	*Let's Make Love* ('60)
Jean-Louis Trintignant	*A Man and a Woman* ('66)

PIROSHKIS

"Why do they always look like unhappy rabbits?"
—Marilyn Monroe, *All About Eve*

Piroshkis . . . juicy Russian meat pies. Tsarist, Red, Leninist, Stalinist, and Mr. Good Guy Russki. No matter which flavor is your choice, they're all available here for your consumption.

Woody Allen	*Love and Death* ('75)
Dana Andrews	*The Iron Curtain* ('48)
Alan Arkin	*The Russians Are Coming! The Russians Are Coming!* ('66)
Lionel Barrymore	*Rasputin and the Empress* ('32)
Mikhail Baryshnikov	*White Nights* ('85)
Alexi Batalov	*The Cranes Are Flying* ('57)
Charles Boyer	*Tovarich* ('37)
Charles Bronson	*Telefon* ('77)
Yul Brynner	*The Brothers Karamazov* ('58); *Anastasia* ('56)
Richard Burton	*Trotsky* ('72)
Louis Calhern	*The Red Danube* ('49)
Richard Chamberlain	*The Music Lovers* ('71)
Nikolai Cherkassov	*Ivan the Terrible, Part One* ('43); *Part Two* ('46)
Sean Connery	*The Hunt for Red October* ('90)
Tom Courtenay	*One Day in the Life of Ivan Denisovich* ('71); *Doctor Zhivago* ('65)
Robert Duvall	*Stalin* ('92)
Nelson Eddy	*Balalaika* ('39)
Mel Ferrer	*War and Peace* ('56)
Peter Firth	*Letter to Brezhnev* ('85)
Henry Fonda	*War and Peace* ('56)
John Gavin	*Romanoff and Juliet* ('61)

Farley Granger	*The North Star* ('43)
Bob Hoskins	*The Inner Circle* ('91)
Whip Hubley	*Russkies* ('87)
Tom Hulce	*The Inner Circle* ('91)
William Hurt	*Gorky Park* ('83)
Walter Huston	*The North Star* ('43)
Michael Jayston	*Nicholas and Alexandra* ('71)
John Phillip Law	*The Russians Are Coming! The Russians Are Coming!* ('66)
Christopher Lee	*Rasputin—the Mad Monk* ('66)
Dolph Lundgren	*Red Scorpion* ('89)
Fredric March	*Anna Karenina* ('35)
Malcolm McDowell	*Gulag* ('85)
Peter McEnery	*I Killed Rasputin* ('67)
Alfred Molina	*Letter to Brezhnev* ('85)
Ron Moody	*The Twelve Chairs* ('70)
Jason Patric	*The Beast* ('88)
George de la Peña	*Nijinsky* ('80)
Nehemiah Persoff	*Francis Gary Powers: The True Story of the U-2 Spy Incident* ('76)
Alexei Petrenko	*Rasputin* ('85)
Roman Polanski	*Back in the USSR* ('91)
Edmund Purdom	*The Cossacks* ('59)
Christopher Reeve	*Anna Karenina* ('85)
Arnold Schwarzenegger	*Red Heat* ('88)
Omar Sharif	*Doctor Zhivago* ('65)
William Shatner	*The Brothers Karamazov* ('58)
Robert Shaw	*From Russia with Love* ('63)
Charles Martin Smith	*Boris and Natasha* ('92)
Anatoli Solonitezine	*Andrei Rublev* ('66)
Max von Sydow	*Red King, White Knight* ('89)
Robin Williams	*Moscow on the Hudson* ('84)

CUISINE EXOTICA

"Persian good-bye?
Why that ain't nuttin' next to an Oklahoma hello."
—Gene Nelson, *Oklahoma*

L'homme exotique—the exotic man. From faraway Araby, mysterious India, and other assorted parts of the globe.

Persian-Arab Melon Balls

Steven Bauer	*The Beast* ('88)
Kabir Bedi	*Ashanti* ('79)
Turhan Bey	*The Mummy's Tomb* ('42)
Ronald Colman	*Kismet* ('44)
Sean Connery	*The Wind and the Lion* ('75)
Tony Curtis	*The Prince Who Was a Thief* ('51)
Douglas Fairbanks	*The Thief of Baghdad* ('24)
Jon Hall	*Arabian Nights* ('42)
Mark Harmon	*Tuareg, the Desert Warrior* ('77)
Paul Henreid	*Thief of Damascus* ('52)
Howard Keel	*Kismet* ('55)
Ben Kingsley	*Harem* ('85)
Franco Nero	*Harold Robbins' The Pirate* ('78)
Anthony Quinn	*Lion of the Desert* ('81)
Steve Reeves	*The Thief of Baghdad* ('61)
Dale Robertson	*Son of Sinbad* ('55)
Omar Sharif	*Lawrence of Arabia* ('62)
Vincent Spano	*The Black Stallion Returns* ('83)
Rudolph Valentino	*The Sheik* ('21)
Eric Vu-An	*The Sheltering Sky* ('90)
Cornel Wilde	*Omar Khayyam* ('57)
Lambert Wilson	*Sahara* ('84)

Indian Curries

Victor Banerjee	*A Passage to India* ('84)
Richard Burton	*The Rains of Ranchipur* ('55)
Shashi Kapoor	*Shakespeare Wallah* ('65)
Ben Kingsley	*Gandhi* ('82)
Victor Mature	*The Bandit of Zhobe* ('59)
Tyrone Power	*The Rains Came* ('39)
Sabu	*The Jungle Book* ('42)
Peter Sellers	*The Millionairess* ('60)
Gordon Warnecke	*My Beautiful Laundrette* ('85)

Polynesian Luau

Jon Hall	*The Hurricane* ('37)
Dayton Ka'ne	*Hurricane* ('79)
Jason Scott Lee	*Rapa Nui* ('94)
Matahi	*Tabu* ('31)

Eskimo Pies

Mikkel Gaup	*Pathfinder* ('88)
Jason Scott Lee	*Map of the Human Heart* ('93)
Toshiro Mifune	*Shadow of the Wolf* ('93)
Lou Diamond Phillips	*Shadow of the Wolf* ('93)
Anthony Quinn	*The Savage Innocents* ('59)

Gypsy Goulashes

Pedro Armendiaz	*From Russia with Love* ('63)
Angelo Evans	*Angelo, My Love* ('83)
Bekim Fehmiu	*I Even Met Happy Gypsies* ('67)
Vittorio Gassman	*The Miracle* ('59)
Sterling Hayden	*King of the Gypsies* ('78)
Judd Hirsch	*King of the Gypsies* ('78)
Harvey Keitel	*Monkey Trouble* ('94)
Christopher Lee	*The Passage* ('79)

Franco Nero	*The Virgin and the Gypsy* ('70)
James Edward Olmos	*Triumph of the Spirit* ('89)
Eric Roberts	*King of the Gypsies* ('78)
Walter Slezak	*The Miracle* ('59)
Cornel Wilde	*Hot Blood* ('56)

DOWN-HOME SOUTHERN COOKING

"Baby, you got me hotter 'n Georgia asphalt."
—Laura Dern, *Wild at Heart*

Stately white columns on big houses, dense vegetation, cotton fields, rednecks, moonshine, and black whips cracking—all southern items. Pick your favorite one, and your southern male to go with it—he's ready, willing, and able to pleasure yo' body.

Fried Fine So'thern Gentlemen

George Brent	*Jezebel* ('38)
Robert Duvall	*Rambling Rose* ('91)
Henry Fonda	*Jezebel* ('38)
Clark Gable	*Gone with the Wind* ('39)
Fred Gwynne	*My Cousin Vinny* ('92)
Rex Harrison	*The Foxes of Harrow* ('47)
Van Heflin	*Tap Roots* ('48)
Leslie Howard	*Gone with the Wind* ('39)
Gregory Peck	*To Kill a Mockingbird* ('62)

Masters

Stephen Boyd	*Slaves* ('69)
Clark Gable	*Band of Angels* ('57)
Perry King	*Mandingo* ('75)
Warren Oates	*Drum* ('76)
Edward Woodward	*Uncle Tom's Cabin* ('87)

Good Ole Boy Potpies

Joe Don Baker	*Walking Tall* ('73)
Marlon Brando	*The Chase* ('66)
Steve McQueen	*The Reivers* ('69)
Robert Redford	*The Chase* ('66)
Burt Reynolds	*W. W. and the Dixie Dancekings* ('75)
Jan-Michael Vincent	*Buster and Billie* ('74)

White Trash Mishmash

Michael Caine	*Hurry Sundown* ('67)
Charley Grapewin	*Tobacco Road* ('41)
Lee Marvin	*The Klansman* ('74)
Robert Mitchum	*Thunder Road* ('58)
Aldo Ray	*God's Little Acre* ('58)
Robert Ryan	*God's Little Acre* ('58)

Everybody's Favorite Southern Uncle
James Baskett, as Uncle Remus, in *Song of the South* ('49).

SHORT ORDERS

"You miserable, cowardly wretched little caterpillar!
Don't you ever want to become a butterfly?"
—Zero Mostel, *The Producers*

Half-pints, peewees, li'l bits of love. They're short men, but these short orders might mean big-sized action when any of them start operating.

Robert Blake	*Electra Glide in Blue* ('73)
Seymour Cassel	*Minnie and Moskowitz* ('71)
Chevy Chase	*Fletch* ('85)
Billy Crystal	*Running Scared* ('86)
Brad Davis	*A Rumor of War* ('80)
Danny DeVito	*Ruthless People* ('86)

Michael J. Fox	*The Secret of My Success* ('87)
Henry Gibson	*Nashville* ('75)
Ben Glass	*Smart Alec* ('86)
Joel Grey	*Cabaret* ('72)
Robert Hays	*Airplane!* ('80)
Dustin Hoffman	*The Graduate* ('67)
Alan Ladd	*Shane* ('53)
Spike Lee	*School Daze* ('88)
Roddy McDowall	*Dead of Winter* ('87)
Dudley Moore	*10* ('79)
Al Pacino	*Panic in Needle Park* ('71)
Michael J. Pollard	*Little Fauss and Big Halsy* ('70)
Steve Railsback	*The Stunt Man* ('80)
Mickey Rooney	*A Family Affair* ('37)
Wallace Shawn	*My Dinner with Andre* ('81)
Russ Tamblyn	*tom thumb* ('58)
Gene Wilder	*Start the Revolution Without Me* ('70)
Paul Williams	*Phantom of the Paradise* ('74)

Little People

Billy Barty	*Rumpelstiltskin* ('87)
Warwick Davis	*Willow* ('88)
Michael Dunn	*Ship of Fools* ('65)
Phil Fondacero	*Troll* ('86)
Ed Gale	*Howard the Duck* ('86)
David Rappaport	*The Time Bandits* ('81)
Angelo Rossitto	*Mad Max Beyond Thunderdome* ('85)
Rene Ruiz	*Under the Volcano* ('84)
Felix Silla	*The She Freak* ('66)
Herve Villechaize	*The Man with the Golden Gun* ('74)

Height Problems

In *Boy on a Dolphin* ('57), Sophia Loren either walked in a ditch or **Alan Ladd** stood on a raised surface so the tall Italian beauty wouldn't tower over the little man.

In *Casablanca* ('42), **Humphrey Bogart** wore large lifts attached to the bottoms of his shoes to achieve some height over costar Ingrid Bergman.

DISGUSTINGLY GROSS

"Did you see his last picture?
I could eat a can of Kodak and puke a better picture."
—Kim Novak, *The Mirror Crack'd*

Repulsive. Awful. Ugh! Can you believe what these men have done? If we hadn't seen it with our own eyes on the screen, we wouldn't have believed it! They vomited, they ate bugs . . . they're the disgustingly gross.

BUG EATERS

Watch out for these guys . . . if they see a bug scampering by, they'll snatch it up and pop it right into their mouths.

Nicolas Cage	*Vampire's Kiss* ('89)
Arte Johnson	*Love at First Bite* ('79)
Brian Thompson	*Fright Night II* ('89)
Tom Waits	*Bram Stoker's Dracula* ('92)

QUEASY STOMACHS

Be careful around these men . . . they're liable to cut loose and throw up all over you.

James Garner	*The Glitter Dome* ('84)
Zach Gilligan	*Round Trip to Heaven* ('91)

Bobcat Goldthwait	*Shakes the Clown* ('91)
Tony Goldwyn	*Kuffs* ('92)
Gregory Harrison	*Razorback* ('84)
Rutger Hauer	*Turkish Delight* ('74)
Don Johnson	*Dead-Bang* ('89)

THE I BET YOU'LL LOVE WHAT'S IN MY PANTS AWARD

Awarded to **Crispin Glover** of *Wild at Heart* ('90), who stuffs cockroaches in his underpants.

DO YOU BELIEVE HE SAID THAT?

"I'd punch you in the nose if I weren't afraid you'd break my jaw."
—Don Beddoe, *The Bachelor and the Bobby-Soxer*

In *Chinatown* ('74) when a policeman asks why he's wearing a bandage on his nose, Jack Nicholson replies: "Your wife closed her legs."

In *Gilda* ('46), Glenn Ford tells George Macready: "I was born the night I met you."

In *Hair* ('79), Don Dacus, as the male character Woof, confides: "Don't get me wrong, I'm not queer, but I wouldn't kick Mick Jagger out of bed."

In *Kiss of Death* ('47), supermacho Richard Widmark assures supermacho Victor Mature: "Dames are no good if you want to have fun."

In *Myra Breckenridge* ('70), Rex Reed, as Myron Breckenridge, wakes up and screams: "My tits! Where are MY TITS!"

In *Partners* ('82), Ryan O'Neal questions his police captain: "Why'd you choose me for this job?" and receives the answer, "Because you're a good cop, and you have a cute ass."

In *Streamers* ('83), Michael Wright, as Carlyle the angry Black recruit, describes his sexuality: "Since I first got on pussy and made it happy to know me."

In *Thunderbolt and Lightfoot* ('74), Jeff Bridges, dressed as a woman, pleads to Clint Eastwood: "We've got to stop meeting like this, you know. After all, where there's smoke, there's fire."

In *Waterhole #3* ('67), James Coburn describes his rape of Margaret Blie as: "An assault with a friendly weapon."

DOCTOR, I DON'T FEEL SO GOOD

"Insanity doesn't run in my family. It practically gallops!"
—Cary Grant, *Arsenic and Old Lace*

THE RETARDATES

Portraying the mentally handicapped presents an actor with the opportunity to literally "chew up the scenery," as witnessed by the performances listed below, two of which won an Oscar for Best Actor.

Norman Alden	*Andy* ('65)
Jim Belushi	*Homer & Eddie* ('90)
Robby Benson	*Two of a Kind* ('82)
Jeff Fahey	*Lawnmower Man* ('92)
Mel Gibson	*Tim* ('79)
Dustin Hoffman	*Rain Man* ('88)
Tom Hulce	*Dominick and Eugene* ('88)
Peter Linari	*Fat Guy Goes Nutzoid* ('86)
Rob Lowe	*Square Dance* ('87)
David Proval	*Nunzio* ('78)
Cliff Robertson	*Charly* ('68)

THE AMNESIACS

Who am I? Where am I? How did I get here? What happened? Who are you? Why am I wearing this? Where are my clothes? Trite questions, but the answers are of vital importance to the amnesiacs.

Tom Berenger	*Shattered* ('91)
Charles Bronson	*Someone Behind the Door* ('71)
Richard Chamberlain	*The Bourne Identity* ('88)
Ronald Colman	*Random Harvest* ('42)
James Garner	*Mister Buddwing* ('66)
John Hodiak	*Somewhere in the Night* ('46)
Zeljko Ivanek	*The Sender* ('82)
Gregory Peck	*Spellbound* ('45)
George Peppard	*The Third Day* ('65)
Michael Sarrazin	*The Groundstar Conspiracy* ('72)
Robert Webber	*Hysteria* ('64)

DON'T MESS WITH THESE MEN

> "You see, I'm not one of those eye-for-an-eye men.
> I always take two eyes."
> —Luther Adler, *Wake of the Red Witch*

They might be handsome, sexy, or intriguing—but is the pleasure worth the trouble?

Steve Martin—*Little Shop of Horrors* ('86)—Martin adds a whole new aura to the art of dental pain as a sadistic, singing, laughing-gas sniffing dentist. He is especially chilling when he sings, "Open wide, here I come." He is definitely not Dr. Prentice, the Painless Dentist.

Richard Roundtree—*Shaft's Big Score* ('72)—In the film's theme song, Shaft (Roundtree) is described by two female singers thusly: "Dat man be trouble, he's been to my house," and "He take a gun, blow a hole 'n yo' mind."

Julian Sands—*Boxing Helena* ('93)—Sands, a physician who's obsessed by Sherilyn Fenn, amputates her arms and legs, then keeps her prisoner until she grows to return his love.

Andrew Stevens—*The Fury* ('78)—Discovering he has been betrayed by his lover, an older woman who's also a scientist charged with monitoring him, Stevens, who possesses psychokinetic powers, causes her to rise into the air. Once she's positioned hanging above him, he berates her for treachery, then rapidly spins her around until she dies, flinging blood and gore about the room.

TRUE EVIL HAS MANY DISGUISES

Powers Boothe	*Guyana Tragedy: The Story of Jim Jones* ('80)
Alec Guinness	*Hitler: The Last Ten Days* ('73)
Christopher Lee	*Rasputin—The Mad Monk* ('66)
Malcolm McDowell	*Caligula* ('80)
Joseph Olita	*Amin—The Rise and Fall* ('81)

No More Mr. Nice Guy

Intimate Strangers ('77) features former all-around Mr. Nice Guy **Dennis Weaver** as a two-fisted wife beater.

THEY'RE WORSE WHEN THEY'RE IN GROUPS

"I'm a ba-a-a-a-ad boy."
—Lou Costello, all his films

Cruising ('80) is a homosexual slasher murder mystery set amid the leather bars of New York. Al Pacino's a hetero detective who's sent undercover into the nether leather world to root out the murderer. Roaming through the nightlife and crowded bars, he sees, and experiences, plenty of action. It's the type of action, along with the male characters, not usually seen in a mainstream film. By the conclusion, Al's discovered new fun-time friends, plus some disturbing new insights into his own hitherto sacrosanct masculinity.

The Leather Boys ('63) peeps into the British motorcycle set. Now that he's married, a new husband has trouble coming to grips with his close relationship with a single, leather buddy from his old motorcycle group. A new variation on the triangle: This time, it's a man, a woman, and a leatherman on a motorcycle.

The Men's Club ('86) begins when an odd assortment of males who loosely form themselves into an unorthodox, impromptu support group, go out into the night seeking some female "company."

Pixote ('81) presents life among underaged and impoverished Brazilian boys of the street who indulge in prostitution to keep alive.

Spetters ('80) features rowdy Dutch motorcyclists rampaging and trying to impress each other and the girls in their lives. Three of the guys even hold a peter-measuring contest to determine who should bed their favorite female first. The term *spetters* is Dutch slang for semen.

Tea and Sympathy ('56) occurs when the "macho" version of manhood conflicts with the "gentler" version, as a group of athletic types harass a less-masculine schoolmate. His fears of any latent homosexuality finally get erased by an encounter with an understanding coach's wife. Pay close attention—and try not to laugh—at her hysterical seduction line, "Years from now when you speak of this—and you will—please be kind."

DOUBLE VISION

"You're as phony to me as an opera soprano."
—Burt Lancaster, *Separate Tables*

Double vision is seeing double, and that means double pleasure. Two performances for the price of one, courtesy of one actor performing twin roles. Or maybe it's real twins—or even different actors pretending to be twins. Whatever the gimmick, it's still double vision for the viewer.

REAL TWINS IN THE SAME FILM

Brian Deacon, Eric Deacon	*A Zed & Two Noughts* ('85)
Mike Gwilym, Roland Gwilym	*On the Black Hill* ('90)
Gary Kemp, Martin Kemp	*The Krays* ('90)
David Paul, Peter Paul	*The Barbarians* ('87)
Chris Udvarnoky, Martin Udvarnoky	*The Other* ('72)

REAL TWINS

Rex Reason	*Band of Angels* ('57)
Rhodes Reason	*Yellowstone Kelly* ('59)

PHONY TWINS

Danny DeVito, Arnold Schwarzenegger	*Twins* ('88)
Tom Hulce, Ray Liotta	*Dominick and Eugene* ('88)
John Hurt, Julian Sands	*After Darkness* ('85)
Donald Sutherland, Gene Wilder	*Start the Revolution Without Me* ('70)

TWIN ROLES

Beau Bridges	*The Fifth Musketeer* ('79)
Barry Crocker	*Barry MacKenzie Holds His Own* ('74)
Jim Dale	*Hot Lead and Cold Feet* ('78)
Cliff de Young	*Shock Treatment* ('81)
Kirk Douglas	*The Man from Snowy River* ('82)
Leon Errol	*Slightly Terrific* ('44)
Trevor Eve	*The Corsican Brothers* ('85)
Douglas Fairbanks Jr.	*The Corsican Brothers* ('41)
Grant Goodeve	*Take Two* ('89)
George Hamilton	*Zorro, the Gay Blade* ('81)
Louis Hayward	*The Man in the Iron Mask* ('39)
Ian Hendry	*Killer with Two Faces* ('74)
Charlton Heston	*Mother Lode* ('82)
Judd Hirsch	*Brotherly Love* ('85)
Jeremy Irons	*Dead Ringers* ('88)
Malcolm Jamieson	*Meridian* ('90)
Boris Karloff	*The Black Room* ('35)
Danny Kaye	*Wonder Man* ('45)

Jean Leclerc	*Whispers* ('90)
Fredric March	*Strangers in Love* ('32)
Lee Marvin	*Cat Ballou* ('65)
Stephen McHattie	*Death Valley* ('82)
Matthew Modine	*Equinox* ('93)
Michael Moriarity	*Blood Link* ('83)
Jack Palance	*House of Numbers* ('57)
Michael Paré	*Killing Streets* ('91)
Elvis Presley	*Kissin' Cousins* ('64)
Aidan Quinn	*Lies of the Twins* ('91)
Steve Railsback	*Scissors* ('91)
James Spader	*Jack's Back* ('88)
Jean-Claude Van Damme	*Double Impact* ('91)
Conrad Veidt	*Nazi Agent* ('42)
Keenan Wynn	*Royal Wedding* ('51)

EGO TRIPS

"In my case, self-absorption is completely justified. I have never discussed any other subject quite so worthy of my attention."
—Clifton Webb, *Laura*

The Taming of the Shrew ('29)—One of the title credits reads: *By William Shakespeare, with additional dialogue by Sam Taylor.* How fortunate that cinema viewers were to have the unknown Shakespeare's atrocious dialogue improved by the words of the world-renowned Sam Taylor!

Withnail and I ('87)—A "Consultant" credit appears for Richard Starkey, M.B.E., who's none other than Ringo Starr. Given that most of the actors who have received actual knighthoods—Olivier, Gielgud, Richardson, for example—often appear in films without their "Sir" prefacing their names, it would have been politic for Starkey to do likewise with his lesser honor.

The World's Greatest Athlete ('73)—At one point in the film, Howard Cosell utters the pompous line: "I've never seen anything like this in my entire *illustrious* career."

DON'T CALL US, WE'LL CALL YOU

The job was to play Jor-el, Superman's father, in *Superman* ('78). Marlon Brando, who signed at a rumored $18 million fee, reportedly tried to talk the director into letting him play it as a "voice" emanating from a suitcase, without ever having to appear on the screen.

WHICH TWO DID HE MISS?

"Let's just get something straight right off the top, babe, huh?
I don't get involved with my women. I'm a short-termed guy.
I don't fall in love. I don't want to get married.
The only thing you can count on me for is sex."
—Cliff Gorman, *An Unmarried Woman*

Supermacho **Steve McQueen** used to boast that he had slept with all his leading ladies. Not so, claimed first wife, Neile Adams McQueen. She said that her husband—who told her about most of his sexual exploits—didn't make the score with two of his costars. Here are Steve's leading ladies in his films in the order in which they were released; which two do you think he missed?

Aneta Corseaut	*The Blob* ('58)
Gina Lollobrigida	*Never So Few* ('59)
Paula Prentiss	*The Honeymoon Machine* ('61)
Shirley Ann Field	*The War Lover* ('62)
Natalie Wood	*Love with the Proper Stranger* ('63)
Tuesday Weld	*Soldier in the Rain* ('63)
Lee Remick	*Baby, the Rain Must Fall* ('65)
Ann-Margret	*The Cincinnati Kid* ('65)
Suzanne Pleshette	*Nevada Smith* ('66)
Candace Bergen	*The Sand Pebbles* ('66)
Faye Dunaway	*The Thomas Crown Affair* ('68)
Jacqueline Bisset	*Bullitt* ('68)

Sharon Farrell	*The Reivers* ('69)
Elga Andersen	*Le Mans* ('71)
Ida Lupino	*Junior Bonner* ('72)
Ali MacGraw	*The Getaway* ('72)
Linda Evans	*Tom Horn* ('80)
Kathryn Harrold	*The Hunter* ('80)

FANGS A LOT,
I HAD A BLOODY SWELL TIME

"At our last meeting, I died. It alters the appearance."
—Deborah Kerr, *The Chalk Garden*

These dudes really know how to boogie all night. They're the kings of the nightlife—the vampires. Here's a selection of the sexiest ones around. But do you really want to hang out with them?

The Bite Me, Bite Me, Oh, Please Bite Me Award
Silvio Oliviero for *Graveyard Shift* ('87)—Oliviero is a hairy-chested, well-built, sexually attractive vampire who works as a cabdriver on the night (get it, *graveyard*) shift, all the better to meet his victims. Naturally, he sleeps in a coffin and really shows off his stuff during several sex scenes in his resting place. This Dark Prince may bring death, but there'll be an orgy of pleasure before it occurs.

The Bela Lugosi-Christopher Lee Merits of Honorable Mention
Christopher Atkins	*Dracula Rising* ('93)
Michael Blodgett	*The Velvet Vampire* ('71)
Steve Bond	*Son of Darkness: To Die For II* ('91)
David Bowie	*The Hunger* ('83)

Nicolas Cage	*Vampire's Kiss* ('89)
Maxwell Caufield	*Sundown: The Vampire in Retreat* ('91)
Ben Cross	*Nightlife* ('89)
Jonathan Frid	*House of Dark Shadows* ('70)
George Hamilton	*Love at First Bite* ('79)
Rutger Hauer	*Buffy, the Vampire Slayer* ('92)
Lance Hendricksen	*Near Dark* ('87)
Edward Herrmann	*The Lost Boys* ('87)
Brendan Hughes	*To Die For* ('89)
Klaus Kinski	*Nosferatu the Vampyre* ('79)
Frank Langella	*Dracula* ('79)
William Marshall	*Blacula* ('72)
David Niven	*Old Dracula* ('74)
Michael Nouri	*The World of Dracula* ('79)
Gary Oldman	*Bram Stoker's Dracula* ('92)
Michael Praed	*Son of Darkness: To Die For II* ('91)
Robert Quarry	*Count Yorga, Vampire* ('70)
Chris Sarandon	*Fright Night* ('85)
Kiefer Sutherland	*The Lost Boys* ('87)

THE FIGHTERS

"This is the only sport in the world where two guys get paid for
doing something they'd be arrested for if they got drunk
and did it for nothing."
—Paul Stewart, *Champion*

Rippling muscles flared, boxers are paradigms of macho power, with
leather gloves slamming in fury against other hard, taut-muscled

male bodies. Then, a bell rings and a champion prances around the ring, his arms raised symbolizing his victorious pounding of another man.

Muhammad Ali	*The Greatest* ('77)
Richard Arlen	*The Leather Pushers* ('40)
Lew Ayres	*The Iron Man* ('31)
Max Baer	*The Prizefighter and the Lady* ('33)
Wallace Beery	*The Champ* ('31)
Tom Berenger	*Flesh & Blood* ('79)
Ruben Blades	*The Last Fight* ('83)
Robert Blake	*Ripped Off* ('71)
Jeff Bridges	*Fat City* ('72)
James Cagney	*City for Conquest* ('40)
Marcel Cerdan Jr.	*Edith and Marcel* ('83)
Jeff Chandler	*Iron Man* ('51)
Dane Clark	*Whiplash* ('48)
Richard Conte	*The Fighter* ('52)
Tim Conway	*The Prize Fighter* ('79)
Tony Curtis	*Flesh and Fury* ('52); *The Square Jungle* ('55)
Willem Dafoe	*Triumph of the Spirit* ('89)
Brad Davis	*Heart* ('87)
Robert De Niro	*Raging Bull* ('80)
John Derek	*The Leather Saint* ('56)
Kirk Douglas	*The Champion* ('49)
Stuart Erwin	*Palooka* ('34)
Erik Estrada	*Honeyboy* ('82)
Jeff Fahey	*Split Decisions* ('88)
Douglas Fairbanks	*The Life of Jimmy Dolan* ('33)
Errol Flynn	*Gentleman Jim* ('42)
Clark Gable	*Cain and Mabel* ('36)
John Garfield	*Body and Soul* ('47)

Harry Hamlin	*Movie Movie* ('78)
Gregory Harrison	*The Fighter* ('83)
William Holden	*Golden Boy* ('39)
James Earl Jones	*The Great White Hope* ('70)
Danny Kaye	*The Kid from Brooklyn* ('46)
Stacy Keach	*Fat City* ('72)
Leon Isaac Kennedy	*Penitentiary* ('79)
Burt Lancaster	*The Killers* ('46)
Harold Lloyd	*The Milky Way* ('36)
Tony Lo Bianco	*Marciano* ('79)
Dolph Lundgren	*Rocky IV* ('85)
William Lundigan	*Sunday Punch* ('42)
Gordon MacRae	*The Big Punch* ('48)
James Marshall	*Gladiator* ('92)
Dewey Martin	*Tennessee Champ* ('54); *The Golden Gloves Story* ('50)
Victor Mature	*Footlight Serenade* ('42)
Greg McClure	*The Great John L.* ('45)
Roddy McDowall	*The Adventures of Bullwhip Griffin* ('67)
Ralph Meeker	*Glory Alley* ('52)
Cameron Mitchell	*Monkey on My Back* ('57)
Sasha Mitchell	*Spike of Bensonhurst* ('88)
Ricardo Montalban	*Right Cross* ('50)
Robert Montgomery	*Here Comes Mr. Jordan* ('41)
Wayne Morris	*Kid Galahad* ('37)
Audie Murphy	*World in My Corner* ('56)
Don Murray	*The Confessions of Tom Harris* ('72)
Liam Neeson	*Crossing the Line* ('91)
Paul Newman	*Somebody Up There Likes Me* ('56)
Pat O'Brien	*The Personality Kid* ('34)
Ryan O'Neal	*The Main Event* ('79)

Adrian Pasdar	*Streets of Gold* ('86)
John Payne	*Kid Nightingale* ('39)
Elvis Presley	*Kid Galahad* ('62)
Dennis Quaid	*Tough Enough* ('83)
Anthony Quinn	*Requiem for a Heavyweight* ('62)
Lalos Rios	*The Ring* ('52)
Mickey Rooney	*Killer McCoy* ('47)
Mickey Rourke	*Homeboy* ('88)
Robert Ryan	*The Set-Up* ('49)
Renato Salvatori	*Rocco and His Brothers* ('60)
O. J. Simpson	*Goldie and the Boxer* ('80)
Sylvester Stallone	*Rocky* ('76), *II* ('79), and *ad nauseum* ('82, '85, '90)
Robert Taylor	*The Crowd Roars* ('38)
Jon Voight	*The Champ* ('79); *The All-American Boy* ('73)
Jimmy Walker	*Let's Do It Again* ('75)
Coley Wallace	*The Joe Louis Story* ('53)
John Wayne	*The Quiet Man* ('52)
Carl Weathers	*Rocky II* ('79)
Treat Williams	*Dempsey* ('83)

FIVE-FINGER EXERCISE

"Hey, don't knock masturbation. It's sex with someone I love."
—Woody Allen, *Annie Hall*

The Good Stroking Grand Prix Award

Dennis Hopper—*Blue Velvet* ('86)—*Masturbatory object*: As he looks between the spread legs of a woman (Isabella Rossellini) he terrorizes, Hopper works himself over while he sniffs laughing gas and calls her "Mommy."

The It Keeps Crawling into My Hand Prize

Michael Woods—*Lady Beware* ('87)—*Where*: (1) While talking on the telephone to a young woman he's pursuing; (2) in the young woman's bed, after he's broken into her apartment. *Masturbatory object*: (1) The young woman's voice, and the thought of what he'd like to do to her; (2) the young woman's nightgown, which he spreads across her bed and humps.

Good Hand Motion Honorable Mentions

Matthew Barry—*Luna* ('79), for letting his mother, played by Jill Clayburgh, lend a helping hand.

Ed Begley Jr.—*Meet the Applegates* ('91) for becoming aroused, in his role as a giant Brazilian cockroach, over a photograph in *Scientific American* of insects mating and rushing off to his typically suburban American bathroom, magazine in hand, to take himself in hand—or wing, as the case may be.

Brad Davis—*Midnight Express* ('78), for cutting loose after seeing his girlfriend's breasts. She's pressed them against the glass partition in the Turkish prison where he's been confined for several years.

Robert Downey Jr.—*Too Much Sun* ('91), for working himself over under the covers of his bed, as a woman, who mistakenly thinks she's his mother, sits on the bed playing her guitar and serenades him with a song.

Peter Firth—*Equus* ('77), for rubbing against the back of a horse he's riding nude outside at night.

Chris Haywood—*Golden Braid* ('90), for spanking his manhood over a golden braid of hair that he's found in an antique chest.

Harvey Keitel—*Bad Lieutenant* ('92), for teasing two young women into having sex with him, then deciding to work himself over instead.

Laurence Luckinbill—*Not For Publication* ('84), for posting a nude centerfold to the wall of his shower stall with soap and moaning "wait for me, baby . . . oh . . . wait for me!" as he climaxes.

Jack Nicholson—*Carnal Knowledge* ('71), for finally getting off with Rita Moreno, a prostitute, because he's become so sexually impotent with women that only manual manipulation works.

Anthony Perkins—*Crimes of Passion* ('84), while viewing a nude dancer in a live porno peep show and concurrently screaming about sin and redemption.

Judge Reinhold—*Fast Times at Ridgemont High* ('82), while hiding in the cabana and watching some females around his parents' pool.

Martin Sheen—*Apocalypse Now* ('79), for rolling around on a hotel bed and rubbing broken pieces of glass into his groin.

Other Hand-Motion Motion Pictures

Masturbation also appears in short scenes of the following films:

Amarcord ('74)

The Apprenticeship of Duddy Kravitz ('74)

Bless the Beasts and Children ('72)

Class of '44 ('73)

Portnoy's Complaint ('72)

MASS-TURBATION

The Filipino film *Macho Dancer* ('88), about the teenage male dancers in a seedy nightclub, features a large group of them seated onstage in a line masturbating together for the audience's pleasure.

A MOST RADICAL CURE

Either ignored or ridiculed by his wife, Gerard Depardieu finally takes up with Ornella Muti as his mistress in the French film *The Last Woman* ('76). Soon, she's treating him as shabbily as his wife did, even forcing Depardieu to masturbate for sexual satisfaction. Finally, the desperate Frenchman decides he's had enough of women and uses an electric knife to amputate his penis.

MATADORS DO IT VIOLENTLY

In *Matador* ('86), a Spanish film, **Nacho Martinez**, playing a retired matador, masturbates while watching the most violent scenes from *Blood and Black Lace* ('64) and *Bloody Moon* ('66), two ultra-bloody, violence-against-women films being shown on TV.

HANDS

"Fill your hands, you son of a bitch!"
—John Wayne, *True Grit*

No idle hands or twiddling thumbs in this bunch. These men know exactly what to do with their hands . . . put them around your neck and strangle. Doobie, doobie, doo . . . stranglers in the night . . . shifting their glance . . . stranglers in the night . . . hoping by perchance . . . a neck to find.

Richard Attenborough	*10 Rillington Place* ('70)
Reb Brown	*Death of a Soldier* ('86)
Victor Buono	*The Strangler* ('64)
Michael Caine	*The Hand* ('81)
Ronald Colman	*A Double Life* ('47)
Laird Cregar	*Hangover Square* ('45)
Tony Curtis	*The Boston Strangler* ('68)
Barry Foster	*Frenzy* ('72)
Allan Goorwitz (Garfield)	*Sketches of a Strangler* ('78)
Farley Granger	*Rope* ('48)
Boris Karloff	*The Haunted Strangler* ('58)
John Loder	*The Brighton Strangler* ('45)
Robert Ryan	*Beware, My Lovely* ('52)
Rod Steiger	*No Way to Treat a Lady* ('68)
Nicholas Worth	*Don't Answer the Phone* ('80)

Serial Killers

"You oughta put handles on that skull.
Maybe you could grow geraniums in it."
—Henry Fonda, *The Lady Eve*

Kill 'em once and kill 'em twice, then kill 'em again and again. One after the other. Serial killers establish a pattern, which they follow over and over. What's the pattern for these serial killers? Well, it varies. But each is a specialist in his own field.

Christopher Atkins	*Fatal Charm* ('92)
Carl Boehm	*Peeping Tom* ('60)
Bud Davis	*The Town That Dreaded Sundown* ('77)
Brian Dennehy	*To Catch a Killer* ('91)
Bobby Di Cicco	*The Baby Doll Murders* ('92)
David Dukes	*The First Deadly Sin* ('80)
Albert Finney	*Night Must Fall* ('64)
Barry Foster	*Frenzy* ('72)
Jeff Goldblum	*Mister Frost* ('90)
Anthony Hopkins	*The Silence of the Lambs* ('91)
Tommy Lee Jones	*The Eyes of Laura Mars* ('78)
David Keith	*White of the Eye* ('87)
Klaus Kinski	*Jack the Ripper* ('79)
Jimmy Laine (Able Ferrara)	*Driller Killer* ('76)
Calvin Levels	*The Atlanta Child Murders* ('85)
Ted Levine	*The Silence of the Lambs* ('91)
Robert Montgomery	*Night Must Fall* ('37)
Judd Nelson	*Relentless* ('89)
Michael Parks	*The China Lake Murders* ('90)
Brad Pitt	*Kalifornia* ('93)
Andy Robinson	*Dirty Harry* ('71)
Michael Rooker	*Henry: Portrait of a Serial Killer* ('90)
Michel Serrault	*Docteur Petiot* ('90)
David Warner	*Time After Time* ('79)
David Wayne	*M* ('51)
Billy Zane	*The Hillside Stranglers* ('89)

THE GALLERY OF PRICELESS ANTIQUES

"Well, at least old age gives tone to certain things—
like violins, old wine."
—Edith Evans, *The Chalk Garden*

Antiques become more priceless as the years pass. What is now an antique was once pristine in its newness—precious, beautiful, desirable. Here is a gallery of now priceless antiques to be admired in their prime.

Marlon Brando	*A Streetcar Named Desire* ('51)
Yul Brynner	*The King and I* ('56)
Rory Calhoun	*River of No Return* ('54)
Tony Curtis	*The Prince Who Was a Thief* ('51)
Kirk Douglas	*The Champion* ('49)
Richard Egan	*The 300 Spartans* ('62)
Douglas Fairbanks	*Thief of Baghdad* ('24)
Douglas Fairbanks Jr.	*Sinbad the Sailor* ('47)
Errol Flynn	*Captain Blood* ('35)
Glenn Ford	*Gilda* ('46)
Clark Gable	*It Happened One Night* ('34)
John Garfield	*The Postman Always Rings Twice* ('46)
Jon Hall	*The Hurricane* ('37)
Charlton Heston	*Ben-Hur* ('59)
Richard Jaeckel	*Come Back, Little Sheba* ('52)
Fernando Lamas	*Dangerous When Wet* ('53)
Burt Lancaster	*The Crimson Pirate* ('52)
Robert Mitchum	*Heaven Knows, Mr. Allison* ('57)
Laurence Olivier	*Wuthering Heights* ('39)

Gregory Peck	*Duel in the Sun* ('46)
Tyrone Power	*Captain from Castile* ('49)
Aldo Ray	*God's Little Acre* ('58)
Ronald Reagan	*King's Row* ('42)
Rudolph Valentino	*The Sheik* ('21)
John Wayne	*Stagecoach* ('39)
Cornel Wilde	*A Thousand and One Nights* ('45)

GREAT DISAPPEARING ACTS

"Go, and never darken my towels again!"
—Groucho Marx, *Duck Soup*

Some things have a way of appearing, and disappearing, depending on the censor's order, the will of the Motion Picture Rating Board, or a distributor's whim. Occasionally, even a film's star gets into the act by making demands about what should or should not appear.

Altered States ('80)—The theatrical print contained a scene where William Hurt's penis was clearly visible. On the videocassette version, Hurt's penis vanished because the print used was not "shadow-boxed" and incapable of showing the film's true width.

Crimes of Passion ('84)—Director Ken Russell made cuts to the theatrical print, the one shown on most premium cable channels, to avoid an X rating. The most infamous scene snipped had hooker China Blue (Kathleen Turner) use a policeman's nightstick on him as a dildo. China Blue's downside job can be viewed on most videocassette prints of the film.

Angel Heart ('87)—Several seconds snipped from Mickey Rourke and Lisa Bonet's sex scene also detoured this devilish film from an X to an R rating. Moviegoers lost sight of Rourke's flabby cheeks slapping together as he plunged between Bonet's spread legs. The footage was restored to the videocassette print release, appearing again when the film made it to cable TV.

Cabaret ('72)—For the film's first showing on network television, ABC deleted all the scenes dealing with Brian's (Michael York's) affair with another man and any mention of the bisexual/homosexual angle to the story.

HAIL TO THE CHIEF

"Don't tell me it's subversive to kiss a Republican."
—John Lund, *A Foreign Affair*

"Why did God make so many dumb fools and Democrats?"
—William Powell, *Life with Father*

Hail to the Chief! Mr. President, Mr. President. The main man at 1600 Pennsylvania Avenue. The occupant of the White House has been played by a variety of actors with varying degrees of success. Here are some.

George Washington	Patrick O'Neal	*Independence* ('76)
John Adams	William Daniels	*1776* ('72)
Thomas Jefferson	Ken Howard	*1776* ('72)
James Madison	Burgess Meredith	*The Magnificent Doll* ('46)
Andrew Jackson	Charlton Heston	*The President's Lady* ('53)
Martin Van Buren	Charles Trowbridge	*The Gorgeous Hussy* ('36)
William Henry Harrison	Douglass Dumbrille	*Ten Gentlemen from West Point* ('42)
James Knox Polk	Addison Richards	*The Oregon Trail* ('59)
Franklin Pierce	Porter Hall	*The Great Moment* ('44)
Abraham Lincoln	Raymond Massey	*How the West Was Won* ('62)
Andrew Johnson	Van Heflin	*Tennessee Johnson* ('42)
Ulysses S. Grant	Jason Robards Jr.	*The Legend of the Lone Ranger* ('81)
Chester Alan Arthur	Larry Gates	*Cattle King* ('63)
Grover Cleveland	Pat McCormick	*Buffalo Bill and the Indians* ('76)

Benjamin Harrison	Roy Gordon	*Stars and Stripes Forever* ('52)
Theodore Roosevelt	Brian Keith	*The Wind and the Lion* ('75)
Woodrow Wilson	Alexander Knox	*Wilson* ('44)
Calvin Coolidge	Ian Wolfe	*The Court Martial of Billy Mitchell* ('55)
Franklin D. Roosevelt	Edward Herrmann	*Annie* ('82)
Harry S. Truman	James Whitmore	*Give 'em Hell, Harry!* ('75)
Dwight D. Eisenhower	Robert Beer	*The Right Stuff* ('83)
John F. Kennedy	James Franciscus	*Jacqueline Bouvier Kennedy* ('81)
Lyndon B. Johnson	Andrew Duggan	*The Private Files of J. Edgar Hoover* ('77)
Richard M. Nixon	Richard M. Dixon	*Where the Buffalo Roam* ('80)
Gerald Ford	Dick Crockett	*The Pink Panther Strikes Again* ('76)
Jimmy Carter	Ed Beheler	*Black Sunday* ('77)

MR. PRESIDENT

Politicians, scamps, scoundrels, heroes, visionaries. Their party doesn't matter, because they're all phonies . . . Mr. President, indeed. Why, it's just somebody imitating a president.

Lloyd Bridges	*Hot Shot! Part Deux* ('93)
Stephen Elliott	*Assassination* ('87)
Henry Fonda	*Fail-Safe* ('64)
Walter Huston	*Gabriel over the White House* ('33)
Christopher Jones	*Wild in the Streets* ('68)
James Earl Jones	*The Man* ('72)
Kevin Kline	*Dave* ('93)
Fredric March	*Seven Days in May* ('64)
Bob Newhart	*First Family* ('80)

Gregory Peck	*Amazing Grace and Chuck* ('87)
Donald Pleasence	*Escape from New York* ('81)
Peter Sellers	*Dr. Strangelove* ('64)
Franchot Tone	*Advise and Consent* ('62)
Lee Tracy	*The Best Man* ('64)
Richard Widmark	*Vanished* ('71)

Quick Quiz

What later president of an African nation starred in a British film during the 1930s?

Jomo Kenyatta, president of Kenya, who played a tribal chief in *Sanders of the River* ('35).

MOVIE STAR AMBASSADORS

John Lodge, who starred with Marlene Dietrich in *The Scarlet Empress* ('34), later served as U.S. ambassador to Spain, Argentina, and Switzerland. Ronald Reagan appointed his friend **John Gavin**, Janet Leigh's lover in *Psycho* ('60), as ambassador to Mexico.

HOUSE BOYS

Three former film stars have served in the U.S. Congress. Shirley Temple's old dancing partner **George Murphy** was a Republican U.S. senator from California, 1964-1970, before being defeated. Olympian **Bob Mathias**, who had a brief career in films, served in the U.S. House as a Republican from California, 1966-1974. Democrat **Will Rogers Jr.**, who starred in his father's film biography, served in the U.S. House of Representatives, 1942-1944, from California.

Unsuccessful candidates for the U.S. House of Representatives have included **Ralph Waite** and sons of both **Gregory Peck** and **Bob Hope**.

John D. Lodge, the brother of Henry Cabot Lodge, and **Ronald Reagan**, both Republicans, are the only film stars to have been elected governor; Lodge in Connecticut and Reagan in California. **Rex Bell**, cowboy star of many films including *She Wore a Yellow Ribbon* (49), and husband of "It Girl" Clara Bow, served as lieutenant governor of Nevada and was running for governor when he died in 1962.

THE HAIRY-BACK BRIGADE

"Beware of men who are hairy on the inside, too."
—Angela Lansbury, *The Company of Wolves*

Do men in the hairy-back brigade excite you? Care for that simian-furry look across a male's back? Try these:

Aldo Ray	*God's Little Acre* ('58)
William Bendix	*The Hairy Ape* ('44)
James Caan	*The Rain People* ('69)
Robert Carradine	*Revenge of the Nerds* ('84)
Andrew Dice Clay	*Casual Sex?* ('88)
Elliott Gould	*Bob & Carol & Ted & Alice* ('69)
Nigel Green	*Let's Kill Uncle* ('66)
Bob Hoskins	*Mona Lisa* ('86)
Steve Martin	*All of Me* ('84)
Craig T. Nelson	*Poltergeist* ('82)
Franco Nero	*The Virgin and the Gypsy* ('70)
Laurence Olivier	*The Betsy* ('78)
John Ritter	*Skin Deep* ('89)
Maximilian Schell	*The Man in the Glass Booth* ('75)
Peter Sellers	*The Bobo* ('67)
Ron Silver	*Eat and Run* ('86)

Special Project

Check out these two stars and see if their backs have gotten less hirsute. First, watch **Mark Harmon** in *Goliath Awaits* ('81), then observe him in *Summer School* ('87). Sure appears that Mark's been depilatoried. Next, catch some of **Chuck Norris**'s really early chop-socky-kung-phooey films—looks like ole Chuck was hairier then than he is now.

ROUGH COMPLEXIONS

If you like your male with a rough complexion, here are six of the roughest around.

Robert Davi	*License to Kill* ('84)
Anthony James	*In the Heat of the Night* ('67)
Tommy Lee Jones	*The Fugitive* ('93)
Richard Lynch	*Scarecrow* ('73)
Edward James Olmos	*Stand and Deliver* ('87)
James Woods	*Fast-Walking* ('82)

LOSING THEIR HAIR

"Men don't get smarter when they get older.
They just lose their hair."
—Claudette Colbert, *The Palm Beach Story*

Hollywood, in its earlier days, had a tremendous struggle deciding how to cope with male body hair—chest hair, in particular. The powers that be obviously felt that it was offensive. So, the '30s, the '40s, and even the '50s presented one male star after another with shiny, clean-shaven chests. It was not until the '60s that chest hair became permissible on male stars. Even today, in occasional lapses, we see it appear and disappear.

Jeff Chandler—Pity Chandler, a nice hirsute Jewish guy covered almost from head to toe with a thick mat of hair. He was permitted to keep some chest hair, with the rest sheared on a regular basis. As a result of his grooming, Chandler walked around itching furiously from the constantly growing stubble covering his body.

Jeff Fahey—Fahey, a dark-haired, hairy-chested man, has appeared shirtless in many of his films. Yet, when he made *The Lawnmower Man* ('92), he was a blond with a clean-shaven chest. What makes the situation all the more puzzling is that there is no reason why Fahey's character—a mental retardate—*should* have been depicted with a hairless chest.

Clark Gable—Gable's studio felt that his fans would never accept his naturally hairy chest, so it was shaven for almost every picture in which it was bared.

William Holden—Holden's naturally hairy chest was one of those on-again, off-again ones. It was left hairy for *The Bridges at Toko-Ri* ('54), but shaved the next year in *Love is a Many Splendored Thing* ('55).

Robert Mitchum—Mitchum, always the rebel even before it was popular, refused to have his chest shaved for screen appearances.

Robin Williams—In *The World According to Garp* ('82), the normally hirsute Williams appeared with his chest shaved.

HAVING THE TABLES TURNED

"There's nothin' I like better than to meet a high-class mama
that can snap 'em back at you. Yessir!
When a cold mama gets hot—boy, how she sizzles!"
—Roscoe Karns, *It Happened One Night*

Having the tables turned, or being raped by a woman, is the fantasy of many a male. It rarely happens—both in real life and on reel life.

Jacques Brel—*Les Risques du Métier* ('67)—Brel, the victim of rape by a group of girls, is left emotionally scarred for life by the incident.

Peter Breck—*Shock Corridor* ('63)—Breck, a journalist, pretends to be insane to be committed to a hospital that he's planning to expose. During his sojourn, he inadvertently enters the wrong room and is attacked by a horde of wild women. Breck has trespassed into the ward of the nymphomaniacs.

Michael Caine—*The Island* ('80)—Caine, a New York writer, is captured along with his son by a band of modern-day, bloodthirsty Caribbean pirates. During his captivity, he is tied up and raped by an atrocious hag.

Seymour Cassel—*Death Game* ('77)—Cassel is teased, titillated, tortured, and raped in his house by two maniacal lesbians (Sondra Locke, Colleen Camp).

Gerard Depardieu—*Bye Bye Monkey* ('78)—Depardieu is raped by a group of actresses in what may—or may not—be a fantasy.

Paul Sorvino—*It Couldn't Happen to a Nicer Guy* ('82)—Sorvino's raped at gunpoint by a beautiful woman. Of course, his tale is so outrageous that no one believes him.

HEAVENLY SPIRITS

"I feel like we've died and gone to heaven—
only we had to climb up."
—Mildred Natwick, *Barefoot in the Park*

Great Caesar's ghost—as Perry White, Clark Kent's boss at the *Daily Planet* would have put it—these guys are really spooky. They're dead, they're ghosts, they're spirits come back from the beyond. It's eerie, it's strange, it's positively ghostly.

Don Ameche	*Heaven Can Wait* ('43)
Alec Baldwin	*Alice* ('90)
Ernest Borgnine	*The Ghost of Flight 401* ('78)
James Caan	*Kiss Me Goodbye* ('82)
Bill Cosby	*Ghost Dad* ('90)
Robert Donat	*The Ghost Goes West* ('36)
Richard Dreyfuss	*Always* ('89)
Redd Foxx	*Ghost of a Chance* ('87)
Cary Grant	*Topper* ('37)
Rex Harrison	*The Ghost and Mrs. Muir* ('47)
Barnard Hughes	*Da* ('88)
Michael Keaton	*Beetlejuice* ('88)
Cecil Kellaway	*I Married a Witch* ('42)
Charles Laughton	*The Canterville Ghost* ('44)
Pepper Martin	*Ghost Fever* ('87)
James Mason	*Pandora and the Flying Dutchman* ('51)
David Niven	*Stairway to Heaven* ('46)
Alan Rickman	*Truly Madly Deeply* ('91)
Patrick Swayze	*Ghost* ('90)
Spencer Tracy	*A Guy Named Joe* ('43)

| Denzel Washington | *Heart Condition* ('90) |
| Jose Wilker | *Dona Flor and Her Two Husbands* ('78) |

ANGELS

Leon Ames	*Yolanda and the Thief* ('45)
Harry Belafonte	*The Angel Levine* ('70)
Jack Benny	*The Horn Blows at Midnight* ('45)
Robert Carradine	*Clarence* ('90)
Robert Cummings	*Heaven Only Knows* ('47)
Richard Dreyfuss	*Always* ('89)
Bruno Ganz	*Wings of Desire* ('88)
Cary Grant	*The Bishop's Wife* ('47)
Paul Hogan	*Almost an Angel* ('90)
John Phillip Law	*Barbarella* ('68)
James Mason	*Forever Darling* ('56)
Harry Morgan	*Charley and the Angel* ('73)
Sidney Poitier	*Brother John* ('72)
Claude Rains	*Here Comes Mr. Jordan* ('41)
Spencer Tracy	*A Guy Named Joe* ('43)
Henry Travers	*It's a Wonderful Life* ('46)
Clifton Webb	*For Heaven's Sake* ('50)

HIGH-FLYING MEN

"Well, from all I've heard about heaven,
it seems to be a pretty unbusinesslike place.
They could probably use a good man like me."
—William Powell, *Life with Father*

Off they go soaring into the heavens. Oh, those daring young men on the high-flying trapeze, how easily they swing through the air. Athletic bodies, their lower limbs sporting tight, tight pants. High flyers . . . they're so nimble, so quick.

Michael Callan	*The Flying Fontaines* ('59)
Keith Carradine	*The Serpent's Egg* ('78)
Tony Curtis	*Trapeze* ('56)
Burt Lancaster	*Trapeze* ('56)
David Nelson	*The Big Circus* ('59)
Elvis Presley	*Fun in Acapulco* ('63)
Cornel Wilde	*The Greatest Show on Earth* ('52)

WHAT GOES UP MUST FALL DOWN—AND HOW!

These guys really fell down . . . and eventually went *splat*! Out of windows, down from buildings; one even rode an atomic bomb down. Oh, please help them, they're falling . . . falling down.

John Huston	*Winter Kills* ('79)
Jack Nicholson	*Batman* ('89)
Slim Pickens	*Dr. Strangelove* ('64)
Alan Rickman	*Die Hard* ('88)
Craig Wasson	*Ghost Story* ('81)

STUNTS

The real daredevils . . . stuntmen of the movies. These films provide the best place to see them in action.

Deathcheaters ('76)

Hooper ('78)

The Stunt Man ('80)

Stunts ('77)

Stunt Seven ('79)

HOLLYWOOD'S BATTLE OF THE BULGE

"Why is it that a woman always thinks the most savage thing she
can say to a man is to impugn his cocksmanship?"
—William Holden, *Network*

Mirror, mirror on the wall, who's the best endowed male star of all?
Only a privileged few know for certain, but rumors do fly. Speculation
has always focused primarily on certain stars, fueled by gossip naturally, especially that from ex-spouses and jilted lovers. Even *Spy*
magazine got into the guessing act when it ran a list of sixteen
names—two fictional—of those abnormally blessed.

These gents represent a compilation of the "old-timers" most
rumored to be among Hollywood's biggest attractions. They're listed
here with one of their films. You might want to catch it to see if you
can spot anything bulging. . . .

Milton Berle	*Tall, Dark and Handsome* ('41)
Humphrey Bogart	*Casablanca* ('42)
Charlie Chaplin	*A King in New York* ('57)
Gary Cooper	*The Plainsman* ('36)
Sammy Davis Jr.	*Johnny Cool* ('63)
Errol Flynn	*Captain Blood* ('35)
John Ireland	*Red River* ('48)
Dean Martin	*Who's Been Sleeping in My Bed?* ('63)
Victor Mature	*Samson and Delilah* ('49)
Roddy McDowall	*Lord Love a Duck* ('66)
Walter Pidgeon	*Mrs. Miniver* ('42)
Anthony Quinn	*Zorba the Greek* ('64)
George Raft	*Scarface* ('32)
Frank Sinatra	*Pal Joey* ('57)
Forrest Tucker	*Auntie Mame* ('58)

NEW CONTENDERS FOR THE TITLE?

Who are the new contenders of today in Hollywood's Battle of the Bulge? Ex-rock groupie Pamela Des Barres touts Don Johnson heavily. *Spy* magazine and other critical observers have selected these "new-timers" as being among the best new contenders for the title:

Warren Beatty	*Dick Tracy* ('90)
Ed Begley Jr.	*Meet the Applegates* ('91)
Willem Dafoe	*Platoon* ('86)
Dolph Lundgren	*Red Scorpion* ('89)
Ryan O'Neal	*Partners* ('82)
Sean Penn	*Bad Boys* ('83)
Tim Robbins	*The Player* ('92)
Paul Williams	*Phantom of the Paradise* ('74)
James Woods	*Salvador* ('86)

And . . . How About These?

Examine the following stars closely in the film listed. Each man displays an attribute that seemingly would make him a possible contender in the Hollywood Battle-of-the-Bulge rumor mill:

- **Kevin Costner** wrapped in a white towel or in a pair of shorts in *Bull Durham* ('88)

- **Steve Guttenberg** in swimming trunks in *Cocoon* ('85)

- **William Petersen** in a pair of shorts in *Manhunter* ('86, aka *Red Dragon*)

Checking Out Don Johnson

Objective: To rate Don Johnson in the Battle of the Bulge

    Reading assignment: *I'm with the Band* by Pamela Des Barres

    Viewing assignments: *The Harrad Experiment* ('73); *The Magic Garden of Stanley Sweetheart* ('70)

    Decision to be made: Well, does Don measure up as Pamela claims?

MEASURING UP

"I like your movies, man. You've got a great penis."
—Val Kilmer, *The Doors*

Put several males together and they'll soon wonder how they "measure up" to each other. The guys in these films certainly couldn't resist pulling it all out and taking measure of each other:

Just One of the Guys ('85)

The Last American Virgin ('82)

Murmur of the Heart ('71)

Porky's ('81)

Spetters ('80)

The Quiet Sheriff Who Packed a Big Pistol

Gary Cooper, the strong, silent sheriff in *High Noon* ('52), packed a sizable pistol in his pants. Coop, famously well endowed, was a nudist and totally uninhibited in his dressing room. He cut a wide swath through Hollywood's females, from Clara Bow and Tallulah Bankhead to Ingrid Bergman and Marlene Dietrich.

Bow, Hollywood's "It Girl" of the '20s, was reported to have described Cooper as "hung like a horse, and he can go all night." Lupe Velez, known as the Mexican Spitfire, with whom Cooper had a long-running affair, babbled all over Hollywood, "Garree has the biggest one in town." Carole Lombard, one of Clark Gable's wives, also had an affair with Coop. According to her, Gary had it all in front but no ass to push it with.

After signing for her first film, the sassy Tallulah cracked, "Darling, they offered me *all* that money, and I thought I'd go to Hollywood to fuck that *divine* Gary Cooper." Off she went, and fuck him she did!

Did any male ever lock lips around Cooper's endowment? One woman he had a long-running affair with commented, "I don't doubt he had a man occasionally. They wouldn't let him alone, you know."

The King: Almost Small Enough to Be a Queen

Clark Gable, acknowledged King of the '40s motion picture industry, had a reputation as a lousy lover. Even his own wife, Carole Lombard, once made the crack to a reporter, "God knows I love Pappy, but he's the worst lay in town." Another time, Lombard was knitting a cock warmer for her husband and showed it around. When someone commented on how small it was, Lombard remarked, "one inch less and he'd be Queen of Hollywood."

LARGE, SMALL, AND UNUSUALLY SHAPED TOOLS

"Now that I see you, let me ask you something. Does that come in
an adult size?"

—Whoopi Goldberg, *Fatal Beauty*

Bachelor Party ('84)—A waiter, nicknamed Nick the Dick for his outrageously
large appendage, is solicited to embarrass the women attending a party in the
same hotel where the bachelor party is being held. Nick unzips his pants and
places his oversized manhood on a sandwich platter, which he then serves to
one of the women.

Brain Damage ('89)—Hunky Brian (**Rick Herbst**) has acquired an AYLMER, a
brain-eating parasite, which resides in his body. On an outing searching for a
brain to eat, Brian picks up a young female punker. They end up in an alley,
where the young lady rubs Brian's crotch and comments, "I bet you've got a
real monster in there!" She kneels before him, slowly lowers his zipper, and
parts his fly. As she slides her hand inside Brian's pants to extract his love
muscle for a little suckie, the AYLMER comes shooting out instead to suck her
brains.

Fatal Beauty ('87)—After detective Whoopi Goldberg has detained a suspect and
threatened to shoot him in the crotch during questioning, she declares disgust-
edly, "You're pathetic, that thing feels like it's only about this big," holding up
her fingers a tiny distance apart.

Full Metal Jacket ('87)—**Dorian Harewood**, one of the soldiers in the film, gets
into an argument with a Vietnamese prostitute who's soliciting business among
the soldiers. According to her, Blacks have large penises, and she doesn't like
their business. Harewood unzips his pants and pulls out his manhood to show
her, referring to it as "nice-sized Black Alabama farm meat."

High Heels ('91)—**Miguel Bosé**, who plays four roles—Hugo, Edwardo, Judge
Dominquez, and Femme Lethal, a drag entertainer—has a large, distinctive
mole on his penis. It causes costar Victoria Abril to exclaim about it when she
pulls his undershorts down.

M*A*S*H ('70)—"Painless," the unit's well-endowed dentist, experiences depres-
sion and considers suicide when his famed organ no longer can get erect.

Patti Rocks ('88)—Billy (**Chris Mulkey**), caught in his underwear on a highway at
night, tells a woman who stops her car and taunts him, "I've got a garden hose
for a penis—twenty-eight inches from base to tip."

Porky's ('81)—When prostitute Cherry Forever (Susan Clark) meets Anthony
Tuperello (**Tony Ganios**), he's introduced as "the pride of Central High, Anthony
Tuperello, affectionately known as Meat." Cherry gazes downward at the nude
Anthony and agrees, saying "this boy is deformed."

   Beulah Ballbricker (Nancy Parsons), the girls' gym instructor, catches
Tommy Turner (Wyatt Knight) with his penis stuck through a hole into the girls'

shower. Even though she grabs it and attempts to hold on, Tommy pulls free and escapes. Beulah then heads to the principal's office, where she attempts to convince him that all the boys in school be ordered to strip for her inspection. According to her, the penis she grabbed has a wart on it, and she can identify it if she sees it again. The principal finally convulses in laughter over the absurdity of her suggestion.

Where's Poppa? ('70)—Senile Ruth Gordon confides to Trish Van Devere that she prefers her eldest son (**Ron Leibman**) to her youngest (**George Segal**), because "he has a pecker this big."

The Witches of Eastwick ('87)—Darryl Van Horne (**Jack Nicholson**) informs Alexandra Medford (Cher) that his manservant Fidel "has a big schlong." In a later scene, Alexandra confides to Sukie (Michelle Pfeiffer) that Darryl himself "has the most amazing penis! It's bent the wrong way!"

You Can't Hurry Love ('88)—At a party, two women are discussing a male guest, when one comments, "Curved? Are you kidding? That thing goes around a house before he does. I haven't been able to walk straight for a week."

One for Each Hand?
Beach House ('80), an Italian film, features a character—a *priest*—who has two penises.

Most Clever Cinematic Display of a Penis
The full-screen wall shadow of William Hurt's penis in *Broadcast News* ('87).

Most Clever Cinematic Euphemism for a Penis
"Bald Avenger," the nickname **Kathleen Turner** uses for hubby **Michael Douglas**'s penis in *War of the Roses* ('89). During one of their brawls, Turner tricks Douglas into thinking she's going to perform fellatio on him, then takes a big bite out of the old Bald Avenger.

Best Penile-Named Character in a Film
"Sweet Dick Willie," played by **Robin Harris** in *Do the Right Thing* ('89).

Steve Martin's Penile Euphemisms
In his movies, Martin's characters use some quaint euphemisms for their penises:

All of Me ('84)	"My little fireman"
The Jerk ('79)	"My special purpose"

UNUSUAL CREATIVITY IN THE CINEMA

A Clockwork Orange ('71)—*Murder weapon:* Malcolm McDowell (Alex) uses a large, white abstract sculpture of an erect penis to bludgeon an exercise guru, known as the Cat Lady, to death after she has attacked him with a statue of Ludwig van Beethoven.

The First Nudie Musical ('76)—*Dancing partner:* The large extravaganza musical number "Dancing Dildoes" features a number of dancing, prancing penises.

Flesh Gordon ('77)—*Air transportation:* Penis-shaped spaceships zoom through outer space.

Groove Tube ('74)—*Puppet:* One of the more humorous segments features a puppet that delivers a television commercial about the dangers of venereal disease. The puppet, shown upside down and through a cutout hole, is male genitalia. Costumed with black glasses and a mustache, and featuring the penis as a rather large nose, it bears an uncanny resemblance to Groucho Marx.

Lisztomania ('75)—*Ground transportation:* Roger Daltrey (Franz Liszt) holds the reins of and rides a giant penis like a charioteer.

STARRING—A MAN'S BEST FRIEND

Only two films, both British releases, have featured the penis as a "star." The first was *Percy* ('71); "Percy" was the nickname the young hero (Hywel Bennett) dubbed the penis he was given as a transplant, after his own was severed in an accident. One critic drubbed the film with the comment that its topic was both penile and puerile.

Despite the overwhelming disdain with which the first film was received, a sequel appeared, *Percy's Progress* ('74)—the title was later changed to *It's Not the Size That Counts*—starring Elke Sommer and Vincent Price.

Another film featuring an "active" role for a penis created a problem for its studio for several years. *Me and Him* ('89), by German director Doris Dorrie, was withheld from release with only a few preview showings before finally being sent directly to video in 1990. The film stars Griffin Dunne as a man whose penis begins to argue with him. The talking penis in this film now has joined the one in *Portnoy's Complaint* ('72) belonging to Portnoy, Richard Benjamin, as an example of men truly being unable to keep their pants zippered shut.

One other example of a "penile" film is *The Amazing Transplant* ('70)—a low-budget semithriller about a penis transplant that gives its new owner a distinctly hard time as it fondly remembers the perversions of its previous owner.

Two Bolinas, California, filmmakers—Jo Monell and B. Moel—premiered their documentary *Dick* ('89) at the San Francisco Gay/Lesbian Film Festival. The short (no pun intended) film consists of frame after frame of various penises. The two filmmakers set up a booth at various outings, inviting males to have their penises photographed as part of a project to cinematically record the differences in the male anatomy.

The Doctor, Please, I'll Do It Myself Award
Awarded to **Jason Edwards** in *Drowning by Numbers* ('87), because he performs a self-circumcision.

THE HOME PEEP SHOW

"Don't look! Whatever you do, don't look at it!
You're safe as long as you don't look at them."
—Christopher Lee, *The Gorgon*

If your VCR is equipped with freeze and frame-advance features, then the following cheap peep shows are available free of charge in your own home.

Kevin Costner puts his pubic hair on display in *No Way Out* ('87).

To see Kevin's pubies: Locate the bedroom scene where he's clad in jeans and is shirtless. At the beginning of the scene, Kevin walks across the room with his jeans unbuttoned and unzipped. Decide on the best view, pause/still and frame advance for a peek at Kev's curlies.

Tom Cruise lets us have a look at his cruise missile in *All the Right Moves* ('83).

To see Tom's weapon: Locate the scene where he and his girlfriend are preparing to make love in the bedroom. Let it run completely through until all their movements are familiar. Rewind and pause/still on the frame where Tom's underpants are about to be peeled down. Then, using the frame advance, move forward one frame at a time. A clear view will soon develop of a cruise missile snuggled between the legs of Tom and his girlfriend.

Willem Dafoe wiggles his willy in *Body of Evidence* ('93).

To see Willem's willy: Locate the sex scene that occurs approximately forty-seven minutes into the film. Now freeze frame and then frame advance all through the sexual action. Willem is supposed to be having sex with Madonna, but you'll see differently. La willy de Willem is most definitely on the outside of the Material Girl and its state of excitement is definitely "low key." What you'll see does appear to confirm some of those rumors that *Spy* magazine was spreading about his endowment, however, as "excited."

Ed Harris flops his privates in *Swing Shift* ('84).

To catch Ed's flopper: Locate the scene (near the beginning of the film) when Ed enters the room wrapped in a towel from taking a shower. Watch the scene and become familiar with his movements as he enters the room and drops himself into a chair. As he drops into the chair, flopping actually, something else emerges from beneath his towel and bounces upward. Now, rewind, and pause/still as he begins his descent into the chair. Then, frame advance until you see Ed's flopper slowly rise and tower above his family jewels.

Brent Huff shows some Huff stuff losing his jockstrap in *The Perils of Gwendoline in the Land of the Yik Yak* ('84).

To check Huff's stuff: Locate the scene (a long-running one) where Brent scampers around in a silver lamé (yes, silver lamé) jockstrap and ends up fighting with some Amazon warriors. (It sounds incredible, but the whole film is!) At the fight's conclusion, one of the Amazons swings her sword at Brent's crotch. Her thrust does no mortal damage, but it does cut the thin waist strap holding his covering in place. As it flies loose, Huff's stuff is semiexposed— curly pubies and the base of his "manhood." Now rerun the scene until the Amazon thrusts with her sword. Pause/still at the sword thrust and frame advance until you've seen enough of Huff.

Tom Towles lets a surprise come flying out of his boxer shorts in *Henry: Portrait of a Serial Killer* ('90).

To examine Tom's surprise: Locate the scene near the end of the film when Tom Towles and Michael Rooker (Henry) get into a fistfight in an apartment. Tom's dressed in boxer shorts, and while fighting, he gets knocked backward onto a sofa. As he hits the sofa, something definitely masculine first tentatively rears its head, then emerges fully from his boxers. Rewind and pause/still on the scene where Tom moves backward onto the sofa. Now, frame advance and see Dick stick his head out for a penile view of Tom and Henry's fight.

Robin Williams shows off his Orkian eggs in *The Survivors* ('83).

To examine the Robin's eggs: Locate the scene when he's in the hospital, wearing only a hospital smock. Watch the scene and become familiar with his movements on the bed. As Robin sits on the bed, he lifts his leg and the eggs de Williams are exposed. Now rewind and pause/still as he sits on the bed. Then frame advance until the Robin uncovers the eggs in his nest.

HOW GREAT THOU ART!

"He's the only man I know who can strut sitting down."
—Gene Kelly, *Inherit the Wind*

They're the greatest. If you don't believe it, then ask them . . . or ask whoever decided to insert the hyperbolic *great* into the title of their film.

Brian Aherne	*The Great Garrick* ('37)
Muhammad Ali	*The Greatest* ('77)
Helmut Berger	*The Great Battle* ('78)
David Brian	*The Great Jewel Robber* ('50)
Lloyd Bridges	*The Great Wallendas* ('78)
Charlie Chaplin	*The Great Dictator* ('40)
Tony Curtis	*The Great Impostor* ('60)
Brian Donlevy	*The Great McGinty* ('40)
Robert Duvall	*The Great Santini* ('79)
Maurice Evans	*The Great Gilbert and Sullivan* ('53)
Jose Ferrer	*The Great Man* ('56)
Paul Michael Glaser	*The Great Houdini* ('76)
Bob Hope	*The Great Lover* ('49)
Allan Jones	*The Great Victor Herbert* ('39)

Alan Ladd	*The Great Gatsby* ('49)
Mario Lanza	*The Great Caruso* ('51)
Larry Mahan	*The Great American Cowboy* ('74)
Greg McClure	*The Great John L.* ('45)
Robert Morley	*The Great Gilbert and Sullivan* ('53)
Pat O'Brien	*The Great O'Malley* ('37)
Jimmy Osmond	*The Great Brain* ('78)
Harold Peary	*The Great Gildersleeve* ('43)
Gregory Peck	*The Great Sinner* ('49)
William Powell	*The Great Ziegfeld* ('36)
Robert Redford	*The Great Gatsby* ('74)
Robert Redford	*The Great Waldo Pepper* ('75)
Erich von Stroheim	*The Great Flamarion* ('45)
Akim Tamiroff	*The Great Gambini* ('37)

I DIDN'T KNOW HE WAS IN A NAKED MOVIE!

"Let's get naked . . . and *smoke!*"
—Pia Zadora, *Hairspray*

Using the word *Naked* in a film's title seems to be nothing more than a ploy to hype prurient interest in the film. In fact, most of these films were released during the 1950s, when nudity was only implied on the screen. Of all the actors who've appeared in films containing *Naked* in the title, only two, Cornel Wilde and Johnny Crawford, actually had nude scenes. Both of those films were released during the 1960s, after on-screen nudity was permitted.

Gary Cooper	*The Naked Edge* ('61)
James Craig	*Naked in the Sun* ('57)
Johnny Crawford	*The Naked Ape* ('73)
Alain Delon	*Naked Under Leather* ('68)
Richard Denning	*Naked Paradise* ('57)
Howard Duff	*The Naked City* ('48)
Anthony Eisley	*The Naked Kiss* ('64)
James Farentino	*Naked Lie* ('89)
Anthony Franciosa	*The Naked Maja* ('59)
Farley Granger	*The Naked Street* ('55)
Sterling Hayden	*Naked Alibi* ('54)
Charlton Heston	*The Naked Jungle* ('54)
Robert Hutton	*Naked Youth* ('59)
William Katt	*Naked Obsession* ('90)
Arthur Kennedy	*The Naked Dawn* ('55)
Scott Marlowe	*The Naked Weekend* ('83)
Kieron Moore	*The Naked Heart* ('49)
Roger Moore	*The Naked Face* ('85)
Esai Morales	*Naked Tango* ('91)
Leslie Nielsen	*The Naked Gun* ('88)
Cliff Robertson	*The Naked and the Dead* ('58)
Frank Sinatra	*The Naked Runner* ('67)
James Stewart	*The Naked Spur* ('53)
Terry-Thomas	*The Naked Truth* ('57)
Richard Todd	*Naked Earth* ('58)
Peter Weller	*Naked Lunch* ('91)
Cornel Wilde	*The Naked Prey* ('66)
Keenan Wynn	*The Naked Hills* ('56)

THE IMPORTANCE OF IMPOTENCE

"Your advertising's great.
People would never guess you got nothing to sell."
—Faye Dunaway, *Bonnie and Clyde*

Can't cut the mustard . . . limp dishrags . . . no lead in their pencils. These men are plagued with a frustrating problem—impotence.

Warren Beatty	*Bonnie and Clyde* ('67)
Hywel Bennett	*The Family Way* ('66)
Rossano Brazzi	*The Barefoot Contessa* ('54)
Richard Burton	*Bluebeard* ('72)
Richard Harris	*Your Ticket Is No Longer Valid* ('79)
Tab Hunter	*The Arousers* ('70)
Walter Huston	*Kongo* ('32)
Marcello Mastroianni	*Bell' Antonio* ('60)
Robert Mitchum	*Ryan's Daughter* ('70)
Greg Morton	*The Adulteress* ('73)
Paul Newman	*Cat on a Hot Tin Roof* ('58)
George Peppard	*Your Ticket Is No Longer Valid* ('79)
Tyrone Power	*The Sun Also Rises* ('57)
John Savage	*Maria's Lovers* ('84)
Sam Shepard	*Resurrection* ('80)
James Spader	*sex, lies, and videotape* ('89)

BEST NICKNAME GIVEN TO AN IMPOTENT MALE

"No Can Do," which is given to **Russell Wong**, by some of his Chinese friends in *Eat a Bowl of Tea* ('89) when he suffers impotence with his new wife.

BEST EXAMPLE OF THE FRUSTRATION OF IMPOTENCE

Performed by **Burt Lancaster** in *1900* ('77), when he squishes his bare feet in a large mound of cow dung and waxes philosophic about his inability to achieve an erection.

KEEP ON TRUCKIN'

> "It had that new car smell.
> Finest smell in the world . . . except maybe pussy."
> —Keith Gordon, *Christine*

Hot men on the move in their big rigs: Diesel fuel burnin' . . . eighteen big wheels a-turnin' . . . here come the truck drivers. Moving constantly, these guys are fueled by coffee, passion for the open road, and the occasional pep pill. What gets them to slow down or stop? An opportunity to swap loads, naturally.

Alan Arkin	*Deadhead Miles* ('72)
Robert Blake	*Coast to Coast* ('80)
Humphrey Bogart	*They Drive by Night* ('40)
Steve Brodie	*Desperate* ('47)
James Brolin	*Steel Cowboy* ('78)
Frank Converse	*In Tandem* ('74)
Robert De Niro	*Jacknife* ('89)
Greg Evigan	*BJ and the Bear* ('79)
Peter Fonda	*High-Ballin'* ('78)
Peter Graves	*Death in Small Doses* ('57)
Ed Harris	*Jacknife* ('89)
David Janssen	*Hijack* ('73)
Sam Jones	*The Highwayman* ('87)
Stacy Keach	*Road Games* ('81)

Kris Kristofferson	*Convoy* ('78)
Burt Lancaster	*The Rose Tattoo* ('55)
Mario Lanza	*That Midnight Kiss* ('49)
Paul Le Mat	*P.K. and the Kid* ('82)
Victor Mature	*The Long Haul* ('57)
Yves Montand	*The Wages of Fear* ('52)
Ed O'Neill	*Dutch* ('91)
David Paul	*Think Big* ('90)
Don Michael Paul	*Rolling Vengeance* ('87)
Peter Paul	*Think Big* ('91)
George Raft	*They Drive by Night* ('40)
Jerry Reed	*High-Ballin'* ('78)
George (Jorge) Rivero	*Killing Machine* ('86)
Kurt Russell	*Big Trouble in Little China* ('86)
Roy Scheider	*Sorcerer* ('77)
Sylvester Stallone	*Over the Top* ('87)
Jan-Michael Vincent	*White Line Fever* ('75)
Ken Watanabe	*Tampopo* ('86)

REVENGE OF THE CAR SALESMEN

Probably the most maligned profession in the United States—the car salesman. Or is it? These characters don't help the reputation.

Ted Danson	*Made in America* ('93)
Kurt Russell	*Used Cars* ('80)
Robin Williams	*Cadillac Man* ('90)

KEEPING IT IN THE FAMILY

"Well, what family doesn't have its ups and downs?"
—Katharine Hepburn, *The Lion in Winter*

These men share a common belief: Vice is nice, but incest is best. Their ranks include fathers diddling their daughters, sons making it with their mothers, brothers satisfying their sisters, and even an uncle acting unnaturally naughty with his nephew.

John Astin	*Candy* ('68)
Helmut Berger	*The Damned* ('69)
Robert Carradine	*Illusions* ('92)
John David Carson	*The Savage Is Loose* ('74)
Ian Charleson	*Jubilee* ('87)
Terence Cooper	*Heart of the Stag* ('84)
Ted Danson	*Something About Amelia* ('84)
Kirk Douglas	*The Last Sunset* ('61)
Benoit Ferreaux	*Murmur of the Heart* ('71)
Frederic Forrest	*Right to Kill?* ('85)
Art Hindle	*Liar, Liar* ('89)
John Huston	*Chinatown* ('74)
Scott Hylands	*Bittersweet Love* ('76)
Curt Jurgens	*Of Love and Desire* ('63)
Stacy Keach	*Butterfly* ('81)
Brian Krause	*Sleepwalkers* ('92)
Rob Lowe	*Hotel New Hampshire* ('84)
Karl Malden	*Nuts* ('87)
Malcolm McDowell	*Cat People* ('82); *Caligula* ('80)
Keith Moon	*Tommy* ('75)
Paul Muni	*Scarface: The Shame of a Nation* ('32)
Per Oscarsson	*My Sister, My Love* ('66)
Peter O'Toole	*Brotherly Love* ('69)

Al Pacino	*Scarface* ('83)
Michel Piccoli	*Themroc* ('72)
Christopher Plummer	*Oedipus the King* ('68)
Martin Potter	*Goodbye Gemini* ('71)
Michael Sarrazin	*Mascara* ('87)
Sam Shepard	*Fool for Love* ('85); *Voyager* ('91)
Nigel Terry	*Excalibur* ('81)
Tom Towles	*Henry: Portrait of a Serial Killer* ('90)

MEN KISSING MEN

"You cad! You swine! . . . It made me sick when I had to let you kiss
me. I only did it because you begged me. You hounded me. You
drove me crazy. And after you kissed me,
I always used to wipe my mouth—wipe my mouth!"
—Bette Davis, *Of Human Bondage*

The Golden Puckered Lips Grand Prix
Harry Hamlin and **Michael Ontkean** in *Making Love* ('82)—probably
the two handsomest men ever to kiss on the silver screen.

The French Tongue of Honorable Mention
Alan Bates and **George de la Peña**—*Nijinsky* ('80)

David Bowie and **Ryuichi Sakamoto**—*Merry Christmas, Mr. Lawrence* ('83)

Marlon Brando and **Robert Forster**—*Reflections in a Golden Eye* ('67)

Marlon Brando and **Matthew Broderick**—*The Freshman* ('90)

Matthew Broderick and **Brian Kerwin**—*Torch Song Trilogy* ('88)

John Cassavetes and **Peter Falk**—*Husbands* ('71)

Gerard Depardieu and **Robert De Niro**—*1900* ('77)

Kirk Douglas and **Alex Cord**—*The Brotherhood* ('68)

Peter Finch and **Murray Head**—*Sunday, Bloody Sunday* ('71)

John Hansen and **Rod McCory**—*The Christine Jorgensen Story* ('70)

John Hansen and **Quinn Redeker**—*The Christine Jorgensen Story* ('70)

Dustin Hoffman and **George Gaynes**—*Tootsie* ('82)

Raul Julia and **William Hurt**—*Kiss of the Spider Woman* ('85)

Mitchell Lichtenstein and **Winston Chao**—*The Wedding Banquet* ('93)

Al Pacino and **John Cazale**—*The Godfather II* ('74)

Stephen Rea and **Jaye Davidson**—*The Crying Game* ('92)

Oliver Reed and **Brian Thompson**—*Hired to Kill* ('91)

Christopher Reeve and **Michael Caine**—*Deathtrap* ('82)

Keanu Reeves and **River Phoenix**—*My Own Private Idaho* ('92)

Rod Steiger and **John Phillip Law**—*The Sergeant* ('68)

Raf Vallone and **Jean Sorel**—*A View from the Bridge* ('62)

Michael York and **Anthony Corlan**—*Something for Everyone* ('70)

And how do male stars feel about having to kiss their fellow male stars? Michael Caine summed it up pretty well by saying, "The most difficult thing I ever did in the cinema was to kiss Christopher Reeve. I said to him, 'If you open your mouth, I'll kill you.' And I said, 'If you stick your tongue out, I'm going to put my leg up backwards—you know, the way Doris Day used to do.' "

LOVE STORIES

In *Triple Echo* ('73), supermacho, ultraheterosexual, burly sergeant **Oliver Reed** falls in love with **Brian Deacon**, who's an AWOL soldier hiding in disguise as a woman friend of his girlfriend's.

In *Rainbow Serpent* ('78), heterosexual cop **Serge Avedikian** falls in love with **Illios Sikimos**, a bodybuilder whom he's investigating.

In *Some Like It Hot* ('59), rich playboy Joe E. Brown falls in love with **Jack Lemmon**, who's pretending to be a woman.

GREAT PUCKERED MOMENTS

Bobby-soxer, teen heartthrob **Frank Sinatra** received his first on-screen kiss in *Step Lively* ('44) from **Gloria DeHaven**.

Ronald Reagan got his first cinematic buss in *Love Is on the Air* ('37), which was also his first film.

The '50s Mr. Super Clean Living **Pat Boone** got his first on-screen smooch from comely **Diane Baker** in *Journey to the Center of the Earth* ('59).

A SEX SYMBOL'S FIRST KISS

Mel Gibson's first screen kiss happens in the backseat of a car in *Summer City* ('76), an Australian—and his first—film, when he quickly kisses another man on the mouth.

DON'T FRENCH-KISS THIS MAN!

In *Warlock* ('91), the evil **Julian Sands** first cuts off the finger of a gay gourmet cook to get his magical ring. Then he forces the cook's mouth open, bites off his victim's tongue, and spits it contemptuously into a nearby frying pan.

THE MOST MEMORABLE KISSES

According to a 1991 Gallup poll, the three most memorable movie kisses were:

1. **Clark Gable** and **Vivien Leigh** in *Gone with the Wind* ('39)

2. **Burt Lancaster** and **Deborah Kerr** surf-smooching in *From Here to Eternity* ('53)

3. **Humphrey Bogart** and **Ingrid Bergman** having a final kiss in *Casablanca* ('42)

THE KISS HE ALWAYS REMEMBERED

During the filming of *Boom Town* ('40), star **Clark Gable** was kissed so hard by costar Claudette Colbert that she broke his porcelain dentures.

LIGHTS! CAMERA! ACTION!

"The director, he should have had his head examined. He shouldn't have shot the picture; he should have shot himself."
—Kirk Douglas, *The Bad and the Beautiful*

I know I'm a really, really big superstar . . . but it's unfulfilling. You know what I *really* want to do? I want to direct! And direct they did. What are the results when a star turns director? A mixed bag, indeed; their results range from awards for Best Director to stinkeroos, as witnessed by these stars turned directors.

Woody Allen	*Bananas* ('71)
Alan Arkin	*Little Murders* ('71)
Lionel Barrymore	*Madame X* ('29)
Warren Beatty	*Reds* ('81)
Richard Benjamin	*Mermaids* ('90)
Bill Bixby	*The Woman Who Loved Elvis* ('91)
Kenneth Branagh	*Dead Again* ('91)
Marlon Brando	*One-Eyed Jacks* ('61)
Beau Bridges	*Seven Hours to Judgment* ('88)
Matthew Broderick	*Infinity* ('95)
Mel Brooks	*The Twelve Chairs* ('70)
Richard Burton	*Dr. Faustus* ('68)
James Caan	*Hide in Plain Sight* ('80)
James Cagney	*Short Cut to Hell* ('57)
Simon Callow	*The Ballad of the Sad Cafe* ('91)
Richard Carlson	*Four Guns to the Border* ('54)
David Carradine	*You and Me* ('91)
John Cassavetes	*Shadows* ('60)
Charlie Chaplin	*A Countess from Hong Kong* ('67)
Jeff Conaway	*Bikini Summer II* ('91)
Robert Conrad	*High Mountain Rangers* ('87)

William Conrad	*Brainstorm* ('65)
Jackie Cooper	*Stand Up and Be Counted* ('72)
Kevin Costner	*Dances with Wolves* ('90)
Noel Coward	*In Which We Serve* ('42)
Helmut Dantine	*Thundering Jets* ('58)
Michael DeLuise	*Almost Pregnant* ('91)
Robert De Niro	*A Bronx Tale* ('93)
John Derek	*Once Before I Die* ('65)
Danny DeVito	*Hoffa* ('92)
Kirk Douglas	*Scalawag* ('73)
Dennis Dugan	*Brain Donors* ('92)
Bob Dylan	*Renaldo and Clara* ('78)
Clint Eastwood	*Play Misty for Me* ('71)
Robert Englund	*976-EVIL* ('88)
Emilio Estevez	*Men at Work* ('90)
Jose Ferrer	*The Great Man* ('56)
Mel Ferrer	*Green Mansions* ('59)
Albert Finney	*Charlie Bubbles* ('68)
Peter Fonda	*Wanda Nevada* ('79)
Al Freeman Jr.	*A Fable* ('71)
Morgan Freeman	*Bopha* ('93)
Andy Garcia	*Cachao (Como Su Ritmo No Hay Dos)* ('92)
Mel Gibson	*The Man Without a Face* ('93)
Terry Gilliam	*Brazil* ('85)
Cuba Gooding Jr.	*Lightning Jack* ('94)
Larry Hagman	*Beware! The Blob* ('72)
Richard Harris	*Bloomfield* ('69)
Laurence Harvey	*The Ceremony* ('63)
David Heavener	*Prime Target* ('91)
David Hemmings	*Running Scared* ('72)
Paul Henreid	*Dead Ringer* ('64)

Charlton Heston	*Antony and Cleopatra* ('73)
Gregory Hines	*White Man's Burden* ('94)
Dennis Hopper	*Kid Blue* ('73)
Leslie Howard	*Pygmalion* ('38)
Ron Howard	*Splash* ('84)
John Huston	*The Misfits* ('61)
Lionel Jeffries	*The Amazing Mr. Blunden* ('72)
Buster Keaton	*The General* ('27)
Gene Kelly	*Gigot* ('62)
Klaus Kinski	*Paganini* ('88)
Fernando Lamas	*The Violent Ones* ('67)
Burt Lancaster	*The Kentuckian* ('55)
Tom Laughlin	*Billy Jack Goes to Washington* ('77)
Charles Laughton	*Night of the Hunter* ('55)
Jack Lemmon	*Kotch* ('71)
Jerry Lewis	*Hardly Working* ('81)
Peter Lorre	*Der Verlorene* ('50)
Karl Malden	*Time Limit* ('57)
Christian Marquand	*Candy* ('68)
Walter Matthau	*The Gangster Story* ('60)
Roddy McDowall	*Tam-Lin* ('72)
Patrick McGoohan	*Catch My Soul* ('74)
Burgess Meredith	*The Man on the Eiffel Tower* ('49)
Ray Milland	*Lisbon* ('56)
Jason Miller	*That Championship Season* ('82)
John Mills	*Gypsy Girl* ('66)
George Montgomery	*From Hell to Borneo* ('64)
Robert Montgomery	*The Lady in the Lake* ('46)
Eddie Murphy	*Harlem Nights* ('89)
Don Murray	*Damien* ('77)
Gene Nelson	*Harum Scarum* ('65)

Anthony Newley	*Summertree* ('71)
Paul Newman	*Rachel, Rachel* ('68)
Jack Nicholson	*The Two Jakes* ('90)
Leonard Nimoy	*Star Trek IV: The Voyage Home* ('86)
Ramon Novarro	*La Sevillana* ('30)
Edmond O'Brien	*Shield for Murder* ('54)
Dennis O'Keefe	*Angela* ('55)
Gary Oldman	*Lords of the Urban Jungle* ('94)
Laurence Olivier	*The Prince and the Showgirl* ('57)
Edward James Olmos	*American Me* ('92)
Ron O'Neal	*Superfly T.N.T.* ('73)
Michael Parks	*The Return of Josey Wales* ('86)
John Payne	*They Ran for Their Lives* ('69)
Sean Penn	*The Indian Runner* ('91)
Anthony Perkins	*Psycho III* ('86)
Lou Diamond Phillips	*Dangerous Touch* ('93)
Sidney Poitier	*Stir Crazy* ('80)
Roman Polanski	*Tess* ('79)
Dick Powell	*The Enemy Below* ('57)
Anthony Quinn	*The Buccaneer* ('58)
Gene Raymond	*Million Dollar Weekend* ('48)
Robert Redford	*Ordinary People* ('80)
Carl Reiner	*Enter Laughing* ('67)
Burt Reynolds	*Stick* ('85)
Ralph Richardson	*Murder on Monday* ('53)
Tim Robbins	*Bob Roberts* ('92)
Cliff Robertson	*J. W. Coop* ('72)
Mickey Rooney	*My True Love* ('51)
Arnold Schwarzenegger	*Christmas in Connecticut* ('92)
Steven Seagal	*On Deadly Ground* ('94)
Peter Sellers	*Mr. Topaze* ('61)

William Shatner	*Star Trek V: The Final Frontier* ('89)
Frank Sinatra	*None But the Brave* ('65)
Charles Martin Smith	*Boris and Natasha* ('92)
Raymond St. Jacques	*The Book of Numbers* ('73)
Sylvester Stallone	*Paradise Alley* ('78)
Daniel Stern	*Rookie of the Year* ('93)
Andrew Stevens	*The Terror Within II* ('92)
Mark Stevens	*Cry Vengeance* ('54)
Jimmy Stewart	*Trail to Christmas* ('68)
Kiefer Sutherland	*Last Light* ('93)
Jacques Tati	*Mon Oncle* ('58)
Robert Townsend	*The Meteor Man* ('93)
John Turturro	*Mac* ('92)
Peter Ustinov	*Memed My Hawk* ('87)
Jean-Claude Van Damme	*The Quest* ('95)
Erich von Stroheim	*Queen Kelly* ('28)
John Wayne	*The Alamo* ('60)
Jack Webb	*Pete Kelly's Blues* ('55)
Orson Welles	*A Touch of Evil* ('58)
Forrest Whitaker	*Strapped* ('94)
Cornel Wilde	*The Naked Prey* ('66)
Henry Winkler	*Cop and a Half* ('93)

FAUX DIRECTORS

"Back home everyone thought I didn't have any talent. They might
be saying the same over here, but it sounds better in French."
—Gene Kelly, *An American in Paris*

The proverbial movie within a movie scenario needs a faux director to
helm the faux film. Some classic interpretations of the tortured, plus
a couple of faux pas.

Danny Aiello	*The Pickle* ('93)
Woody Allen	*Stardust Memories* ('80)

Humphrey Bogart	*The Barefoot Contessa* ('54)
Maurice Chevalier	*Man About Town* ('47)
Charles Dance	*Good Morning, Babylon* ('87)
Peter Finch	*The Legend of Lylah Clare* ('68)
Marcello Mastrioanni	*8½* ('63)
Peter O'Toole	*The Stunt Man* ('80)
Anthony Perkins	*Destroyer* ('88)
George C. Scott	*Movie Movie* ('78)
Peter Sellers	*After the Fox* ('66)
Donald Sutherland	*Alex in Wonderland* ('70)
Francois Truffaut	*Day for Night* ('73)
Erich von Stroheim	*The Last Squadron* ('32)

LOVE FOR SALE

"I loaf—but I do it in a highly decorative and charming manner."
—Zachary Scott, *Mildred Pierce*

The All-Fucked-Out Grand Prize
Michael Paré—*The Women's Club* ('87)—Poor, poor Paré. He's a struggling writer who falls prey to a sophisticated businesswoman, who sets him up in a mansion where he has to service a large female clientele. By the end of the film, his ordeal has him all screwed up—and fucked out.

The Oh, How the Women Sing His Praises Runner-Up
David Bowie—*Just a Gigolo* ('79)—Bowie doesn't really possess the body or looks to make his role believable, but Marlene Dietrich (in her last film appearance) does sing the theme song, "Just a Gigolo."

The I Peddle My Love for Cash Honorable Mentions

William Baldwin	*Three of Hearts* ('93)
Warren Beatty	*The Roman Spring of Mrs. Stone* ('61)
Charles Boyer	*Love for Sale* ('38)
Jeff Bridges	*Cutter's Way* ('81)
Richard Burton	*Boom!* ('68)
Mathieu Carriere	*A Woman in Flames* ('82)
George Chakiris	*The Big Cube* ('69)
John Garfield	*Humoresque* ('46)
Richard Gere	*American Gigolo* ('80)
Mark Harmon	*Sweet Bird of Youth* ('89)
William Holden	*Sunset Blvd.* ('50)
Leigh J. McCloskey	*Alexander: The Other Side of Dawn* ('77)
Paul Newman	*Sweet Bird of Youth* ('62)
Hugh O'Brien	*Love Has Many Faces* ('65)
George Peppard	*Breakfast at Tiffany's* ('61)
River Phoenix	*My Own Private Idaho* ('91)
Prince	*Under the Cherry Moon* ('86)
Keanu Reeves	*My Own Private Idaho* ('91)
Cliff Robertson	*Love Has Many Faces* ('65)
Oliver Tobias	*The Stud* ('78)
Jon Voight	*Midnight Cowboy* ('69)

THE MR. MACHO PLAYS *MISS NELLIE* AWARD

Frequently, a truly embarrassing moment occurs for a male film star. For example, like when a well-known star has developed an "image," then an earlier film that he's made with him in an unlikely role surfaces. Supermacho, kick-fighting, Mr. Muscles from Brussels **Jean-Claude Van Damme** suffered that moment in 1992, when *Monaco Forever* ('85), one of his earlier films appeared. In it, Mr. Macho-today plays a gay male hustler.

YO' BETTER PEDDLE YO' ASS WHORE

"Politicians, ugly buildings, and whores all get respectable,
if they last long enough."
—John Huston, *Chinatown*

If prostitution is the world's oldest profession, then pimping must be the oldest management skill. Presented here are some of the meanest, nastiest pimps who have ever threatened poor working girls on the screen.

The Joan Crawford Memorial Golden Coat Hanger

Wings Hauser in *Vice Squad* ('82)—When his girls get out of line, Hauser, a despicable character, punishes them by tying them up, then beating the little money-makers between their legs with a heated coat hanger.

Honorable Mentions

Morgan Freeman in *Street Smart* ('87)

Bo Hopkins in *Dawn: Portrait of a Teenage Runaway* ('76)

Clifton James in *Ladies of the Night* ('85)

Harvey Keitel in *Taxi Driver* ('76)

Dale Midkiff in *Streetwalkin'* ('84)

Roscoe Ormon in *Willie Dynamite* ('74)

James Spader in *Less than Zero* ('87)

MAGAZINE POSES

"Why didn't you take all your clothes off?
That way you could have stopped forty cars."
—Clark Gable, *It Happened One Night*

Beginning in the mid-1970s cinema celebrities (some famous, and some not so famous) began to bare all their charms in the new group of magazines on the market, which were aimed primarily at the liberated woman.

Legend: a = ass, b = body, p = penis:

Phil Avalon (a, b, p)—*Playgirl*—11/74
Pose: Multipage layout; full frontal; variety of poses
Film: *Summer City* ('76, Australian)

Robby Benson (p)—*In Touch* #92
Pose: Rear nude
Films: *Running Brave* ('83), *Harry and Son* ('84)
Note: The photo is a "blowup still" from *Running Brave*, a scene that did not appear in the film.

Chuck Berry (p)—*High Society*—1/90
Pose: One-page frontal
Film: *Chuck Berry Hail! Hail! Rock 'n' Roll* ('87)

Steve Bond (a, b, p)—*Playgirl*—10/75, 2/77, 8/83, 12/84
Pose: Multipage layout; full frontal; variety of poses
Films: *Massacre at Central High* ('76), *H.O.T.S.* ('79), *Picasso Trigger* ('89)
TV Series: "General Hospital"

Jim Brown (a, b, p)—*Playgirl*—6/74, 4/76, 1/81, 1/82, 1/83, 1/84, 1/85
Pose: Multipage layout; full frontal; variety of poses
Films: *Riot* ('69), *Kid Vengeance* ('77)

Dennis Cole (a, b, p)—*Ultra*—2/77
Pose: Rear shot
Film: *Powderkeg* ('70)
TV Series: "The Felony Squad," "The Bearcats," "Bracken's World"

Gary Conway, (a, b)—*Playgirl*—8/73
Pose: Multipage layout; variety of poses; mostly covered
Film: *I Was a Teenage Frankenstein* ('57)
TV Series: "Land of the Giants"

Joe Dallesandro (a, b, p)—*After Dark*, 8/72, 5/74, 5/78; male physique magazines
Pose: Full-frontal nudity; variety of poses
Films: *Andy Warhol's Heat* ('72), *Dracula* ('74), *Frankenstein* ('74), et al.

John Davidson (b)—*Cosmopolitan*, 1973
Pose: Too-cute, full-page, show-nothing nude
Film: *The Concorde—Airport '79* ('79)
TV Series: "That's Incredible"

John Ericcson (a, b, p)—*Playgirl*—1/74
Pose: Multipage layout; variety of poses; mostly covered
Films: *The Money Jungle* ('68), *Oregon Passage* ('57)
TV Series: "Honey West"

Fabian Forte (a, b, p)—*Playgirl*—9/73
Pose: Multipage layout; variety of poses; mostly covered
Films: *Little Laura & Big John* ('73), *Ride the Wild Surf* ('64), *Thunder Alley* ('67)
Other Appearances: singer, entertainer

Christopher George (a, b, p)—*Playgirl*—6/74
Pose: Multipage layout; variety of poses; mostly covered
Films: *The Gentle Rain* ('66), *Day of the Animals* ('77), *Grizzly* ('76)
TV Series: "The Immortal," various guest appearances

Howie Gordon (a, b, p)—*Playgirl*—11/78
Pose: Multipage layout; full frontal; variety of poses
Films: *Purple Haze* ('82), *Simply Irresistible* ('83), various "adult" films, using the name Richard Pacheco

David Hasselhof (b)—*Cosmopolitan*—6/90
Pose: Multipage layout; variety of poses; mostly covered
Films: *Revenge of the Cheerleaders* ('76), *Witching* ('88)
TV Series: "Knightrider"

Richard Hench (a, b, p)—*Playgirl*—4/84
Pose: Multipage layout; full frontal; variety of poses
Posing Name: Richard Alan
Film: *Scalps* ('83)

Sam Jones (a, b, p)—*Playgirl*—6/75, 1/81, 1/83; *In Touch*—8/84
Playgirl Posing Name: Andrew Cooper III
Pose: Multipage layout; full frontal; variety of poses
Films: *Flash Gordon* ('80), *My Chauffeur* ('86), *Jane and the Lost City* ('87)
TV Series: "Code Red," "The Highwayman"

Greg Louganis (a, b)—*Playgirl*—8/87
Pose: Multipage layout; variety of poses; rear shot
Film: *Dirty Laundry* ('87)

Peter Lupus (a, b, p)—*Playgirl*—4/74
Pose: Multipage layout; full frontal; variety of poses
Films: *Muscle Beach Party* ('64), Italian-muscle flicks under name of "Rock Madison"
TV Series: "Mission Impossible"

George Maharis (a, b, p)—*Playgirl*—7/73; *In Touch*—8/84
Pose: Multipage layout; variety of poses; mostly covered
Films: *Look What's Happened to Rosemary's Baby* ('76), *Land Raiders* ('70), *The Satan Bug* ('65)
TV Series: "Route 66"

Biff Manard (a, b, p)—*Playgirl*—5/75
Pose: Multipage layout; full frontal; variety of poses
Films: *The Zone Troopers* ('85), *Shanks* ('74), *Trancers* ('85)
TV Series: "Mission Impossible" episode

Steve Mateo (a, b, p)—*Playgirl*—9/86
Pose: Multipage layout; variety of poses
Film: *Vice Academy III* ('91)

Jaime Moreno (a, b, p)—*Playgirl*—9/75, 4/77
Pose: Multipage layout; full frontal; variety of poses
Films: *Amor Clego, La India, Las Del Talon, El Sex Sentido* (all Mexican)

Ben Murphy (a, b)—*Viva*—11/73
Pose: Multipage layout; mostly covered
Films: *Time Walker* ('82), *Sidecar Racers* ('75)
TV Series: "Alias Smith and Jones," "Griff," "Gemini Man"

Rudolph Nureyev (a, b, p)—*After Dark*—mid-'70s
Pose: Full-frontal nude
Films: *Valentino* ('77), *Exposed* ('83)

Andrew Prine (b, p)—*Viva*—5/74
Pose: Multipage nude layout; variety of poses
Films: *Grizzly* ('76), *The Town That Dreaded Sundown* ('77)

Ted Prior (a, b)—*Playgirl*—3/83, 10/83, 1/84
Pose: Multipage nude layout; full frontal; variety of poses
Films: *Aerobi-cide* ('90), *Hardcase and Fist* ('91)

Steve Rally (a, b, p)—*Playgirl*—9/84; 1/85 (Man of the Year)
Pose: Multipage layout; full frontal; variety of poses
Video: "Playgirl on the Air"
Film: *Overkill* ('86)
TV Series: "Young and the Restless"

Keanu Reeves (a, b)—*Detour*—5/93
Pose: Multipage layout; rear shots
Films: *Point Break* ('91), *My Own Private Idaho* ('91)

Burt Reynolds (b)—*Cosmopolitan*—1973
Pose: Too-cute, full-page, show-nothing nude
Films: *The End* ('78), *Cannonball Run* ('81)

Arnold Schwarzenegger (b, p)—*After Dark*—2/77; *Playgirl*—4/86
Pose: Full-page, partial-frontal nude
Films: *The Terminator* ('84), *Conan the Barbarian* ('82)

Don Stroud (a, b, p)—*Playgirl*—11/73
Pose: Multipage layout; mostly covered
Films: *The House by the Lake* ('77), *Bloody Mama* ('70)

Lyle Waggoner (a, b)—*Playgirl*—7/73
Pose: Multipage layout; mostly covered
Films: *The Love Boat II* ('77), *Surf II* ('84), *Journey to the Center of Time* ('67)
TV Series: "Carol Burnett Show"

Fred Williamson (a, b, p)—*Playgirl*—10/73, 4/76
Pose: Multipage layout; full frontal; variety of poses
Films: *The Last Fight* ('83), *1990: The Bronx Warriors* ('83)

STAR PHOTOGRAPH SOURCES

Male "star gazers" should pay attention to the following magazines in their quest to see more of their favorite stars:

Hollywood Rated X—A special one-issue publication featuring scores of nude photographs of stars ranging from Errol Flynn and Burt Lancaster to Rudolph Nureyev and Don Johnson.

In Touch—Contains frequent articles on films and male film stars, often accompanied by nude stills from the films. Of particular interest to voyeurs is Issue 94 (August '84). This issue features an article, "Celebrity Dicks," which includes purported nude photographs of many stars including Alain Delon, Vince Edwards, and Guy Madison, plus others.

Playboy—Its annual "The Sex in Cinema" feature contains stills from many of the best nude scenes of the year.

Playgirl—The oldest mainstream magazine featuring male nudes. Don't discard any of the back issues, for the "unknown" male model of today might be a star of tomorrow.

Other Sources—Also check the "Resources" listing (at the back of this book) for agencies that specialize in selling back issues of magazines or search for "star" photographs.

THE CONNOISSEUR SUPREME OF CINEMATIC MALE NUDES

Jimmy Wah, the effeminate Saigon bar owner in *Good Morning, Vietnam* ('87), played by **Cu Ba Nguyen**. Wah is obsessed with obtaining nude photographs of then seventyish Walter Brennan, three-time winner of the Oscar for Best Supporting Actor in the '30s and '40s, and better remembered as Grandpa McCoy on the TV series, "The Real McCoys."

HE POSED FOR NUDE PHOTOGRAPHS!

In *The Oscar* ('66), one of the major subplots revolves around the disclosure that **Stephen Boyd**, as Frank Fontaine—a glamour-boy who's just received his first nomination for the big O—had posed for nude photographs earlier in his career.

During the early 1940s in New York City, **Yul Brynner** often posed nude for photographers as a model. Other actors who have served stints as either artist's models or modeled for art classes include both **Sean Connery** and **Ronald Reagan**, in his younger years, leaving the avid voyeur to wonder if any *undraped* poses of them lay hidden somewhere.

Many actors—especially when younger and "between roles"—have posed for *athletic* (i.e., undraped—or jockstrap) photos. The Athletic Model Guild (AMG) was among the largest, and best known, of the photo studios producing these pictures. Their models included **Ed Fury** and **Richard Harrison**, who later appeared in Italian "sandal and muscle" epics; **Joe Dallesandro**, who became a staple in Andy Warhol's avant-garde films; plus **Gary Conway** and **Glenn Corbett**.

Quick Quiz

What male porno film star appeared on the cover of *Newsweek* and when?

Cal (Casey Donovan) Culver, on the 1972 cover, "The New Sex Therapy."

MAMA'S BOYS

"I wear the pants, and she beats me with the belt."
—Edward G. Robinson, *All My Sons*

The Big Simpering Heap of Mother Love Grand Prize

Rod Steiger in *The Loved One* ('65)—Pudgy body, a head full of golden ringlets, and with a lisping voice, Mr. Joyboy, Steiger's mortician character, is someone only a mother could love. He simpers, arches his eyebrows, and parades around in skimpy briefs while working out. He's supposed to be straight—with a fixation on Amy Thanatogenes, the heroine—but, Mr. J. is one real tutti-frutti. He's the type that gives respectable homosexuals a bad name. He even has a nauseating little song, "Mama's Little Joyboy," that he sings for *mater*.

The only thing more disgusting than Mr. Joyboy is his mother, Mama Joyboy, an extralarge eating machine who drools over television commercials for King's Chicken. Joyboy *père* is unseen, thank goodness.

The I Love My Mama in an Unhealthily Abnormal Way Honorable Mentions

John Drew Barrymore	*While the City Sleeps* ('56)
Victor Buono	*The Strangler* ('64)
Danny DeVito	*Throw Momma from the Train* ('87)
Timothy Greeson	*The Disturbance* ('90)
Michael Lerner	*Anguish* ('87)
John Savage	*The Killing Kind* ('73)
Dick Shawn	*It's a Mad Mad Mad Mad World* ('63)
Robert Wagner	*A Kiss Before Dying* ('56)

MOMMY STUFFERS

They loved their mommies so much, they couldn't live without them . . . so when they died, they stuffed their bodies and kept them around for company.

Roberts Blossom	*Deranged* ('74)
Roddy McDowall	*It!* ('67)
Anthony Perkins	*Psycho* ('60)

SHE'S DEAD, BUT I STILL LOVE HER

In **Sweet Kill** ('70), impotent mama's boy **Tab Hunter** pays a prostitute to pretend to be the body of his dead mother while he masturbates over the fantasy.

MEN WHO REALLY KNOW HOW

"I know. You know I know. I know you know I know.
We know Henry knows, and Henry knows we know it.
We're a knowledgeable family."
—John Castle, *The Lion in Winter*

The following gents really know how. Of course, there may be scant demand for some of these skills, but at least they've proven that they have the know-how in these films.

THE MOST USELESS SKILL OF ALL

How to Frame a Figg ('73)—**Don Knotts**

TRULY AWFUL SOCIAL SKILLS

How to Make a Monster ('58)	Robert Harris
How to Make It ('69)	Vic Morrow
How to Make Love to a Negro Without Getting Tired ('89)	Isaach Bankolé
How to Pick Up Girls! ('78)	Desi Arnaz Jr.
How to Stuff a Wild Bikini ('65)	Dwayne Hickman
How to Be Very, Very Popular ('55)	Robert Cummings

FINANCIAL AND BUSINESS SKILLS

How to Beat the High Co$t of Living ('80)	Richard Benjamin
How to Get Ahead in Advertising ('89)	Richard E. Grant

How to Succeed in Business (Without Really Trying) ('67)	Robert Morse

MARITAL SKILLS

How to Break Up a Happy Divorce ('76)	Hal Linden
How to Commit Marriage ('69)	Bob Hope
How to Save a Marriage ('68)	Dean Martin

CRIMINAL SKILLS

How to Murder a Rich Uncle ('57)	Anthony Newley
How to Murder Your Wife ('65)	Jack Lemmon
How to Steal an Airplane ('71)	Peter Deuel
How to Steal a Million ('66)	Peter O'Toole

WELL EXCUSE ME!
JUST IGNORE THIS MISTAKE

"I should have anticipated this. Twenty years ago, I made a pardonable mistake of thinking I could civilize a girl who bought her hats out of a Sears, Roebuck catalog."
—Clifton Webb, *Titanic*

Deadly Force ('83)—Male lead **Wings Hauser** is soaking in the bathtub, located in the middle of the room of a loft apartment. As gunfire suddenly erupts through the windows, Hauser leaps from the tub and flings himself to the floor.

Wiggling around on the floor and trying to cover himself with a white towel, Hauser returns the assailant's fire. In some frames, Hauser's bare ass is exposed; in others, a black jockstrap can be seen beneath the towel with which he attempts to cover himself. Never during all the action does Hauser cease his fire and don the black jockstrap.

How Funny Can Sex Be? ('76)—In this Italian film, a young country lad falls madly in love with a beautiful Roman girl, before discovering that: (a) she is a prostitute; (b) she is really a he, a transvestite; (c) the transvestite is actually his brother.

THE MOST POPULAR AMATEUR VIDEO AWARD

Awarded to **Rob Lowe** for his anatomically upstanding—as it most certainly was—performance in an amateur video, which he never dreamed would air on TVs and VCRs across America.

THE THAT WAS NO MISTAKE—HE WASN'T ACTING AWARD

Rock Hudson plays a playboy character who pretends to be gay for the first part of *Pillow Talk* ('59) to fool his leading lady, Doris Day. Aw, come on now, Rock, we knew you were a good actor, but we never realized you were that good!

MONSTER MISHMASH

"I know you have a civil tongue in your head.
I sewed it there myself."
—Whit Bissell, *I Was a Teenage Frankenstein*

Even a mother would be hard-pressed to love some of these big ugly oafs. Creepy, crawly, hairy, misshapen—truly the stuff of which nightmares are made.

James Arness	*The Thing* ('51)
Peter Boyle	*Young Frankenstein* ('74)
Lon Chaney	*The Phantom of the Opera* ('25)

Gary Conway	*I Was a Teenage Frankenstein* ('57)
Jeff Goldblum	*The Fly* ('86)
Louis Gossett Jr.	*Enemy Mine* ('85)
Kevin Peter Hall	*Predator* ('87)
David Hedison	*The Fly* ('58)
John Hurt	*The Elephant Man* ('80)
Boris Karloff	*Frankenstein* ('31)
Klaus Kinski	*Nosferatu the Vampyre* ('79)
Michael Landon	*I Was a Teen-age Werewolf* ('57)
Charles Laughton	*The Hunchback of Notre Dame* ('39)
Christopher Lee	*Dracula—Prince of Darkness* ('66)
Bela Lugosi	*Dracula* ('31)
Fredric March	*Dr. Jekyll and Mr. Hyde* ('32)
David Naughton	*An American Werewolf in London* ('81)
Vincent Price	*The Abominable Dr. Phibes* ('71)
Randy Quaid	*Frankenstein* ('93)
Anthony Quinn	*The Hunchback of Notre Dame* ('57)
Dean Stockwell	*The Werewolf of Washington* ('73)
Eric Stoltz	*The Fly II* ('89)
Spencer Tracy	*Dr. Jekyll and Mr. Hyde* ('41)

The That's *Mr.* Monster to You Award

Awarded to **Michael Palazzolo** in *Curse of the Queerwolf* ('83), who plays a *straight* male who turns into a *gay* werewolf.

MECHANICAL MEN

Who are the mechanical men? No, not the screen's best mechanics— they're the androids, robots. Part machine and part man.

Kenny Baker	*Star Wars* ('77)
Bruce Boxleitner	*TRON* ('82)

Yul Brynner	*Westworld* ('73)
Anthony Daniels	*Star Wars* ('77)
Johnny Depp	*Edward Scissorhands* ('90)
Robert Foxworth	*The Questor Tapes* ('74)
Jack Haley	*The Wizard of Oz* ('39)
Rutger Hauer	*Blade Runner* ('82)
Lance Hendriksen	*Aliens* ('86), *Alien³* ('92)
Robert Hutton	*Torture Garden* ('68)
Robert Joy	*Millennium* ('89)
Andy Kaufman	*Heartbeeps* ('81)
Harvey Keitel	*Deathwatch* ('80)
Barret Oliver	*D.A.R.Y.L.* ('85)
Don Opper	*Android* ('82)
Robert Patrick	*Terminator 2: Judgment Day* ('91)
Arnold Schwarzenegger	*The Terminator* ('84); *Terminator 2: Judgment Day* ('91)
George Segal	*The Terminal Man* ('74)
Peter Weller	*Robocop* ('87)
Frank Zagarino	*Project Shadowchaser* ('89)

MOON SHOTS

"And, waiter, you see that moon? I want to see
that moon in the champagne."
—Herbert Marshall, *Trouble in Paradise*

The best moon shots were not the Apollo missions; they are those asses directed in a moment of frivolity toward cinema audiences. The films that follow present an opportunity for the viewer to be mooned by groups of actors.

Fandango ('85)

Fraternity Vacation ('85)

The Hollywood Knights ('80)

Porky's ('81)

Revenge of the Nerds ('84)

Slapshot ('77)

BEST OVERALL MOON SHOT

Bachelor Party ('84)—One of the guys is stripped by his buddies and hung outside his hotel window. As he dangles on the rope, his bare butt presses against the window of a room on the floor below, occupied by a young couple. Telling his girlfriend, "There's a lovely moon out tonight," the man in the room snatches open the curtain. Seeing a different moon than what she expected sends the woman into shrieks of hysteria. As he looks, the man begins screaming, too. Later, shaken by their experience, the couple leave the hotel and go to their car. While they are sitting there discussing what happened, they lean over to kiss. Just as they do, the dangling nude falls and his butt plunges through the top of their convertible, where the couple each kisses one of his cheeks.

THE SITTING ON THE THRONE AWARD

The Office Picnic ('72), from Australia, was the first film to show someone actually seated on a toilet.

MR. MUSCLES AND HIS BROTHERS

"I never see pictures where the man's tits are bigger than
the woman's."
—Groucho Marx, commenting on Victor Mature in
Samson and Delilah

For the devotee of the muscular male body there exists a whole genre of film, dubbed "breasterns" by *Variety*, for the overdeveloped pecs of the male stars. Beginning in the early 1950s, the Italian film industry produced a plethora of breasterns, usually about legendary heroes such as Sampson, Ulysses, and others. Many American musclemen, such as Steve Reeves and Peter Lupus, later to gain fame as Willy on TV's "Mission Impossible," strapped on sandals and roamed down the Appian Way to Italian studios to appear in these less-than-epic concoctions.

Even though this type of film eventually slipped in popularity, "full-figured" guys still find employment in the cinema.

Lex Barker	*Tarzan's Savage Fury* ('52)
	Tarzan and the She-Devil ('53)
	Tarzan and the Slave Girl ('50)
Reb Brown	*Yor, the Hunter from the Future* ('83)
Lou Ferrigno	*Hercules* ('83)
	Hercules II ('85)
Mike Henry	*Tarzan and the Great River* ('67)
	Tarzan and the Jungle Boy ('68)
	Tarzan and the Valley of Gold ('66)
Victor Mature	*Hannibal* ('60)
	Samson and Delilah ('49)
Miles O'Keefe	*Tarzan, the Ape Man* ('81)
Steve Reeves	*Hercules* ('59)
Gordon Scott	*Tarzan the Magnificent* ('60)
	Tarzan's Fight for Life ('58)
	Tarzan's Greatest Adventure ('59)
	Tarzan's Hidden Jungle ('55)
	Tarzan and the Trappers ('58)
Arnold Schwarzenegger	*Predator* ('87)
	The Terminator ('84)
	Twins ('88)

WHOLE LOTTA MUSCULAR BODIES

"Physical ed? Who's he?"
—Spencer Tracy, *Pat and Mike*

Wanna see a lotta muscular bodies at once? Then try any one of these selections to get your fill of pumped-up bodies:

Aria ("Armide" segment) ('88)

Muscle Beach Party ('64)

Pumping Iron ('77)

Stay Hungry ('76)

The Most Bulging Biceps Collected in One Film
Hercules, Sampson, and Ulysses ('65)

The Hunk of Hunk
John Allen Nelson, who played a hunk named Hunk, in *Hunk* ('87).

NERDS, GEEKS, WIMPS, AND PESTS

"How do you get a guy to be a geek? Is that the only one?
I mean, is a guy born that way?"
—Tyrone Power, *Nightmare Alley*

Horror of all horrors . . . it's the truly horrible: the nerds, geeks, wimps, and pests of the world. They'll plague your every step, annoy you to death, ruin your life.

Dan Aykroyd	*Neighbors* ('81)
Woody Allen	*Take the Money and Run* ('69)
Albert Brooks	*Real Life* ('79)

John Candy	*Planes, Trains & Automobiles* ('87)
Robert Carradine	*Revenge of the Nerds* ('84)
Patrick Dempsey	*Can't Buy Me Love* ('87)
Pee-wee Herman	*Pee-wee's Big Adventure* ('85)
Jerry Lewis	*The Stooge* ('53)
Keanu Reeves	*The Night Before* ('88)
Peter Sellers	*The Party* ('68)
Jim Varney	*Ernest Goes to Camp* ('87)
Gedde Watanabe	*Vamp* ('86)

TWO SUPER SISSIES

Sissy britches, Miss Marys, girlie boys . . . that was their specialty. **Franklin Pangborn** and **Grady Sutton** were always simply tooooo much in whatever film they appeared. If you don't believe it, then see them both perform in *The Bank Dick* ('40).

A DUMMY'S BEST FRIEND

He's always putting words in a dummy's mouth . . . it's his job to do so. Why? Because he's the ventriloquist, you dummy.

Edgar Bergen	*Charlie McCarthy, Detective* ('39)
Lon Chaney	*The Unholy Three* ('30)
Anthony Hopkins	*Magic* ('78)
Danny Kaye	*Knock on Wood* ('54)
Michael Redgrave	*Dead of Night* ('45)
Erich von Stroheim	*The Great Gabbo* ('29)

PREACHERMEN

"My religion? My dear, I'm a millionaire. That's my religion."
—Robert Morley, *Major Barbara*

Preacherman, preacherman, stop passing that collection plate and pray for me. Please save my soul; help heal me, make me whole. I don't know if I can wait until you're finished on the floor, ministering to that moaning whore.

Ned Beatty	*Pray TV* ('82)
Julian Beck	*Poltergeist II* ('86)
Dirk Bogarde	*The Vision* ('87)
Richard Burton	*Night of the Iguana* ('64)
Tim Curry	*Pass the Ammo* ('88)
Timothy Daly	*In the Line of Duty: Ambush in Waco* ('93)
Dom DeLuise	*The Twelve Chairs* ('70)
Brian Dennehy	*Prophet of Evil: The Ervil LeBaron Story* ('93)
Fabian	*Soul Hustler* ('86)
Jose Ferrer	*Miss Sadie Thompson* ('53)
Marjoe Gortner	*Marjoe* ('72)
Spaulding Gray	*Stars and Bars* ('88)
Tom Irwin	*Light of Day* ('87)
Burt Lancaster	*Elmer Gantry* ('60)
Calvin Lockhart	*Cotton Comes to Harlem* ('70)
Stephen McHattie	*Salvation!* ('87)
Robert Mitchum	*Night of the Hunter* ('55)
Michael O'Keefe	*Unholy Matrimony* ('88)
Anthony Perkins	*Crimes of Passion* ('84)
Richard Pryor	*Car Wash* ('76)
Oliver Reed	*The Devils* ('71)

Christopher Reeve	*Monsignor* ('82)
Rod Steiger	*Guilty as Charged* ('92)
Richard Thomas	*Glory! Glory!* ('89)
Dick Van Dyke	*The Runner Stumbles* ('79)
Stuart Whitman	*Guyana: Cult of the Damned* ('80)

Best Propagator of a New Religion

Brad Dourif, the founder of The First Church *Without* Christ, a truly back to the nitty-gritty, fundamentalist sect in John Huston's gothic southern comedy, *Wise Blood* ('79).

MARY'S KID

"Come on Jesus, show me you're cool,
walk across my swimming pool."
—Josh Mostel, *Jesus Christ Superstar*

I don't care if it rains or freezes, long as I got my celluloid Jesus, flickering on the movin' picture screen. He's up there along with his sweet mother Mary, Heaven's queen.

Lothaire Bluteau	*Jesus of Montreal* ('89)
Claude Brooks	*The Life of Jesus* ('80)
Willem Dafoe	*The Last Temptation of Christ* ('88)
Brian Deacon	*Jesus* ('79)
Victor Garber	*Godspell* ('73)
Jeffrey Hunter	*King of Kings* ('61)
Enrique Irazoqui	*The Gospel According to St. Matthew* ('66)
Zalman King	*The Passover Plot* ('76)
John Krish	*Jesus* ('79)
Ted Neely	*Jesus Christ Superstar* ('73)
Peter O'Toole	*The Ruling Class* ('72)
Robert Powell	*Jesus of Nazareth* ('76)
Max von Sydow	*The Greatest Story Ever Told* ('65)

Best Alternative Savior
Graham Chapman, as Brian, in *Life of Brian* ('79).

Jesus Tried to Go to Congress
In 1992, **Claude Heater**, who played Jesus in *Ben-Hur* ('59), ran for the Republican nomination for a seat in the U.S. House of Representatives in a northern California district. Jesus saves, but Heater lost.

Rabbis
"We are all as God made us, and many of us much worse."
—Michael MacLiammoir, *Tom Jones*

Reform, Conservative, and Orthodox . . . with an occasional totally unorthodox leader of the Jewish faith.

Alan King	*Enemies, a Love Story* ('89)
Kenneth More	*Radio Days* ('87)
Saul Rubinek	*The Outside Chance of Maximillian Glick* ('88)
Rod Steiger	*The Chosen* ('81)
Sam Waterston	*Crimes and Misdemeanors* ('89)

Oh! Sweet Jesus, I'm Coming, I'm Coming
"I always said if I had a choice of death, I wanted to be screwed to death. I think I was."
—Eric Bogosian, *Special Effects*

They died—and presumably went to meet their savior—during an orgasm.

Albert Brooks	*Private Benjamin* ('80)
Sam Elliott	*Sibling Rivalry* ('90)
Jose Ferrer	*A Midsummer Night's Sex Comedy* ('82)

Coming Attractions
"You're a real blue-flame special: young, dumb, and full of cum."
—Gary Young, *Point Break*

When a male star reaches orgasm during a sex scene on-camera, the camera can't show the action. It usually just rests on the actor's face as he contorts his features and moans expressively. Here's a few Coming Attractions to watch out for:

Antonio Banderas	*The Mambo Kings* ('92)
Marlon Brando	*Last Tango in Paris* ('73)
Nicolas Cage	*Zandalee* ('91)
Brad Davis	*Midnight Express* ('78)
Bruce Dern	*Coming Home* ('78)
Michael Douglas	*Basic Instinct* ('92)
Ed Harris	*To Kill a Priest* ('88)
Al Pacino	*Frankie and Johnny* ('91)
Luke Perry	*Terminal Bliss* ('92)
River Phoenix	*My Own Private Idaho* ('91)
Mickey Rourke	*9½ Weeks* ('86)
Chris Sarandon	*Whispers* ('90)
Robert Wuhl	*The Hollywood Knights* ('80)

EQUAL TIME: GIVING THE DEVIL HIS DUE

"Oh dear, oh dear. I have a queer feeling there's going to be a
strange face in heaven in the morning."
—J. M. Kerrigan, *The Informer*

Old Mr. Scratch. Lucifer. Beelzebub. Mephistopheles. The Great Horned One. The Fallen Angel. Evil Incarnate. Asmodeus. He carries many names, but he's still the devil.

Patrick Bergin	*Highway to Hell* ('92)
Ernest Borgnine	*The Devil's Rain* ('75)
George Burns	*Oh, God! You Devil* ('84)
James Coco	*Hunk* ('87)
Peter Cook	*Bedazzled* ('67)
Bill Cosby	*The Devil and Max Devlin* ('81)
Robert De Niro	*Angel Heart* ('87)

Stanley Holloway	*Meet Mr. Lucifer* ('53)
Walter Huston	*The Devil and Daniel Webster* ('41)
Burgess Meredith	*The Sentinel* ('77)
Ray Milland	*Alias Nick Beal* ('49)
Jack Nicholson	*The Witches of Eastwick* ('87)
Oliver Reed	*Two of a Kind* ('83)
Mickey Rooney	*The Private Lives of Adam and Eve* ('60)
Max von Sydow	*Needful Things* ('93)
Ray Walston	*Damn Yankees* ('58)
Simon Ward	*Holocaust 2000* ('78)

POPERY POTPOURRI: POPES—REAL AND PRETEND

"These hands can heal the sick, raise the dead,
and make little girls talk right outta their head."
—Dennis Quaid, *Great Balls of Fire*

The throne of St. Peter's. The Most Holy Father. *Il Papa*. The head of Mother Church and Most Divine Propagator of the Holy Faith.

Robby Coltrane	*The Pope Must Die* ('91)
Tom Conti	*Saving Grace* ('86)
Albert Finney	*Pope John Paul II* ('84)
John Gielgud	*The Scarlet and the Black* ('83)
Alec Guinness	*Brother Sun, Sister Moon* ('73)
Rex Harrison	*The Agony and the Ecstasy* ('65)
Cyril Magnin	*Foul Play* ('78)
Anthony Quinn	*The Shoes of the Fisherman* ('68)
Liv Ullman	*Pope Joan* ('72)

FORGIVE ME, FATHER, FOR I HAVE SINNED

"I can afford a blemish on my character,
God will understand. But not on my clothes."
—Clifton Webb, *Laura*

Forgive me, Father, for I have sinned. Please hear my confession: I had impure thoughts about you, even though you are a priest of the Roman Catholic Church. Please, Father, I couldn't contain myself. . . . I kept wondering what's under your cassock that bulges.

Tom Berenger	*Last Rites* ('88)
Richard Burton	*Becket* ('64)
Richard Chamberlain	*The Thorn Birds* ('83)
Montgomery Clift	*I Confess* ('53)
Bing Crosby	*The Bells of St. Mary's* ('45)
Ben Cross	*The Unholy* ('88)
Tom Courtenay	*I Heard the Owl Call My Name* ('73)
Robert De Niro	*True Confessions* ('81)
William Holden	*Satan Never Sleeps* ('62)
Jeremy Irons	*The Mission* ('86)
Zeljko Ivanek	*Mass Appeal* ('84)
Tommy Lee Jones	*Broken Vows* ('87)
Raul Julia	*Romero* ('89)
Jason Miller	*The Exorcist* ('73)
Sean Penn	*We're No Angels* ('89)
Oliver Reed	*The Devils* ('71)
Christopher Reeve	*Monsignor* ('82)
Martin Sheen	*Catholics* ('73)
Frank Sinatra	*Miracle of the Bells* ('48)
Jeremy Slate	*The Lawnmower Man* ('92)
Donald Sutherland	*The Rosary Murders* ('87)
Spencer Tracy	*Boys Town* ('38)
Tom Tryon	*The Cardinal* ('63)

A RANDOM MENAGERIE OF MALES

"If there's one thing I know, it's men. I ought to.
It's been my life's work."
—Marie Dressler, *Dinner at Eight*

The films listed below present an opportunity to view a male sex symbol in his prime physical condition. All of them contain lengthy segments where Mr. Beautiful's body is displayed to full advantage.

Jean-Paul Belmondo	*Borsalino* ('70)
Pierce Brosnan	*The Fourth Protocol* ('87)
Horst Buchholz	*The Empty Canvas* ('64)
Richard Chamberlain	*Joy in the Morning* ('65)
Sean Connery	*Dr. No* ('62)
Alain Delon	*Borsalino* ('70)
Sam Elliott	*The Lifeguard* ('76)
Mark Harmon	*The Prince of Bel Air* ('86)
Gregory Harrison	*For Ladies Only* ('81)
Sal Mineo	*Dino* ('57)
Don Murray	*Bus Stop* ('56)
Paul Newman	*Sweet Bird of Youth* ('62)
Nick Nolte	*North Dallas Forty* ('79)
Elvis Presley	*Jailhouse Rock* ('57)
Robert Redford	*The Way We Were* ('73)
Burt Reynolds	*Deliverance* ('72)
Tom Selleck	*A Washington Affair* ('77)
Marc Singer	*The Beastmaster* ('82)
Fabio Testi	*China 9, Liberty 37* ('78)
Jan-Michael Vincent	*The World's Greatest Athlete* ('73)

ROCKIN' AND ROLLIN'

THE ROCKERS

"His parents met at one of dem Grateful Dead concerts. You know,
dat hippie shit what killed de Motown."
—Charlie Barnett, *My Man Adam*

Rock stars: screen biographies, rock-type roles, and real rockers in rock roles. Singing, screaming, wailing, moaning. Oh, get down and get funky—wail and moan some more for me, Daddy!

Neil Barry	*Joey* ('85)
The Beatles	*Help!* ('65)
David Bowie	*Ziggy Stardust and the Spiders from Mars* ('83)
Eric Burton	*Comeback* ('78)
Gary Busey	*The Buddy Holly Story* ('78)
Ray Charles	*Blues for Lovers* ('66)
Michael Chiklis	*Wired* ('89)
Jimmy Clanton	*Teen-age Millionaire* ('61)
Dave Clark Five	*Having a Wild Weekend* ('65)
The Clash	*Rude Boy* ('80)
Jimmy Cliff	*The Harder They Come* ('73)
Bruce Davison	*Deadman's Curve* ('78)
Neil Diamond	*The Jazz Singer* ('80)
Stephen Dorff	*Backbeat* ('94)
Bob Dylan	*Renaldo and Clara* ('78)
David Essex	*That'll Be the Day* ('74), *Stardust* ('75)
Michael J. Fox	*Light of Day* ('87)
Leif Garret	*Thunder Alley* ('67)
Gerrit Graham	*Phantom of the Paradise* ('74)
Bill Haley	*Rock Around the Clock* ('56)

Richard Hatch	*Deadman's Curve* ('78)
Richie Havens	*Catch My Soul* ('74)
Mick Jagger	*Performance* ('70)
Don Johnson	*Elvis and the Beauty Queen* ('81)
Paul Jones	*Privilege* ('67)
David Keith	*Heartbreak Hotel* ('88)
Val Kilmer	*Top Secret* ('84), *The Doors* ('91), *True Romance* ('93)
KISS	*KISS Meets the Phantom of the Park* ('78)
Kris Kristofferson	*A Star Is Born* ('76)
Paul McCartney	*Give My Regards to Broad Street* ('84)
Malcolm McDowell	*Get Crazy* ('83)
Meat Loaf	*Roadie* ('80)
Dale Midkiff	*Elvis and Me* ('88)
Sal Mineo	*Rock, Pretty Baby* ('56)
The Monkees	*Head* ('68)
Willie Nelson	*Honeysuckle Rose* ('80)
Jack Nicholson	*Psych-Out* ('82)
Harry Nilsson	*Son of Dracula* ('74)
Gary Oldman	*Sid and Nancy* ('86)
Michael Ontkean	*Voices* ('79)
Michael Paré	*Eddie and the Cruisers* ('83)
Jesse Pearson	*Bye Bye Birdie* ('63)
Lou Diamond Phillips	*La Bamba* ('87)
Brad Pitt	*Johnny Suede* ('91)
Elvis Presley	*Jailhouse Rock* ('57)
Prince	*Purple Rain* ('84)
Dennis Quaid	*Great Balls of Fire!* ('89)
Cliff Richard	*Expresso Bongo* ('60)
Kurt Russell	*Elvis* ('79)
Paul Simon	*One-Trick Pony* ('80)

Rick Springfield	*Hard to Hold* ('84)
Tommy Steele	*Rock Around the World* ('57)
Parker Stevenson	*This House Possessed* ('85)
Sting	*Bring on the Night* ('85)
Yutaka Tadokara	*Tokyo Pop* ('88)
The Village People	*Can't Stop the Music* ('80)
Leroy Wallace	*Rockers* ('78)
The Who	*Tommy* ('75)
Michael York	*The Guru* ('69)
Neil Young	*Human Highway* ('82)
Rob Youngblood	*Elvis and the Colonel* ('92)
Frank Zappa	*200 Motels* ('71)

Best Retrospective of Rock
Tim McIntire, as Alan Freed, the deejay daddy of radio rock, in *American Hot Wax* ('78).

Most Nudes in a Rock Film
All the hippie/yippie nudes in *Woodstock* ('70).

Funniest Rock Film
I Wanna Hold Your Hand ('78), a comedy about a group of teens attempting to get tickets for the Beatles' '64 appearance on the Ed Sullivan show.

Best Tongue-in-Cheek Rock Madness
This Is Spinal Tap ('84), Rob Reiner's parody of a rock concert tour film.

THE ROLLERS

"Mein Führer! I can valk!"
—Peter Sellers, *Dr. Strangelove*

Do paraplegics interest you? Or are quadraplegics more to your taste? Whichever, the following dudes in their wheelchairs range from youngsters to "hunks on wheels."

Jason Beghe	*Monkey Shines* ('88)
Marlon Brando	*The Men* ('50)
Lloyd Bridges	*Devlin* ('92)
Raymond Burr	*Ironside* ('67)
Bernie Casey	*Maurie* ('73)
Robert Conrad	*Coach of the Year* ('80)
Tom Cruise	*Born on the Fourth of July* ('89)
Daniel Day-Lewis	*My Left Foot* ('89)
Corey Haim	*The Silver Bullet* ('85)
Devin Hoelscher	*Wired to Kill* ('86)
Malcolm McDowell	*Long Ago Tomorrow* ('70)
Lawrence Monoson	*Gaby—A True Story* ('87)
Robert Moore	*Tell Me That You Love Me, Junie Moon* ('70)
Tony Musante	*The Desperate Miles* ('75)
Peter Sellers	*Dr. Strangelove* ('64)
James Stewart	*Rear Window* ('54)
Eric Stoltz	*The Waterdance* ('92)
Jan-Michael Vincent	*Enemy Territory* ('87)
Jon Voight	*Coming Home* ('78)
Paul Winfield	*It's Good to Be Alive* ('74)

STUMP-HUMPERS' DELIGHT

"Where's the rest of me?"
—Ronald Reagan, *Kings Row*

For "stump-humpers"—those devotees of amputated limbs—the thrills from Hollywood have been sparse. The most notable exception was **Harold Russell**, who won an Oscar for Best Supporting Actor in *The Best Years of Our Lives* ('46). In addition to his regular Oscar, Russell—a double-hand amputee—also was awarded a "special"

Oscar. After his double win (for his double loss?), Russell disappeared and wasn't seen on the screen again until *Inside Moves* ('80). In 1992, he auctioned off one of his awards to provide financial security for him and his wife.

Honorable Mentions

William Bendix	*Lifeboat* ('44)
Timothy Bottoms	*Johnny Got His Gun* ('71)
Nicolas Cage	*Moonstruck* ('87)
Michael Caine	*The Hand* ('81)
Keith Carradine	*A Winner Never Quits* ('86)
Damian Chapa	*Bound by Honor* ('93)
Chuck Connors	*99 and $^{44}/_{100}$% Dead* ('74)
Kirk Douglas	*Scalawag* ('73)
Clint Eastwood	*The Beguiled* ('71)
Rupert Everett	*The Right Hand Man* ('87)
Eric Fryer	*The Terry Fox Story* ('83)
John Heard	*Cutter's Way* ('81)
Patrick O'Neal	*Chamber of Horrors* ('66)
Gregory Peck	*Moby Dick* ('56)
Ronald Reagan	*Kings Row* ('42)
James Stacy	*Just a Little Inconvenience* ('77)
Spencer Tracy	*Bad Day at Black Rock* ('55)

He's Got an Eye Out for You!

Catch the films of one of these stars and see if you can spot his missing eye. Yes, that's right . . . these men have got an eye out (for you, maybe?) and it's been replaced with a "glass" one. Catch them in the film listed and see if you can spot the artificial eye.

Peter Falk	*Murder, Inc.* ('60)
Rex Harrison	*The Honey Pot* ('67)

SEX BEHIND BARS

"If you don't keep yourself in good condition to fight,
then you have to spread ass."
—Tom Berenger, *Looking for Mr. Goodbar*

Men behind bars. Rough dudes with tattoos who play a constant game of jockeying for masculine supremacy against their fellow inmates. Hollywood didn't discover sex in men's prisons until the early '70s. Wonder what Spencer Tracy and George Raft did in their '30s cinematic prisons once the lights went out at night?

Hi Guys! I'm the New Hot Stuff in the Cellblock

Fortune and Men's Eyes ('71)—Cute, blond **Wendell Burton** is tossed into prison on a minor drug charge, which changes his whole life. As soon as he arrives, he's attacked in the shower and forced to defend his ass. Then, a striptease during a Christmas party by **Michael Greer** (as the acid-tongued pseudo-drag queen Queenie) incites the prisoners to a riot. By the film's end, Burton is as bad as the guy who first attacked him. In between, Burton's attitude changes, and there are various rapes and humiliations enough to make anyone want to avoid being sentenced to do time in this prison.

The Glass House ('72)—Young, new prisoner **Kristofer Tabori** is anally raped and humiliated by old-timer **Vic Morrow**. Distressed by his fate, Tabori leaps to his death in a dramatic suicide.

Other Unsavory Movie Prisons
American Me ('92)

Bad Boys ('83)

Bound by Honor ('93)

Ghosts of the Civil Dead ('87)

Lock Up ('89)

Moon 44 ('90)

Night Zoo ('87)

Penitentiary ('79)

Riot ('69)

Short Eyes ('77)

OSCAR'S REAR ENTRY

Undoubtedly, many actors have felt that they were screwed out of an Academy Award, but **William Hurt** was the first one to be screwed *into* the award. In his Academy Award-winning role for *Kiss of the Spider Woman* ('85), a prison drama, Hurt had his buns plunged by cellmate **Raul Julia**.

THE SEXUAL INDIGNITIES AWARDS

"They used me! Like a woman!"
—Sal Mineo, *Exodus*

The following actors are awarded an "Attaboy!" for the sexual indignities that they've suffered.

Ned Beatty in *Deliverance* ('72)—After being made to squeal like a pig, Beatty is anally assaulted by Georgia rednecks. Finishing with Beatty, one particularly toothless member of the clan approaches Jon Voight and, while unzipping his bib overalls, comments on Voight's pretty mouth. Butch Burt Reynolds saves Voight in the nick of time, however.

Marlon Brando in *Last Tango in Paris* ('73)—Maria Schneider spreads butter on her fingers and gives Marlon's more than ample posterior a true finger wave. Watch this woman if she ever comes to dinner at your house and wants to butter the bread—Lord only knows where her fingers have been.

Wendell Burton in *Fortune and Men's Eyes* ('71)—Blond, mild-mannered Wendell has to fight in the showers to resist the unwanted attentions of fellow prison inmate David (Zooey) Hall. Then, in a turnabout, Wendell forces one of the few likable characters in the film, a poor soul named Mona, to orally service him and promises that as long as Mona continues the ministrations he'll be Mona's protector.

Richard Chamberlain in *Shogun* ('80)—Annoyed by his lack of good manners, a Japanese samurai urinates on Chamberlain's back to convince him to act more like a gentleman.

Sean Connery in *Goldfinger* ('64)—Auric Goldfinger ties James Bond (Connery) to a large metal table and positions a laser beam above him. The laser beam is turned on and begins cutting up the table aimed straight for Bond's crotch.

Richard Crenna in *The Rape of Richard Beck* ('85)—Crenna plays a policeman who's captured by two real cop-hating thugs, one dressed in black leather. The leather-clad baddie forces Crenna to his knees and rapes him.

Brad Davis in *Midnight Express* ('78)—Having spurned the advances of the Turkish prison commander (Paul Smith), Davis is hung upside down nude and given a good beating on his ass and the soles of his feet.

Richard Harris in *A Man Called Horse* ('70)—Harris, an English lord captured by an American Indian tribe, has large hooks sunk into his pectoral muscles and is then lifted into the air as part of an Indian tribal initiation ceremony.

Roger Herren in *Myra Breckenridge* ('70)—Herren, playing Rusty, an acting student, is strapped to an examining table by Myra (Raquel Welch), who jerks his trousers down and rapes him with a large, wicked dildo.

William Hurt in *Kiss of the Spider Woman* ('85)—Prisoner Hurt alternately taunts, bores, and talks incessantly to his cellmate, Raul Julia, until he finally gets humped in his bunk.

Harvey Korman in *High Anxiety* ('77)—Psychiatrist Korman, playing a bit of a kinky character himself, is tied up in a large wooden wardrobe and thrashed with a riding crop by Nurse Diesel (Cloris Leachman), who's dressed à la Nazi in an SS uniform with high black leather boots.

George Lazenby in *On Her Majesty's Secret Service* ('69)—Bond is back for more, and he gets whacked on the testicles with a carpet beater.

Ron Leibman in *Where's Poppa?* ('70)—Ron makes several late night trips across Central Park, where he is accosted by a gang of young toughs. After robbing him, the gang makes Ron rape a woman who's walking in the park. She turns out to be a male undercover policeman in disguise, who "enjoys" the assault so much that he sends Ron roses and thanks him for the most wonderful evening of his life.

Jack Lemmon in *Buddy Buddy* ('81)—Lemmon suffers the ultimate marital indignity, when wife Paula Prentiss melts down her gold wedding band into a replica of the genitals of Klaus Kinski, a sex therapist, who has taken her to the fourth plateau (of a possible nine) in sexual excitement.

Marc McClure in *Grim Prairie Tales* ('90)—McClure meets a pregnant woman alone on the prairie. That night, she becomes visibly less pregnant all the while talking about how men have "treated" her. She arouses McClure, who lies on top of her and they begin to have sex. His ecstasy, however, is abruptly ended when he is sucked whole into her vagina. The woman is seen the next morning wandering away from the campsite once again very pregnant—with McClure.

Tim McIntire in *The Choirboys* ('77)—Policeman McIntire is left bare-assed and handcuffed to a tree in a park by some of his policeman buddies. While attached to the tree, he is accosted by that most dread of all creatures, an effeminate male walking a poodle.

Ryan O'Neal in *Partners* ('82)—While pretending to be a gay couple with fellow undercover policeman John Hurt, O'Neal has to pose nude for the cover of *Man's Man* magazine in a effort to trap a killer of male models. During the photography session, the female photographer tells O'Neal to stop being nervous and advises that he "concentrate HARDER, if you know what I mean."

Peter O'Toole in *Lawrence of Arabia* ('62)—Captured by Turkish soldiers, O'Toole is led away to the office of Commandant Jose Ferrer for questioning. During the interrogation, the soldiers push O'Toole facedown on a bench and sexually assault him as the camera discreetly withdraws to a view of the building's exterior.

Al Pacino in *Scarecrow* ('73)—Meeting up in a prison work camp with Pacino, pock-marked bad guy Richard Lynch rubs his crotch and asks Al to give him some "relief." When Pacino refuses, Lynch tries to physically force his much-needed relief out of him.

Bill Pullman in *The Serpent and the Rainbow* ('88)—While in Haiti investigating the secret of the zombies, Pullman has a nail driven through his scrotum by the leader of President Duvalier's "tonton macoutes" (secret police).

Oliver Reed in *Venom* ('82)—The world's deadliest snake crawls up Reed's pants leg and bites him on a most sensitive organ, causing him an agonizing death.

Sylvester Stallone in *First Blood (Rambo I)* ('82)—Arrested in a small southern town, Stallone is taken into a shower by a group of redneck police officers, stripped naked, and thrown against the wall. As they turn a powerful water hose on him, the policemen make jeering remarks about Stallone liking "water sports."

Unknown Actor in *Crimes of Passion* ('84)—Hooker China Blue (Kathleen Turner) takes a policeman back to her room, cuffs him to the bed, and uses his nightstick to anally make her point.

Unknown Actor in *The Evil That Men Do* ('84)—During the opening title credits, an arrested journalist is shown being tortured, while a group of interested onlookers watches. The torture concludes with the insertion of a metal rod in the newsman's ass, to which electric current is applied.

Cornel Wilde in *The Naked Prey* ('66)—Attacked by a band of native warriors in Africa, white hunter Wilde is stripped naked, then forced to run cross-country with them in murderous pursuit.

Robert Wuhl in *The Hollywood Knights* ('80)—Wuhl's character, Turk, finally lures the object of his affection into the back of his van. While she writhes on the floor of the van shedding her clothes and telling him how much she wants him, Wuhl, sitting behind the steering wheel, has a premature ejaculation. In consolation, the young lady tells Turk, "You're so immature!"

THE YEAH, WELL SHIT HAPPENS MAN AWARD

Awarded to **Neil Morrisey** in *I Bought a Vampire Motorcycle* ('82), when a character, who's been reincarnated as a giant turd, leaps out of a toilet bowl and crams itself down Morrisey's throat.

SEX PERVERTS, WEIRDOS, AND OUTRIGHT LOONIES

"Forty-two percent of all liberals are queer. That's a fact.
George Wallace's people took a poll."
—Peter Boyle, *Joe*

Special Male Sickie Award

Peter Brown in *Rape Squad* ('74)—Brown, an especially sick rapist, makes all his victims sing "Jingle Bells" while he rapes them.

Honorable Mentions

Ken King in *Polyester* ('81)—King, playing Divine's son, which is enough to give a male problems anyway, receives his sexual kicks by stomping on women's feet in public.

Tim Curry in *The Rocky Horror Picture Show* ('75)—Curry, as Dr. Frank-N-Furter, a demented scientist, spends the film swishing around wearing women's black underwear, eyeshadow, lipstick, and heavy makeup. Though outrageously garbed, he still manages to seduce both Brad and Janet, the male and female romantic leads of the film, by pretending to be Brad to Janet and Janet for Brad.

Gene Davis in *Ten to Midnight* ('83)—Davis, an attractive but nerdy office boy, kills several female coworkers who resist his advances. He always strips naked before attacking his victims, spending quite a bit of time in the film padding around in the nude. An amusing highlight in the film occurs when during a search of Davis's apartment, the investigating detective, Charles Bronson, discovers his store-bought "jack-off device."

Bruce Dern in *Tattoo* ('81)—Bruce, a tattoo artist, kidnaps Maud Adams to use her body as a canvas for his tattoo artistry. During the publicity tour for the film, Dern alleged that he and Adams actually had sex as part of the filming. Adams firmly denied the allegation.

Clint Eastwood in *Tightrope* ('84)—Eastwood, playing a New Orleans cop, departs from his usual "straight-guy" image to portray one of the kinkier heroes seen in recent American films. His character likes to play sexual bondage games—handcuffing prostitutes to the bed before having sex with them.

Ted Levine in *The Silence of the Lambs* ('91)—Levine, a serial killer, is a repressed transsexual, who slaughters his female victims and then skins them. He likes to parade around his home wearing the skins of his victims.

David Lochary in *Pink Flamingos* ('72)—Lochary (Raymond Marble) and his wife are engaged in a contest with Divine to see who is the "filthiest person in the world." The male half of the Marble duo ties a turkey neck to his penis, then frightens women in a local park, using his novel manner of wienie wagging as a distraction to steal their purses. As a final note to creating a memorable character, Lochary dyed his pubic hair blue for the role of Raymond Marble.

Alan Ormsby in *Children Shouldn't Play with Dead Things* ('72)—As the leader of a rowdy group of pseudofilmmakers in a cemetery, Ormsby has his band of cretins perform a voodoo spell to raise the dead. After the rite, Ormsby takes one of the moldering bodies, a male he names Orville, back to his bedroom in a nearby cabin. Once there, Ormsby lies next to Orville on the bed murmuring sweet nothings about how "close" they're going to be to one another. His dreams of necrophilic bliss shatter abruptly when Orville, whom the spell has transformed into a ghoul, rises up and begins munching away at him.

Michael Sklar in *Andy Warhol's Trash* ('70)—During an interview with Joe Dallesandro and Holly Woodlawn, Sklar, a social worker, refuses to permit them to collect their benefits unless Holly gives him her high-heel shoes. She vows not to part with them, but Dallesandro forces her to relinquish them. Pleased with his victory, Sklar tries on the shoes and models them triumphantly.

Robert Vaughn in *S.O.B.* ('81)—Vaughn, the powerful head of a movie studio who double-deals and reigns supreme, overappears in several bedroom scenes with his mistress garbed strangely. During them, he wears female black-lace undergarments and high-heeled shoes, even while he's on the telephone berating his staff and plotting against the other cast members. To make the situation even funnier, no reference is ever made to his bizarre mode of dress by either him or his mistress.

IF ALL ELSE FAILS

In *Shadey* ('85), **Anthony Sher** as Shadey, who's been prevented from having a sex change by his mentor, insidious **Patrick Macnee**, provokes Macnee's wife—Katherine Helmond in a hilariously unpredictable loony role—into cutting off his penis in the kitchen with a knife during a chic cocktail party.

BEST COLLECTION OF SEXUAL WEIRDOS

Eating Raoul ('82), a tasty little dish directed by Paul Bartel, combines the hazards of sexual swinging with a look at real all-American entrepreneurship.

THE SPECIALISTS

> "I used to make obscene phone calls to her—collect—and she
> used to accept the charges all the time."
> —Woody Allen, *Take the Money and Run*

When it comes to sexual perversions, these men are all specialists—each one's outstanding in his field.

Obscene Callers

Stephen McHattie	*Call Me* ('88)
Sal Mineo	*Who Killed Teddy Bear?* ('65)
Robert Reed	*The Secret Night Caller* ('75)
Michael Woods	*Lady Beware* ('87)

The Voyeurs

William Baldwin	*Sliver* ('93)
Richard Benjamin	*The Marriage of a Young Stockbroker* ('71)
Michel Blanc	*Monsieur Hire* ('89)
Carl Boehm	*Peeping Tom* ('60)
Lou Castel	*Rorret* ('87)
Charles Cyphers	*Someone's Watching Me!* ('78)
Charles Dance	*The McGuffin* ('85)
John Di Santi	*Eyes of a Stranger* ('81)
Kenneth Gilman	*Bedroom Eyes* ('86)
Trevor Howard	*White Mischief* ('88)
Buck Kartalian	*Please Don't Eat My Mother!* ('72)
Klaus Kinski	*Crawlspace* ('86)
John Lithgow	*Mesmerized* ('86)

Karl Malden	*Baby Doll* ('56)
Anthony Perkins	*Crimes of Passion* ('84)
David Soul	*Through Naked Eyes* ('83)
Andrew Stevens	*The Seduction* ('82)
Preston Sturges Jr.	*Strange Compulsion* ('81)
Henry Thomas	*Psycho IV: The Beginning* ('90)
Craig Wasson	*Body Double* ('84)

Masochism—Burning Self with Cigarettes

Clint Kimbrough	*Bloody Mama* ('70)
James Woods	*Best Seller* ('87)

SOME VERY SPECIAL AND UNUSUAL AWARDS

"I gave you that prize years ago. There isn't an abomination award
going that you haven't won."
—Richard Burton, *Who's Afraid of Virginia Woolf?*

THE THEY ALL STOOD UP AND APPLAUDED ME AWARD

The Draughtsman's Contract ('82)—The Statue, an unnamed
male, spends the entire film scampering around a wealthy estate in
Restoration England, assuming poses like a statue for the amuse-
ment of the estate's owner and his guests. During one memorable
scene, a dinner party is being held by candlelight outside at night.
The statue positions himself on top of a marble column in the dark
and asks for light to be shined upon him. As he's illuminated, he faces
the guests nude and sends a golden stream of urine arching from his
body. Pleased by his inventiveness in arranging an unusual diversion
from their meal, all the guests stand to applaud the Statue.

THE REALLY TALL STORY AWARD

Diner ('82)—*What happened:* Mickey Rourke's date reaches into the box of popcorn he's holding at the movies and finds his penis inside it.

His explanation: Mickey claims he got an erection while watching the movie *A Summer Place.* It was pushing against his leg and hurting badly, so he pulled it out—as he phrases it—"for some air." The erection subsided, but he became so engrossed in the movie again he forgot it was still hanging out. Then, another love scene in the movie caused a second, harder erection. The hardness of this one just pushed his penis right through the bottom flap of the popcorn box before he knew it. And before he could stop her, his date reached in the popcorn box for another handful of popcorn.

THE WE REALLY CAUSED THE BITCH TO ROLL HER EYEBALLS AWARD

Death on the Nile ('78)—While on the deck of a tourist riverboat cruising down the Nile, Bette Davis, not the most congenial of traveling companions in the film, is mooned by a group of young Arab boys prancing along the riverbank. The look on Davis's face is priceless when she realizes what she is being shown. Davis's eyeballs have rarely rolled more effectively to register her distaste with the matter at hand.

THE MOST BARE MALE BUTTS AWARD

Mel Brooks's *History of the World: Part I* ('81)—The Empress Messalina (Madeline Kahn), a notorious wanton, has assembled a large group of Roman centurions for her inspection. The warriors are lined up, nude from the waist down with their rears facing the camera. Messalina reviews the troops, one by one, passing in front of them and examining their assets. Those meeting her high (and large) expectations are being selected to have an opportunity later to become better acquainted with the Empress. Using a combination of a few choice remarks, coupled with facile facial expressions, Kahn manages to make the Empress's selection scene quite humorous.

THE MOST UNUSUAL OCCUPATION AWARD

The Loved One ('65)—When Robert Morse passes through U.S. immigration on his way into Los Angeles, he's asked for his occupation. Morse, smiling devilishly, replies, "sperm bank donor."

THE DEDICATED TO THE ONE I LOVE AWARD

Going Berserk ('83)—At his prenuptial rehearsal party, the groom—John Candy—gets quite drunk and dedicates a love song he's going to sing to the one thing in his life that means the most to him—his dick.

THE I LOVE WRINKLED OLD FLESH AWARD

Harold and Maude ('72)—Harold (Bud Cort)—who's in his twenties—is one of the few leading men in film who's sexually attracted to elderly women, namely octogenarian Maude (Ruth Gordon), in a truly black comedy of love.

STUDS

"Look, he probably gets more ass than a toilet seat."
—Bill Rusconi, *Out of the Dark*

Studs, men who think they're God's gift to everybody. Studs, who'll try to bed anything breathing. Studs, possessed of egos large to the extreme.

Warren Beatty	*Shampoo* ('75)
Tom Berenger	*In Praise of Older Women* ('78)
Marlon Brando	*A Streetcar Named Desire* ('51)
Michael Caine	*Alfie* ('66)

Andrew Dice Clay	*Casual Sex?* ('88)
Patrick Dempsey	*In the Mood* ('87)
James Farentino	*The Pad—And How to Use It* ('66)
Paul Newman	*Hud* ('63)
Terence Stamp	*Teorema* ('68)
Donald Sutherland	*Fellini's Casanova* ('76)
Richard Tyson	*Two-Moon Junction* ('88)
Michael York	*Something for Everyone* ('70)

STUDS WITH THE BEST-DRESSED PENISES

John Ritter and **Bryan Genessee** in *Skin Deep* ('89), for wearing fluorescent condoms—Ritter in blue, Genessee in red—during their in-the-dark "cockfight."

TATTOOS

"Never could understand the quaint habit of making a billboard out of one's torso. I must say, however, you've shown the most commendable delicacy in just tattooing the initials of your lovers and not printing the names, addresses, and telephone numbers."
—Tallulah Bankhead, *Lifeboat*

Alec Baldwin in *Miami Blues* ('90) has a big tattoo on a bicep that reaches almost onto his shoulder.

Dirk Benedict in *Mark of the Devil* ('74) parades around in ultraskimpy black briefs as an evil tattoo spreads across his face and body.

Robert De Niro in *Cape Fear* ('91) plays a just-released-from-prison convict with myriad tattoos on his body.

Johnny Depp in *Cry-Baby* ('90) is a "bad boy" delinquent, who has an electric chair etched on his chest, in memory of his Dad, who fried on the hot seat.

Bruce Dern in *Tattoo* ('81) is a tattoo artist who sports several artistic renderings on his own body.

Divine (Glenn Milstead) in *Lust in the Dust* ('85) has a tattoo on his/her butt, which is one-half of a treasure map. The other half appears on the ample rear of archrival Lainie Kazan, who's also a longlost sibling.

Lance Hendricksen in *Hit List* ('89) is a Mafia hit man whose back is covered with tattoos.

Lorenzo Lamas in *Snake Eater* ('89) has a large snake that coils around his upper arm onto his shoulder.

Burt Lancaster in *The Rose Tattoo* ('55) has a large red rose tattooed on his chest to honor his love for Anna Magnani.

Robert Mitchum in *Night of the Hunter* ('55) is a murderous backwoods ex-convict preacher, with tattoos that spell "Hate" and "Love" on his fingers.

Ryan O'Neal in *Tough Guys Don't Dance* ('87) wakes up with "Madeleine" tattooed on his arm. He claims to have no recollection of who she is or how he got the tattoo.

Kurt Russell in *Escape from New York* ('81) plays a character named Snake Plisken, who has a snake tattooed on his abdomen.

Rod Steiger in *The Illustrated Man* ('69) has a body covered with tattoos, several of which introduce the short stories that make up the film.

REAL TATTOOS

A few of Hollywood's real tattooed attractions are:

Adam Ant	"Pure Sex"
Orson Bean	a rose
Glen Campbell	a dagger
Sean Connery	"Mum and Dad"; "Scotland Forever"
Tony Danza	"Keep on Truckin' "; cartoon man
Johnny Depp	"Winona Forever"; Indian chief; "Betty Sue"
Peter Fonda	dolphins, three stars
Lorenzo Lamas	Harley-Davidson emblem
Robert Mitchum	obscene word
Sean Penn	"Madonna"
Michael J. Pollard	heart with girl's name
Gene Simmons	rose
Ringo Starr	half moon; shooting star

THANK HEAVEN FOR LITTLE GIRLS

"She was fifteen, going to thirty-five, Doc, and she told me she was
eighteen, and she was very willing, you know what I mean. Matter
of fact, I would have had to take to sewing my pants shut."
—Jack Nicholson, *One Flew over the Cuckoo's Nest*

These men just can't get enough of young, nubile girls . . . they're
fascinated with them, infatuated with them, in love with them . . . and
a couple of them even molest them.

The Dirty Old Man Grand Prize
James Mason in *Lolita* ('62)—Vladimir Nabokov's novel *Lolita* introduced a new term to describe the nubile young female: *nymphet*.
James Mason, as the nymphet-loving Humbert Humbert, paints an
engaging portrait of a stolid professor obsessed by desire for Sue
Lyon (Lolita), the pubescent daughter of Shelley Winters, in this
screen adaption of Nabokov's sex classic. Listen to the theme song,
"Lolita Ya-Ya." Sung by Sue Lyon, it's regarded as one of the more
sensual movie themes.

The Slobbering Lips of Honorable Mention

Felix Alymer	*Never Take Sweets from a Stranger* ('83)
Helmut Berger	*The Damned* ('69)
Charles Bronson	*Lola* ('69)
Michael Caine	*Blame It on Rio* ('84)
Ted Danson	*Something About Amelia* ('84)
Bruce Davison	*Short Eyes* ('77)
Keith Carradine	*Pretty Baby* ('78)
Zooey Hall	*I Dismember Mama* ('72)
William Holden	*Breezy* ('73)
Ian Holm	*DreamChild* ('85)
Hardy Kruger	*Sundays and Cybele* ('62)

Ed Marinaro	*Lethal Lolita—Amy Fisher: My Story* ('93)
Marcello Mastroianni	*Stay as You Are* ('78)
Richard Masur	*Fallen Angel* ('81)
Robert Mitchum	*Cape Fear* ('62)
Dennis Quaid	*Great Balls of Fire!* ('89)
Jack Scalia	*Casualties of Love: The "Long Island Lolita" Story* ('93)
William Shatner	*Impulse (aka Want a Ride, Little Girl?)* ('74)
Martin Sheen	*The Little Girl Who Lives Down the Lane* ('76)
Stuart Whitman	*The Mark* ('61)
Nicol Williamson	*Laughter in the Dark* ('69)

TIMBER!

"Well, we've been shaken out of the magnolias."
—Lucile Watson, *Watch on the Rhine*

Big men and tall trees. . . . Timber! Watch out below, there's tall trees falling and big, burly lumberjacks stomping around.

Bruce Boxleitner	*Happily Ever After* ('91)
George Brent	*God's Country and the Woman* ('36)
Kirk Douglas	*The Big Trees* ('52)
Sterling Hayden	*Timberjack* ('55)
Richard Jaeckel	*Sometimes a Great Notion* ('71)
Alan Ladd	*Guns of the Timberland* ('60)
Joel McCrea	*Come and Get It* ('36)
Wayne Morris	*Valley of the Giants* ('38)

Paul Newman	*Sometimes a Great Notion* ('71)
Michael Sarrazin	*Sometimes a Great Notion* ('71)
Forrest Tucker	*Girl in the Woods* ('58)
Martin West	*Freckles* ('60)

TITLES CAN BE MISLEADING

"How could this happen? I was so careful. I picked the wrong play,
the wrong cast, the wrong director. Where did I go right?"
—Zero Mostel, *The Producers*

Fist in His Pocket ('66)—Is not a heart-wrenching drama about a chronic masturbator's attempts to overcome his addiction.

Five Finger Exercise ('62)—Is not an educational cartoon that features the various ways young boys may keep themselves amused.

Head ('68)—Is not an instructional film for learning to give fellatio.

The Last Hard Men ('76)—Is not a science-fiction film about the effects of radiation on the male's ability to achieve erections.

Moby Dick ('56)—Is not a disaster epic about a virulent new venereal disease decimating males.

So Big ('53)—Is not a comedy about what Pee-wee Herman discovers in his pants.

HOW'D YOU LIKE TO GO SWINGING ON A STAR?

"What if I were to say 'Take it in your mouth, or you die'? Would
you take my Pride and Joy in your mouth?"
—John Bedford Lloyd, *Tough Guys Don't Dance*

Somebody went swinging on these stars! And they didn't use their hands to hold on to them.

Warren Beatty, in *Shampoo* ('75), under the table in a Hollywood restaurant, by **Julie Christie**, who prefaces her action by exclaiming, "I wanna suck his cock!"

Dirk Bogarde, in *The Night Porter* ('74), by **Charlotte Rampling**, who's playing an ex-prisoner in a concentration camp where Bogarde was an SS officer during World War II.

Wendell Burton, in *Fortune and Men's Eyes* ('71), in his prison cell by another male prisoner, nicknamed Mona by the other inmates.

Jim Carrey, in *Once Bitten* ('85), on a living room sofa, by **Lauren Hutton**, who's a vampire and needs the blood of a virgin. She bites the buttons off his shirt as she descends on the object of her desire. Later, when she attacks him a second time, Carrey begs her not to bite his buttons off again.

Joe Dallesandro, in *Flesh* ('68), while lying on a daybed in a sleazy apartment, by a demented go-go dancer.

Clint Eastwood in *The Rookie* ('90), while tied to a chair, by sultry **Sonia Braga**.

Jeff Goldblum, in *Death Wish I* ('74), in the living room of a Manhattan apartment building, by **Kathleen Tolan**, who's being sexually assaulted by Goldblum and his friends.

William Hurt, in *Body Heat* ('81), outside on a patio at nighttime, by **Kathleen Turner**.

Don Johnson, in *Hot Spot* ('90), gets it from **Virginia Madsen**, who's kneeling in front of it.

William Katt, in *Naked Obsession* ('90), gets it from a stripper, who's tied him to a chair—with a noose around his neck, which she keeps tightening to give him the ultimate orgasm.

Fred Lincoln, in *Last House on the Left* ('72), outdoors at night by a pond, by **Cynthia Carr**. She plays the mother of a young girl Lincoln's character, Weasel, has brutally slain earlier in the film. As he climaxes, she bites off his penis in revenge.

Steve Martin in *Parenthood* ('89), in the front seat of a van he's driving, by **Mary Steenburgen**. Martin's so surprised by his wife's unexpected act, that he wrecks the van. When the investigating police officer asks how the accident happened, Martin turns to Steenburgen and says, "Show him, Honey."

Danny Mills, in *Pink Flamingos* ('72), on a living room sofa, by **Divine**, who plays his mother. All during the episode, Mills keeps moaning, "Oh, Mama, you're the best . . . you're the best."

Gary Oldman, in *Prick Up Your Ears* ('87), in the darkened men's room of a public toilet, by several other men and again in *Bram Stoker's Dracula* ('92), when **Winona Ryder** puts her own kind of bite on his Count Dracula.

River Phoenix, in *My Own Private Idaho* ('91), by a male "customer" while sitting in a chair as the film opens.

Charlie Sheen, in *Wall Street* ('87), in the rear of a limousine, by a high-class hooker hired by his mentor, Gordon Gekko (Michael Douglas).

James Spader, in *White Palace* ('90), early one morning while still asleep in bed, by **Susan Sarandon**, who's giving him a very special wake-up call.

John Travolta, in *Carrie* ('76), in a car at the drive-in, by **Nancy Allen**, who's attempting to persuade him to help her humiliate her classmate Carrie at the prom.

Jon Voight, in *Midnight Cowboy* ('69), in a darkened movie theater, by a young male who promises him $25 and accompanies him to the theater.

Jason Williams, in *Flesh Gordon* ('77), in a bedroom, by another male, who needs a favor from his character Flash.

LONGEST SINGLE SEX ACT IN A FILM

Andy Warhol's Blow Job ('63), black/white, 35 minutes—In this underground film by Mister Pop Art, the camera focuses on the rugged face of a black leather jacket-clad male, standing in front of a brick wall, as he receives a blow job. As the film begins, the camera briefly glimpses the shoulder of a second black leather jacket in the bottom left of the screen before traveling upward to the standing male's face, where it remains for the film's entire 35 minutes, recording his every facial emotion during the sexual encounter.

Warhol engaged five males to perform fellatio and offered an actor friend the opportunity to be the recipient. When his friend declined, Warhol said he "used a kid who was hanging around that day."

THE COITUS VIOLENT INTERRUPTUS AWARD

Pierce Brosnan in *The Fourth Protocol* ('87)—A young homosexual spots Brosnan, clad in a black leather jacket, and follows him to a public restroom. There he witnesses an exchange between Brosnan, a secret KGB agent, and a Soviet courier. Not realizing what he has seen, and assuming Brosnan is not interested in him, he leaves hurriedly.

Brosnan follows quickly and asks if the young man "is looking for someone." He first demurs, until Brosnan inquires if he has a room, whereupon he volunteers that he has a car outside.

The duo proceed to car and once inside, Brosnan puts his arm around the other's shoulder. Asked what he likes, Brosnan gently lowers his newfound friend's head into his crotch, holding it there while he slits the young man's throat.

THE PARADE OF THE UNDERPANTS

"Something tells me you could really fit
into a pair of Jockey shorts."
—Tammy Grimes, *Can't Stop the Music*

Award-winning performances by the Grand Marshals in the Cinematic Parade of the Underpants. Their individual parading styles can be viewed as follows:

Kevin Bacon	*She's Having a Baby* ('88)
Alec Baldwin	*Married to the Mob* ('88)
Pierce Brosnan	*The Lawnmower Man* ('92)
Kevin Costner	*Fandango* ('85)
Tom Cruise	*Risky Business* ('83)
Robert De Niro	*Taxi Driver* ('76)
Johnny Depp	*Cry-Baby* ('90)
Matt Dillon	*Little Darlings* ('80)
Robert Downey Jr.	*Rented Lips* ('87)
Michael J. Fox	*Back to the Future* ('85)
Mel Gibson	*Lethal Weapon 3* ('92)
Jeff Goldblum	*The Fly* ('86)
Mark Hamill	*Black Magic Woman* ('90)
Tom Hanks	*Turner & Hooch* ('89)
Dustin Hoffman	*The Graduate* ('67)

Michael Keaton	*Touch and Go* ('86)
Nick Nolte	*North Dallas Forty* ('79)
Michael O'Keefe	*Caddyshack* ('80)
Brad Pitt	*Johnny Suede* ('91)
Keanu Reeves	*Parenthood* ('89)
John Ritter	*Skin Deep* ('89)
Charlie Sheen	*Three for the Road* ('87)
Martin Sheen	*Apocalypse Now* ('79)
John Travolta	*Saturday Night Fever* ('77)

MR. MACHO WEARS A JOCKSTRAP

"Hey, kid. Whadda you use for a jockstrap?
A rubber band and a peanut shell?"
—Robert Archambault, *Porky's*

A jockstrap is the quintessential male garment. However, cinematic appearances in this most masculine piece of clothing aren't very commonplace.

The Dancin', Prancin', and Struttin' My Hot Stuff Award
Richard Gere in *Looking for Mr. Goodbar* ('77)—Gere prances around the room, does push-ups, and performs an athletic dance brandishing a switchblade with a fluorescent blade—all to impress a woman (Diane Keaton) who's picked him up in a bar.

Honorable Mentions

Kevin Bacon	*Pyrates* ('91)
David Alan Grier	*Streamers* ('83)
Charlton Heston	*Number One* ('69)
Paul Holland	*Polyester* ('81)
Rob Lowe	*Hotel New Hampshire* ('84), *Youngblood* ('86)
Franco Nero	*The Salamander* ('81)
Michael Ontkean	*Slap Shot* ('77)
Tom Selleck	*Mr. Baseball* ('92)

The opportunity to see groups of guys in jockstraps occurs in:

Just One of the Guys ('85)

North Dallas Forty ('79)

One Night Only ('87)

Semi-Tough ('77)

The Real-Life Hollywood Hot-Cup Award
Awarded to **Henry Fonda**, because during the filming of *Daisy Kenyon* ('47), Fonda's costar, **Joan Crawford**, presented him with a jockstrap of rhinestones, gold sequins, and red beads—then led him off the set to model and pose in it for her.

WATER SPORTS

"I don't hold with too much water, anyhow. Rusts the bones."
—Percy Kilbride, *The Egg and I*

No, not Johnny Weissmuller's swimming; it's the other, more raunchy kind of water sports. The one that features the most common of all bodily functions.

Caligula ('80)—**Malcolm McDowell** does the deed.

Canterbury Tales ('71)—**Robin Askwith** cuts loose from the balcony of a bordello onto the guests in a tavern below.

Greystoke: The Legend of Tarzan, Lord of the Apes ('84)—The young Tarzan, high up in a tree, does it on an ape's head.

Liebenstraum ('91)—**Graham Beckel** does it on-camera while pausing outside his police car.

My Own Private Idaho ('91)—**River Phoenix** does it on the highway. (And close observers of the scene claim that the tip of the water nozzle used to make his stream is visible.)

Personal Best ('82)—**Kenny Moore** is led nude from bed by **Mariel Hemingway** and into the bathroom, where she holds it for him while he relieves himself.

Screen Test ('86)—Three guys together at a urinal, with two playing games and directing their streams to a cigarette butt.

Short Cuts ('93)—**Huey Lewis** does it and discovers a dead body nearby.

Taxi Zum Klo ('81)—**Frank Ripploh** does it into the mouth of one of his many pickups.

War of the Roses ('89)—**Michael Douglas** does it on the fish course his wife, a caterer, is preparing for a group of her clients.

Some other notable watery performances are:

Emilio Estevez	*Young Guns* ('88)
Jackie Earle Haley	*Losin' It* ('83)
Michael Keaton	*Touch and Go* ('86)
Cheech Marin	*Up in Smoke* ('78)
Sean Penn	*Taps* ('81)
Dennis Quaid	*Dreamscape* ('84)

MOST WATERY FILM

Sweet Movie ('74) is a urination extravaganza. Almost every male character, at one time or another, in the film—and most in extreme close-up—is shown urinating. They perform their water stunts at the dining table (onto the food, no less), while in bed, and even outside in full public view.

MOST ELECTRIFYING PERFORMANCE BY A WATER SPRITE

Awarded to **Scott "Bam Bam" Bigelow** for his role in *Snake Eater III: His Law* ('92). Bigelow, playing an ultralarge, outlaw biker gets electrocuted while urinating in his own bathroom. It's seems that **Lorenzo Lamas** has rigged up Bigelow's toilet so that his urine stream conducts a massive jolt of electricity when it strikes the water in his commode.

KING ORSON'S THRONE

Orotund **Orson Welles**, among his other many accolades, bears the distinction of being the first male to be shown sitting on a throne in an American film. In *Catch-22* ('70), His Largeness is seated on a toilet having a bowel movement.

WHERE HAVE ALL THE EX-HUNKS GONE?

"With all these successful people around, where are all of our
young failures going to come from?"
—Jason Robards, *A Thousand Clowns*

And whatever happened to these young hunky numbers whose stars
seemed so bright once upon a time? Where are they now? Has their
male beauty survived intact?

Scott Anthony	*Savage Messiah* ('72)
John Beck	*The Other Side of Midnight* ('77)
Michael Callan	*Gidget Goes Hawaiian* ('61)
Troy Donahue	*A Summer Place* ('59)
Ron Ely	*Tarzan's Deadly Silence* ('70)
Chad Everett	*The Last Challenge* ('67)
Farley Granger	*Strangers on a Train* ('51)
Ty Hardin	*The Chapman Report* ('62)
Brent Huff	*The Perils of Gwendoline in the Land of the Yik Yak* ('84)
John Kerr	*Tea and Sympathy* ('56)
Guy Madison	*Drums in the Deep South* ('51)
Dewey Martin	*Land of the Pharaohs* ('55)
Denny Miller	*Tarzan, the Ape Man* ('59)
George Nader	*The Female Animal* ('58)
Michael Parks	*Bus Riley's Back in Town* ('65)
Johnny Sheffield	*Bomba and the Hidden City* ('50)
Klinton Spilsbury	*The Legend of the Lone Ranger* ('81)
Clint Walker	*Yellowstone Kelly* ('59)

THE GROTESQUE HUNK

Rondo Hatton, a once handsome young actor who suffered from acromegaly, a progressive bone disease that causes enlargement and distortion of the bones, was used in several Universal B thrillers of the '40s, because he was so grotesque no makeup was required. Hatton the hunk can be caught as the Oxton creeper in *Pearl of Death* ('44) and as the scientist's assistant in *Jungle Captive* ('45). The B feature *Brute Man* ('46) is a fictionalized account of the tragedy that was Hatton's life.

THE CINEMATIC MALE NUDITY PIONEERS

"Young man, you can be grateful that my invention is not for sale,
for it would undoubtedly ruin you. It can be exploited for a
certain time as a scientific curiosity, but apart from that
it has no commercial value whatsoever."
—August Lumiere, pioneer of cinematography, 1895

Full-Frontal Male Nudity
The first full-frontal male nudity appeared fleetingly in an Italian silent film, *Dante's Inferno* ('12).

Nudity by Major Male Star
Michael Parks in *The Bible* ('66), directed by John Huston, became the first major actor since the '20s to perform nude on-screen. Parks, playing Adam as created by God, was shot without any camouflage, although only full length from the rear or side.

Prior to his appearance, the only American audiences to catch a glimpse of male nudity were these devotees of foreign "art" films, which occasionally afforded a quick view of a nude actor. For example, in Ingmar Bergman's *The Virgin Spring* ('59, Swedish), **Max von**

Sydow, later to become an international star, had a nude bathing scene. While it appeared in some prints shown to American audiences, von Sydow's nude dip was clipped from other prints distributed in the American market.

Richard Harris's role in *This Sporting Life* ('63, British) was the first in which the actor who appeared in a nude scene (although only fleetingly) was nominated for an Oscar.

Explicit Male Genitalia

The first explicit scene of male genitalia in a modern commercial feature occurred when **Alan Bates** and **Oliver Reed** stripped down, for a nude wrestling bout in front of a roaring fire, in Ken Russell's *Women in Love* ('69).

Male Nudity on a Movie Poster

The poster for *Thunderball* ('65), a James Bond film, was the first to contain male nudity. On it, a sketch of **Sean Connery** as Bond showed the superspy lying nude on his stomach, while a comely young female hovered above him, cradling a gun. The poster was a tease to entice Connery's fans, as no scene like the one depicted on it appeared in the film.

AND THE NAKED MALE BODIES RUNNETH RAMPANT

"This is filth—pure filth.
I sat through every disgusting frame—twice."
—Gary Young, *Porky's Revenge*

Caligula ('80)—The real Caligula, the third Roman emperor, was overly fond of his sister, had a sexual field day among Roman citizens of both sexes, established a brothel staffed by the wives of the Senate members, made his horse a senator, and was generally an actual pain in everyone's ass (not to mention the indignities he performed on the other parts of their bodies during his reign).

Justly regarded as the most repulsive "mainstream" film ever released, **Caligula**, the brainchild of *Penthouse* publisher Bob Guccione and bearing a screenplay credit for Gore Vidal, does full justice to the depraved emperor. It begins as the not-yet emperor dallies with his sister under a tree. That tree is the last natural sight in the film. From then onward only unnatural sights prevail. The audience is treated to Caligula's gratuitous violence (smothering his grandfather to ensure his succession, binding a man's penis and pouring water down his throat to bloat him before cutting him open), interspersed with his sexual frolics.

Particularly humorous (in a thoroughly tasteless manner) are two of the many, many sex scenes in the film. In the first, Caligula visits one of his mistresses, who's in her bathtub surrounded by several handsome men masturbating. As each climaxes, their ejaculate is directed onto the lady in the tub, who believes it gives her healthier skin. Caligula fingers their drippings asking, "Is it good to grow hair, too?" (He has been mocked over his inability to grow a proper beard and has resorted to a false one.)

In the second scene, Caligula attends a wedding, where he takes the nuptial couple into another room to bestow his imperial blessing. This consists of taking the bride's virginity himself, and when he's finished with her, using his fist to anally assault the groom (leaving the viewer with the suspicion that secret wedding ceremonies proba- bly were very much in vogue during Caligula's reign).

The Devils ('71). Ken Russell's cinematic exercise in exorcism, based on Aldous Huxley's *The Devils of Loudon*, is probably the most blasphemous and censorable film in existence.

Featuring Oliver Reed as the lecherous Father Urbain Grandier and Vanessa Redgrave as a hunchbacked Mother Superior whose advances he ignores, Russell presents a film with something to offend everyone's religious sensibilities (even those who don't pos- sess any!). The plot is seemingly simple but actually intricate. It's set in a French convent, where the nuns have become "possessed." The Inquisition is involved in helping rid the good sisters of their demons, while political intrigue runs rife.

Hundreds dance naked, torture permeates the screen, Redgrave lopes about acting weird, and Reed is finally burned at the stake in a fiery finale.

Salo (The 120 Days of Sodom) ('75)—Based on de Sade's posthumous novel, *Salo* was directed by Pier Paolo Pasolini. The film is set in a northern Italian town, where the Italian Fascists, under Mussolini, established their stronghold after the fall of Rome. The screen is filled with rampant sex and sadism, with a plethora of male nude bodies.

Rumors flew during filming that the erotic, highly sexual scenes were played with complete truth by the actors. Pasolini supposedly took a perverse pleasure in convincing the primarily heterosexual actors to kiss and indulge in sexual relations with each other for the sake of reality in art.

The film's hallmarks are its overabundant nudity and the crudity of the sexual situations. (Play close attention during the coprophagy scenes; it's easy to see that chocolate was used to represent feces.) Pasolini's own peculiar sexual tastes are probably well represented in the film: he died in November 1975 on a secluded road, bludgeoned to death with a fence stake wielded by a male hustler he had picked up for a midnight snack.

Honorable Mentions of Gratuitous Nudity

The Arabian Nights ('74)

The Canterbury Tales ('71)

The Decameron ('70)

Woodstock ('70)

Nudus Latinum

Sebastiane ('76)—The only film ever released in Latin (with English subtitles), it purports to be the story of St. Sebastian, but in reality seems only an excuse for the all-male cast to appear almost entirely nude throughout the film.

What Are You Trying to Hide?

"Yes, it's true. This man has no dick. Well . . . that's what I heard."
—Bill Murray, *Ghostbusters*

Do these sex symbols have something they're trying to hide? Strange tattoos perhaps? All the viewer saw in their films was a nude side view. No front, no rear . . . no fun at all! Aw, come on guys, what are you trying to hide?

Adam Baldwin	*Bad Guys* ('86)
Erik Estrada	*Light Blast* ('87)
Harrison Ford	*Frantic* ('88)
Mick Jagger	*Performance* ('70)
Steve Martin	*The Jerk* ('79)
Omar Sharif	*MacKenna's Gold* ('69)

| Kiefer Sutherland | *Promised Land* ('88) |
| Patrick Swayze | *Dirty Dancing* ('87) |

Porno's Big Three

Three of porno's "biggest" male stars have each made at least one venture into the commercial mainstream cinema. Even in these films, they couldn't resist the opportunity to expose the assets for which they are famed.

Jamie Gillis	*Dracula Exotica* ('81)
John Holmes	*Dracula Sucks* ('78)
Harry Reems	*The Case of the Full Moon Murders* ('71)

Longest Nude Exposure in a Film

"I don't do horror movies."
—James Garner, telling why he doesn't do nude scenes

Taylor Mead's Ass ('64), black & white, 70 minutes, silent—Famous for its nonaction, this underground film by pop artist Andy Warhol features the bare bottom of pseudoactor **Taylor Mead** for its entire running time.

THE GOLDEN BUTTOCKS HALL OF FAME

"If we can bring a little joy into your humdrum lives, it makes us feel our work ain't been for nothin'."
—Jean Hagen, *Singin' in the Rain*

Beginning in the mid-1960s, there was a rush by filmmakers to undrape as many actors as possible. Of course, this onslaught of male nudity in the cinema would have been impossible without the full cooperation of the actors involved. A glance through the following pages shows that almost every male considered to be a "star" appears on this dubious honor roll.

Male film nudity differs from that of the female in one almost startling aspect. While most female film nudity is presented in a frankly sexual nature, that of the male is overwhelmingly gratuitous— or comedic. Scenes that could have been filmed in almost any other location seem to have been switched to one—the locker room, for example—which almost inspires the male to drop his pants and bare his buns. But did filmgoers really see what they thought they saw?

No, quite often they did not. Many films today are available in several formats: the theatrical release, a laser-disk version, a video-tape version for the domestic market, "spicier" versions for the overseas (primarily European) theatrical and videotape markets, and the oft-truncated version used by commercial television. Each of these versions can differ markedly; scenes are shortened or cut entirely, especially those containing nudity. This censorship depends on reasons as varied as the whims of a laser-disk manufacturer to the amount of time needed to insert commercials for television.

With this plethora of versions available, the film viewer frequently has to see a film three or four times—with each viewing being a different version—before finally being allowed a full unexpurgated "little peek" at all the male star's assets.

Two other points also should be made about the Golden Buttocks Hall of Fame. Many actors are reluctant to do nude scenes and are replaced by uncredited "body doubles." Undoubtedly, that is true of some of the names on the following pages. Also, no attempt has been made to include the multitude of males who have appeared in "porno" films.

Come now and browse through the Golden Buttocks Hall of Fame . . . with profound apologies to any who have been included by mistake . . . and abject mortification over those who we have failed to honor by inadvertently omitting their names.

THE GOLDEN BUTTOCKS
HALL OF FAME

LEGEND

(Ar)	Argentinian	(D)	Dutch	(I)	Italian	(P)	Philippine
(A)	Australian	(F)	French	(Jm)	Jamaican	(R)	Russian
(B)	British	(G)	German	(J)	Japanese	(SA)	South African
(Br)	Brazilian	(Gr)	Greek	(M)	Mexican	(Sp)	Spanish
(C)	Canadian	(H)	Hungarian	(NZ)	New Zealand	(S)	Swedish
(Da)	Danish	(Is)	Israeli	(N)	Norwegian	(Y)	Yugoslavian

a = ass revealed; p = penis shown; * = footage shot, not used in film

Aames, Willie	*Paradise* ('82)	a, p
Abatantuono, Diego	*Mediterraneo* (I) ('91)	a
Abbott, Michael D.	*Satisfaction Guaranteed* ('73)	a
Abele, Jim	*Student Affairs* ('87)	a
Abelew, Alan	*The All-American Girl* ('72)	a
Abelew, Alan	*The First Nudie Musical* ('75)	a
Aberdeen, Robert	*Saturday Night at the Baths* ('75)	a, p
Abraham, Ken	*Creepozoids* ('87)	a
Abraham, Ken	*Deadly Embrace* ('88)	a
Acovone, Jay	*Cruising* ('80)	a
Adams, Mark	*Manageress II*	a
Addabbo, Anthony	*Inside Out 4* ('92)	a
Adelin, Jean-Claude	*Chocolat* (F) ('88)	a, p
Adell, Steve	*Almost Pregnant* ('91)	a
Adler, Bill	*Malibu Beach* ('78)	a
Adler, Bill	*Van Nuys Blvd.* ('79)	a
Adley, Frank	*Boardinghouse* ('82)	a
Agenso, Anders	*You Are Not Alone* (S) ('80)	a, p
Agterberg, Toon	*Spetters* (D) ('80)	a, p
Aguirre, Cesar	*La Tentacion*	a, p
Ahlstead, Borje	*I Am Curious—Blue* (S) ('68)	a, p
Ahlstead, Borje	*I Am Curious—Yellow* (S) ('67)	a, p
Albee, Josh	*Slaughterhouse-Five* ('72)	a
Albert Jr., Eddie	*The Fool Killer* ('64)	a
Albert Jr., Eddie	*The House Where Evil Dwells* ('82)	a
Albertini, Michel	*Jury of One* (F/I) ('75)	a
Alberto, Daniel	*Satanico Pandemonium* (M)	a

Alden, John	*Young Warriors* ('83)	a
Alderman, John	*Little Miss Innocence* ('73)	a
Alejandro, Miguel	*Popi* ('69)	a, p
Alejandro, Oscar	*Playa Prohibide* (M)	a
Alexander, Jason	*The Burning* ('81)	a
Alexander, Sandy	*The People Next Door* ('70)	a, p
Alfaire, Claude	*Betty Blue* (F) ('86)	a, p
Alfieri, Richard	*Echoes* ('83)	a
Alin, Jeff	*A Matter of Love* ('78)	a
Alkerton, Carl	*It's All In Good Taste*	p
Allande, Fernando	*El Pacto* (M)	a
Allande, Fernando	*Vereno Salvaje* (M)	a
Allen, Ron	*Angel, Angel, Down We Go* ('69)	a
Alonzo, Jose	*El Vuelo De La Ciguena* (M)	a, p
Alonzo, Jose	*La Derrota* (M)	a, p
Alonzo, Jose	*Motel* (M) ('83)	a, p
Alonzo, Jose	*Naufragio* (M)	a, p
Alonzo, Jose Luis	*The Deputy* (Sp) ('78)	a, p
Altamura, John	*The Marilyn Diaries* ('90)	a
Altamura, John	*Party Inc.* ('89)	a
Alton, Walter George	*Heavenly Bodies* ('85)	a
Alvernez, Carlos	*El Chico Temido*	a, p
Ambrus, Andras	*Forgotten Prisoners* ('90)	a
Amidou	*Life, Love, Death* (F)	a
Amigo, Hank	*Computer Beach Party* ('85)	a
Amodio, Amedeo	*The Night Porter* (I) ('73)	a
Anacnina, Richard	*Se Lo Scopre Garguilo*	a
Anastasonthlos, Nikos	*To Soguien* (F)	a, p
Anderson, John	*March of the Falsettos* (A)	a, p
Anderson, Kevin	*Liebestraum* ('91)	a
Anderson, Kevin	*Orpheus Descending* ('90)	a
Anderson, Marc	*A Matter of Love* ('78)	a
Anderson, Peter	*Freud Leaving Home* (S)	a
Andre, Robert	*Garden of Beauty*	a
Andres, Valeriom	*Las Eroticas Vacaiones de Stela* (M) ('75)	a, p
Andrew, Michael	*Hollywood Hot Tubs* ('84)	a
Andrews, Anthony	*Brideshead Revisited* (B) ('81)	a
Andrews, Anthony	*Z Is for Zachariah*	p
Andrews, Chris	*The Immoral One* (F)	a
Angelini, Frank	*Fear of Scandal* (I)	a
Anglade, Jean Hugues	*Betty Blue* (F) ('86)	a, p
Anglade, Jean Hugues	*L'Homme Blesse* (F) ('88)	a
Anglade, Jean Hugues	*Maladie d'Amour* (F) ('87)	a, p
Anglade, Jean Hughes	*One Summer Night in Town* (F)	a
Anthony, Corwyn	*Student Confidential* ('87)	a
Anthony, David	*Take Time to Smell the Flowers*	a

Antin, Steve	*The Accused* ('88)	a
Antin, Steve	*The Last American Virgin* ('82)	a
Aragon, Alejandro	*Pueblo Maldito* (M)	a, p
Arantes, Romulo	*Hell Hunters* ('86)	a
Archibek, Ben	*The Dirt Gang* ('71)	a
Arditi, Pierre	*La Passerelle* (F) ('88)	a
Arenda, Angel	*Escalofrio* (M)	a, p
Argenzianno, Carmen	*Not My Daughter!* ('70)	a
Arias, Imanol	*Camila* (Sp) ('84)	a
Arias, Imanol	*La Muerte de Mikel* (M)	a, p
Arkin, Alan	*Catch-22* ('70)	a
Armstrong, R. G.	*Stay Hungry* ('76)	a
Armstrong, Vic	*Expose*	a
Arnaz Jr., Desi	*A Wedding* ('78)	a
Arngrim, Stefan	*Fear No Evil* ('81)	a
Arnott, Mark	*Return of the Secaucus 7* ('80)	a, p
Arquette, Alexis	*Grief* ('93)	a
Arquette, Alexis	*Jumpin' at the Boneyard* ('93)	a, p
Ashby, Linden	*Night Angel* ('89)	a
Asher, Michael	*Tender Loving Care* ('73)	a
Ashley, John	*Beast of the Yellow Night* ('73)	a
Ashmore, Frank	*The Clonus Horror* ('78)	a
Askwith, Robin	*Canterbury Tales* (I) ('71)	a, p
Askwith, Robin	*Confessions of a Driving Instructor* (B) ('71)	a, p
Askwith, Robin	*Confessions of a Holiday Camp* (B) ('77)	a
Askwith, Robin	*Confessions of a Pop Performer* (B) ('75)	a
Askwith, Robin	*Confessions of a Window Cleaner* (B) ('74)	a
Askwith, Robin	*Cool It Carol* (B) ('68)	a
Askwith, Robin	*Dirtiest Girl I Ever Met* (B) ('70)	a
Askwith, Robin	*The Love Trap* (B)	a
Askwith, Robin	*Tower of Evil* (B) ('72)	a
Asparagus, Fred	*Surf II* ('83)	a
Assante, Armand	*I, the Jury* ('81)	a
Astan, Thomas	*The Three Cornered Bed* (G) ('71)	a
Astin, Sean	*Toy Soldiers* ('91)	a
Atherton, William	*Looking for Mr. Goodbar* ('77)	a
Atkins, Christopher	*The Blue Lagoon* ('80)	a, p
Atkins, Christopher	*A Night in Heaven* ('83)	a, p
Atkins, Christopher	*The Pirate Movie* ('82)	a
Atkins, Tom	*Halloween III* ('83)	a
Atzorn, Robert	*From the Life of the Marionettes* (G) ('80)	a, p
Aubrey, James	*Home Before Midnight* ('79)	a

Aurialt, Phillipe	*Glass House* ('72)	a
Aurialt, Philippe	*Secret of Love* (F)	a
Auteuil, Daniel	*Tempeches Tous le Monde de Dormir* (F) ('82)	a, p
Auyer, George	*New York Nights* ('83)	a
Avedikan, Serge	*We Were One Man* (F/G) ('79)	a, p
Ayres, Lew	*All Quiet on the Western Front* ('30)	a
Azra, Jean Luc	*Comment Draguer Tortes les Filles* (F)	a
Baad, Harold	*The Master Beater* ('68)	a
Babb, Roger	*Working Girls* ('87)	a, p
Babilee, Yann	*True Story of the Lady aux Camilias* (F)	a
Backer, Brian	*The Burning* ('81)	a
Bacon, Kevin	*Friday the 13th* ('80)	a
Bacon, Kevin	*Pyrates* ('91)	a
Bacon, Kevin	*Queens Logic* ('91)	a
Badolisani, Vincenzo	*I Ragazzi di Torino* (I)	a
Baggetta, Vincent	*The Man Who Wasn't There* ('83)	a
Bahner, Blake	*Sensations* ('88)	a
Bail, Rod	*Porky's* ('81)	a
Baim, John	*While the Cat's Away*	a
Baio, Scott	*I Love N.Y.* ('87)	a
Bajrovic, Izudin	*Games of Desire* ('68)	a
Bakaba, Sidiki	*Descente aux Enfers* (F) ('86)	p
Baker, Henry Judd	*Clean and Sober* ('88)	a
Baker, Scott	*Cleo/Leo* ('89)	a
Baker, Tom	*Canterbury Tales* (I) ('71)	a, p
Baker, Tom	*I, a Man* (B)	a, p
Baker, Tom	*The Life & Loves of a She-Wolf* (B)	a
Bakewell, William	*All Quiet on the Western Front* ('30)	a
Balatzovicz, Lajos	*Private Vices, Public Virtue*	a, p
Baldwin, Alec	*Working Girl* ('88)	a
Baldwin, Stephen	*Bitter Harvest*	a
Baldwin, William	*Backdraft* ('91)	a
Baldwin, William	*Sliver* ('93)	a, p*
Baldwin, William	*Three of Hearts* ('93)	a
Balko, Dave	*Strikeback* ('84)	p
Ball, Vincent	*Not Tonight, Darling* (B) ('71)	a, p
Ballatare, Thomas	*Once Bitten* ('85)	a
Bancroft, Bradford	*Damned River* ('89)	a
Banderas, Antonio	*Baton Rouge* ('88)	p
Banderas, Antonio	*Law of Desire* (Sp) ('86)	a, p
Banderas, Antonio	*The Mambo Kings* ('92)	a
Banderas, Antonio	*Matador* (Sp) ('86)	a
Banderas, Antonio	*Shopping Down South*	a
Banderas, Antonio	*Tie Me Up! Tie Me Down!* (Sp) ('90)	a

Bane, Monte	*Up!* ('76)	p
Banneberg, Ulf	*Liz* (S)	a
Banner, Steve	*Les Fou de Bassan* (F)	a
Banta, Pat	*Fear City* ('85)	a
Barbareschi, Luca	*Bye Bye Baby* ('88)	a
Barbareschi, Luca	*Romance*	a, p
Barber, Paul	*The Long Good Friday* (B) ('80)	a
Bardem, Javier	*Jamon, Jamon* (Sp) ('93)	a
Bardonnet, Phillipe	*Love Circles* (F) ('85)	a
Barnes, Julian	*Mistress Pamela* (B) ('81)	a
Barnes, Rick	*Carnival of Fools* ('63)	a
Barrett, Lance	*Not Tonight, Darling* (B) ('71)	a, p
Barrett, Roy	*Don's Party* (A) ('76)	a, p
Barro, Cesare	*My Father's Wife* (I) ('76)	a
Barry, Neill	*O.C. & Stiggs* ('85)	a
Bassett, Steve	*Spring Break* ('83)	a
Bates, Alan	*The Fixer* ('69)	a
Bates, Alan	*Georgy Girl* (B) ('66)	a
Bates, Alan	*The Go-Between* (B) ('71)	a
Bates, Alan	*King of Hearts* (F) ('66)	a
Bates, Alan	*Women in Love* (B) ('69)	a, p
Battaglia, Mat	*Chantilly Lace* ('93)	a
Bauer, Steven	*Red Shoe Diaries: Safe Sex* ('92)	a
Bauer, Steven	*Sweet Poison* ('91)	a
Bauer, Steven	*Thief of Hearts* ('84)	a
Bean, Sean	*Stormy Monday* (B) ('88)	a
Beard, Chuck	*Filthiest Show in Town* ('82)	a
Beard, Peter H.	*Hallelujah the Hills* ('63)	a, p
Beargatto, Thierry	*Augustine* (F)	a, p
Beatty, Ned	*Deliverance* ('72)	a
Beatty, Warren	*Shampoo* ('75)	a
Beausoleil, Bobby	*Lucifer Rising* ('67)	a, p
Beck, Julian	*Paradise Now*	a, p
Beckel, Graham	*Liebestraum* ('91)	p
Beckel, Graham	*The Paper Chase* ('73)	a
Beckley, Tony	*Life of Brian* (B) ('79)	a
Beckley, Tony	*When a Stranger Calls* ('79)	a
Beghe, Jason	*Monkey Shines* ('88)	a
Begley Jr., Ed	*Amazon Women on the Moon* ('88)	a
Begley Jr., Ed	*Meet the Applegates* ('89)	a
Begley Jr., Ed	*She-Devil* ('89)	a
Beilike, Frank	*Robby Kallepaul*	a, p
Belafonte, Harry	*Buck and the Preacher* ('71)	a
Belden, Danny	*A Night in Heaven* ('83)	a
Bell, Marshall	*Nightmare on Elm Street II* ('85)	a
Bell, Tom	*Straight on Till Morning* (B) ('72)	a
Bell, Tom	*Wish You Were Here* (B) ('87)	a

Belle, Ekkehardt	*Julia* (G) ('74)	a
Beller, Georges	*The Legend of Frenchie King* (F) ('72)	a
Bellini, Cal	*Little Big Man* ('74)	a
Belmondo, Jean-Paul	*Doctor Popoul* (F) ('72)	a
Beltran, Robert	*Latino* ('85)	a
Beltran, Robert	*Scenes from the Class Struggle in Beverly Hills* ('89)	a
Belushi, Jim	*Salvador* ('86)	a
Belzer, Richard	*The Groove Tube* ('72)	a, p
Benedict, Dirk	*Sssssss* ('73)	a
Benigno, Francesco	*Ragazzi Fuori* (I)	p
Benjamin, Richard	*Goodbye, Columbus* ('69)	a
Bennent, David	*The Tin Drum* (G) ('79)	a
Bennett, Hywel	*Loot* (B) ('70)	a
Bennett, Hywel	*Percy* (B) ('71)	a
Bennett, Hywel	*The Virgin Soldiers* (B) ('69)	a
Bennett, Hywel	*Twisted Nerve* (B) ('68)	a
Bennett, Matt	*Hickey and Boggs* ('72)	a
Benneytton, Yves	*Broken Dreams* (F)	a, p
Benneytton, Yves	*The Lacemaker* (F) ('77)	a
Benson, Robbie	*Invasion of Privacy* ('92)	a
Benson, Robbie	*Jeremy* ('73)	a
Benson, Robbie	*Modern Love* ('90)	a
Benson, Robbie	*Running Brave* ('83)	a
Benson, Robbie	*White Hot* ('88)	a
Bentivoglio, Fabrizio	*Via Montenapoleone* (I)	a
Berenger, Tom	*At Play in the Fields of the Lord* ('91)	a, p
Berenger, Tom	*In Praise of Older Women* (C) ('77)	a, p
Berenger, Tom	*Looking for Mr. Goodbar* ('77)	a
Berg, Peter	*Aspen Extreme* ('93)	a
Berg, Peter	*Genuine Risk* ('89)	a
Berg, Peter	*The Last Seduction* ('93)	a
Berger, Helmut	*Conversation Piece* (I) ('74)	a, p
Berger, Helmut	*The Damned* (I/G) ('69)	a
Berger, Helmut	*Dorian Gray* (I/G) ('71)	a
Berger, Helmut	*Fatal Fix* ('80)	a
Berger, Helmut	*Garden of the Finzi-Continis* (I) ('71)	a
Berger, Helmut	*Merry-Go-Round* (I)	a
Berger, Helmut	*Salon Kitty* (G) ('75)	a, p
Bergin, Patrick	*Love Crimes* ('91)	a
Bergin, Patrick	*Sleeping with the Enemy* ('91)	a
Berhardt, Stephane	*Le Feu Sous la Peau* (F)	a
Berkrot, Peter	*Caddyshack* ('80)	a
Berling, Peter	*Julia* (G) ('74)	a
Bern, Thomas	*Dreamaniac* ('88)	a
Bernard, Erick	*Passion of Beatrice* (F) ('88)	a

Bernhardt, Kevin	*Hellraiser III: Hell on Earth* ('92)	a
Bernsen, Collin	*Puppetmaster II* ('90)	a
Bernsen, Corbin	*Major League* ('89)	a
Berri, Claude	*Le Sex Shop* (F) ('73)	a
Berri, Claude	*Stan the Flasher* (F)	p
Berry, Paul	*The All-American Girl* ('72)	a
Bhaskar	*I Drink Your Blood* ('71)	a
Bianchi, Franco	*Parci Con la Ali* (I)	a, p
Bianci, Tommaso	*Immacolata e Cocetta* (I)	a
Bideau, Jean Luc	*Et la Tandresse Bordel* (F) ('79)	a, p
Bideman, Robert	*Skull* ('88)	a
Biehn, Michael	*The Coach* ('78)	a
Biehn, Michael	*K2* ('91)	a
Biehn, Michael	*The Martyrdom of St. Sebastian*	a
Biehn, Michael	*The Terminator* ('84)	a
Biehn, Michael	*Timebomb* ('90)	a
Biggs, Jerry	*Mercenary Fighters* ('88)	a
Bignamini, Nino	*The Night Porter* (I) ('73)	a, p
Bill, John	*Draft Dodger* ('72)	a
Binder, Arthur	*The Sinful Bed* (G) ('78)	a
Birchard, Paul	*Black Magic Mansion* ('92)	p
Birket, Jack	*The Tempest* (B) ('82)	a
Bisley, Steve	*The Chain Reaction* (A) ('80)	a, p
Bisley, Steve	*Summer City* (A) ('77)	a
Bjerg, Peter	*You Are Not Alone* (S) ('80)	a, p
Blackburn, Ken	*Skin Deep* (NZ) ('78)	a
Blades, Ruben	*Dead Man Out* ('89)	a
Blaise, Pierre	*Lacombe, Lucien* (F) ('74)	a
Blake, Jon	*Freedom* ('81)	a, p
Blake, Robert	*Tell Them Willie Boy Is Here* ('70)	a
Blake, Stephen	*Mad at the Moon* ('92)	a
Blakely, Colin	*This Sporting Life* (B) ('63)	a
Blanc, Michel	*Les Bronzes* (F) ('79)	a
Blanc, Michel	*A Night at the Congress*	a, p
Blankfield, Mark	*Jekyll and Hyde Together Again* ('82)	a
Blaustein, Jeff	*One Night Only* ('89)	a
Blech, Hans Christian	*Colonel Redl* (G/H) ('84)	a
Blodgett, Michael	*Beyond the Valley of the Dolls* ('70)	a, p
Blodgett, Michael	*There Was a Crooked Man* ('70)	a
Blodgett, Michael	*The Trip* ('67)	a
Blodgett, Michael	*The Velvet Vampire* ('71)	a
Blum, Jack	*East End Hustle* (B) ('76)	a
Blumenfield, Alan	*Out Cold* ('89)	a, p
Blundell, Graeme	*Alvin Purple* (A) ('73)	a, p
Blundell, Graeme	*Alvin Rides Again* (A) ('74)	a
Blundell, Graeme	*Pacific Banana* (A) ('80)	a

Blundell, Graeme	*The Odd Angry Shot* (A) ('79)	a
Blutheau, Lothair	*The Black Robe* (C) ('91)	a
Blutheau, Lothair	*Jesus of Montreal* (C) ('89)	a, p
Blythe, Robert	*Experience Preferred, Not Essential* (B) ('83)	a
Bocher, Christian	*Secret Games* ('91)	a
Bochner, Hart	*And the Sea Will Tell* ('91)	a
Bochner, Hart	*Mad at the Moon* ('92)	a
Bockner, Michael	*Graveyard Shift* ('86)	a
Boddy, Michael	*Age of Consent* (A) ('69)	a
Bogarde, Dirk	*Despair* (G) ('79)	a
Bogosian, Eric	*Special Effects* ('85)	a
Bohringer, Richard	*Cent Francs l'Amour* (F) ('85)	a
Bolano, Tony	*Cat Chaser* ('88)	a
Boldi, Massimo	*Yuppies II*	a
Boles, Eric	*Great Texas Dynamite Chase* ('76)	a
Bonacelli, Paolo	*Francesco* (I) ('89)	a
Bonaduce, Danny	*H.O.T.S.* ('79)	a
Bonaffe, Jacques	*Le Meilleurie Pa Vie* (F)	a
Bonanno, Louie	*Wimps* ('86)	a
Bond, Steve	*H.O.T.S.* ('79)	a
Bond, Steve	*Massacre at Central High* ('76)	a, p
Bond, Tony	*Desert Passion* ('92)	a
Bondy, Christopher	*Deadly Illusions* (aka *Deadly Surveillance*) ('91)	a
Bonetti, Massimo	*La Bocca* (I)	a
Bongbigio, Andres	*Muerte en la Playa* (M)	a
Bonilla, Hector	*El Cumpleaños del Perro* (M)	p
Bonin, Arturo	*Otra Historia de Amor* (I)	a
Boniscalzi, Luca	*Ultimo Giorno* (I)	a, p
Bonnafol, Jacques	*Prenom Carmen* (F) ('83)	a, p
Bonnet, Stephane	*Paprika*	a, p
Bonuglia, Maurizio	*The Seducers* (I) ('70)	a
Boone, Randy	*The Minx* (aka *Dr. Minx*) ('68)	a
Boorman, Charley	*The Emerald Forest* ('85)	a
Boothe, James	*The Man Who Had Power Over Women* ('70)	a
Boothe, Powers	*A Breed Apart* ('84)	a
Boretski, Paul	*Perfect Timing* ('84)	a, p
Borghetto, Bruno	*King of the Bean*	a
Borisenico, Sacha	*Love Camp* (F) ('76)	a
Borjoniogidia, Draz	*Hey Babu Riba* (Y) ('86)	a
Borromeo, Christian	*Nest of Vipers* (I)	a, p
Bory, Jean-Marc	*The Lovers* (F) ('59)	a
Bose, Miguel	*Family Portrait*	a
Bostwick, Barry	*Jail Bait* ('90)	a
Bottoms, Joseph	*Born to Race* ('88)	a

Bottoms, Joseph	*Inner Sanctum* ('91)	a
Bottoms, Joseph	*Liar's Edge* ('92)	a
Bottoms, Joseph	*Surfacing* ('74)	a
Bottoms, Sam	*The Last Picture Show* ('71)	a
Bottoms, Timothy	*High Country* ('81)	a
Bottoms, Timothy	*In the Shadow of Kilimanjaro* (B) ('86)	a
Bottoms, Timothy	*Johnny Got His Gun* ('71)	a
Bottoms, Timothy	*The Last Picture Show* ('71)	a
Bottoms, Timothy	*The Paper Chase* ('73)	a
Bouchitey, Patrick	*The Best Way* (F) ('76)	a, p
Boussa, Halim	*Les Hors La Loi* (F) ('84)	a
Bouvier, Jean Pierre	*Goodbye Emmanuelle* (F) ('81)	a, p
Bouvier, Tommy	*Nightmare* ('82)	a
Bowen, Dennis	*Van Nuys Blvd.* ('79)	a
Bowen, Michael	*Mortal Passions* ('90)	a
Bowie, David	*Just a Gigolo* (G) ('79)	a
Bowie, David	*The Man Who Fell to Earth* ('76)	a, p
Bowles, Billy	*The Todd Killings* ('71)	a
Boxleitner, Bruce	*Double Jeopardy* ('92)	a
Boxleitner, Bruce	*Six-Pack Annie* ('75)	a
Boyle, Lance	*Long, Swift Sword of Siegfried* (G) ('71)	a
Boyle, Peter	*The Dream Team* ('89)	a
Boyle, Peter	*Joe* ('70)	a
Bracken, Jimmy	*With Six You Get Eggroll* ('68)	a
Bradford, Greg	*Let's Do It* ('82)	a
Bradley, David	*Cyborg Cop* ('91)	a
Bradley, David	*Kes* (B) ('70)	a, p
Bradshaw, Bill	*The Other Woman* ('92)	a
Bradshaw, Carl	*The Lunatic (Jam)* ('92)	a
Bradshaw, Carl	*Smile Orange* (B) ('76)	a
Brady, Randell	*Jaded*	a
Braeden, Eric	*Colossus, the Forbin Project* ('70)	a
Branagh, Kenneth	*High Season* (B) ('88)	a
Branagh, Kenneth	*Much Ado About Nothing* ('93)	a
Brancia, Armando	*Amarcord* (I) ('74)	a
Branciaroli, Franco	*The Key* (I)	a
Branciaroli, Franco	*Miranda* (I)	a, p
Brando, Marlon	*Last Tango in Paris* ('73)	a, p
Brando, Marlon	*The Nightcomers* ('71)	a, p
Brando, Marlon	*Reflections in a Golden Eye* ('67)	a
Brandon, Cory	*Auditions* ('78)	a
Brandon, David	*Naked Sun* ('76)	a
Brandy, Mycle	*Flesh Gordon* ('72)	a, p
Brannan, Gavin	*Private Passions* ('83)	a
Brasseur, Claude	*Aragoste a Colazione* (I)	a

Brasseur, Claude	*The Detective* (F) ('85)	a
Breeding, Larry	*Street Music* ('82)	a
Brel, Jacques	*Mon Oncle Benjamin* (F)	a
Breland, Mark	*The Lords of Discipline* ('83)	a
Brennan, Frank	*The Girl* ('86)	a, p
Brenner, Christopher	*The Exterminator* ('80)	a
Bridges, Beau	*Gaily, Gaily* ('69)	a
Bridges, Beau	*Hammersmith Is Out* ('72)	a
Bridges, Jeff	*Against All Odds* ('84)	a
Bridges, Jeff	*The Last American Hero* ('73)	a, p*
Bridges, Jeff	*Rancho Deluxe* ('75)	a, p
Bridges, Jeff	*Starman* ('84)	a
Bridges, Jeff	*Winter Kills* ('79)	a
Brieux, Berard	*The Rascals* (F) ('84)	a, p
Briski, Norman	*Psexoanaliois*	a
Britton, Raphael	*Calendar Girls*	a, p
Britton, Raphael	*Pin Up Playmates*	a, p
Brizzar, Phillipe	*Letrio Infernal*	a, p
Broaderup, Brend	*Taxi Zum Klo* (G) ('81)	a, p
Broadway, Christophe	*Bloodmoon* ('89)	a
Brockette, Gary	*The Last Picture Show* ('71)	a, p
Broderick, Matthew	*Out on a Limb* ('92)	a
Brojobie, Bladimer	*Caligula and Messalina* (I)	a
Brolin, James	*Ted & Venus* ('91)	a
Brooks, David	*Scream for Help* ('86)	a, p
Brooks, Wayne	*The 14* (B) ('73)	a
Brosnan, Pierce	*The Deceivers* ('88)	a
Brosnan, Pierce	*The Heist* ('89)	a
Brosnan, Pierce	*Live Wire* ('92)	a
Brosnan, Pierce	*Nomads* ('85)	a, p
Broust, Jean-Louis	*To Live and Die in Bangkok* (F)	a, p
Brown, Barnaby	*Tree of Hands* (B) ('89)	a
Brown, Bryan	*The Odd Angry Shot* (A) ('79)	a
Brown, Bryan	*Palm Beach* (A) ('84)	a, p
Brown, Bryan	*The Winter of Our Dream* (A) ('81)	a
Brown, Clancy	*Blue Steel* ('90)	a
Brown, Dwier	*The Guardian* ('90)	a
Brown, Eric	*Private Lessons* ('80)	a
Brown, Jim	*I Escaped from Devil's Island* ('73)	a
Brown, Lou	*Final Cut* (A) ('88)	a
Brown, Max M.	*Wolfen* ('81)	p
Brown, Murray	*Vampyres* (B) ('74)	p
Brown, Peter	*Bleep* ('70)	a
Brown, Reb	*Mercenary Fighters* ('88)	a
Brown, Reb	*Sssssss* ('73)	a
Brown, Timothy	*Sweet Sugar* ('72)	a
Brown, Woody	*The Accused* ('88)	a

Brown, Woody	*The Rain Killer* ('89)	a
Bruel, Patrick	*La Maison Assassinée* (F) ('88)	a
Buchanan, David	*The Curious Female* ('68)	a
Buchholz, Horst	*The Confessions of Felix Krull* (G) ('58)	a
Buchholz, Horst	*Le Sauveur* (F)	a, p
Buchholz, Horst	*How, Why and with Whom*	a
Buckert, Martin	*Martin's Day* ('85)	a
Buckley, Jim	*WR: Mysteries of the Orgasm* ('71)	a, p
Buenfil, Raul	*El Chico Temido*	a, p
Buenfil, Raul	*Operacion Asisinito*	a, p
Bullington, Perry	*Chatterbox* ('77)	a
Bumiller, William	*Overexposed* ('90)	a
Burghoff, Gary	*B.S. I Love You* ('71)	a
Burghoff, Gary	*Steam Room*	a
Burke, Brandon	*The Odd Angry Shot* (A) ('79)	p
Burke, Robert	*Dust Devil*	a
Burke, Simon	*The Devil's Playground* (A) ('76)	a, p
Burke, Simon	*Slate, Wyn, and Me* (A) ('87)	a
Burlinson, Tom	*Windrider* ('86)	a
Burlyayev, Kolya	*My Name Is Ivan* (R) ('62)	a
Burnett, Cliff	*A Prayer for the Dying* (B) ('87)	a
Burns, Mark	*The Stud* (B) ('78)	a
Burns, Mark	*The Virgin and the Gypsy* ('70)	a
Burns, Michael	*That Cold Day in the Park* ('69)	a
Burns, Stephan	*Spiker* ('84)	a
Burns, Wally	*Death Blow* ('87)	a
Burns, William	*Play Murder for Me* ('91)	a
Burr, Butch	*Genesis Children* ('71)	a, p
Burrows, Martin	*Sex with the Stars* ('81)	a
Burrus, Slade	*The Boys of Cellblock Q*	a
Burton, Jeff	*Planet of the Apes* ('68)	a
Burton, Robert	*Linda Lovelace for President*	a
Burton, Wendell	*Fortune and Men's Eyes* ('71)	a
Bury, Sean	*Friends* ('71)	a
Bury, Sean	*Paul and Michelle* ('74)	a
Bush, Chuck	*Fandango* ('85)	a
Butcher, Glenn	*Young Einstein* (A) ('88)	a
Butler, William	*Inner Sanctum* ('91)	a
Butow, Steve	*Desperate Living* ('77)	a
Butterworth, Tyler	*What the Butler Saw* (B)	a
Buzalski, Johannes	*Los Encantos de un Alpinesta* (M)	a, p
Buzzanco, Lando	*Bello Come un Arcangelo* (I)	a, p
Buzzanco, Lando	*Man of the Year* (I) ('71)	a
Buzzanco, Lando	*Playing the Field* (I) ('74)	a
Byrd, George	*The Marriage of Maria Braun* (G) ('79)	a, p

Byrd, Tom	*Out Cold* ('89)	a, p
Byrne, Gabriel	*A Dangerous Woman* ('93)	a
Byrne, Gabriel	*Dark Obsession* (B) ('90)	a
Byrne, Gabriel	*Siesta* ('87)	a, p
Byrnes, Burke	*Thumb Tripping* ('72)	a, p
Caan, James	*Rabbit Run* ('70)	a
Caan, James	*The Rain People* ('69)	a
Cable, Bill	*Basic Instinct* ('91)	p
Cada, Jerry	*Vago a Viviere da Solo* (I)	a
Cadman, Josh	*Going All the Way* ('81)	a
Cadman, Josh	*Surf II* ('83)	a
Cage, Nicolas	*Zandalee* ('90)	a
Caine, Michael	*Get Carter* ('71)	a
Calderon, Paul	*Q & A* ('90)	a
Calfa, Don	*Chopper Chicks in Zombietown* ('91)	a
Cali, Joseph	*The Lonely Lady* ('83)	a
Calignon, Yves	*Police des Moeuves* (F) ('85)	a, p
Callow, Simon	*A Room with A View* (B) ('85)	a, p
Calmeyer, Joachim	*On the Threshold*	a, p
Calvi, John	*March of the Falsettos* (A)	a, p
Calvin, John	*Almost Pregnant* ('91)	a
Calvin, John	*California Dreaming* ('79)	a
Calvin, John	*The Siege of Firebase Gloria* ('89)	a
Cameron, David	*Salome* (I) ('85)	a
Camp, Rod	*Night of the Demon* ('79)	p
Campanaro, Phillip	*Slammer Girls* ('86)	a
Campbell, Bill	*Tales of the City* (B) ('93)	a
Campbell, Nicholas	*Certain Fury* ('85)	a
Campbell, Nicholas	*The Dead Zone* ('83)	a
Campbell, Nicholas	*Naked Lunch* ('91)	a
Campbell, Paul	*The Lunatic (Jam)* ('92)	a
Capellupo, Michael	*Venus Flytrap* ('88)	a
Capolicchio, Lino	*Calamo* (I)	p
Caprinteiro, Victor	*El Chico Temido*	a, p
Cardy, David	*Xtro* ('83)	a
Cargol, Jean Pierre	*The Wild Child* (F) ('70)	a, p
Cariou, Len	*The Four Seasons* ('81)	a
Carlson, Shane	*Possessions: Until Death Do You Part* ('90)	a
Carlton, Jerry	*Spirit of 76* ('91)	a
Carpenter, Peter	*Blood Mania* ('69)	a
Carr, Paul	*The Dirt Gang* ('71)	a
Carradine, David	*Box Car Bertha* ('72)	a
Carradine, David	*On the Line* ('84)	a
Carradine, David	*The Serpent's Egg* (S) ('77)	a
Carradine, Keith	*An Almost Perfect Affair* ('79)	a
Carradine, Keith	*Backfire* ('87)	a

Carradine, Keith	*Capone* ('89)	a
Carradine, Keith	*Choose Me* ('85)	a
Carradine, Keith	*Grassland*	a
Carradine, Keith	*The Moderns* ('88)	a
Carradine, Keith	*Nashville* ('74)	a
Carradine, Keith	*Payoff* ('91)	a
Carradine, Keith	*Streets of No Return* ('89)	a
Carradine, Robert	*Massacre at Central High* ('76)	a
Carradine, Robert	*The Pom Pom Girls* ('76)	a
Carrey, Jim	*Ace Ventura, Pet Detective* ('94)	a
Carrey, Jim	*It's All in Good Taste*	a, p
Carrey, Jim	*Once Bitten* ('85)	a
Carrier, Tim	*Night of the Living Dead* ('90)	a
Carriere, Mathieu	*Blondy* (F) ('76)	a, p
Carriere, Mathieu	*Charlotte* (F) ('86)	a, p
Carriere, Mathieu	*Tout Disparaitra* (F)	a
Carriere, Mathieu	*A Woman in Flames* (G) ('84)	a
Carson, John David	*Pretty Maids All in a Row* ('70)	a
Carven, Mircha	*Bad Thoughts* (I)	a
Carven, Mircha	*A Man for Sale* (I) ('82)	a
Casal, Gregorio	*El Llanto de la Tortuga* (M)	a
Casas, Edwyn	*Rich Boy, Poor Boy* (Pl)	a, p
Case, Robert	*Hot Blood* (Sp) ('89)	a
Casey, Bernie	*Hit Man* ('72)	a
Casey, Bernie	*The Man Who Fell to Earth* ('76)	a
Casey, Larry	*The Gay Deceivers* ('69)	a
Casey, Lawrence	*Daughter of Emmanuelle*	a
Casey, Lawrence	*Student Nurses* ('70)	a
Cassavetes, Nick	*Body of Influence* ('92)	p
Cassavetes, Nick	*Sins of the Night* ('92)	a
Cassel, Alan	*Dark Room* ('84)	a
Cassel, Jean-Pierre	*Who Is Killing the Great Chefs of Europe?* ('78)	a
Cassidy, Patrick	*Nickel Mountain* ('85)	a
Cassidy, Rick	*Auditions* ('78)	a, p
Castel, Lou	*The Eyes, The Mouth* (F/I) ('83)	a
Castel, Lou	*Francis of Assisi* (I)	a
Castelli, Paulo	*Happily Ever After* (Br) ('86)	a
Castellitto, Sergio	*La Carne* (I)	a
Castellitto, Sergio	*Magic Moments* (I)	a
Castelnuovo, Nino	*Camille 2000* (I) ('69)	a
Castillo, Braulio	*El Cielo y Tu* (M)	a
Castillo, Eduardo	*Food of the Gods, Part 2* ('89)	a
Castillo, Gregory	*Cat Murkil and the Silks*	a
Castle, John	*The Adventures of Eliza Fraser* (B) ('76)	a
Catalifo, Patrick	*Sand and Blood* (F) ('89)	a, p

Caufield, Maxwell	*Dance with Death* ('91)	a
Caufield, Maxwell	*In a Moment of Passion*	a
Caufield, Maxwell	*Midnight Witness*	a
Caufield, Maxwell	*Sundown, the Vampire in Retreat* ('91)	p
Cavina, Gianni	*La Bella Otera* (I)	a
Cazenove, Christopher	*Heat and Dust* (B) ('82)	a
Ceccaldi, Daniel	*Charles and Lucie* (I) ('79)	a
Ceinos, Jose Antonio	*Black Venus* (B) ('83)	a, p
Ceinos, Jose Antonio	*Orgasmo Caliente* (M)	a
Cele, Henry	*Shaka Zulu* ('83)	a
Celozzi, Nick	*Carnal Crimes* ('91)	a
Celozzi, Nicholas	*Pretty Smart* ('86)	a
Chabrol, Thomas	*The Rascals* (F) ('84)	a
Chadwick, Justin	*London Kills Me* (B) ('91)	a
Chamberlain, Richard	*Julius Caesar* ('70)	a
Chambers, Steve	*The First Turn On* ('84)	a
Chambragne, Didier	*Les Hors La Loi* (F) ('84)	a
Chan, Jackie	*Fearless Hyena: Part II* ('84)	a
Chapa, Damien	*Bound by Honor* ('93)	a
Chapman, Graham	*Life of Brian* (B) ('79)	a, p
Chapman, Sean	*Hellraiser* ('87)	a
Charles, Bobby H.	*C.O.D.* ('81)	a
Charles, Emile	*The Fruit Machine* (aka *Wonderland*) ('88)	a, p
Charles, Gordon	*Felicity* (F) ('79)	a
Charles, Timothy	*Angel in Red* (aka *Uncaged*) ('91)	a
Charleson, Ian	*Jubilee* ('77)	a, p
Charlesworth, John	*Tom Brown's School Days* ('51)	a
Chase, Steve	*Eden 2* ('92)	a
Chase, Steve	*Eden 3* ('93)	a
Chatlos, Tom	*King Frat*	a
Chelsom, Peter	*A Woman of Substance* ('84)	a
Chew, Simon Leu	*Shadow of China* ('91)	a, p
Chicot, Etienne	*36 Fillette* (F) ('88)	a
Chiklis, Michael	*Wired* ('89)	a
Chirizzi, Gianluigi	*Scandal in the Family* (I)	a
Chitty, Chris	*Sex Games of the Very Rich*	a
Chong, Tommy	*Cheech & Chong's Nice Dreams* ('81)	a
Christian, Michael	*Hard Knocks* ('77)	a
Christian, Michael	*Hollywood Knight* ('77)	a
Christopher, Andrew	*While the Cat's Away*	a, p
Christopher, Bojesse	*Point Break* ('91)	a
Christopher, Dennis	*The Young Graduates* ('71)	a
Christopher, Gerard (Jerry Dimone)	*Tomboy* ('85)	a

Christopher, Jordan	*Angel, Angel, Down We Go* ('69)	a
Christopher, Jordan	*Pigeons*	a
Ciamaca, Julien	*My Father's Glory* (F) ('91)	p
Ciarro, Gianni	*Ferragasto OK* (I)	a
Ciccio, Vic	*Party Games for Adults* ('83)	a
Cilento, Angelo	*Death Kiss* (I)	a
Citti, Franco	*Arabian Nights* (I) ('74)	a
Ciulla, Tommy	*The Pursuit of D. B. Cooper* ('81)	a
Clapp, Gordon	*Return of the Secaucus 7* ('80)	a
Clark, Brett	*Alien Warrior* (B) ('85)	a
Clark, Brett	*Young Lady Chatterly, Part II* (B) ('85)	a
Clark, Dort Donald	*Cameron's Closet* ('88)	a
Clark, John	*Blood Frenzy* ('87)	a
Clavier, Christian	*Les Bronzes* (F) ('79)	a
Clavier, Christian	*Quand Tu Seras Debloque Fais Moi Seigne* (F)	a
Clay, Andrew Dice	*Casual Sex?* ('88)	a
Clay, Nicholas	*Excalibur* ('81)	a
Clay, Nicholas	*Lady Chatterly's Lover* (B) ('81)	a, p
Cleese, John	*A Fish Called Wanda* ('88)	a, p
Cleese, John	*Monty Python's The Meaning of Life* (B) ('83)	a
Cleese, John	*Romance with a Double Bass* (B) ('74)	a
Clementi, Pierre	*Benjamin* (F) ('68)	a
Clementi, Pierre	*Cannibals* (I)	a
Clementi, Pierre	*Pigsty* (I) ('69)	a
Clementi, Pierre	*Steppenwolf* ('74)	a, p
Clennon, David	*He's My Girl* ('87)	a
Cliff, Jimmy	*The Harder They Come* ('72)	a
Cliver, Al	*Forever Emmanuelle* ('82)	a, p
Cliver, Al	*The Head Hunters*	a
Cliver, Al	*Il Saprofita* (I)	a
Clough, Donaldo	*El Chico Temido*	a, p
Cluzet, François	*Chocolat* (F) ('88)	a, p
Cluzet, François	*Cocktail Molotov* (F) ('80)	a, p
Cluzet, François	*One Deadly Summer* (F) ('83)	p
Coates, Kim	*Red-Blooded American Girl* ('90)	a
Coburn, David	*Born American* ('86)	a
Coburn, James	*Last of the Mobile Hotshots* ('69)	a
Coburn, James	*Pat Garrett and Billy the Kid* ('73)	a
Coby, Michael	*The Bitch* (B) ('78)	a
Coca, Richard	*American Me* ('92)	a
Cochran, Rory	*Father/Son*	a
Cochrane, Ian	*Bolero* ('84)	a
Coe, George	*Cousins* ('89)	a

Coffrey, Scott	*Il Peccato di Lola* (I)	a, p
Cohen, Alain	*The Two of Us* (F) ('68)	a, p
Colaiacomo, Enzo	*Love Lessons* (I) ('85)	a, p
Colasanti, Arderino	*How Tasty Was My Little Frenchman* (F) ('71)	a, p
Colbert, Ray	*RSVP* ('84)	a
Cole, John	*Adventures of Sadie* (B) ('55)	a
Coleman, Dabney	*Modern Problems* ('81)	a
Coleman, John	*Angel Eyes* ('91)	a
Coleman, Kyle	*Run Virgin Run* ('90)	a
Coleman, Warren	*Young Einstein* (A) ('88)	a
Colignon, Yves	*Scirocco* (F)	a
Collado, Tony	*Feelin' Up!* ('76)	a
Collard, Cyril	*Les Nuits Fauves (Savage Nights)* (F) ('93)	a
Collet, Christopher	*Sleepaway Camp* ('83)	a
Collins, Bubba	*Genesis Children* ('71)	a, p
Collver, Mark	*There's Nothing Out There* ('90)	a
Colman, Roger	*The Baby Doll Murders* ('92)	a
Colvig, Vance	*Track 29* ('88)	a
Comber, Warwick	*Double Deal* (A) ('81)	a
Combs, Frederick	*Boys in the Band* ('70)	a
Conaway, Jeff	*Almost Pregnant* ('91)	a
Conaway, Jeff	*Covergirl* ('82)	a, p
Conaway, Jeff	*I Never Promised You a Rose Garden* ('77)	a
Congbon, James	*Refuge*	a
Conlan, Christopher	*Boardinghouse* ('82)	a
Conlon, Tim	*Prom Night III* ('89)	a
Connery, Jason	*The Boy Who Had Everything* (A) ('84)	a, p
Connery, Jason	*La Veneziana* (I) ('86)	a
Connery, Jason	*Winner Takes All* (I) ('86)	a
Connery, Sean	*Man Who Would Be King* ('75)	a
Connery, Sean	*Robin and Marian* ('75)	a
Connery, Sean	*Zardoz* ('73)	a
Connors, Kenneth	*Carry on Constable* (B)	a
Conrad, Robert	*Murph the Surf* ('74)	a
Conroy, Kevin	*Chain of Desire* ('92)	a
Conti, Tom	*Shirley Valentine* (B) ('89)	a
Coogan, Keith	*Toy Soldiers* ('91)	a, p
Cook, Paul	*The Great Rock and Roll Swindle* ('79)	a, p
Cooper, George	*Lassiter* ('84)	a
Cooper, Jeff	*Circle of Iron* ('79)	a
Cooper, Terence	*Heart of the Stag* (NZ) ('83)	a
Cooper, Trevor	*Drowning by Numbers* (B) ('88)	a, p

Corbo, Robert	*Last Rites* ('88)	a
Cordell, Chase	*Double Infidelity* ('71)	a
Cordero, Joaquin	*Lio de Faldas* (M)	a
Cordova, Pancho	*Acto de Posesion* (M)	a
Corlan, Anthony	*Flavia, the Rebel Nun* ('74)	a, p
Cornillac, Clovis	*Les Hors la Loi* (F) ('84)	a
Corot, Alair	*Madame Kitty*	a, p
Corrado, Gabriele	*Apartment Zero* ('88)	a
Corri, Nick	*Tropical Snow* ('89)	a
Corri, Nick	*Wildcats* ('86)	a, p
Corrnero, Roberto	*Il Diavolo Sulle* (I)	a, p
Cory, Henry	*Hot Times* ('74)	a
Costello, Anthony	*Doctor's Wives* ('71)	a
Costigan, George	*Rita, Sue and Bob Too* (B) ('86)	a
Costner, Kevin	*American Flyers* ('85)	a
Costner, Kevin	*Dances with Wolves* ('90)	a
Costner, Kevin	*Revenge* ('90)	a
Courtena, Tom	*The Day the Fish Came Out* (Gr) ('67)	a
Coutant, Marc	*Beyond Love and Evil* ('69)	a, p
Covert, Con	*Hollywood High, Part II* ('81)	a
Cox, Richard	*Cruising* ('80)	a
Coyote, Peter	*Bitter Moon* (F) ('94)	a
Coyote, Peter	*A Man in Love* (F/I) ('87)	a
Crabbe, Larry (Buster)	*King of the Jungle* ('33)	a
Crabbe, Larry (Buster)	*Tarzan the Fearless* ('33)	a
Cramer, Grant	*Hardbodies* ('84)	a
Cranston, Kyle Edward	*10 to Midnight* ('83)	a
Crawford, Johnny	*Great Texas Dynamite Chase* ('76)	a
Crawford, Johnny	*The Naked Ape* ('73)	a, p
Crawford, Michael	*Some Mothers Do 'Ave Em* (B)	a
Crew, Carl	*Blood Diner* ('87)	a
Crick, Ed	*Naked Vengeance* ('86)	a
Crocetti, Vincenzo	*La Supplente Vaincitta* (I)	a, p
Crocker, Barry	*Barry McKenzie Holds His Own* (B) ('74)	a
Cromer, Michael	*French Pussycat*	a, p
Cromwell, James	*Tank* ('74)	a
Cross, Ben	*L'Attenzione* (I)	a
Cross, Harvey	*Convict's Women* ('72)	a, p
Crowe, Russell	*Proof* (A) ('91)	a
Crowe, Russell	*Romper Stomper* ('92)	a
Cruciani, Mario	*Warrior Queen* ('87)	a
Cruise, Tom	*All the Right Moves* ('83)	a, p
Cruise, Tom	*Far and Away* ('92)	a
Cruise, Tom	*Taps* ('81)	a
Crystal, Billy	*Rabbit Test* ('78)	a

Cullen, Max	*Sunday Too Far Away* (A) ('75)	a
Cullinane, David	*Play Dead* ('81)	a
Culp, Robert	*A Name for Evil* ('73)	a, p
Culver, Cal	*Eleana* ('70)	a
Culver, Cal	*Ginger* ('70)	a, p
Culver, Cal	*Score* ('73)	a
Cummings, Burton	*Melanie* ('82)	a
Curreri, Lee	*Crystal Heart* ('85)	a
Curry, Steven	*Glen and Randa* ('71)	a, p
Curzi, Pierre	*Decline of the American Empire* (C) ('86)	a
Cutuni, Mario	*Nathalie* (I) ('88)	a
Cvetkovic, Svetozar	*Montenegro* (Sw/B) ('81)	a, p
Cypher, Jon	*Valdez Is Coming* ('71)	a
D'Inzeo, David	*Hard Car*	a
D'Inzeo, David	*Casa di Piaccre*	a
da Silva, Fernando	*Pixote* (Br) ('81)	a, p
Dacus, Don	*Hair* ('79)	a
Dafoe, Willem	*Body of Evidence* ('93)	a
Dafoe, Willem	*The Last Temptation of Christ* ('89)	a
Dafoe, Willem	*Light Sleeper* ('93)	a
Dafoe, Willem	*The Loveless* ('81)	a
Dafoe, Willem	*To Live and Die in L.A.* ('85)	a
Dafoe, Willem	*Roadhouse 66* ('84)	a
Dagelet, Hans	*Dear Boys* (D) ('80)	a
Dahl, Lisbet	*Topsy Turvy* ('84)	a, p
Dallesandro, Joe	*Andy Warhol's Dracula* ('74)	a
Dallesandro, Joe	*Andy Warhol's Flesh* ('68)	a, p
Dallesandro, Joe	*Andy Warhol's Frankenstein* ('74)	a, p
Dallesandro, Joe	*Andy Warhol's Heat* ('72)	a, p
Dallesandro, Joe	*Andy Warhol's Trash* ('76)	a, p
Dallesandro, Joe	*Donna e Bello* (I)	a
Dallesandro, Joe	*Je T'Aime Mai Non Plus* (F)	a, p
Dallesandro, Joe	*The Margin*	a, p
Dallesandro, Joe	*The Seeds of Evil* ('74)	a, p
Daltrey, Roger	*Lisztomania* (B) ('75)	a, p
Daltrey, Roger	*McVicar* (B) ('81)	a
Damian, Leo	*Ghosts Can't Do It* ('90)	a
Damon, Matt	*School Ties* ('92)	a
Danare, Malcolm	*Heaven Help Us* ('85)	a
Danburger, Francis	*Running Brave* ('83)	a
Dance, Charles	*White Mischief* (B) ('88)	a
Dane, Karl	*The Big Parade* (silent) ('26)	a
Daniel, Dany	*Teenage Teasers*	a
Daniels, Gary	*Final Reprisal*	a
Daniels, Jack	*The Devastator* ('85)	a
Daniels, Jack	*Wheel of Fire* ('84)	a

Daniels, Jeff	Checking Out ('93)	a
Daniels, Jeff	Love Hurts ('89)	a
Daniels, Jeff	Something Wild ('86)	a
Daniels, John	Black Shampoo ('76)	a
Daniels, John	Tender Loving Care ('73)	a
Daniels, Phil	Class of Miss MacMichaels (B) ('78)	a
Daniels, Phil	Quadrophenia (B) ('79)	a, p
Danon, Rami	Beyond the Walls (Is) ('84)	a, p
Darby, Ron	The Honeymoon Is Over	a
Dario, Luciano	I Ragazzi di Torino (I)	a
Daughton, James	Beach Girls ('82)	a, p
Daughton, James	Malibu Beach ('78)	a
Davanzati, Stefano	Cartoline Italiane (I)	a
Daveau, Alan	Screwballs ('83)	a
Davidson, Jaye	The Crying Game (B) ('92)	p
Davie, Stephen	Inserts ('75)	a, p
Davies, James	Pledge Night ('88)	a
Davies, John Howard	Tom Brown's School Days ('51)	a
Davis, Brad	Midnight Express ('78)	a
Davis, Brad	A Small Circle of Friends ('80)	a
Davis, Gene	10 to Midnight ('83)	a
Davis, Gene	Night Games ('79)	a
Davis, Mac	North Dallas Forty ('79)	a
Davis, Mark	Edward II (B) ('92)	a
Davis, Oscar	The Legend of Frenchie King (F) ('72)	a
Davison, Bruce	Last Summer ('69)	a
Davison, Bruce	Lathe of Heaven ('80)	a
Davison, Bruce	The Misfit Brigade ('87)	a
Davison, Bruce	The Strawberry Statement ('70)	a
Davoli, Ninetto	Arabian Nights (I) ('74)	a, p
Davoli, Ninetto	Canterbury Tales (I) ('71)	a, p
Davoli, Ninetto	Wicked Stories (I)	a
Day, Clayton	Deep in the Heart (aka The Handgun) ('83)	a, p
Day-Lewis, Daniel	In the Name of the Father (B) ('93)	a
Day-Lewis, Daniel	Stars and Bars ('88)	a, p
Day-Lewis, Daniel	The Unbearable Lightness of Being ('88)	a
de la Peña, George	Nijinsky ('80)	a
de Lint, Derek	Soldier of Orange (D) ('79)	a
de Lint, Derek	Stealing Heaven (D) ('88)	a, p
de Padua, Guilherme	Via Appia (G)	a, p
de Sica, Christian	Casta e Pura (I)	a
de Sica, Christian	Compagni di Scuola (I) ('85)	a
de Sica, Christian	The Sex Machine (I) ('76)	a
De Bartolli, Moreno	When Father Was Away on Business (Y) ('85)	a, p

De Cicio, Bob	*Thieves After Dark*	p
De Giorgi, Grazia	*Nathalie* (I) ('88)	a, p
De la Brosse, Simon	*The Little Thief* (F) ('89)	a
De Luc, Xavier	*Captive* ('86)	p
De Luc, Xavier	*On Ne Meurt Que Deux Fois* (F)	a
De Meijo, Carlo	*Teorema* (I) ('68)	a
De Meijo, Carlo	*Twelveth Night* (B) ('88)	a
Deacon, Brian	*A Zed & Two Noughts* (B) ('85)	a, p
Deacon, Eric	*A Zed & Two Noughts, A* (B) ('85)	a, p
Deas, Justin	*Dream Lover* ('86)	a
Debon, Frederic	*Kill Nani*	p
Degand, Michel	*Le Cavaleur* (F) ('80)	a, p
DelConte, Ken	*Working Girls* ('74)	a
Delger, Jeff	*On the Line* ('84)	a
Delon, Alain	*Girl on a Motorcycle* (B) ('68)	a
Delon, Alain	*Le Battant* (F)	a
Delon, Alain	*Le Choc* (F) ('74)	a, p
Delon, Alain	*M. Klein* (aka *Monsieur Klein*) (F) ('75)	a
Delon, Alain	*Shock Treatment* (F) ('81)	a, p
Dempsey, Mark	*Oh! Calcutta* ('72)	a, p
Dempsey, Patrick	*Meatballs III* ('84)	a
Dempsey, Patrick	*Some Girls* ('89)	a, p
De Niro, Robert	*1900* (I) ('77)	a, p
De Niro, Robert	*Bloody Mama* ('70)	a
De Niro, Robert	*The Deerhunter* ('78)	a, p
Denison, Anthony John	*Little Vegas* ('90)	a
Dennehy, Brian	*The Belly of an Architect* (B) ('87)	a
Dennehy, Brian	*Semi-Tough* ('77)	a
Denney, David	*Undercover* ('87)	a
Depardieu, Gerard	*1900* (I) ('77)	a, p
Depardieu, Gerard	*Fort Saganne* (F) ('85)	a
Depardieu, Gerard	*Germinal* (F) ('93)	a, p
Depardieu, Gerard	*Going Places* (F) ('74)	a, p
Depardieu, Gerard	*Hurricane Rosey* (F)	a
Depardieu, Gerard	*The Last Woman* (F) ('76)	a, p
Depardieu, Gerard	*Loulou* (F) ('80)	a
Depardieu, Gerard	*Maitresse* (F) ('76)	a
Depardieu, Gerard	*Menage* (F) ('86)	a
Depardieu, Gerard	*Moon in the Gutter* ('84)	a
Depardieu, Gerard	*Pas Si Merchant Que Ca (Wonderful Crook)* (F) ('75)	p
Depardieu, Gerard	*Rude Journée Pour la Ville* (F) ('73)	a, p
Depardieu, Gerard	*Vincent, Francois, Paul and the Others* (F) ('76)	p
Depp, Johnny	*Private Resort* ('85)	a
Dern, Bruce	*Coming Home* ('69)	a

Dern, Bruce	*On the Edge* ('85)	a
Dern, Bruce	*Silent Running* ('71)	a
Dern, Bruce	*Tattoo* ('81)	a
Dern, Bruce	*The Twist* (F) ('72)	a
Desarthe, Gerard	*A Love in Germany* (F) ('84)	a
Deshors, Eric	*Cain's Laughter*	a
Devincentis, Maurice	*Moving Out* (A) ('83)	a
Dewaere, Patrick	*The Best Way* (F) ('76)	a, p
Dewaere, Patrick	*Going Places* (F) ('74)	a
Dewaere, Patrick	*Heat of Desire* (F) ('84)	a, p
Dewaere, Patrick	*Hot Head* (aka *Coup de Tête*) (F) ('79)	a, p
Dewaere, Patrick	*La Stanza del Vescovo* (I)	a
Dewaere, Patrick	*Paradise Pour Tous* (F) ('83)	a
Dewaere, Patrick	*Psy* (F) ('80)	a, p
Dewaere, Patrick	*Victory March* (I) ('76)	a, p
Dewee, Martin	*Master of Dragonard Hill* (B) ('87)	a
Di Francesco, Maudo	*Ferragasto OK* (I)	a
Di Lorenzo, Rocky	*New York's Finest* ('88)	a
Di Sanzo, Alessandro	*Ragazzi Fuori* (I)	p
Dickson, David	*Over the Summer* ('85)	a
Diego, Juan	*La Criatrua* (M)	a
Diehl, John	*Angel* ('83)	a
Dietz, Evans	*Teen Vamp* ('88)	a
Dignam, Arthur	*Jock Peterson* (A) ('74)	a
Dignam, Arthur	*The Devil's Playground* (A) ('76)	a, p
Dillon, Kevin	*Heaven Help Us* ('85)	a
Dillon, Matt	*A Kiss Before Dying* ('91)	a
Dillon, Stephen	*Business as Usual* (B) ('87)	a
Dimone, Jerry (Gerard Christopher)	*Tomboy* ('85)	a
Dingwall, Kelly	*Around the World in 80 Ways* ('86)	a
Dini, Memo	*Mediterraneo* (I) ('91)	a
Dionisi, Stefano	*Rose* (I)	a, p
Disanti, John	*King Frat*	a
DiStefano, Len	*Naked Instinct* ('93)	a
Divine (Glenn Milstead)	*Female Trouble* ('74)	a, p
Divine (Glenn Milstead)	*Lust in the Dust* ('85)	a
Divoff, Andrew	*Another 48 HRS* ('90)	a
Dixon, Gallum	*Waterland* ('92)	a
Djela, Badja Medu	*The Main Event* ('79)	a
Dolan, Michael	*Necessary Roughness* ('91)	a
Domadoni, Maurizio	*She Also Smoked a Cigar* (I)	a, p
Domadoni, Maurizio	*Storua di Piera* (I)	a, p
Donnelly, Tim	*The Clonus Horror* ('78)	a
D'Onofrio, Vincent	*Fires Within* ('91)	a
Donovan, Jason	*The Heroes* ('72)	a

Donovan, Tate	*Vietnam War Stories* ('88)	a
Dorison, Zag	*Deadly Innocents*	a
dos Santos, Joao Carlos	*Wild Orchid* ('90)	a
Douglas, Kirk	*The Arrangement* ('69)	a
Douglas, Kirk	*Draw* ('84)	a
Douglas, Kirk	*Holocaust 2000* ('78)	a
Douglas, Kirk	*Saturn 3* ('80)	a
Douglas, Kirk	*There Was a Crooked Man* ('70)	a
Douglas, Kirk	*Tough Guys* ('86)	a
Douglas, Kirk	*The War Wagon* ('67)	a
Douglas, Michael	*Basic Instinct* ('91)	a
Douglas, Michael	*Fatal Attraction* ('87)	a
Douglas, Michael	*Hail Hero!* ('69)	a
Douglas, Michael	*The War of the Roses* ('89)	a
Douglas, Stephen	*Skin Deep* (NZ) ('78)	a
Dourif, Brad	*One Flew over the Cuckoo's Nest* ('75)	a
Downey Jr., Robert	*Less than Zero* ('87)	a
Downey Jr., Robert	*Rented Lips* ('88)	a
Downing, Derrich	*While the Cat's Away*	a
Draeger, Jurgen	*My Swedish Meatball* (S) ('71)	a
Drake, Dennis	*Preppies* ('84)	a
Drivas, Robert	*The Illustrated Man* ('68)	a
Drivas, Robert	*Where It's At* ('69)	a
Duchovny, David	*Julia Has Two Lovers* ('90)	a
Duchovny, David	*Kalifornia* ('93)	a
Duchovny, David	*New Year's Day* ('89)	a, p
Duchovny, David	*The Rapture* ('91)	a
Duffy, Patrick	*Vamping* ('84)	a
Duffy, Thomas	*Death Wish II* ('82)	a
Dukes, David	*The First Deadly Sin* ('80)	a
Dullea, Keir	*De Sade* ('69)	a
Dullea, Keir	*The Next One* ('83)	a
Dullea, Keir	*Paperback Hero* (C) ('73)	a
Dumont, J. K.	*The Pamela Principle* ('92)	a
Duncan, Peter	*The Lifetaker* ('75)	a
Dunham, Donald	*Sebastiane* (B) ('79)	a, p
Dunn, Matthew Cary	*Bikini Carwash Company* ('92)	a
Dunning, Judd	*Cabin Fever*	a
Dupois, Roy	*Being at Home with Claude* (C) ('92)	a
Dupuich, Jean-Marc	*Andrea* (F) ('75)	a, p
Durham, Steve	*Born American* ('86)	a
Dutton, Simon	*Lion and the Hawk* ('83)	a, p
Duvall, Robert	*THX-1138* ('71)	a
Dyce, Hamilton	*Unman, Wittering and Zigo* (B) ('71)	a
Dye, Cameron	*Fraternity Vacation* ('85)	a
Dye, Cameron	*Out of the Dark* ('88)	a

Dytri, Mike	*The Living End* ('92)	a
Earhar, Kirt	*Summer Job* ('89)	a
East, Jeff	*The Hazing* ('78)	a
East, Jeff	*Tom Sawyer* ('73)	a
Eastland, Todd	*Pledge Night* ('88)	a
Eastwood, Clint	*Escape from Alcatraz* ('79)	a
Eastwood, Clint	*Tightrope* ('84)	a
Eastwood, Clint	*The Witches* (I) ('67)	a
Eccles, Teddy	*My Side of the Mountain* ('67)	a
Eckhart, Paul Matthew	*The Dirtiest Show in Town*	a
Eden, Daniel	*Fear No Evil* ('81)	a, p
Edmondson, Dennis	*The Supergrass* (B) ('85)	a
Edwards, Anthony	*Downtown* ('90)	a
Eek-A-Mouse	*New Jack City* ('91)	a
Egan, Peter	*The Perfect Spy*	a
Egon, Robert	*Profumo* (B)	a, p
Eguia, Jose L. F.	*Colegas* (aka *Pals*) (Sp) ('82)	a
Ehlers, Jerome	*Fatal Bond* ('91)	a
Ehlers, Jerome	*Weekend with Kate* (A) ('90)	a
Eisenberg, Ned	*The Burning* ('81)	a
Ekland, Ben	*Master of Love* (I) ('81)	a
Ekman, Kristen	*Maid in Sweden* (S) ('83)	a
El Mino, Lalo	*El Sex Sentido* (M)	a
Eld, William	*Deadly Alliance* ('78)	a
Elemendorf, Raymond	*Bloody Wednesday* ('85)	a
Elholm, Thomas	*Friends Forever* (Da) ('86)	a
Elliott, Chris	*Cabin Boy* ('93)	a
Elliott, David	*The Possession of Joel Delaney* ('71)	a, p
Elliott, Denholm	*The Apprenticeship of Duddy Kravitz* (C) ('74)	a
Elliott, Sam	*The Games* ('69)	a
Elliott, Sam	*The Legacy* ('79)	a
Ellsworth, Scott	*Girls Are for Loving*	a
Elrechery, Rich	*Cage* ('89)	a, p
Elvegard, Charlie	*What the Swedish Butler Saw* (Da)	a
Elwes, Cary	*The Crush* ('93)	a
Elwes, Cary	*Lady Jane* (B) ('86)	a
Emil, Michael	*Sitting Ducks* ('78)	a
Englund, Bryan	*Slumber Party '57* ('76)	a
Eperjes, Karoly	*Tight Quarters*	a, p
Eric, Antonio	*El Chico Temido*	a, p
Eric, Antonio	*La Tentacion*	a, p
Eric, Antonio	*Muerte en la Playa* (M)	a, p
Ernback, Hans	*Fanny Hill* (S) ('69)	a
Erskine, Timothy	*Paradise* ('91)	a
Esposito, Giancarlo	*Taps* ('81)	a
Esposito, Michael	*Fatal Skies* ('89)	a

Estevez, Emilio	*Freejack* ('92)	a, p*
Estevez, Emilio	*National Lampoon's Loaded Weapon 1* ('93)	a
Estevez, Emilio	*Young Guns* ('88)	a
Estevez, Emilio	*Young Guns II* ('90)	a
Estrada, Tommy	*Party Games for Adults* ('83)	a
Estrowitz, Daniel	*Camorra* (I) ('85)	a
Eubanks, Cory Michael	*Payback* ('91)	a
Evans, Barry	*Adventures of a Taxi Driver* (B) ('76)	a, p
Evans, Barry	*Doctor on Call* (B)	a
Evans, Barry	*Here We Go Round the Mulberry Bush* (B) ('67)	a
Evans, Barry	*Under the Doctor* (B) ('76)	a
Evans, Brian	*The Book of Love* ('90)	a
Evans, David	*Leonora*	a
Evans, Mark	*Group Marriage* ('71)	a
Everett, Rupert	*The Comfort of Strangers* ('91)	a
Everett, Rupert	*Gli Occhiali d'Oro* (I)	a
Fabian (Forte)	*The Devil's 8* ('69)	a
Fahey, Jeff	*Backfire* ('87)	a
Fahey, Jeff	*The Hit List* ('93)	a
Fahey, Jeff	*The Sketch Artist* ('92)	a
Fairbanks, Douglas	*The Half Breed* (silent) ('16)	·a
Fairbanks Jr., Douglas	*Brother, Can You Spare a Dime?* ('75)	a
Fairbanks-Fogg, Kirk	*Alien Space Avenger* ('88)	a
Faith, Adam	*McVicar* (B) ('81)	a
Falconetti, Sonny	*Angel of Passion* ('91)	a
Falk, Eric	*Sensual Partners* ('87)	a
Falk, Peter	*In the Spirit* ('90)	a
Farias, Reginaldo	*Lucio Flavio* (I)	p
Farkas, James	*Jungle Man* ('88)	a
Farmer, Gary	*Powwow Highway* ('89)	a
Farron, Nicola	*Golden Rimmed Eyeglasses*	a, p
Farron, Nicola	*A Passionate Woman*	a, p
Fassbinder, Rainer Werner	*Fox and His Friends* (G) ('75)	a, p
Faucher, Cory	*One on One* ('77)	a
Faulkner, Graham	*Brother Sun, Sister Moon* (I/B) ('73)	a
Fawcett, Daniel	*Teenage Teasers*	p
Fawcett, Greg	*Naked Instinct* ('93)	a
Feast, Al	*The Draughtsman's Contract* (B) ('82)	a, p
Febles, Jose	*Al Sur del Eden* (M)	a, p
Fehmiu, Bekim	*The Adventurers* ('70)	a
Fehmiu, Bekim	*Salon Kitty* (G) ('75)	a, p
Feldman, Cory	*Blown Away* ('92)	a
Feldman, Marty	*The Adventures of Sherlock Holmes' Smarter Brother* ('75)	a

Feldman, Marty	*Think Dirty* (B) ('70)	a
Felix, Enrique Alvarez	*La Primavera de los Escorpiones* (M)	a
Fenton, Kim	*Unmasked* ('87)	a
Fernando, Daniel	*Macho Dancers* (P) ('88)	a
Ferrache, Rachid	*My Other Husband* (F) ('85)	a
Ferreaux, Benoit	*Murmur of the Heart* (F) ('71)	a, p
Ferrera, Stephane	*Kiss of the Tiger*	a, p
Ferrera, Stephane	*Mon Bel Amour Ma Dechirure*	a
Ferri, Michael Alan	*Getting It On* ('83)	a
Ferris, John	*Monique* ('83)	a, p
Ferris, Larry	*Penthouse Love Stories* ('86)	a, p
Fiedler, John	*Harper Valley PTA* ('78)	a
Fiachi, Stephen	*Animal Instincts* ('91)	a
Field, Todd	*Back to Back* ('90)	a
Fields, Dave	*Ghosts of the Civil Dead*	a, p
Fields, Robert	*The Sporting Club* ('71)	a
Figgs, George	*Desperate Living* ('77)	a, p
Figueroa, Ruben	*Popi* ('69)	a
Fimple, Dennis	*Bootleggers* ('74)	a
Finch, Jon	*Game of Seduction* (B) ('86)	a, p
Finch, Jon	*The Last Days of Man on Earth* (B) ('75)	a
Findlay, Bob	*Chances*	a
Findlay, Bob	*The Heroes* ('72)	a
Finlay, Frank	*Fellini's Casanova* (I) ('75)	a
Finlay, Frank	*The Key* (B) ('85)	a
Finney, Albert	*Under the Volcano* ('84)	a, p
Firth, Colin	*Hostages* ('93)	a
Firth, Colin	*Tumbledown*	a
Firth, Peter	*Daniele and Maria*	a
Firth, Peter	*Equus* ('77)	a, p
Firth, Peter	*Joseph Andrews* (B) ('77)	a, p
Fish, Tony	*Madman* ('82)	a
Fishbourne, Stuart K.	*Death Wish II* ('82)	a
Fisher, Bruce M.	*Escape from Alcatraz* ('79)	a, p
Fisher, Gordon	*Loving and Laughing*	a
Fisher, Jasen	*The Witches* ('90)	a
Fitzpatrick, Bob	*If Looks Could Kill* ('86)	a
Fletcher, Dexter	*The Rachel Papers* (B) ('89)	a
Fletcher, Dexter	*Raggedy Rawney* ('90)	a
Fletcher, Page	*A Matter of Cunning*	a
Flower, George "Buck"	*Innocent Sally* ('73)	a, p
Flower, George "Buck"	*Video Vixens* ('73)	a, p
Flugum, Tim	*The Underachievers* ('88)	a
Folk, Abel	*El Escote* (M)	a
Fonda, Peter	*Easy Rider* ('69)	a
Fonda, Peter	*Fighting Mad* ('76)	a

Fonda, Peter	*The Hired Hand* ('71)	a
Fonda, Peter	*Killer Force* ('75)	a
Fonda, Peter	*The Trip* ('67)	a
Fontana, Alessandro	*Il Diavolo Sulle* (I)	a, p
Fontana, Alessandro	*Il Diavolo Sulle Colline* (I)	a
Fontes, Guilhermes	*Subway to the Stars* (Br) ('87)	a
Ford, Mick	*Naming the Names*	a
Forest, Pierce	*The Eye of the Birds*	a, p
Foronjy, Richard	*Once Upon a Time in America* ('84)	a
Forrest, Andy J.	*Appunamento in Nero*	a
Forrest, Andy J.	*Capriccio* (I)	a, p
Forrest, Andy J.	*Love and Passion* (I)	a
Forrest, Andy J.	*Miranda* (I)	a
Forrest, Andy J.	*The Scorpion*	a
Forrest, Frederic	*The Dion Brothers* (aka *The Gravy Train*) ('74)	a
Forrest, Frederic	*The Missouri Breaks* ('76)	a
Forristal, John	*The Doors* ('91)	a
Forster, Robert	*Cover Me Babe* ('72)	a
Forster, Robert	*Hollywood Harry* ('85)	a
Forster, Robert	*Medium Cool* ('69)	a, p
Forster, Robert	*Reflections in a Golden Eye* ('67)	a
Forster, Robert	*Vigilante* ('83)	a
Forsyth, Tony	*The Fruit Machine* (aka *Wonderland*) ('88)	a, p
Forsythe, Colin	*The Houseman's Tale* (B)	a
Forte, Alexander	*She-Wolf of London* ('90)	a
Foschi, Massimo	*Jungle Holocaust* (I) ('85)	a
Foster, Jeremy	*Black Oak Conspiracy* ('77)	a
Foster, Robert	*Botas Negras Latigo de Cuerio*	a, p
Foster, Robert	*Macoma Sexual* (I)	a
Fourton, Eric	*On Se Calme et On Boit* (F)	a
Fox, Colin	*My Pleasure Is My Business* ('74)	a
Fox, Edward	*Day of the Jackal* ('73)	a
Fox, Edward	*Shaka Zulu* ('83)	a
Fox, James	*Performance* (B) ('70)	a, p
Fox, Michael J.	*Back to the Future III* ('90)	a
Fox, Michael J.	*Greedy* ('94)	a
Fox, Peter	*Mother's Day* ('80)	a
Foxworth, Robert	*The Invisible Strangler* (aka *Astral Factor*) ('76)	a
Francella, Guillermo	*Los Colgials* (M)	a, p
Franco, Angel F.	*Street Warriors* ('87)	a, p
Frank, Billy	*Nudity Required* ('89)	a
Frank, Edward	*Zero in and Scream* ('71)	a
Frappat, Francis	*Black and White in Color* (F) ('77)	a, p
Fraser, Brendan	*School Ties* ('92)	a

Fraser, Todd	*The Clay Farmers*	a
Fratkin, Stuart	*Valet Girls* ('83)	a
Frazer, Rupert	*Girl in a Swing* (B) ('89)	a
Frechete, Peter	*Paint It Black* ('89)	p
Frechette, Mark	*Zabriski Point* ('70)	a
Freedman, Dan	*Fortune and Men's Eyes* ('71)	a
Freiss, Stephane	*Does This Mean We're Married?* (F) ('90)	a
Freitag, Robert	*Nea* (F) ('76)	a
Freixas, Rocio	*Genidos de Placer* (M)	a
Frey, Sami	*The Black Widow* ('87)	a
Frieberger, Alex	*Casa di Piaccre*	a
Friedrich, John	*The Wanderers* ('79)	a
Friels, Colin	*Kangaroo* (A) ('87)	a, p
Friels, Colin	*Monkey Grip* (A) ('83)	a
Friels, Colin	*Weekend with Kate* (A) ('90)	a
Frigel, Thomas	*The Inheritors* (G) ('84)	a, p
Fringle, Bryan	*Drowning by Numbers* (B) ('88)	a
Frittella, Mauro	*La Supplente Vaincitta* (I)	a
Frye, Brittain	*Hide and Go Shriek* ('87)	a
Fryer, Eric	*The Terry Fox Story* ('83)	a
Fuentes, Tony	*Hidden Pleasures* (Sp)	a
Fuji, Tatsuya	*In the Realm of the Senses* (J) ('76)	a
Fuller, Brook	*The Christmas Tree* ('69)	a
Furrh, Chris	*Lord of the Flies* ('90)	a
Furst, Carl	*California Manhunt*	a
Fux, Herbert	*The Three-Cornered Bed* (G) ('71)	a
Gabela, Glen	*Shaka Zulu* ('83)	a
Gable, Christopher	*Women in Love* (B) ('69)	a
Gadjakov, Valentin	*The Berlin Conspiracy* ('91)	a
Gagen, Tom	*Everything Goes*	a
Gaines, Boyd	*Call Me* ('88)	a
Gaines, Tyler	*Novel Desires* ('91)	a
Gallagher, Peter	*Summer Lovers* ('82)	a, p
Galland, Philippe	*Overseas* (F) ('91)	a, p
Gallion, Randy	*Valet Girls* ('83)	a
Gambieri, Giuseppe	*Yellow Emmanuelle* (F)	a
Gamelon, Laurent	*P.R.O.F.S.*	p
Gammon, James	*Crisscross* ('92)	a
Ganios, Tony	*Porky's* ('81)	a
Ganios, Tony	*Porky's Revenge* ('85)	a
Ganz, Bruno	*Circle of Deceit* (F/G) ('81)	a, p
Ganz, Bruno	*Strapless* (B) ('90)	a
Garcia, Andres	*Carnada* (M)	a
Garcia, Andres	*Chili Picanto* (M)	a, p
Garcia, Andres	*El Macho Bionico* (M)	a
Garcia, Andres	*El Sex Sentido* (M)	a

Garcia, Andres	El Sexologo (M)	a
Garcia, Andres	Llegamos los Fregamos (M)	a, p
Garcia, Andres	Mirano con Pornagraficos (M)	a
Garcia, Andres	Paraiso (M)	a, p
Garcia, Andres	Sexo Contro Sexo (M)	a
Garcia, Andres	Tintorera (B/M) ('77)	a, p
Garcia, Javier	El Pico (M)	a, p
Garcin, Henri	Jury of One (F/I) ('75)	a
Gareth, Curt	A Very Natural Thing ('74)	a, p
Garfield, Allen	Cry Uncle ('71)	a
Garfunkel, Art	Bad Timing: A Sensual Obsession (B) ('80)	a
Garfunkel, Art	Carnal Knowledge ('71)	a
Garko, Gianni	Joy of Flying (I)	a, p
Garnier, Phillipe	Island of 1000 Delights (I/F/G)	a, p
Garrison, Bob	Hollywood Hot Tubs 2 ('89)	a
Garza, Jaime	Nana (M)	a, p
Garza, Jaime	Playa Prohibide (M)	a, p
Gas, Mario	L'Amore Sporco (I)	a
Gaste, Phillipe	House of 1000 Pleasures (F)	a
Gates, Rick	Kentucky Fried Movie ('77)	a
Gates, Rick	So Long, Blue Boy ('73)	a
Gavazzi, Francesco	The Decameron (I) ('71)	a
Gaylord, Mitch	American Rickshaw (aka American Tiger) ('90)	a
Gaylord, Mitch	Animal Instincts ('91)	p
Gaynes, James	Final Reprisal	a
Geary, Anthony	Scorchers ('92)	a
Geary, Tony	Blood Sabbath ('72)	a
Gedrick, Jason	Backdraft ('91)	a
Gedrick, Jason	Heavenly Kid ('85)	a
Gee, Robbie	Manageress II	a
Gelfant, Alan	The Other Woman ('92)	a
Gelin, Manuel	One Deadly Summer (F) ('83)	a, p
Gemma, Guiliano	The Bastards (I)	a
Gentry, Jim	Savage Passion	a
Gentry, Richard (Peter)	All the Loving Kinfolk ('89)	a
Genzano, Filippo	Ragazzi Fuori (I)	a
Geoffreys, Stephen	Fright Night ('85)	a
Gerber, Mark	Sirens ('94)	a, p
Gere, Richard	American Gigolo ('79)	a, p
Gere, Richard	Beyond the Limit ('83)	a
Gere, Richard	Breathless ('83)	a, p
Gere, Richard	Final Analysis ('92)	a
Gere, Richard	Looking for Mr. Goodbar ('77)	a
Gere, Richard	Yanks ('79)	a
Gerreaud, Jean-François	Violette (F) ('78)	a

Getty, Balthazar	*The Pope Must Die* ('91)	a
Getz, Stuart	*The Van* ('77)	a
Gewerty, Perry	*The Love Thrill Murders* ('71)	a
Ghadban, Alfe	*Prom Night IV: Deliver Us from Evil* ('91)	a
Giallelis, Anthony	*Panagoalis Zei*	a, p
Giamatti, Marcus	*Necessary Roughness* ('91)	a
Giamo, Anthony	*Deadly Rivals (aka Rivals)* ('72)	a
Giannini, Giancarlo	*Seven Beauties* (I) ('76)	a
Giannini, Giancarlo	*Swept Away* (I) ('75)	a
Gibb, Donald	*Revenge of the Nerds* ('84)	a
Gibson, Henry	*The Last Remake of Beau Geste* ('77)	a
Gibson, Mel	*Bird on a Wire* ('90)	a
Gibson, Mel	*Forever Young* ('92)	a
Gibson, Mel	*Gallipoli* (A) ('81)	a, p
Gibson, Mel	*Lethal Weapon* ('87)	a
Gibson, Mel	*Summer City* (A) ('77)	a
Gibson, Thomas	*Tales of the City* (B) ('93)	a
Gift, Roland	*Sammy and Rosie Get Laid* (B) ('87)	a
Gift, Roland	*Scandal* (B) ('89)	a
Gilbert, Michel	*Fortune and Men's Eyes* ('71)	a
Gilles, Millinaire	*Miami Blues* ('90)	a
Gilligan, Zach	*Mortal Passions* ('90)	a
Gillis, Jamie	*Deranged* ('87)	a
Gilmore, Craig	*The Living End* ('92)	a
Gilmour, George	*The Apple* ('80)	a
Ginsburg, Allen	*Ciao, Manhattan* ('72)	a, p
Girard, Remy	*The Decline of the American Empire* (C) ('86)	a, p
Girardot, Hippolite	*L'Amant Magnifique* (F) ('86)	a, p
Gismondo, Antonio	*Black Emmanuelle, White Emmanuelle* (F)	a
Gitlin, Rick	*Squeeze Play* ('80)	a
Giusti, Paul	*Emmanuelle on Taboo Island* (F) ('76)	a, p
Glawson, Peter	*Genesis Children* ('71)	a, p
Glenn, Scott	*The Baby Maker* ('70)	a, p
Glenn, Scott	*Past Tense* ('94)	a
Glenn, Scott	*The Right Stuff* ('83)	a
Glover, Bruce	*Uncommon Bonds*	a
Glover, Kevin	*Love Bites* ('88)	a
Glover, Kevin	*Venus Flytrap* ('88)	a
Gobbi, Marco	*The Statue* (B) ('70)	a
Goddard, Trevor	*Inside Out* ('92)	a
Godreau, Miguel	*Altered States* ('81)	a, p
Goldan, Wolf	*Melody in Love* ('78)	a
Goldblum, Jeff	*Death Wish* ('74)	a

Goldblum, Jeff	*The Fly* ('86)	a
Goldblum, Jeff	*The Tall Guy* (B) ('90)	a
Goldenburg, Devin	*Savage Weekend* ('79)	a
Goldwyn, Tony	*Love Matters* ('92)	a
Goldwyn, Tony	*Traces of Red* ('92)	a
Gomez, Jaime	*The Silencer* ('92)	a
Gomez, Oscar	*El Chico Temido*	a, p
Gomez, Panchito	*American Me* ('92)	a
Goncic, Svetislav	*Secerna Vodica* (Y)	a, p
Gonzales, Antonio	*Colegas* (aka *Pals*) (Sp) ('82)	a, p
Gonzales, Joe	*Brain Damage* ('87)	a
Gonzales, Will	*White Slave* ('86)	a, p
Good, Jack	*Genesis Children* ('71)	a, p
Good, Mike	*Genesis Children* ('71)	a, p
Goodeve, Grant	*Take Two* ('87)	a
Gooding Jr., Cuba	*Daybreak* ('93)	a
Gooding Jr., Cuba	*Boyz N the Hood* ('91)	a
Goodman, Caleb	*Up Your Ladder* (B)	a
Goodrow, Michael	*The Sweater Girls* ('78)	a
Gordon, Barry	*Out of It* ('69)	a
Gordon, Evan H.	*Hometown U.S.A.* ('79)	a
Gordon, Phillip	*Bridge to Nowhere* (NZ) ('85)	a, p
Gori, Gabrielle	*La Monaca Nel Peccato*	a
Gortner, Marjoe	*When You Comin' Back, Red Ryder?* ('79)	a
Gossart, Jean Rene	*Emmanuelle VI* ('92)	a
Gothard, Michael	*The Valley* (F) ('72)	a
Gould, Elliott	*Getting Straight* ('70)	a
Gould, Elliott	*I Will, I Will . . . for Now* ('76)	a
Gould, Elliott	*Move* ('70)	a
Grabrow, Mike	*King Frat*	a
Graf, Peter	*3 Musketeers & Their Sexual Adventures*	a
Graham, Gary	*The Last Warrior* ('89)	a
Graham, Gary	*Robot Jox* ('89)	a
Graham, Gerrit	*Used Cars* ('80)	a
Graham, Gerrit	*Hi, Mom!* ('70)	a, p
Grannell, William	*Ginger* ('70)	a, p
Grant, Andrew	*Girl from Starship Venus*	a, p
Grant, David Marshall	*American Flyers* ('85)	a, p
Grant, Gerald	*Score* ('73)	a, p
Grant, Gordon	*Both Sides*	a, p
Grant, Richard	*How to Get Ahead in Advertising* ('89)	a
Grant, Rupert	*Possessions: Until Death Do You Part* ('90)	a
Gras, Jose	*Al Sur Del Eden* (M)	a

Gravance, Louie	*Evilspeak* ('81)	a
Graves, Rupert	*A Room with a View* (B) ('85)	a, p
Graves, Rupert	*Maurice* (B) ('87)	a, p
Greenall, Douglas	*Riding Fast* ('82)	a
Greene, Daniel	*Stitches* ('85)	a
Greene, Daniel	*Weekend Warriors* ('86)	a
Greene, Matt	*Dreamy Desire*	a
Greene, Matt	*I Remember Love*	a
Greene, Michael	*The Harrad Experiment* ('73)	a, p
Greene, Michael	*Naked Angels* ('69)	a
Greenleaf, Jim	*Surf II* ('83)	a
Greenleaf, Jim	*The Vals* ('83)	a
Greenquist, Brad	*The Bedroom Window* ('86)	a
Greenwood, Bruce	*Wild Orchid* ('90)	a, p
Greer, Michael	*Fortune and Men's Eyes* ('71)	a, p
Greeson, Timothy	*The Disturbance* ('89)	a
Gregauff, Paul	*A Piece of Pleasure* (F) ('70)	a, p
Gregory, André	*Some Girls* ('89)	a
Gregory, Mark	*Blue Paradise* ('86)	a
Gress, Googy	*The First Turn On* ('84)	a
Grieco, Richard	*Tomcat* ('93)	a
Griem, Helmut	*Malou* (G) ('83)	a
Grier, David Alan	*Streamers* ('82)	a
Griffith, Gordon	*Tarzan of the Apes* (silent) ('18)	a
Griggs, Jeff	*Eden* ('92)	a
Griggs, Jeff	*Eden 2* ('92)	a
Griggs, Jeff	*Eden 3* ('93)	a
Grimes, Gary	*The Spikes Gang* ('74)	a
Groat, Rick	*L.A. Goddess* ('92)	a
Groome, Malcolm	*Feelin' Up!* ('76)	a
Gross, Paul	*Aspen Extreme* ('93)	a
Gross, Paul	*Buffalo Jump* ('90)	a
Gross, Peter	*Virgin Territory*	a, p
Guerin, Bruce	*Country Kid* ('23)	a
Grumelli, Aldo	*El Topo* ('70)	a
Grundberg, Klaus	*More* (G) ('69)	a
Gruner, Olivier	*Nemesis* ('92)	a
Guest, Christopher	*Girlfriends* ('78)	a
Guest, Cliff	*The Disturbance* ('89)	a
Guest, Nicholas	*My Daughter's Keeper*	a
Guglielmi, Marco	*Copenhagen Nights* ('87)	a
Guillen, Fernando	*Cuero la Senora*	a
Guillen, Fernando	*Depravation*	a
Gulager, Clu	*Tapeheads* ('89)	a
Gulp, Eisi	*Sugarbaby* (G) ('85)	a
Gulpilil, David	*The Last Wave* (A) ('77)	a
Gulpilil, David	*Walkabout* (A) ('70)	a

Gunner, Robert	*Planet of the Apes* ('68)	a
Guthrie, Arlo	*Alice's Restaurant* ('69)	a
Guthrie, Bob	*Coed Dorm* ('71)	a
Guttenberg, Steve	*The Bedroom Window* ('86)	a
Guttenberg, Steve	*The Chicken Chronicles* ('77)	a
Guttenberg, Steve	*The Man Who Wasn't There* ('83)	a, p
Haag, Romy	*Mascara* (F) ('87)	a, p
Haak, Todd	*State Park*	a
Haas, Lukas	*Testament* ('83)	a
Haase, Rod	*Candy Stripe Nurses* ('74)	a
Haase, Rod	*If You Don't Stop You'll Go Blind* ('74)	a
Haber, Paul	*Fear No Evil* ('81)	a, p
Hackett, Jay	*One Night Stand* ('84)	p
Hackett, Jay	*Puberty Blues* (A) ('84)	a
Hafiel, Matthias	*A Corps Perdu* (F)	a
Hagen, Ross	*The Devil's 8* ('69)	a
Haggerty, Dan	*Bury Me an Angel* ('72)	a
Haim, Cory	*Blown Away* ('92)	a
Haines, Zachery	*Guess What We Learned in School Today?* ('70)	a
Hajek, Ron	*Swinging Cheerleaders* ('74)	a
Hall, Frank	*While the Cat's Away*	a
Hall, Michael Keyes	*Blackout* ('89)	a
Halm, Martin	*Ernesto* (I) ('79)	a
Halsey, Brett	*Dangerous Obsession* (I) ('88)	a
Ham, Peter	*Happy Gigolo* ('75)	a
Hamill, John	*Tower of Evil* (B) ('72)	a
Hamill, Mark	*Body Bags* ('93)	a
Hamill, Mark	*Corvette Summer* ('78)	a
Hamilton, Dan	*Opposing Force* ('87)	a
Hamilton, Gary	*Tower of Evil* (B) ('72)	a
Hamilton, Neil	*The Tall Guy* (B) ('90)	a, p
Hamilton, Tony	*Nocturna* ('81)	a
Hamlin, Harry	*Laguna Heat* ('87)	a, p
Hamlin, Harry	*Save Me* ('93)	a
Hand, Chip	*The Wild McCullochs* ('75)	a
Haney, Daryl	*Daddy's Boys* ('87)	a
Hanks, Jim	*Buford's Beach Bunnies* ('92)	a
Hanks, Mark	*Night Games* ('79)	p
Hannawald, Ernst	*The Consequence* (G) ('77)	a
Hardwick, Derek	*Among the Cinders* ('84)	a, p
Harenstam, Magnus	*Father to Be*	a, p
Hargreaves, John	*Don's Party* (A) ('76)	a, p
Hargreaves, John	*Hoodwink* (A)	a
Harkness, Percy	*Caged Terror* ('72)	a
Harmon, Mark	*Fourth Story* ('90)	a, p

Harmon, Mark	*Sweet Bird of Youth* (European version) ('89)	a
Harmstorf, Raymond	*Long, Swift Sword of Siegfried* (G) ('71)	a
Harpaz, Shraga	*The Secret of Yolanda* ('82)	a
Harpaz, Shraga	*The Vulture* ('67)	a
Harrelson, Woody	*The Cowboy Way* ('94)	a
Harrelson, Woody	*White Men Can't Jump* ('92)	a
Harris, Ed	*Knightriders* ('81)	a
Harris, Ed	*Swing Shift* ('84)	p
Harris, Gregory Alan	*Conflict of Interest* ('92)	a
Harris, Jim	*Squeeze Play* ('80)	a
Harris, Ralph	*Loose Shoes* ('80)	a
Harris, Richard	*99 and 44/100 % Dead* ('74)	a
Harris, Richard	*A Man Called Horse* ('69)	a
Harris, Richard	*Return of a Man Called Horse* ('76)	a
Harris, Richard	*Tarzan, the Ape Man* ('81)	a
Harris, Richard	*This Sporting Life* (B) ('63)	a
Harris, Richard	*Wrestling Ernest Hemingway* ('94)	a
Harris, Richard	*Your Ticket Is No Longer Valid* ('84)	a
Harrison, Gregory	*Body Chemistry 2: Voice of a Stranger* ('91)	a
Harrison, Gregory	*For Ladies Only* (European version) ('81)	a
Harrison, Gregory	*The Harrad Experiment* ('73)	a, p
Harrison, Sebastian	*White Apache*	a
Harrschmann, Johannes	*Der Philosop* (G)	a
Hart, Geno	*Takin' It All Off* ('87)	a
Hart, Ian	*The Hours and Times* (B) ('93)	a
Hartman, Billy	*Slaughter High* ('85)	a
Hartman, Don	*The Feud* ('89)	a
Harvey, Laurence	*The Magic Christian* ('69)	a
Harvey, Laurence	*Night Watch* (B) ('73)	a
Harvey, Rodney	*La Bocca* (I)	a, p
Haslund, Mangus	*On the Threshold*	a
Hasselhoff, David	*Revenge of the Cheerleaders* ('76)	a, p
Hatch, Richard	*Heated Vengeance* ('84)	a
Hauer, Rutger	*Blind Side* ('92)	a
Hauer, Rutger	*Cold Blood* ('75)	a
Hauer, Rutger	*Dandelions* (G) ('74)	a
Hauer, Rutger	*Flesh + Blood* ('85)	a
Hauer, Rutger	*Mysteries* (D) ('79)	a, p
Hauer, Rutger	*Soldier of Orange* (D) ('79)	a
Hauer, Rutger	*Turkish Delight* (D) ('73)	a, p
Haughton, David Cain	*Emperor Caligula* ('86)	a
Hauser, Patrick	*Hot Dog—The Movie* ('83)	a
Hauser, Wings	*Art of Dying* ('91)	a

Hauser, Wings	*Deadly Force* ('83)	a, p
Hawtrey, Charles	*Carry On Constable* (B)	a
Hayes, Alan	*Friday the 13th: the Final Chapter* ('84)	a
Haygarth, Anthony	*Unman, Wittering and Zigo* (B) ('71)	a
Haysbert, Dennis	*Mr. Baseball* ('92)	a
Hayward, Charles	*Nightfall* ('88)	a
Hayward, David	*Delusion* ('81)	a
Haywood, Chris	*Golden Braid* (A) ('90)	a
Haywood, Chris	*Razorback* (A) ('84)	a
Head, Anthony	*A Prayer for the Dying* (B) ('87)	a
Head, Murray	*The French Woman* (B) ('77)	a
Head, Murray	*Sunday, Bloody Sunday* (B) ('71)	a
Headley, James	*Strangers* ('90)	a, p
Headrick, Richard	*The Little Minister* ('21)	a
Heard, John	*Between the Lines* ('77)	a
Heard, John	*Heart Beat* ('79)	a
Heard, John	*Cat People* ('82)	a
Hearn, Mark	*Party Games for Adults* ('83)	a
Hearns, Michael	*Young Lady Chatterly* (B) ('76)	a
Hegyes, Robert	*Just Tell Me You Love Me* ('78)	a
Hehn, Sascha	*High Season* (G) ('82)	a
Hehn, Sascha	*Melody in Love* ('78)	a, p
Hehn, Sascha	*The Naughty Nymphs* (G) ('72)	a
Hehn, Sascha	*Patricia* ('84)	a
Heintzman, Michael	*Slammer Girls* ('86)	a
Hembrow, Mark	*Out of the Body* ('88)	a
Hemmings, David	*Blow-Up* (I) ('66)	a
Hench, Richard	*Scalps* ('83)	a
Henderson, Eric	*A Night in Heaven* ('83)	a
Henderson, Ty	*The Competition* ('80)	a
Hennessy, Michael	*Transformations* ('88)	a
Henry, Buck	*Taking Off* ('71)	a
Henry, Gregg	*The Patriot* ('86)	a
Henshaw, Jim	*Snapshot* ('77)	a
Herbst, Rick	*Brain Damage* ('87)	a
Herra, Rigoberto	*Mujer de Fuego* (M)	a, p
Herren, Roger	*Myra Breckenridge* ('70)	a
Herrier, Mark	*Porky's Revenge* ('85)	a
Herrman, Herbert	*Spare Parts* ('85)	a
Hershburger, Gary	*Paradise Motel* ('84)	a
Hess, David A.	*The House on the Edge of the Park* ('84)	a
Heston, Charlton	*Antony and Cleopatra* ('73)	a
Heston, Charlton	*Julius Caesar* ('70)	a
Heston, Charlton	*Number One* ('69)	a
Heston, Charlton	*Planet of the Apes* ('68)	a

Hewitt, Martin	*Carnal Crimes* ('91)	a
Hewitt, Martin	*Crime Lords* ('90)	a
Hewitt, Martin	*Endless Love* ('81)	a
Hewitt, Martin	*Night Rhythms* ('91)	a
Hewitt, Martin	*Secret Games* ('91)	a
Hewlett, David	*Where the Heart Is* ('90)	a
Hicks, Ken	*Sebastiane* (B) ('79)	a, p
Hicks, Kevin	*Blood Relations* ('87)	a
Higgins, Mike	*Party Games for Adults* ('83)	a
Hill, Bernard	*Drowning by Numbers* (B) ('88)	a
Hill, Bernard	*Mountains of the Moon* (B) ('89)	a
Hill, Greg	*Genesis Children* ('71)	a, p
Hill, Nicholas	*Desert Passion* ('92)	a
Hillel, Stephane	*Summer Night Fever* (G) ('85)	a
Hindley, Tommy	*Silent Night, Deadly Night 4* ('90)	a
Hines, Gregory	*Wolfen* ('81)	a
Hines, Robert	*The Insurance Man* (B) ('85)	a, p
Hinton, Darby	*Firecracker* ('81)	a
Hinton, Darby	*Malibu Express* ('84)	a
Hiroyugi-Togawa, Carey	*The Last Warrior* ('89)	a
Hockney, David	*A Bigger Splash* ('74)	a, p
Hodern, Michael	*Joseph Andrews* (B) ('77)	a
Hodges, Tom	*The Baby Doll Murders* ('92)	a
Hodges, Tom	*Excessive Force* ('93)	a
Hoffman, Dustin	*John and Mary* ('69)	a
Hoffman, Dustin	*Lenny* ('74)	a
Hoffman, Dustin	*Little Big Man* ('74)	a
Hoffman, Dustin	*Marathon Man* ('76)	a
Hoffman, Dustin	*Straight Time* ('78)	a, p
Hoffman, Thom	*Lily Was Here* (D) ('89)	a, p
Hoffman, Thom	*The Fourth Man* (D) ('79)	a, p
Hofmann, Josef	*Robby Kallepaul*	a
Hofschneider, Marco	*Europa, Europa* (G) ('91)	a, p
Hogan, Bosco	*The Outsider* (B) ('79)	a
Hogdon, John Phillip	*Visit to a Chief's Son* ('74)	a
Holbrook, Hal	*The Girl from Petrovka* ('74)	a
Holbrook, Hal	*Natural Enemies* ('79)	a
Holden, Bob	*Deadly Vengeance* ('85)	a
Holder, Roy	*Loot* (B) ('70)	a
Holiday, Bill	*Pretty Baby* ('78)	a
Holland, Paul	*Polyester* ('81)	a
Holmebakk, Torstein	*Burning Flowers*	a, p
Holt, Steven	*Preppies* ('84)	a
Hompertz, Tom	*Lonesome Cowboys* ('68)	a
Honaerts, Gerrt	*To Play or to Die* (D) ('91)	a, p
Honesseau, Mikael	*Anita Dances Nude*	a, p
Hönig, Heinz	*The Matchmaker* (G)	a, p

Hooker, Buddy Joe	*Cheech & Chong's Nice Dreams* ('81)	a
Hooten, Peter	*Fantasies* ('74)	a
Hooten, Peter	*Slashed Dream* ('74)	a
Hoover, Phil	*Policewomen* ('74)	a, p
Hopkins, Harold	*Don's Party* (A) ('76)	a, p
Hopkins, Harold	*The Picture Show Man* (A) ('77)	a
Hopman, Jan	*Dear Boys* (D) ('80)	a, p
Hoppe, Nickolas	*Night Club* ('89)	a
Hopper, Dennis	*The American Friend* ('77)	a
Hopper, Dennis	*Chattahoochee* ('90)	a
Hopper, Dennis	*Easy Rider* ('69)	a
Hopper, Dennis	*Kid Blue* ('73)	a
Hopper, Dennis	*The Last Movie* ('71)	a
Hopper, Dennis	*Nails* ('92)	a
Hopper, Dennis	*Tracks* ('76)	a, p
Horenstein, Jay	*American Taboo* ('84)	a, p
Horgaard, Carsten	*The Fruit Machine* (aka *Wonderland*) ('88)	a
Hostalot, Luis	*What Have I Done to Deserve This?* (Sp) ('85)	a, p
Houseman, David	*Mrs. Barrington*	a
Houser, Patrick	*Hot Dog—The Movie* ('83)	a
Houston, Robert	*Cheerleaders' Wild Weekend* ('85)	a
Howard, Alan	*The Cook, The Thief, His Wife & Her Lover* (B) ('90)	a, p
Howard, Alan Coleman	*Slaves of New York* ('89)	a
Howard, Clint	*Evilspeak* ('81)	a
Howard, John	*The Club* (A) ('80)	a
Howard, Ken	*Tell Me That You Love Me, Junie Moon* ('70)	a
Howard, Kevyn Major	*Death Wish II* ('82)	a
Howell, C. Thomas	*Acting on Impulse* ('93)	a
Howell, C. Thomas	*A Tiger's Tale* ('87)	a
Howell, C. Thomas	*To Protect and Serve* ('92)	a
Howes, Dougie	*Salome's Last Dance* (B) ('87)	a
Howitt, Peter	*Ball Trap on the Cote Sauvage*	a
Howitt, Peter	*Bread*	a
Howman, Karl	*The House on Straw Hill* (B) ('76)	a
Hoyes, Chuck	*Angel of H.E.A.T.* ('82)	a
Huart, Gerard Antonio	*Joy*	a
Hubert, Antoine	*Le Grand Chemin* (aka *The Grand Highway*) (F) ('87)	a, p
Hudson, Brett	*Hysterical* ('82)	a
Hudson, Gary	*Roadhouse* ('89)	a
Hudson, Gary	*Wild Cactus* ('92)	a
Hudson, Rock	*Embryo* ('76)	a

Huff, Brent	The Perils of Gwendoline in the Land of the Yik Yak ('84)	a
Hugh, Soto Joe	The Killing of a Chinese Bookie ('76)	a
Hughes, Brendan	To Die For ('88)	a
Hulce, Tom	The Inner Circle ('91)	a
Hunold, Rainer	The Matchmaker (G)	a, p
Hunter, Larry	The Amazing Transplant ('70)	a, p
Hunter, Thomas	Il Sorriso del Ragno	a
Hurst, Jeffrey	Mrs. Barrington	a, p
Hurst, Michael	Death Warmed Up (NZ) ('85)	a
Hurt, John	1984 (B) ('85)	a
Hurt, John	East of Elephant Rock (B) ('76)	a, p
Hurt, John	The Naked Civil Servant (B) ('75)	a
Hurt, John	The Osterman Weekend ('83)	a
Hurt, William	Altered States ('81)	a
Hurt, William	Body Heat ('81)	a
Hurt, William	Broadcast News ('87)	a
Hurt, William	Until the End of the World ('91)	a
Hurwitz, Stan	Necromancer ('88)	a
Huster, Francis	Equciter (F)	a, p
Huster, Francis	L'Amour Braque (F)	a, p
Huster, Francis	L'Amour d'Orphic (F)	a
Huster, Francis	Le Femme Publique (F)	a, p
Hutchison, Ken	The Wrath of God ('72)	a
Hutton, Timothy	Made in Heaven ('87)	a
Hutton, Timothy	Q & A ('90)	a
Hvenegaard, Pelle	Pelle the Conqueror (Da) ('88)	a, p
Hylands, Scott	Daddy's Gone A-Hunting ('69)	a
Hylands, Scott	Passengers	a
Hyry, David	The Northfield Cemetery Massacre ('76)	a
Idle, Eric	Splitting Heirs (B) ('93)	a
Imaros, Richard	Labyrinth of Passion (Sp) ('92)	a, p
Incerto, Carlo	Men in Love ('90)	a, p
Inclan, Rafael	La Pulquera II (M)	a
Inclan, Rafael	Los Modeles de Desnudos (M)	a
Inclan, Rafael	Los Movidos del Mofles (M)	a
Inclan, Rafael	Nos Reimos de la Migra (M)	a
Infanti, Angelo	Black Emmanuelle (F) ('76)	a
Inman, James	The Detective ('68)	a
Interlandi, Maurizio	Senza Buccia (aka Skin Deep) (I)	a, p
Iorio, Jeff	Deadly Obsession ('88)	a
Ipalé, Aaron	Too Hot to Handle ('76)	a
Irons, Jeremy	Brideshead Revisited (B) ('81)	a
Irons, Jeremy	Damage (B) ('92)	a
Irons, Jeremy	Dead Ringers ('88)	a
Irons, Jeremy	Landrishe Go Down	a

Ironside, Michael	*Mind Field* ('90)	a
Isherwood, Mark	*Mondo Trasho* ('70)	a, p
Ismael, Gerard	*The Last Romantic Lover* (F) ('79)	a
Ismael, Gerard	*Les Heroines du Mal* (F)	a
Ivgi, Moshe	*Cup Final* (Is) ('92)	a
Jacot, Michael	*Hot Sex in Bangkok* (F)	a, p
Jacot, Michael	*Tempting Roommates* (F) ('86)	a
Jaeckel, Richard	*Once Before I Die* ('66)	a
Jagger, Mick	*Performance* (B) ('70)	a
Jagger, Mick	*Running Out of Luck* ('86)	a
James, Barney	*Sebastiane* (B) ('79)	a, p
James, Michael	*Warriors of the Apocalypse* ('85)	a
Janes, Tom	*Nemesis* ('92)	a
Jansen, Ton	*Loos*	a, p
Janssen, David	*Jacqueline Susann's Once Is Not Enough* ('75)	a
Janssen, David	*Where It's At* ('69)	a
Jarrett, John	*Australian Dream* (A)	a
Jarrett, John	*The Odd Angry Shot* (A) ('79)	a, p
Jarrett, John	*A Salute to the Great McCarthy* (A)	p
Jastrow, Terry	*Waltz Across Texas* ('82)	a
Javorsky, Vladmir	*Krali*	a
Jeavons, Colin	*Stalin* ('92)	a
Jeffrey, Douglas	*Chain of Desire* ('92)	a
Jenkins, Daniel H.	*O. C. & Stiggs* ('85)	a
Jenkins, John	*Patti Rocks* ('87)	a
Jenkins, Ralph	*Ribald Tales of Robin Hood* ('69)	a
Jensini, Joey	*Party Games for Adults* ('83)	a
Jeter, Michael	*Hair* ('79)	a
Jiminez, Carlos	*Poison* ('91)	a
Joamie, Robert	*Map of the Human Heart* ('92)	a, p
Jodorowsky, Axel	*Santa Sangre* ('89)	a
Jodorowsky, Brontis	*El Topo* ('70)	a, p
Joel, Robert	*A Very Natural Thing* ('74)	a, p
Johansson, Paul	*Soapdish* ('91)	a
John, Lucien	*Walkabout* (A) ('70)	a
Johnson, Claude	*The Moonshine War* ('70)	a
Johnson, David	*Genesis Children* ('71)	a, p
Johnson, Don	*The Harrad Experiment* ('73)	a, p
Johnson, Don	*Hot Spot* ('90)	a
Johnson, Don	*The Magic Garden of Stanley Sweetheart* ('70)	a, p
Johnson, Don	*Sweet Hearts Dance* ('88)	a
Johnson, E. Lamont	*Death Wish II* ('82)	a
Johnson, Jesse	*Chillers* ('88)	a
Johnson, Joseph Alan	*Beserker* ('87)	a
Johnson, Joseph Alan	*Iced* ('88)	a, p

Johnson, Karl	*The Tempest* (B) ('82)	a
Johnson, Kelly	*Utu* (NZ) ('83)	a
Johnson, Kyle	*The Learning Tree* ('69)	a
Johnston, Bobby	*Animal Instincts* ('91)	a
Johnston, Bobby	*Maximum Breakout* ('91)	a
Jolivet, Pierre	*Le Dernier Combat* (F) ('84)	a
Jones, Christopher	*Three in the Attic* ('68)	a
Jones, Christopher	*Wild in the Streets* ('68)	a
Jones, Dean	*Mr. Super-Invisible* ('73)	a
Jones, Griff Rhys	*The Misadventures of Mr. Wilt* (B) ('89)	a
Jones, James Earl	*Claudine* ('74)	a
Jones, L. Q.	*The Hunting Party* ('71)	a
Jones, Mark	*Girl from Starship Venus*	a, p
Jones, Mark	*Keep It Up Jack* (B) ('75)	a, p
Jones, Michael	*Opposing Force* ('87)	a
Jones, Sam	*My Chauffeur* ('86)	a
Jones, Sam	*Under the Gun* ('88)	a
Jones, Steve	*The Great Rock and Roll Swindle* ('79)	a, p
Jones, Terry	*Life of Brian* (B) ('79)	a
Jones, Tommy Lee	*Back Roads* ('81)	a
Jones, Tommy Lee	*The Executioner's Song* ('82)	a
Jones, Tommy Lee	*Gotham* ('88)	a
Jones, Tyrone	*Angel III* ('88)	a
Joshua, Larry	*The Burning* ('81)	a
Josse, Fabrice	*Les Exploits d'un Jeune Don Juan* (F)	a
Jouffroy, Yves	*The Immoral One* (F)	a
Joyce, William	*Young Nurses* ('73)	a
Joynt, Paul	*Opposing Force* ('87)	a
Judd, Stephen	*Bridge to Nowhere* (NZ) ('85)	a, p
Jugnot, Geral	*Pour 100 Briques* (F)	a, p
Julia, Raul	*Kiss of the Spider Woman* (Br) ('85)	a
Julia, Raul	*One from the Heart* ('82)	a
Juliano, Al	*True Love* ('89)	a
Junior, Fabio	*Bye, Bye Brazil* (Br) ('80)	a
Ka'ne, Dayton	*Beyond the Reef* ('81)	a
Kabouche, Aziz	*A Flame in My Heart* (F) ('87)	a, p
Kalfon, Jean Pierre	*Le Declic* (aka *The Turn-On*) (F) ('85)	a
Kalfon, Jean Pierre	*The Valley* (F) ('72)	a, p
Kalinski, Edward	*Home Before Midnight* ('79)	a
Kanan, Sean	*Hide and Go Shriek* ('87)	a
Kane, Big Daddy	*Posse* ('93)	a
Kani, John	*Killing Heat* ('84)	a
Kantor, Richard	*Out of Control* ('85)	a
Karja, S. Yriwana	*At Play in the Fields of the Lord* ('91)	a

Karlen, John	*Daughters of Darkness* ('71)	a
Karsen, Emmanuel	*Comment Draguer Tortes les Filles* (F)	a, p
Kask, Scott	*Jaded*	a
Kastner, Peter	*B.S. I Love You* ('71)	a
Kastner, Peter	*Steam Room*	a
Katcher, Adam	*Beneath the Valley of the Ultravixens* ('79)	a
Katt, William	*First Love* ('77)	a
Katt, William	*Last Call* ('90)	a
Katt, William	*Naked Obsession* ('90)	a
Katzur, Yaftach	*Baby Love* (Is) ('83)	a
Katzur, Yaftach	*Going Steady* (Is) ('80)	a
Katzur, Yaftach	*Private Popsicle* (Is) ('82)	a
Kaufman, Bruce	*Brute Corps* ('71)	a
Kay-Hune, Charles	*Affairs of the Heart* ('92)	a
Kaye, Norman	*Lonely Hearts* (A) ('83)	a, p
Kaye, Norman	*Man of Flowers* (A) ('83)	a, p
Keach, Stacy	*Doc* ('71)	a
Keach, Stacy	*The Dion Brothers* (aka *Gravy Train*) ('74)	a
Keach, Stacy	*The Squeeze* (I) ('77)	a, p
Kearns, Michael	*Kentucky Fried Movie* ('77)	a
Keaton, Buster	*The Cameraman* ('28)	a
Keitel, Harvey	*Bad Lieutenant* ('92)	a, p
Keitel, Harvey	*Fingers* ('78)	a, p
Keitel, Harvey	*The Men's Club* ('86)	a
Keitel, Harvey	*The Piano* (NZ) ('93)	a, p
Keitel, Harvey	*Who's That Knocking at My Door?* ('68)	a
Keith, David	*Gulag* ('84)	a
Keith, David	*Liar's Edge* ('92)	a
Keith, David	*An Officer and a Gentleman* ('82)	a
Keller, Hiram	*Fellini Satyricon* (I) ('69)	a
Keller, Hiram	*Lifespan* ('75)	a
Keller, Hiram	*Rosina Fumo* (I)	a
Keller, Todd	*Penthouse Love Stories* ('86)	a, p
Kelly, Andrew	*For a Lost Soldier* (D) ('93)	a
Kelly, David	*Zero In and Scream* ('71)	a
Kelly, Tommy	*The Adventures of Tom Sawyer* ('38)	a
Kemp, Martin	*The Krays* ('90)	a
Kennedy, George	*Zig Zag* ('70)	a
Kennedy, Graham	*The Club* (A) ('80)	a
Kennedy, Graham	*Don's Party* (A) ('76)	a
Kennedy, Leon Isaac	*Penitentiary* ('79)	a
Kennedy, Marklen	*Witchcraft V: Dance with the Devil* ('93)	a

Kennedy, Neil	*Sebastiane* (B) ('79)	a, p
Kenney, Sean	*Terminal Island* ('73)	a
Kenny, Lee	*The Revenger* ('90)	a
Kent, Peter	*Re-Animator* ('85)	a
Keoys-Bryne, Hugh	*Stone*	a, p
Kerr, Herbert	*Ginger* ('70)	a
Kerr, Ken	*Beneath the Valley of the Ultravixens* ('79)	a, p
Kerwin, Brian	*Hometown U.S.A.* ('79)	a
Kerwin, Brian	*Murphy's Romance* ('85)	a
Kessler, Rick	*Slammer Girls* ('86)	a
Kierney, Tyde	*I Drink Your Blood* ('71)	a
Kilmer, Val	*The Doors* ('91)	a
Kimbrough, Clint	*Bloody Mama* ('70)	a
Kime, Jeffrey	*Quartet* (B) ('81)	a
King, Freeman	*Long Live the King* ('77)	a, p
King, Perry	*A Different Story* ('78)	a
King, Perry	*The Killing Hour* (aka *The Clairvoyant*) ('82)	a
King, Perry	*Mandingo* ('75)	a, p
King, Perry	*The Possession of Joel Delaney* ('71)	a
King, Perry	*The Wild Party* ('74)	a
King, Tony	*Gordon's War* ('73)	a
King, Zalman	*You Gotta Walk It Like You Talk It* ('68)	a
Kingsley, Ben	*The Fifth Monkey* ('90)	a
Kingsley, Ben	*Murderers Among Us* ('89)	a, p
Kingsley, Ben	*Necessary Love* (I) ('91)	a
Kingsley, Ben	*Oxbridge Blues, Part 2*	a
Kinski, Klaus	*The Main Thing Is to Love* (F) ('75)	a
Kinski, Klaus	*The Story of "O" Continues* (F) ('81)	a
Kirby Jr., Bruno	*The Harrad Experiment* ('73)	a, p
Kirby, Michael	*My Pleasure Is My Business* ('74)	a
Kirk, David	*Cry Uncle* ('71)	a
Kitaoji, Kina	*Himatsuri (Fire Festival)* (J) ('85)	a
Kivirinta, Niilo	*At Play in the Fields of the Lord* ('91)	a, p
Klar, Norman	*The Hitchhikers* ('71)	a, p
Kleeman, Gunther	*I Spit on Your Grave* ('78)	a
Klein, Robert	*Deadly Rivals* (aka *Rivals*) ('72)	a
Kline, Kevin	*Consenting Adults* ('92)	a
Kline, Kevin	*Dave* ('93)	a
Kline, Kevin	*I Love You to Death* ('90)	a
Kline, Kevin	*Violets Are Blue* ('86)	a
Klisser, Evan J.	*Prey for the Hunter* ('92)	a
Knell, David	*Spring Break* ('83)	a
Knight, Peter	*Slammer Girls* ('86)	a
Knight, Wyatt	*Porky's* ('81)	a

Knight, Wyatt	*Porky's Revenge* ('85)	a
Knoph, Greg	*Ilsa, She-Wolf of the SS* ('74)	a
Knox, Norman	*Forever Young, Forever Free* (SA) ('76)	a
Knox, Terence	*Rebel Love* ('85)	a
Koenig, Tommy	*Stitches* ('85)	a
Kohan, Glenn	*The Blue Lagoon* ('80)	a
Kohler, Giles	*The Last Romantic Lover* (F) ('79)	a
Kohler, Giles	*The Marvelous Visit* (F) ('74)	a
Kologie, Ron	*Iced* ('88)	a
Koryzev, Volodya	*Freedom Is Paradise* (R) ('89)	a, p
Kosio, Paul	*Bootleggers* ('74)	a
Kosloff, Dan	*Torment* ('86)	a
Kotto, Yaphet	*Drum* ('76)	a
Kove, Martin	*Death Race 2000* ('75)	a
Kove, Martin	*White Light* ('90)	a
Kove, Martin	*Women in Revolt* ('72)	a, p
Krabbe, Jeroene	*The Fourth Man* (D) ('79)	a, p
Kraft, Michael	*Husbands, Wives, Lovers*	a
Krause, Brian	*Liar's Club*	a
Krause, Brian	*Return to the Blue Lagoon* ('91)	a
Kresting, Bob	*Class of '74* ('71)	a
Krim, Tom	*Campus Confidential* ('68)	a
Kristofferson, Kris	*Pat Garrett and Billy the Kid* ('73)	a
Kristofferson, Kris	*The Sailor Who Fell from Grace with the Sea* ('76)	a
Kristofferson, Kris	*Semi-Tough* ('77)	a
Kroger, Marco	*First Polka*	a
Krone, Marc	*Party in Paris*	a, p
Krowchuk, Chad	*Bye Bye Blues* (C) ('89)	a
Kuhlman, Ron	*Shadow Play* ('86)	a
La Doire, Oscar	*Les Etades de Lulu* (F)	a, p
La Gunez, Guillermo	*Las Mujeras de Jeremias* (M)	a
La Porte, Jean	*Romero and Julia* (F)	a, p
Labato, Humberto	*Muerte en la Playa* (M)	a
Lablais, Michel	*Beyond Love and Evil* ('69)	a, p
LaBruce, Bruce	*No Skin Off My Ass* (C)	a
Lacher, Taylor	*Devil Times Five* ('74)	a
Lackey, Skip	*Once Bitten* ('85)	a
LaDage, Duane	*The Hollywood Knights* ('80)	a
Ladd, Christopher	*Love Bites* ('88)	a, p
Lados, Takis	*Erotic Passions*	a, p
Laezza, Luigi	*Capriccio* (I)	a, p
Lafayette, John	*The Sin* (C) ('79)	a
Lagache, Frederic	*Emmanuelle, Joys of a Woman* (F) ('75)	a, p
Lamas, Lorenzo	*Night of the Warrior* ('90)	a

Lambert, Christopher	*Greystoke, the Legend of Tarzan* ('84)	a
Lambert, Christopher	*Highlander* ('86)	a
Lambert, Christopher	*I Love You* ('86)	a
Lambert, Christopher	*The Sicilian* ('87)	a
Lamden, Derek	*Baby Love* ('68)	a
Lancaster, Burt	*Cattle Annie and Little Britches* ('80)	a
Lancaster, Burt	*Go Tell the Spartans* ('78)	a
Lancaster, Burt	*The Swimmer* ('68)	a
Lancaster, Burt	*Valdez Is Coming* ('71)	a
Lancaster, Stuart	*Supervixens* ('75)	a
Lander, Ned	*Starstruck* (A) ('82)	a
Landers, Steve	*Wager of Love* ('90)	a
Landi, Sal	*Savage Streets* ('84)	a
Landis, Mark	*Computer Beach Party* ('85)	a
Landrum, Bill	*The Doors* ('91)	a
Landzaat, Andrew	*Female Animal*	a
Lane, Charles	*Sidewalk Stories* ('89)	a
Lane, Dickson	*Echoes* ('83)	a, p
Lang, Perry	*Spring Break* ('83)	a
Lang, Perry	*Teen Lust* ('78)	a
Langa, Steven	*Eden 3* ('93)	a
Langdon, Greg	*Night of the Demon* ('79)	a
Lange, Erich	*Love Bites* ('88)	a, p
Lange-Nielsen, Nicolay	*A Handful of Fire* (N)	a, p
Langenstein, Felix	*The Sinful Bed* (G) ('78)	p
Langlois, Eric	*Greystoke, The Legend of Tarzan* ('84)	a
Langmann, Thomas	*Night and Day* (F)	a
Lanno, Jay	*Slammer Girls* ('86)	a
Lanoux, Victor	*Cousin, Cousine* (F) ('76)	a
Lanoux, Victor	*Pardon Mon Affaire* (F) ('76)	a
Lanza, Paolo	*Cosi fan Tutte* (I)	a
LaPaglia, Anthony	*Innocent Blood* ('92)	a
Larson, Eric	*The Demon Wind* ('89)	a
Lattanzi, Matt	*Rich and Famous* ('81)	a
Lauer, Andrew	*Necessary Roughness* ('91)	a
Laughlin, Brad	*Dreamaniac* ('88)	a
Laughlin, John	*Crimes of Passion* ('84)	a
Laughlin. John	*Footloose* ('84)	a
Lauservic, Zarko	*Officer with a Rose*	a
Lauterbach, Heiner	*Men* (G) ('85)	a, p
Lavant, Dennis	*Les Amants du Pont Neuf* (F) ('84)	a, p
Lavoy, Zachary	*Parenthood* ('89)	a
Law, John Phillip	*Angel Eyes* ('91)	a
Law, John Phillip	*The Eye on the Wall*	a, p
Law, John Phillip	*The Love Machine* ('71)	a

Law, John Phillip	*Open Season* (Sp) ('74)	a
Lawrence, Andre	*Loving and Laughing*	a, p
Lawrence, Bruno	*Smash Palace* (A) ('81)	a, p
Lawrence, Bruno	*The Quiet Earth* (A) ('85)	a, p
Laws, Barry	*Shadow Play* ('86)	a
Lawson, Dennis	*Dead Head*	a
Layne, Scott	*Vice Academy II* ('90)	a
Lazaroff, Steve	*Slammer Girls* ('86)	a
Lazenby, George	*Last Harem*	a
Lazovic, Danilo	*The Golden Apple*	a, p
Le Bel, Roger	*Night Zoo* (C) ('87)	a
Le Duc, Richard	*Le Plaisir Serieux* (F)	a
Le Fay, Justine	*Toga Party* ('79)	a
Le Fever, Chuck	*Naked Gun 2½* ('91)	a
Lefevre, Adam	*Return of the Secaucus 7* ('80)	a, p
Le Moine, Jean Rene	*Cosi fan Tutte* (I)	a
Leaud, Jean-Pierre	*The 400 Blows* (F) ('59)	a
Lee, Christopher	*To the Devil—A Daughter* (B) ('76)	a
Lee, Donnie	*Mini-Skirt Love* ('68)	a
Lee, Jason Scott	*Map of the Human Heart* ('92)	a
Lee, John	*The Master Beater* ('68)	a
Lee, Mark	*The Everlasting Secret Family* (A) ('89)	a
Lee, Mark	*Gallipoli* (A) ('81)	a, p
Lee, Sheldon	*Blazing Stewardesses* ('75)	a
Legarrata, Juan Carlos	*La India* (M)	p
Legein, Marc	*Secrets of Love* (F) ('86)	a
LeGros, James	*Point Break* ('91)	a
Leguary, Jean Claude	*Scout Toujours* (F)	a, p
Leguizamo, John	*Casualties of War* ('89)	a
Leibman, Ron	*Norma Rae* ('79)	a
Leibman, Ron	*Where's Poppa?* ('70)	a
Leibman, Ron	*Your Three Minutes Are Up* ('73)	a
Leina, Jonathan	*Police* (F) ('85)	a
Leinert, Mike	*Easy Wheels* ('89)	a
Lemieux, Vincent	*Desert Passion* ('92)	a
Lemmon, Jack	*Avanti* ('72)	a
Lemmon, Jack	*Save the Tiger* ('73)	a
Lena, Lorenzo	*The Flavor of Corn*	a
Lena, Lorenzo	*Fotografando Patrizia* (I)	a
Lena, Lorenzo	*Via Montenapoleone* (I)	a
Lenhart, Lane	*Prototype X29A* ('92)	p
Lennon, John	*Imagine* ('88)	a, p
Leonard, Robert Sean	*Much Ado About Nothing* ('93)	a
Leonardi, Marco	*Fernandino* (I)	a
Leonardi, Marco	*Like Water for Chocolate* (M) ('93)	a, p
Leonardi, Marco	*Ultimo Minuto* (I)	a

Lepetit, Xavier	*Les Branches à Saint Tropez* (F)	a
Leroy, Phillippe	*The Frightened Woman*	a
Lester, Jeff	*In the Cold of the Night* ('90)	a
Lester, Mark	*La Prima Volta Sull Erba* (I)	a
Lester, Mark	*Redneck* (I) ('73)	a, p
Leung, Tony	*L'Amant* (aka *The Lover*) (F) ('92)	a
Levine, Ben	*Drifting* (Is) ('82)	a, p
Levine, Jerry	*Casual Sex?* ('88)	a
Levine, Mark	*Spring Fever* ('88)	a
Levine, Ted	*The Silence of the Lambs* ('91)	a
Levisetti, Emile	*Sexual Response* ('92)	a
Levitt, Steve	*Blue Movies* ('87)	a
Levy, Dani	*Robby Kallepaul*	a, p
Levy, Dani	*Same to You*	a, p
Levy, Eugene	*Armed and Dangerous* ('86)	a
Lewis, Huey	*Short Cuts* ('93)	p
Lewis, Russell	*Young Winston* (B) ('72)	a
Lewis, Tim	*The Minx* (aka *Dr. Minx*) ('68)	a, p
Lhermitte, Thierry	*Fucking Fernard* (F) ('87)	a, p
Lhermitte, Thierry	*The Last Romantic Lover* (F) ('79)	a
Lhermitte, Thierry	*Les Bronzes* (F) ('79)	a
Lhermitte, Thierry	*Until September* ('84)	a
Lichtenstein, Mitchell	*Streamers* ('82)	a
Ligarche, Sebastian	*La Tentacion*	a, p
Lindhart, Buzzy	*The Groove Tube* ('72)	a, p
Lindon, Vincent	*Half Moon Street* ('86)	a
Lindstrom, Jorgen	*Night Games* (S) ('67)	a, p
Lionello, Alberto	*'Til Marriage Do Us Part* (I) ('74)	a
Liotta, Ray	*Unlawful Entry* ('92)	a
Lipton, Robert	*Lethal Woman* ('88)	a
Lithgow, John	*Traveling Man* ('89)	a
Lloyd, Christopher	*Track 29* ('88)	a
LoBianco, Tony	*The Honeymoon Killers* ('69)	a
Lockhart, Calvin	*Melinda* ('72)	a
Lockwood, Paul	*Finders Keepers, Lovers Weepers* ('68)	a
Loeffer, Peter	*Wager of Love* ('90)	a
Loggia, Robert	*An Officer and a Gentleman* ('82)	a
Lone, John	*M. Butterfly* ('93)	a
Long, Alan	*The Pickup* ('75)	a
Lonsdale, Michael	*The Phantom of Liberty* (F) ('68)	a
Lopez, Carlos	*Les Nuits Fauves (Savage Nights)* (F) ('93)	a
Lopez, Sergio	*Los Colgials* (M)	a, p
Louden, Jay	*Opposing Force* ('87)	a
Louganis, Greg	*Inside Out 3* ('92)	a
Love, Allen	*The Apple* ('80)	a

Lovelock, Ray	*At Last, at Last*	a
Lovelock, Ray	*Autopsy* ('78)	a
Lovelock, Ray	*L'Annello Matrimoniale* (I)	a
Lovelock, Ray	*To Be Twenty* ('81)	a, p
Lowe, Rob	*About Last Night* ('86)	a, p
Lowe, Rob	*Bad Influence* ('90)	a
Lowe, Rob	*Masquerade* ('88)	a
Lowe, Rob	*The Outsiders* ('83)	a
Lowe, Rob	*Youngblood* ('86)	a
Lowell, Skip	*The Sweater Girls* ('78)	a
Lowitsch, Klaus	*Despair* (G) ('79)	a
Lubac, Bob	*Stitches* ('85)	a
Luchini, Fabrice	*Et La Tendresse Bordel #2* (F) ('84)	a
Lukaszewicz, Algiero	*The Story of Sin*	a, p
Luke, Benny	*La Cage aux Folles* (F) ('78)	a
Luke, Jorge	*La Horas Jaguar* (M)	a
Luke, Jorge	*Pueblo Maldito* (M)	a, p
Lumsden, David	*A Prayer for the Dying* (B) ('87)	a
Lundgren, Dolph	*The Punisher* ('82)	a
Lundgren, Dolph	*Showdown in Little Tokyo* ('91)	a, p
Lundy, Wayne	*Wild Gypsies* ('69)	a
Luther, Michael	*Malibu Beach* ('78)	a
Lutz, Rick	*Auditions* ('78)	a, p
Luz, Franc	*Love Scenes* ('84)	a
Lycos, Tom	*Sweetie* (A) ('89)	a, p
Lynas, Jeffrey	*Lies My Father Told Me* ('75)	a
Lynch, Barry	*Small World*	a
Lynch, John	*Cal* (B) ('84)	a
Lynch, John	*Railway Station Man* ('92)	a
Lynch, Richard	*Open Season* (Sp) ('74)	a
Lyon, Steve	*Campus Man* ('87)	a
Lyon, Steve	*Valet Girls* ('83)	a
Lyons, James	*Poison* ('91)	a
Lyons, Robert F.	*Dealing* ('72)	a
Lyons, Robert F.	*The Todd Killings* ('71)	a
Lys, Agata	*La Iniciacion en el Amor* (M)	a
Maccanti, Roberto	*1900* (I) ('77)	p
Macchia, Gianni	*Emanuelle Perche Vilenza Alledonnne* (I)	a
Macchia, Gianni	*Fiorina la Vacca* (I)	a
Macchia, John	*Pink Motel* ('82)	a
Maccione, Aldo	*Il Piatto Piange* (I)	a
MacCorkindale, Simon	*Riddle of the Sands* (B) ('84)	a
MacCorkindale, Simon	*Robbers of the Sacred Mountain* (B) ('83)	a
MacDonald, Gordon	*Brain Damage* ('87)	a
MacDonald, Ian	*Snake Eater III: His Law* ('92)	a

MacDonald, Ryan	*Future Kick* ('91)	a
MacFayden, Angus	*The Lost Language of Cranes* (B) ('92)	a, p
MacGowan, Jack	*Age of Consent* (A) ('69)	a
MacGuire, Gerald	*Kitty and the Bagman* (A) ('82)	a, p
MacKay, Geoffrey	*One Night Only* ('89)	a
Mackintosh, Steven	*London Kills Me* (B) ('91)	a, p
MacLachlan, Kyle	*Blue Velvet* ('86)	a, p
Macy, Bill	*Oh! Calcutta* ('72)	a, p
Madsen, Michael	*Fatal Instinct* (aka *To Kill For*) ('92)	a
Madsen, Michael	*House in the Hills*	a
Maetro, Carlos	*Desiderando Giulia* (I)	a, p
Magwaza, Conrad	*Shaka Zulu* ('83)	a
Maheu, Gilles	*Night Zoo* (C) ('87)	a
Mahinda, Edwin	*The Kitchen Toto* ('87)	a, p
Maia, Nino Leal	*Lady on the Bus* (Br) ('78)	a
Maiden, Tony	*Spaced Out* (B) ('80)	a
Maie, Hiromi	*Lady Chatterly in Tokyo* (J)	a
Maien, Michael	*2069: A Sex Odyssey* (G)	a
Major, Richard	*While the Cat's Away*	p
Malavoy, Christopher	*Peril* (F) ('85)	a, p
Malavoy, Christopher	*Rebus*	p
Malet, Laurent	*Invitation au Voyage* (F) ('83)	a
Malet, Laurent	*Jacko & Lise* (F) ('82)	a
Malik, Art	*Jewel in the Crown* ('84)	a
Malis, Steve	*Can't Stop the Music* ('80)	a
Malis, Steve	*Venus Flytrap* ('88)	a, p
Malkovich, John	*Making Mr. Right* ('86)	a
Malkovich, John	*Queens Logic* ('91)	a
Malkovich, John	*The Sheltering Sky* ('90)	a, p
Malone, Joseph	*Inside Out* ('92)	a
Mancuso, Nick	*Nightwing* ('79)	a
Maniatis, Mihalis	*Angel* (Gr)	a, p
Mann, Kris	*Slugs* ('87)	a, p
Mann, Ray	*King Frat*	a
Manson, Andrew	*Love Trap*	a
Mansort, George	*Le Plaisir Serieux* (F)	a
Mantee, Paul	*Robinson Crusoe on Mars* ('64)	a*
Mantegna, Joe	*Queens Logic* ('91)	a
Manzano, Jose Luis	*Colegas* (aka *Pals*) (Sp) ('82)	a, p
Manzano, Jose Luis	*El Chico Temido*	p
Manzano, Jose Luis	*El Pico* (M)	a
Manzano, Jose Luis	*Gentle Knives* (Sp) ('81)	a, p
Manzano, Jose Luis	*Navajaros* (Sp)	a, p
Manzon, Norman	*What Do You Say to a Naked Lady?* ('69)	a, p
Marachuk, Steve	*Hot Target* ('84)	a

Marcano, Joss	*Delivery Boys* ('84)	a
March, John	*Moon 44* (G) ('90)	a, p
Marchand, Guy	*Loulou* (F) ('80)	a
Marchinko, Ken	*Thrilled to Death* ('89)	a
Marcus, Stephen	*My Beautiful Laundrette* ('85)	a
Marecek, Heinz	*Tea for Three* (G) ('84)	a
Margold, William	*Auditions* ('78)	a, p
Margotta, Michael	*Breach of Contract*	a
Margotta, Michael	*Drive, He Said* ('72)	a, p
Marin, Cheech	*Cheech & Chong's Nice Dreams* ('81)	a
Marin, Cheech	*Things Are Tough All Over* ('82)	a
Marinaro, Ed	*Dead Aim* ('87)	a
Marion, Jean Marie	*Una Donna da Scoprire* (I)	a
Markle, Stephen	*Perfect Timing* ('84)	a
Marks, Alfred	*Fanny Hill* (S) ('83)	a
Marotte, Carl	*Pick-Up Summer* (C) ('79)	a
Marquette, Ron	*Red Shoe Diaries: Bounty Hunter* ('93)	a
Mars, Kenneth	*Desperate Characters* ('71)	a
Marsh, Gary	*Shampoo* ('75)	a
Marshall, Bryan	*Because of the Cats* ('73)	a, p
Marshall, Bryan	*Bliss* (A) ('85)	a
Marshall, David Anthony	*Another 48 HRS* ('90)	a
Marshall, James	*Gladiator* ('92)	a
Marsina, Antonio	*Gran Bollito* (I)	a, p
Martial, Jacques	*White and Black* (F)	a, p
Martin, Claude	*Hot Sex in Bangkok* (F)	a, p
Martin, Ray	*Young Lady Chatterley* (B) ('76)	a, p
Martinez, Nacho	*Matador* (Sp) ('86)	a
Martinez, Ricardo	*Muerte en la Playa* (M)	a
Marvell, Leon	*Leonora*	a, p
Marx, Horst-Gunter	*Venus Trap* (G)	a
Marzio, Duileo	*Two to Tango* (I) ('88)	a
Mase, Marino	*Summer Temptations* (I)	a
Massino, Foschi	*Orlando Furioso* (I)	a
Masters, Ben	*Key Exchange* ('85)	a
Mastroianni, Marcello	*Henry IV* (I) ('85)	a
Mastroianni, Marcello	*Kiss the Other Sheik* (I/F) ('68)	a
Mastroianni, Marcello	*La Grande Bouffe* (F) ('73)	a
Mastroianni, Marcello	*Leo the Last* (B) ('70)	a
Mastroianni, Marcello	*What?* (I) ('73)	a, p
Mateau, Sergi	*Laura: Del Ciel Llega de Noche*	a, p
Mateo, Steve	*Vice Academy III* ('91)	a
Mateos, Julian	*Kashmiri Run* ('69)	a, p
Mathers, James	*Aria* ('87)	a, p
Matheson, Tim	*Animal House* ('78)	a

Matheson, Tim	*Impulse* ('84)	a
Mathews, Christopher	*Some Like It Sexy*	a
Mathews, Stephen Kean	*Young Lady Chatterley, Part II* (B) ('85)	a
Matshikiza, John	*Dust* (F) ('85)	a
Matsunaga, Teruho	*Lady Chatterly in Tokyo* (J)	a
Matthau, Walter	*Pete 'n' Tillie* ('72)	a
Matthey, Peter	*New York Nights* ('83)	a
Mattia, Joe	*East End Hustle* (B) ('76)	a
Mauch, Billy	*Anthony Adverse* ('36)	a
Maunder, Wayne	*The Seven Minutes* ('71)	a
Maurel, Julien	*In Extremis*	a
Maury, Derrel	*Massacre at Central High* ('76)	a
Mauro, Joseph E.	*Affairs of the Heart* ('92)	a
Max, Ron	*Heated Vengeance* ('84)	a
Maya, Ariel	*Machos*	a
Mazmanian, Marius	*Video Vixens* ('73)	a
McAllister, Dennis	*Baring It All* ('85)	a
McCarthy, Andrew	*Heaven Help Us* ('85)	a
McCarthy, Andrew	*Less Than Zero* ('87)	a
McCarthy, Andrew	*Year of the Gun* ('91)	a
McCarthy, Brett	*The Doors* ('91)	a
McClean, Warren	*Opposing Force* ('87)	a
McCleery, Gary	*Hard Choices* ('84)	a
McCloskey, Leigh	*Fraternity Vacation* ('85)	a
McClure, Doug	*The Bananas Boat* (B) ('78)	a
McClure, Doug	*The House Where Evil Dwells* ('82)	a
McClure, Marc	*Grim Prairie Tales* ('90)	a
McCoy, Matt	*Fraternity Vacation* ('85)	a
McCracken, Jeff	*Running Brave* ('83)	a, p
McCrane, Paul	*Hotel New Hampshire* ('84)	a
McCrea, Joel	*The Palm Beach Story* ('42)	a, p
McDermott, Dylan	*Hardware* ('90)	a
McDermott, Dylan	*The Fear Inside* ('92)	a
McDermott, Pat	*Joe* ('70)	a
McDonald, Bruce	*Return of the Secaucus 7* ('80)	a, p
McDonald, Christopher	*Conflict of Interest* ('92)	a
McDonald, Joshua	*11 Days, 11 Nights* ('88)	a, p
McDowell, Malcolm	*Britannia Hospital* (B) ('82)	a, p
McDowell, Malcolm	*Caligula* ('79)	a, p
McDowell, Malcolm	*Cat People* ('82)	a, p
McDowell, Malcolm	*A Clockwork Orange* ('71)	a, p
McDowell, Malcolm	*Gulag* ('84)	a
McDowell, Malcolm	*if. . . .* (B) ('68)	a
McDowell, Malcolm	*Jezebel's Kiss* ('90)	a
McDowell, Malcolm	*O Lucky Man* (B) ('73)	a
McDowell, Malcolm	*The Passage* (B) ('79)	a

McDowell, Malcolm	*Voyage of the Damned* ('76)	a
McElroy, Scott	*Desert Passion* ('92)	a
McEnery, Peter	*Entertaining Mr. Sloane* (B) ('70)	a
McGann, Paul	*The Rainbow* (B) ('89)	a, p
McGavin, Darren	*Zero to Sixty* ('78)	a
McGill, Bruce	*Out Cold* ('89)	a, p
McGill, Everett	*Field of Honor* ('86)	a
McGill, Everett	*Quest for Fire* ('82)	a
McGill, Everett	*The Silver Bullet* ('85)	a
McGinley, Ted	*Revenge of the Nerds* ('84)	a
McGlashan, Don	*Linda's Boy*	a
McGrath, Liam	*The Clay Farmers*	a
McGuire, Mitchell	*Oh! Calcutta* ('72)	a, p
McIntyre, Tim	*The Choirboys* ('77)	a
McKechnie, J. R.	*The Burning* ('81)	a
McKellan, Ian	*The Priest of Love* (B) ('81)	a, p
McKellan, Ian	*Walter* (B) ('82)	a
McKellar, Don	*Highway 61* ('91)	a
McKenna, T. P.	*Ulysses* (B) ('67)	a
McKenna, Travis	*Cheerleader Camp* ('88)	a
McKeon, Doug	*Mischief* ('85)	a
McLane, Robert	*Up!* ('76)	a
McLean, Brandon	*King of the Bean*	a
McMahon, Julian	*Wet and Wild Summer* (A)	a
McNally, Kevin	*Not Quite Paradise* (B) ('86)	a
McNamara, Brian	*When the Party's Over* ('91)	a
McNeice, Ian	*The Lonely Passion of Judith Hearne* (B) ('87)	a
McNichol, Jimmy	*Night Warning* ('81)	a
McNicoll, Peter	*Dragonslayer* (B) ('81)	a
McShane, Ian	*Pussycat, Pussycat I Love You* ('70)	a
McShane, Ian	*Yesterday's Hero* (B) ('79)	a
McWilliams, Joss	*The Gold and the Glory* (A)	a
Meader, Vaughn	*Linda Lovelace for President*	a, p
Meadows, Stephen	*Night Eyes* ('90)	a
Meek, Jeff	*Night of the Cyclone* ('90)	a
Melani, Danele	*Salome* (I) ('85)	a
Melcher, John	*Opposing Force* ('87)	a
Melvin, Murray	*Joseph Andrews* (B) ('77)	a
Melymick, Mark	*Devlin* ('92)	a
Mendelsohn, Ben	*The Year My Voice Broke* ('87)	a
Meredith, Burgess	*Such Good Friends* ('71)	a
Merenda, Luc	*Action* (I)	a, p
Merenda, Luc	*Bad Thoughts* (I)	a, p
Merenda, Luc	*Pensione Paura* (I)	a, p
Merino, Ricardo	*Las Eroticas Vacaiones de Stela* (M) ('75)	a

Merlo, Luis	*La Señora*	a
Metrano, Art	*Police Academy II* ('85)	a
Metsers, Hugo	*Dear Boys* (D) ('80)	a
Meyer, Fabio	*Blue Island*	a
Meyer, Michael	*Mirror Images* ('91)	a
Meyers, Anthony	*Hamlet* (B) ('69)	a, p
Meyers, David	*Hamlet* (B) ('69)	a, p
Meyers, David	*The Tempest* (B) ('82)	p
Meza, Arthur	*Dona Herlinda and Her Son* (M) ('86)	a, p
Mezzobuorno, Vittorio	*L'Homme Blesse* (F) ('88)	a, p
Michieli, Danilo	*Love, Lust & Ecstasy* (Gr)	a
Michlin, Barry	*Wild Gypsies* ('69)	a, p
Migicovsky, Alan	*Snapshot* ('77)	a
Mikulski, Mark	*Stuck on You* ('84)	a
Milian, Thomas	*Cat Chaser* ('88)	p
Milian, Thomas	*Identification of a Woman* (I)	a, p
Milione, Lou	*Six Degrees of Separation* ('93)	a, p
Militi, Ricardo	*Cat Murkil and the Silks*	a
Militi, Ricardo	*Cruisin' High* ('76)	a
Miller, Dennis	*Last of the Knucklemen* (A)	a
Miller, Jason	*Vengeance* ('86)	a, p
Miller, Scott	*Play Dirty* (B) ('68)	a
Mills, Danny	*Pink Flamingos* ('72)	a, p
Mills, Joel W.	*Student Confidential* ('87)	a, p
Mills, Thomas	*Luther the Geek* ('88)	a
Milne, Christopher	*Felicity* (F) ('79)	a, p
Minervini, Ulisse	*Biccolt Fuochi* (I)	a
Minsker, Andy	*Broken Noses* ('92)	a
Mioni, Stefano	*Unragazzo* (I)	a, p
Mirandola, Vasco	*Mediterraneo* (I) ('91)	a
Mitchell, Albert	*Naked Instinct* ('93)	a
Mitchell, Cameron	*The Midnight Man* ('74)	a
Mitchell, Mark	*The Outing* ('86)	a, p
Mitchell, Scott	*Inside Out* ('92)	p
Mitchell, Warren	*The Bananas Boat* (B) ('78)	a
Mitchell, Warren	*Norman Loves Rose* ('82)	a
Mitchell, Warren	*Stand Up Virgin Soldiers* (B)	a, p
Mitchum, Christopher	*Once* ('74)	a
Modesto	*Fortune and Men's Eyes* ('71)	a
Modine, Matthew	*Birdy* ('85)	a
Modine, Matthew	*Hotel New Hampshire* ('84)	a
Modine, Matthew	*Private School* ('83)	a
Modine, Matthew	*Streamers* ('82)	a, p
Modine, Matthew	*Vision Quest* ('85)	a
Moeller, Flemmin Quist	*Ladies on the Rocks* (Da) ('83)	a
Moir, Richard	*Heatwave* (A) ('83)	a

Moir, Richard	*Indecent Obsession* (A) ('85)	a
Mol, Albert	*Dear Boys* (D) ('80)	a
Molfesi, Fabio	*Il Buon Soldato* (I)	a
Molina, Alfred	*Manifesto* (Y) ('88)	a
Molina, Alfred	*Prick Up Your Ears* (B) ('87)	a
Molina, Pedro	*Depravation*	a, p
Molinas, Joris	*My Father's Glory* (F) ('91)	a
Monahan, Dan	*Porky's* ('81)	a
Monahan, Dan	*Porky's II* ('83)	a, p
Monahan, Dan	*Porky's Revenge* ('85)	a
Monoson, Lawrence	*Friday the 13th, Part IV* ('84)	a
Monoson, Lawrence	*The Last American Virgin* ('82)	a
Montagnani, Renzo	*Fiorina la Vacca* (I)	a
Montana, Michael	*Affairs of the Heart* ('92)	a
Montanary, Michel	*Jacko & Lise* (F) ('82)	a
Montand, Yves	*Claire de Femme* (F)	a
Montesi, Jorge	*Sentimental Reasons*	p
Montgomery, Chad	*Nightmare at Shadow Woods* ('83)	a
Montgomery, Lee	*Prime Risk* ('84)	a
Montgomery, Mark	*Thunderbolt and Lightfoot* ('75)	a
Montgomery, Nick	*Torch Song Trilogy* ('88)	a
Montilla, Carlos	*Mujer de Fuego* (M)	a
Monty, Mike	*Bloodline* ('79)	a
Moore, Dickie	*Blonde Venus* ('32)	a
Moore, Dudley	*10* ('79)	a
Moore, Kenny	*Personal Best* ('82)	a, p
Moore, Michael	*Border Heat* ('88)	a
Moore, Michael	*Cheating Hearts*	a
Moore, Robert	*Tell Me That You Love Me, Junie Moon* ('70)	a
Moore, Stephen	*Under Suspicion* (B) ('91)	p
Morales, Esai	*Naked Tango* ('91)	a
Moran, Paco	*Las Que Enpiezan a los 15 Anos*	a
More, Kenneth	*Adventures of Sadie* (B) ('55)	a
Morena, Claudio	*The Emerald Forest* ('85)	a
Moreno, Jaime	*Amor Clego* (M) ('80)	a, p
Moreno, Jaime	*El Sex Sentido* (M)	a
Moreno, Jaime	*La India* (M)	a
Moreno, Jaime	*Las del Talon* (M)	a
Moreno, Jaime	*Las Fabulosas del Reventon* (M)	a
Moreno, Jaime	*Solo Para Damas* (M)	a
Moresti, Nanni	*Bianca*	p
Morgan, Stafford	*Exotic Image III*	a
Mori, Richard	*Wrong World*	a
Moriarity, Daniel	*The Other Woman* ('92)	a
Moriarty, Michael	*My Old Man's Place* ('72)	a
Moriarity, Michael	*Reborn* ('78)	a

Moridis, Theodore	*The Woman Who Dreamed*	a
Morissey, David	*Drowning by Numbers* (B) ('88)	a
Morressey, David	*Waterland* ('92)	a
Morrow, Rob	*Private Resort* ('85)	a
Mortensen, Claus Bender	*Friends Forever* (Da) ('86)	p
Mortensen, Viggo	*The Indian Runner* ('91)	a, p
Mortensen, Viggo	*The Reflecting Skin* ('90)	a
Moses, Mark	*The Tracker* ('88)	a
Mosley, Roger	*Drum* ('76)	a
Moss, Robert	*Spring Fever* ('88)	a
Moss, Warrick	*Candy Regentag* (A)	a, p
Mossley, Robin	*Riding Fast* ('82)	a
Mossy, Carlo	*Her Summer Vacation*	a
Mostel, Joshua	*Harry and Tonto* ('74)	a
Moulder-Brown, John	*Claudia* ('89)	a
Moulder-Brown, John	*The Confessions of Felix Krull* (B) ('82)	a, p
Moulder-Brown, John	*The Deep End* (B) ('70)	a
Moulder-Brown, John	*King Queen Knave* (B) ('72)	a
Moulder-Brown, John	*Ludwig* (I/G/F) ('73)	a
Mouton, Benjamin	*Sister, Sister* ('87)	a
Moyle, Allan Bozo	*East End Hustle* (B) ('76)	a
Mozzilo, Brian	*A Night in Heaven* ('83)	a
Mpofu, Bekhithemba	*A Dry White Season* ('89)	a
Mucari, Carlo	*La Lingua* (I)	a
Mucari, Carlo	*Lady Chatterly's Story*	a
Mulcahy, Jack	*Porky's* ('81)	a
Mulder, Paul	*Silent Night, Deadly Night* ('84)	a
Mulkey, Chris	*Patti Rocks* ('87)	a, p
Mullaly, Richard	*Street Smart* ('87)	a
Mullinar, Rod	*Breakfast in Paris* ('81)	a
Mullins, Michael	*The Pom-Pom Girls* ('76)	a
Munne, Pep	*L'Amore Sporco* (I)	a
Munster, Klaus	*2069: A Sex Odyssey* (G)	a
Murata, Takehiro	*Okoge* (J)	a
Murdocco, Vince	*Flesh Gordon 2* ('90)	a
Mure, Stefano	*La Lingua* (I)	a
Musante, Tony	*The Detective* ('68)	a
Music, Al	*California Girls* ('84)	a
Mutrux, Floyd	*Cover Me Babe* ('72)	a
Muxeneder, Franz	*2069: A Sex Odyssey* (G)	a
Muxeneder, Franz	*Los Encantos de un Alpinista* (M)	a, p
Myers, Michael	*So I Married an Axe Murderer* ('93)	a
N!xau	*The Gods Must Be Crazy* (SA) ('81)	a
Nagurney, Nickolas	*Fun Down There* ('88)	p
Nail, Jimmy	*Auf Weiderzen, Pet*	a, p

Nakahara, Takeo	*Okoge* (J)	a
Namath, Joe	*C.C. and Company* ('70)	a
Napier, Charles	*Harry, Cherry & Raquel* ('69)	a
Nash, Danny	*The Clinic* (A) ('82)	a, p
Nassi, Joe	*Sorority House Massacre* ('87)	a
Naughton, David	*An American Werewolf in London* ('81)	a, p
Naughton, David	*The Boy in Blue* ('86)	a
Naya, Juan Carlos	*Senza Buccia (aka Skin Deep)* (I)	a, p
Nazario, Al	*Incoming Freshman* ('79)	a
Ndebele, Ben Louis	*Forever Young, Forever Free* (SA) ('76)	a
Neary, Robert	*Torch Song Trilogy* ('88)	a
Nedrow, Craig	*A Night in Heaven* ('83)	a
Neeson, Liam	*City of Darkness* (B)	a
Neeson, Liam	*Duet for One* ('86)	a
Neeson, Liam	*Under Suspicion* (B) ('91)	a, p
Negret, François	*Night and Day* (F)	a
Neidorf, David	*Rainbow Drive* ('90)	a
Neidorf, Ron	*Guistano* (I)	a
Neil, Christopher	*Adventures of a Plumber's Mate* (B) ('78)	a
Neil, Christopher	*Adventures of a Private Eye* (B) ('77)	a
Neill, Sam	*The Piano* (NZ) ('93)	a
Neill, Sam	*Possession* (F/G) ('81)	a
Neill, Sam	*Reilly, Ace of Spies* ('84)	a
Neilson, John	*Shark's Treasure* ('75)	a
Nelevic, Mladen	*Heads or Tails* (F) ('82)	a, p
Nelson, Bob	*Sorceress* ('82)	a
Nelson, Haywood	*Evilspeak* ('81)	a
Nelson, Haywood	*Mixed Company* ('74)	a
Nelson, Judd	*Fandango* ('85)	a
Nene, Oliver	*Thieves of Fortune* ('89)	a
Nero, Franco	*A Flower in His Mouth* (I) ('75)	a
Nero, Franco	*Redneck* (I) ('73)	a
Nero, Franco	*The Salamander* (I/B)	a
Nero, Franco	*Submission* (I) ('77)	a
Nero, Franco	*Victory March* (I) ('76)	a
Nero, Franco	*The Virgin and the Gypsy* ('70)	a
Newley, Anthony	*Hieronymus Merkin* (B) ('69)	a
Newman, Paul	*Cool Hand Luke* ('67)	a
Nichols, Wade	*Teenage Runaway*	a, p
Nicholson, Jack	*Carnal Knowledge* ('71)	a
Nicholson, Jack	*Chinatown* ('74)	a
Nicholson, Jack	*The Passenger* ('75)	a
Nicholson, Jack	*The Postman Always Rings Twice* ('79)	a

Nicholson, Jack	*Prizzi's Honor* ('85)	a
Nicholson, Jack	*Reds* ('81)	a
Nicholson, Stephan	*I Remember Love*	a
Niklas, Jan	*Colonel Redl* (G/H) ('84)	a
Nilsson, Kjell	*The Road Warrior* (aka *Mad Max 2*) (A) ('81)	a
Nilsson, Rob	*Heat and Sunlight* ('88)	a, p
Nimoy, Leonard	*Catlow* ('71)	a
Nock, Thomas	*Alpine Fire* ('86)	a, p
Nock, Thomas	*Gemini the Twin Star*	a
Nolan, John	*The World Is Full of Married Men* (B) ('79)	a, p
Nolan, Tom	*School Spirit* ('84)	a
Nolan, Tom	*Yanks* ('79)	a
Nolte, Nick	*Down and Out in Beverly Hills* ('86)	a
Nolte, Nick	*North Dallas Forty* ('79)	a
Nolte, Nick	*Return to Macon County* ('75)	a
Nolte, Nick	*Weeds* ('87)	a, p
Nolte, Nick	*Who'll Stop the Rain* ('78)	a, p
Nomicas, Chris	*To Kopitai Bomba*	a
Nomikos, Christos	*Midnight Strangers* (Gr)	a
Nordling, Jeffrey	*And the Band Played On* ('93)	a
Noriega, Ricardo	*Mariposa Dilleadas*	a, p
Norman, Zack	*Sitting Ducks* ('78)	a
Norris, Mike	*Born American* ('86)	a
North, Jay	*Maya* ('66)	a
Norton, Ken	*Drum* ('76)	a
Norton, Ken	*Mandingo* ('75)	a
Norton, Richard	*Lady Dragon* ('92)	a
Noteas, Elias	*Chain of Desire* ('92)	a
Noth, Christopher	*Jakarta* ('88)	a
Nouri, Michael	*Thieves of Fortune* ('89)	a
Novi, Enrique	*Las Mujeras de Jeremias* (M)	a
Noy, Zachi	*Baby Love* (Is) ('83)	a
Noy, Zachi	*Going Steady* (Is) ('80)	a
Noy, Zachi	*Hot Bubblegum* (Is) ('83)	a
Noy, Zachi	*Private Maneuvers* (Is)	a
Noy, Zachi	*Private Popsicle* (Is) ('82)	a
Nozick, Bruce	*Hit the Dutchman* ('92)	a
Nureyev, Rudolf	*Exposed* ('83)	a
Nureyev, Rudolf	*Nureyev*	a, p
Nureyev, Rudolf	*Valentino* ('77)	a, p
O, George	*Summer Job* ('88)	a
O'Brien, Myles	*Evil Laugh* ('86)	a
O'Brien, Tom	*The Big Parade* (silent) ('26)	a
O'Bryan, Patrick	*Relentless* ('89)	a
O'Donnell, Chris	*School Ties* ('92)	a

O'Donovan, Ross	*Starstruck* (A) ('82)	a
O'Hara, Adore	*Auditions* ('78)	a
O'Keefe, Michael	*Finders Keepers* ('84)	a
O'Keefe, Miles	*Dead On: Relentless II* ('91)	a, p
O'Keefe, Miles	*The Drifter* ('88)	a
O'Keefe, Miles	*S.A.S San Salvador* ('82)	a
O'Keefe, Miles	*Tarzan, the Ape Man* ('81)	a
O'Leary, Michael	*Fatal Games* ('84)	a
O'Leary, William	*Bull Durham* ('88)	a
O'Leary, William	*Nice Girls Don't Explode* ('87)	a
O'Malley, Michael	*Not Tonight, Darling* (B) ('71)	a, p
O'Neal, Griffin	*Night Children*	a, p
O'Neal, Ron	*Superfly* ('72)	a
O'Neal, Ryan	*The Big Bounce* ('69)	a
O'Neal, Ryan	*Oliver's Story* ('78)	a
O'Neal, Ryan	*Partners* ('82)	a
O'Neal, Ryan	*The Wild Rovers* ('71)	a
O'Neil, Paddy	*Fanny Hill* (S) ('83)	a
O'Neill, Michael	*Sea of Love* ('89)	a
O'Quinn, Terry	*The Forgotten One* ('90)	a
O'Quinn, Terry	*The Stepfather* ('87)	a, p
O'Reilly, Cyril	*Bloody Birthday* ('80)	a
O'Reilly, Cyril	*Porky's* ('81)	a
O'Ross, Ed	*Play Nice* ('92)	a
O'Shea, Paul	*Among the Cinders* ('84)	a, p
Obalshir, Claus	*Mieux Vaux Etie Riche at Bien Portant* (F)	a
Occhipinti, Andrea	*Bolero* ('84)	a
Occhipinti, Andrea	*Miranda* (I)	a, p
Ochsenknecht, Uwe	*Men* (G) ('85)	a, p
October, Gene	*Jubilee* ('77)	a
Ohlers, Hendrik	*Friends Forever* (Da) ('86)	a, p
Okada, Eiji	*Hiroshima, Mon Amour* (F) ('59)	a
Okada, Eiji	*Woman in the Dunes* (J) ('64)	a
Okay, Yaman	*40 Square Meters of Germany*	a
Olaivar, Brian	*A Boy Named Cocoy* (Pl)	a, p
Olandt, Ken	*Summer School* ('87)	a
Olbrychski, Daniel	*La Truite* (F) ('83)	a
Olbrychski, Daniel	*The Tin Drum* (G) ('79)	a
Oldman, Gary	*Chattahoochee* ('90)	a, p
Oldman, Gary	*Prick Up Your Ears* (B) ('87)	a
Oldman, Gary	*Track 29* ('88)	a
Olds, Gabriel	*Calendar Girl* ('93)	a
Olin, Ken	*Queens Logic* ('91)	a
Olivier, Laurence	*The Betsy* ('78)	a
Olivieri, Dennis	*Centerfold Girls* ('74)	a
Olivieri, Dennis	*The Naked Ape* ('73)	a

Oliviero, Silvio	*Graveyard Shift* ('86)	a
Oliviero, Silvio	*Graveyard Shift II: The Understudy* ('88)	a
Olkewicz, Walter	*Circle of Power* ('83)	a, p
Olmos, James Edward	*Wolfen* ('81)	a, p
Olmos, James Edward	*Zoot Suit* ('81)	a
Olsen, Arne	*Black Ice* ('92)	a
Olson, James	*The Andromeda Strain* ('70)	a
Ontkean, Michael	*Slapshot* ('77)	a
Ontkean, Michael	*Willie and Phil* ('80)	a
Orlando, Antonio	*Il Buon Soldato* (I)	a, p
Orlando, Antonio	*Rosen Kavalier* (I)	a, p
Orsini, Umberto	*Emmanuelle, Joys of a Woman* (F) ('75)	a
Orsini, Umberto	*Goodbye Emmanuelle* (F) ('81)	p
Osbon, Harry	*Auditions* ('78)	a
Osborn, Bill	*Double Jeopardy* ('92)	a
Oscarsson, Per	*Secrets* (Sw) ('71)	a
Osmond, Steve	*Recruits* ('86)	a
Ostan, Boris	*Years of Decision*	a
Otto, Barry	*Bliss* (A) ('85)	a
Owen, Clive	*Close My Eyes* (B) ('91)	a, p
Owens, Gary	*Midnight Cowboy* ('69)	a
Ozzimo, Carlos	*Andrea* (F) ('75)	a
Pace, Richard	*I Spit on Your Grave* ('78)	a, p
Pacino, Al	*Cruising* ('80)	a
Pacino, Al	*Panic in Needle Park* ('71)	a
Pacino, Al	*Scarecrow* ('73)	a
Pack, Roger	*The Man Who Couldn't Get Enough*	a
Packer, David	*Trust Me* ('87)	a
Packer, David	*You Can't Hurry Love* ('87)	a
Pagey, Florent	*Les Fauves* (F)	a, p
Palance, Jack	*The Mercenary* ('69)	a
Palese, Joe	*Sinners!* ('90)	a
Palillo, Ron	*Hellgate* ('89)	a
Palin, Michael	*American Friends* ('93)	a
Palin, Michael	*Life of Brian* (B) ('79)	a, p
Palin, Michael	*Monty Python's The Meaning of Life* (B) ('83)	a
Palin, Michael	*Pole to Pole* ('92)	a
Palmer, Gregg	*Flirting* (A) ('90)	a
Palomo, Armando	*Machos*	a, p
Panebianco, Richard	*China Girl* ('87)	a
Pankow, John	*To Live and Die in L.A.* ('85)	a
Pantsari, Buddy	*Legend of the Golden Goddess*	a
Pantsari, Buddy	*Trader Hornee* ('70)	a
Paole, Allen	*Macho Dancers* (P) ('88)	a

Pap, Enrico	La Bocca (I)	a
Paramore, Kiri	Flirting (A) ('90)	a
Pardo, Angel	The Deputy (Sp) ('78)	a, p
Pardo, Angel	Hidden Pleasures (Sp)	a
Paré, Michael	Instant Justice ('86)	a
Paré, Michael	Point of Impact	a
Paré, Michael	Sunset Heat ('91)	a
Paré, Michael	The Women's Club ('87)	a
Parisini, Daniele	Employees	a
Parker, Carl	Punishment of Anne	a, p
Parker, Carl	Score ('73)	a
Parker, Jameson	The Bell Jar ('79)	a, p
Parker, Nathaniel	Wide Sargasso Sea ('93)	a, p
Parks, Michael	The Bible ('66)	a
Parrish, Steve	Island of Love	a, p
Parrish, Steve	Midnight ('89)	a
Parrish, Steve	Scanners III: The Takeover ('92)	a
Parvin, Steve	Wheel of Fire ('84)	a
Pasdar, Adrian	Made in USA ('88)	a
Pasdar, Adrian	Vital Signs ('90)	a
Pasik, Mario	Otra Historia de Amor (I)	a
Pastore, Charles	A Night in Heaven ('83)	a
Patinkin, Mandy	Yentl ('84)	a
Patric, Jason	After Dark, My Sweet ('90)	a
Patrick, Alain	Thar She Blows	a
Patrick, Randal	By Dawn's Early Light ('90)	a
Patrick, Robert	Terminator 2: Judgment Day ('91)	a
Patrizi, Stefano	Conversation Piece (I) ('74)	a
Patrizi, Stefano	Fear (I)	a
Patrizi, Stefano	Nest of Vipers (I)	a, p
Patterson, Jimmy	Young Warriors ('83)	a
Patterson, Steve	Au Pair Girls (B) ('72)	a
Patton, Mark	Nightmare on Elm Street II ('85)	a
Pauer, Henrik	Time Stands Still (H) ('82)	a, p
Paul, Brian	Sea of Love ('89)	a
Paul, David	The Barbarians ('87)	a
Paul, Peter	The Barbarians ('87)	a
Paulin, Scott	The Last of Phillip Baxter ('86)	a, p
Pavel, Sami	L'Asino d'Oro (F)	a
Pavesi, Paolo	1900 (I) ('77)	a, p
Paxton, Bill	Boxing Helena ('93)	a
Paxton, Bill	Brain Dead ('90)	a
Paxton, Bill	The Dark Backward ('91)	a
Paxton, Bill	Monolith ('93)	a
Paxton, Bill	Weird Science ('85)	a
Payne, Dell	Buster and Billie ('74)	a
Peacock, Daniel	The Supergrass (B) ('85)	a

Pearl, Barry	*Grease* ('78)	a
Pearson, Christopher	*Frank and I* (B) ('83)	a
Peck, Bob	*Parker* ('84)	a, p
Peck, Brian	*The Last American Virgin* ('82)	a
Pegge, Edmund	*Stage Fright* ('87)	a
Pegram, Nigel	*Riders of the Storm* (B) ('86)	a, p
Peleki, Kamill	*The Philadelphia Act*	p
Pelhize, Daryl	*The Clinic* (A) ('82)	a, p
Penn, Bob	*The Hang-Up* ('69)	a
Penn, Christopher	*Made in USA* ('88)	a
Penn, Sean	*Bad Boys* ('83)	a
Penn, Sean	*Racing with the Moon* ('84)	a
Penn, Sean	*Taps* ('81)	a
Penner, Jonathan	*Amityville 1992: It's About Time* ('92)	a
Pepe, Paul	*Saturday Night Fever* ('77)	a
Peranio, Eddie	*Desperate Living* ('77)	a, p
Pereio, Paulo Cesar	*I Love You* (Br) ('82)	a, p
Perkins, Anthony	*Phaedra* (Gr) ('62)	a
Perkins, Anthony	*Ten Days Wonder* (F) ('72)	a
Perrin, François	*Le Roidescon* (F)	a, p
Perriz, Miguel Angel	*Las Mujeras de Jeremias* (M)	a
Perry, Jeff	*Naked Instinct* ('93)	a
Perze, Lazaro	*Fortune and Men's Eyes* ('71)	a
Peter, Bocsar	*The Annunciation*	a, p
Peter, Jens	*Wild Orchid* ('90)	a
Petersen, William	*Curacao* ('93)	a
Petersen, William	*To Live and Die in L.A.* ('85)	a, p
Phelen, Mark	*Sea of Love* ('89)	a
Phelps, Matthew	*Nightmare Sisters* ('87)	a
Phelps, Peter	*The Lighthorsemen* (A) ('87)	a, p
Phillips, Lou Diamond	*Dangerous Touch* ('93)	a
Piccoli, Michel	*Maladie d'Amour* (F) ('87)	a, p
Piccoli, Michel	*One Strange Affair*	a
Pichette, Jean-François	*A Corps Perdu* (F)	a, p
Picker, Josh	*Flirting* (A) ('90)	a
Pilon, Donald	*Two Women in Gold* ('70)	a, p
Pinchette, Jean-François	*Being at Home with Claude* (C) ('92)	a
Pineiro, Antonio B.	*Colegas* (aka *Pals*) (Sp) ('82)	a, p
Pintos, Adelo Garcia	*Night of the Pencils*	a, p
Pitt, Brad	*Kalifornia* ('93)	a
Pitt, Brad	*Thelma & Louise* ('91)	a
Pitts, Charles	*Supervixens* ('75)	a
Pitzalis, Federico	*Devil in the Flesh* (I) ('86)	a, p
Placido, Donato	*Caligula* (I) ('79)	a, p
Placido, Michele	*'Til Marriage Do Us Part* (I) ('74)	a
Placido, Michele	*Casotto* (I) ('77)	p
Placido, Michele	*Come Meet My Wife* ('77)	a

Placido, Michele	*Leap into the Void* (I) ('79)	a, p
Plank, Scott	*Red Shoe Diaries: Accidents Happen* ('93)	a
Po, Tang	*Kickboxer* ('89)	a
Poeschl, Hanno	*Querelle* (G) ('82)	a
Poindexter, Larry	*Toy Soldiers* ('91)	a
Polando, Ben	*Cat Murkil and the Silks*	a
Polden, Russel	*Games Lovers Play* (B)	a, p
Polkakof, Michael	*The Vals* ('83)	a
Pollard, Thommy	*Penitentiary* ('79)	a
Poncela, Eusebio	*Law of Desire* (Sp) ('86)	a, p
Pontremoli, David	*To Forget Venice* (I) ('79)	a, p
Poole, David	*Naked Instinct* ('93)	a
Popper, Alan	*Small Kill* ('91)	a
Porel, Marc	*The Innocent* (I) ('76)	a
Porel, Marc	*Una Spirale di Nebbia* (I) ('78)	a, p
Posse, Roberto	*Year of the Gun* ('91)	p
Potter, Michael	*Cruising* ('80)	a
Potter, Michael	*Female Trouble* ('74)	a, p
Potts, Cliff	*Cry for Me, Billy* ('72)	a
Potts, Daniel	*Greystoke, the Legend of Tarzan* ('84)	a
Pradal, Bruno	*The Contract* ('72)	a, p
Praed, Michael	*Son of Darkness: To Die For II* ('91)	a
Pratt, Robert	*The Hired Hand* ('71)	a, p
Prejean, Patrick	*The Legend of Frenchie King* (F) ('72)	a
Prentice, Keith	*Cruising* ('80)	a
Prescott, Robert	*Bachelor Party* ('84)	a
Pressman, Lawrence	*Hanoi Hilton* ('87)	a
Preston, Michael	*Last of the Knucklemen* (A)	a, p
Prete, Giancarlo	*Street Law* ('79)	a
Price, Alan	*Oh, Alfie* (B) ('75)	a
Price, Brendan	*Naughty Wives* (B)	a, p
Price, Mark	*Trick or Treat* ('86)	a
Priestly, Jason	*Calendar Girl* ('93)	a
Primus, Barry	*Autopsy* ('78)	a
Primus, Barry	*Been Down So Long It Looks Like Up* ('71)	a, p
Primus, Barry	*Night Games* ('79)	p
Prine, Andrew	*Simon, King of the Witches* ('71)	a
Pringle, Brian	*Drowning by Numbers* (B) ('88)	a, p
Prinz, Dietmar	*Beethoven's Nephew* (G) ('86)	a, p
Prochnow, Jurgen	*The Consequence* (G) ('77)	a
Prochnow, Jurgen	*Killing Cars* ('86)	a
Prochozia, John	*Taxi to Cairo* (G)	a
Profumo, Serfina	*Mandinga* (I) ('77)	a

Proval, David	*Nunzio* ('78)	a
Pryce, Jonathan	*Praying Mantis* (B) ('83)	a
Pryor, Richard	*Jo Jo Dancer, Your Life Is Calling* ('86)	a
Pucci, Robert	*Concrete War* (aka *Last Hour*) ('90)	a
Pucholt, Vladimir	*Loves of a Blonde* (Cz) ('65)	a
Purcell, James	*Playroom* ('89)	a
Purcell, James	*Schizo* ('77)	a
Putnam, Johnny	*Trash* ('70)	a, p
Quaid, Dennis	*The Big Easy* ('87)	a
Quaid, Dennis	*Everybody's All-American* ('88)	a
Quaid, Dennis	*Gorp* ('79)	a
Quaid, Dennis	*Innerspace* ('87)	a
Quaid, Dennis	*The Night the Lights Went Out in Georgia* ('81)	a
Quaid, Randy	*Frankenstein* ('93)	a
Quaid, Randy	*The Last Picture Show* ('71)	a
Quarter, James	*Intimate Obsession* ('92)	a
Queiro, Ignacio	*Los Colgials* (M)	a
Quester, Hughues	*Je T'Aime Mai Non Plus* (F)	a, p
Quigley, Paxton	*The Boob Tube* ('75)	a
Quill, Tom	*Staying Together* ('89)	a
Quinn, Aidan	*Blink* ('93)	a
Quinn, Aidan	*Crusoe* ('88)	a
Quinn, Aidan	*Desperately Seeking Susan* ('85)	a
Quinn, Aidan	*Reckless* ('84)	a, p
Quinn, Anthony	*Zorba the Greek* (Gr) ('64)	a
Quinn, I. William	*Love Me Deadly* ('72)	a, p
Quinn, J. C.	*Crisscross* ('92)	a
Quinoz, Luis Mario	*Playa Prohibide* (M)	a
Quintero, Lorenzo	*Man Facing Southeast* (Ar) ('86)	a
Race, Hugo	*In Too Deep* (A) ('90)	a, p
Raggetti, Tony	*Emmanuelle in the Country* (I) ('80)	a
Rajot, Pierre-Loup	*A Nos Amours* (F) ('84)	a, p
Railsback, Steve	*Lifeforce* ('85)	a
Rally, Steve	*Playgirl on the Air* ('86)	a, p
Ramos, Sergio	*El Sex Sentido* (M)	a
Ramsey, David	*The Killing Hour* (aka *The Clairvoyant*) ('82)	a, p
Rand, Jonathon	*Skeleton Coast* ('89)	a
Ranieri, Massimo	*Bubu*	a
Rannow, Les	*Summer Affair* ('79)	a
Rano, Corey	*Predator 2* ('90)	a, p
Rapport, Michael	*Hardbodies* ('84)	a
Rasche, David	*Made in Heaven* ('87)	a
Rassimov, Ivan	*The Eerie Midnight Horror Show* ('82)	a

Rassimov, Ivan	*Emmanuelle in Bangkok* ('78)	a
Rassimov, Ivan	*The Man from Deep River* ('77)	a
Ratray, Peter	*Young Lady Chatterley* (B) ('76)	a
Raum, Warren	*Robby* ('67)	a, p
Rawls, Lou	*Angel, Angel, Down We Go* ('69)	a
Reardon, Peter Brady	*Preppies* ('84)	a
Reckert, Winston	*Your Ticket Is No Longer Valid* ('84)	a
Reconti, Paco	*Francesco* (I) ('89)	a, p
Redding, Nick	*Forbidden Passions: Oscar Wilde* ('87)	a
Redford, Ian	*Antonia & Jane* (B) ('91)	a
Reding, Nick	*Captive* ('86)	a
Redpath, Ralph	*Filthiest Show in Town* ('82)	a, p
Reed, Matthew	*Perfect* ('85)	a
Reed, Oliver	*Castaway* ('86)	a, p
Reed, Oliver	*Women in Love* (B) ('69)	a, p
Reems, Harry	*RSVP* ('84)	a
Rees, Roger	*Ebony Tower* (B) ('86)	a
Reeves, Keanu	*Much Ado About Nothing* ('93)	a
Reeves, Keanu	*My Own Private Idaho* ('91)	a
Reeves, Keanu	*Point Break* ('91)	a
Regehr, Duncan	*The Banker* ('89)	a
Regent, Benoit	*A Flame in My Heart* (F) ('87)	p
Reigrod, Jon	*The Boob Tube* ('75)	a
Reilly, Tom	*Animal Instincts* ('91)	a
Reinhold, Judge	*Roadhouse 66* ('84)	a
Reinhold, Judge	*Zandalee* ('90)	a
Reisch, Steve	*Partners* ('82)	a
Reiser, Robert	*The Harrad Summer* ('74)	a
Remar, James	*Cruising* ('80)	a
Remar, James	*The Tigress* ('92)	a
Rempel, Nicholas	*The Clay Farmers*	a
Renucci, Robin	*Mawques*	a
Reschse, Knut	*The Sinful Bed* (G) ('78)	a
Rethmeer, Gary	*Oh! Calcutta* ('72)	a, p
Rey, Alejandro	*High Velocity* ('77)	a
Rey, Fernando	*Cabo Blanco* (Sp) ('81)	a
Reyne, David	*Frenchman's Farm* ('87)	a
Reynolds, Burt	*Fade-In* ('68)	a
Reynolds, Burt	*Impasse* ('69)	a
Reynolds, Burt	*The Man Who Loved Women* ('83)	a
Reynoso, Jorge	*Las Mujeras de Jeremias* (M)	a
Rhodes, Donnelly	*A Change of Mind* ('69)	a
Rhoe, Jeff	*Puberty Blues* (A) ('84)	a
Rialet, Daniel	*Le Grand Chemin* (aka *The Grand Highway*) (F) ('87)	a
Ribeirio, Marcelo	*Love Strange Love* (I) ('83)	p

Ribon, Diego	*Francesco* (I) ('89)	a, p
Ricard, Eduardo	*Last Resort* ('86)	a
Rice, Randy	*Pumping Iron II: The Women* ('85)	a
Rich, Christopher	*Prisoners of Inertia* ('89)	a
Rich, Mark A.	*Bound by Honor* ('93)	a
Richard, Pierre	*The Tall Blond Man with One Black Shoe* (F) ('72)	a
Richardson, Ian	*Marat/Sade* (B) ('67)	a
Rijn, Brad	*Perfect Strangers* ('84)	a
Rijn, Brad	*Smithereens* ('82)	a
Rijn, Brad	*Special Effects* ('85)	a
Rios, Javier	*Q & A* ('90)	a
Ripploh, Frank	*Taxi to Cairo* (G)	a, p
Ripploh, Frank	*Taxi Zum Klo* (G) ('81)	a, p
Riton	*Get Out Your Handkerchiefs* (F) ('78)	a
Rivals, Jean Luc	*Beatrice* (aka *The Passion of Beatrice*) (F) ('88)	p
Rivas, Ernesto	*La Tentacion*	a, p
Rivas, Ernesto	*Machos*	a
Rivera, Keith	*Inside Out 3* ('92)	a, p
Rivero, Jorge	*Como Pesiar Malide* (M)	a
Rivero, Jorge	*El Angel Negro* (M)	a
Rivero, Jorge	*El Llanto de la Tortuga* (M)	a
Rivero, Jorge	*La Pulquera*	a
Rivero, Jorge	*The Sin of Adam and Eve* (M) ('72)	a, p
Rivero, Jorge	*Vereno Salvaje* (M)	a
Rives, Robbie	*Shadowzone* ('89)	p
Rives, Robbie	*Waves of Passion*	a
Roarke, Adam	*The Stunt Man* ('80)	a
Robards, Sam	*Fandango* ('85)	a
Robbins, Tim	*Bull Durham* ('88)	a
Robbins, Tim	*Jacob's Ladder* ('90)	a
Robbins, Tim	*The Player* ('92)	a, p
Roberts, Derek	*Party Inc.* ('89)	a
Roberts, Eric	*Descending Angel* ('90)	a
Roberts, Eric	*Star 80* ('83)	a
Robertson, Clift	*Out of Season* (B) ('75)	a
Robinson, Bruce	*Kleinhoff Hotel*	a, p
Robinson, Chris	*Cycle Savages* ('69)	a
Robinson, David	*Revenge of the Cheerleaders* ('76)	a
Robinson, Leon	*Colors* ('88)	a
Robinson, Stuart K.	*Death Wish II* ('82)	a
Robles, Jorge Humberto	*The Evil That Men Do* ('84)	a
Robles, Jorge Humberto	*Vereno Salvaje* (M)	a, p
Rocco, Alex	*The Godfather* ('72)	a
Rocha, Enrique	*Satanico Pandemonium* (M)	p
Rodriquez, Miguel	*El Chico Temido*	a, p

Rodway, Norman	*Chimes at Midnight* (aka *Falstaff*) (B/Sp) ('66)	a
Roeves, Maurice	*Ulysses* (B) ('67)	a
Rohner, Clayton	*Masked Target* (Sp)	a
Roll, Michel	*It Has to Be Murder*	a
Rolland, Jean-Louis	*One More Encore* (I)	a, p
Rolston, Mark	*Weeds* ('87)	a
Roman, Alex	*The Voluptuary* ('71)	a, p
Romanus, Robert	*Fast Times at Ridgemont High* ('82)	a, p*
Rosa, Robby	*Salsa* ('88)	a
Rose, Michael	*Breakfast in Bed* ('90)	a
Rosen, Eric	*The Wooden Gun* (Is) ('79)	a
Ross, Chelchie	*One More Saturday Night* ('86)	a
Ross, Gerry	*The Kid and the Killers* ('74)	a
Ross, Guy	*if. . . .* (B) ('68)	a
Ross, Howard	*Uomo Che Sfido Organizzazione* (I)	a
Ross, Stan	*Hollywood Zap* ('86)	a
Ross, Willie	*The Cook, The Thief, His Wife & Her Lover* (B) ('90)	p
Rosseau, Pierre	*Sensual Awakening* (F)	a, p
Rossi, Jorge	*Los Colgials* (M)	a, p
Rossi, Leo	*Halloween II* ('81)	a
Rossiter, Leonard	*The Pink Panther Strikes Again* ('77)	a
Rossovich, Rick	*Paint It Black* ('89)	a
Rossovich, Rick	*Tales from the Crypt Trilogy* ('90)	a
Rossovich, Rick	*Tropical Heat* ('93)	a
Roundtree, Richard	*Shaft* ('71)	a
Roundtree, Richard	*Shaft in Africa* ('73)	a
Roundtree, Richard	*Shaft's Big Score!* ('72)	a
Rourke, Mickey	*9½ Weeks* ('86)	a, p*
Rourke, Mickey	*Angel Heart* ('87)	a
Rourke, Mickey	*Francesco* (I) ('89)	a, p
Rourke, Mickey	*Wild Orchid* ('90)	a
Rourke, Mickey	*The Year of the Dragon* ('85)	a
Rouveni, Avi	*Young Love* ('87)	a
Rowlatt, Michael	*Spaced Out* (B) ('80)	a
Rowley, Richard	*So Long, Blue Boy* ('73)	a
Roya, David	*Billy Jack* ('71)	a
Roya, David	*The Outrageous Mechanical Love Machine* ('70)	a
Roya, David	*The Very Friendly Neighbors*	a
Rozakis, Gregory	*Abduction* ('75)	a
Rubbo, Joe	*Hot Chili* ('85)	a
Rubbo, Joe	*The Last American Virgin* ('82)	a
Rubinek, Saul	*By Design* (C) ('81)	a
Rudder, John	*Nail Gun Massacre* ('85)	a
Rudin, Stuart	*The Silence of the Lambs* ('91)	a

Ruiz, Jose Carlos	*Luna De Sangre* (M)	a
Rusler, Robert	*Final Embrace* ('92)	a
Russ, Tim	*Night Eyes II* ('91)	a
Russell, Kurt	*Silkwood* ('84)	a
Russell, Kurt	*Tango & Cash* ('89)	a
Russell, Kurt	*Used Cars* ('80)	a
Russo, James	*Cold Heaven* ('90)	a
Russo, James	*Freeway* ('88)	a
Rust, Richard	*Student Nurses* ('70)	a
Ruston, Jared	*A Cry in the Wild* ('90)	a
Ryan, Eric	*Bikini Carwash Company* ('92)	a
Ryan, Mitchell	*My Old Man's Place* ('72)	a
Rydell, Christopher	*Blood and Sand* ('89)	a
Rylance, Mark	*Prospero's Books* (B) ('91)	a
Rynka, Ron	*Panic in the City* ('68)	a
S, Bruno	*Stroszek* (G) ('77)	a
Sabol, Dick	*Cotton Comes to Harlem* ('70)	a
Sabourin, Marcel	*Two Women in Gold* ('70)	a, p
Sacks, Michael	*Slaughterhouse-Five* ('72)	a
Sacristan, Jose	*The Deputy* (Sp) ('78)	a, p
Sadler, William	*Die Hard 2* ('90)	a
Sador, Daniel	*Sugar Cookies* ('73)	a
Sadurny, Massimo	*Love, Lust & Ecstasy* (Gr)	a
Safilli, Stefano	*I Ragazzi della Periferia Sird*	a, p
Sakiss, Frederick	*Her, She and Him* ('70)	a
Saladar, Fred	*Waitress!* ('81)	a
Salinger, Matt	*Revenge of the Nerds* ('84)	a
Sallahan, Loris	*Sleepaway Camp* ('83)	a
Salverno, Sergio	*Carnal Crimes* ('91)	a
Salvino, Richard	*The Legend of Frenchie King* (F) ('72)	a
Sanders, Scott	*Opposing Force* ('87)	a
Sands, Julian	*After Darkness* (B) ('85)	a, p
Sands, Julian	*Boxing Helena* ('93)	a
Sands, Julian	*Gothic* (B) ('87)	a
Sands, Julian	*Husbands and Lovers* (I) ('92)	a, p
Sands, Julian	*A Room with a View* (B) ('85)	a, p
Sanford, Garvin	*Quarantine* ('89)	a
Santana, Arnaldo	*Cruising* ('80)	a
Santos, Bert	*Harry, Cherry & Raquel* ('69)	a
Sanudo, Rafael	*Lawless Land* ('88)	a
Sanville, Michael	*Dreams Come True* ('85)	a
Sanville, Michael	*The First Turn On* ('84)	a
Sanz, Jorge	*Lovers* (Sp) ('92)	a, p
Sarafian, Deran	*10 to Midnight* ('83)	a
Sarandon, Chris	*Lipstick* ('76)	a
Sargent, Richard	*Tanya's Island* ('81)	a, p

Sarno, John	*The Seven Minutes* ('71)	a
Sarrazin, Michael	*Eye of the Cat* ('69)	a
Sarrazin, Michael	*In Search of Gregory* ('70)	a
Sarrazin, Michael	*The Pursuit of Happiness* ('70)	a
Sarrazin, Michael	*The Seduction* ('82)	a
Sarrazin, Michael	*The Sweet Ride* ('68)	a
Sarrera, Anthony	*Waitress!* ('81)	a
Satterfield, Paul	*Arena* ('88)	a
Savage, John	*Cattle Annie and Little Britches* ('80)	a
Savage, John	*Hair* ('79)	a
Savage, John	*The Killing Kind* ('73)	a
Savage, John	*Sister-in-Law* ('74)	a
Saxon, John	*Una Donna Dietro la Porto* (I)	a
Sayles, John	*Return of the Secaucus 7* ('80)	a, p
Scalia, Jack	*Illicit Behavior* ('92)	a
Scarbrough, Don	*Beneath the Valley of the Ultravixens* ('79)	a
Scheider, Roy	*All That Jazz* ('79)	a
Schell, Maximilian	*Together* (I) ('79)	a
Schell, Rene	*First Polka*	a, p
Schellenberg, August	*The Black Robe* (C) ('91)	a
Schenk, Udo	*Taxi to Cairo* (G)	a, p
Schick, Benjamin	*The Shooters* ('90)	a
Schlatter, Charlie	*The Delinquents* (A) ('89)	a
Schlesinger, Peter	*A Bigger Splash* ('74)	a
Schneider, John	*Cocaine Wars* ('85)	a
Schneider, John	*Eddie Macon's Run* ('83)	a
Schonenberger, Rene	*The Three Cornered Bed* (G) ('71)	a
Schott, Bob	*Working Girls* ('74)	a
Schroder, Ricky	*The Champ* ('79)	a
Schuck, John	*M*A*S*H* ('70)	a
Schultz, Jeff	*Buying Time* ('89)	a
Schuster, Thomas	*Psycho IV: The Beginning* ('90)	a
Schwartz, Neil	*Steam Baths*	a
Schwarzenegger, Arnold	*Red Heat* ('88)	a
Schwarzenegger, Arnold	*Terminator 2: Judgment Day* ('91)	a
Schwarzenegger, Arnold	*The Terminator* ('84)	a, p
Schwickert, Vincent	*Men in Love* ('90)	a, p
Scofield, Dean	*Eden 2* ('92)	a
Scorpio, Bernie	*Video Vixens* ('73)	a
Scorpio, Lennie	*Video Vixens* ('73)	a
Scott, Campbell	*Dying Young* ('91)	a
Scott, Campbell	*Longtime Companion* ('90)	a
Scott, Campbell	*The Sheltering Sky* ('90)	p
Scott, Joe	*While the Cat's Away*	p
Scott, Kirk	*Cinderella* ('77)	a, p
Scott, Larry B.	*A Hero Ain't Nothing But a Sandwich* ('77)	a, p

Scotti, Alessandro	*Casa di Piaccre*	a
Scotti, Joe	*Saturday Night at the Baths* ('75)	a
Scuddamore, Simon	*Slaughter High* ('85)	a, p
Seal, Frederick	*The Onion Field* ('79)	a, p
Segado, Alberto	*Two to Tango* (I) ('88)	a
Segal, George	*Born to Win* ('71)	a
Segal, George	*The Girl Who Couldn't Say No* ('69)	a
Segal, George	*The Terminal Man* ('74)	a
Segal, George	*Where's Poppa?* ('70)	a
Segal, Jonathan	*Baby Love* (Is) ('83)	a
Segal, Jonathan	*Drifting* (Is) ('82)	a
Segal, Jonathan	*Going Steady* (Is) ('80)	a
Segal, Jonathan	*Young Love* ('87)	a
Selby, David	*The Girl in Blue* ('73)	a
Self, Doug	*Men in Love* ('90)	a
Selleck, Tom	*Lassiter* ('84)	a
Selleck, Tom	*Mr. Baseball* ('92)	a
Sellier, Pascal	*L'Amant de Poche* (F)	a, p
Senner, Peter	*Via Appia* (G)	a, p
Sera, Ian	*Pieces* (I/Sp) ('83)	a, p
Serbedzna, Rade	*Manifesto* (Y) ('88)	a
Serna, Pepe	*Day of the Locust* ('75)	a
Serna, Pepe	*The Killer Inside Me* ('75)	a, p
Serrault, Michel	*On Ne Meurt Que Deux Fois* (F)	a
Severns, Darl	*Sweet Sugar* ('72)	a
Seymour, Ralph	*Meatballs II* ('84)	a
Shad, Daniel	*Miss Mona*	a
Shane, Michael	*Do or Die* ('91)	a
Shane, Michael	*Savage Beach* ('89)	a
Shaner, Michael	*American Me* ('92)	a
Shannon, George	*Sugar Cookies* ('73)	a
Shannon, Mark	*Island of the Living Dead*	a
Sharkey, Ray	*Act of Piracy* ('90)	a
Sharkey, Ray	*Scenes from the Class Struggle in Beverly Hills* ('89)	a
Sharkey, Ray	*Willie and Phil* ('80)	a
Shatner, William	*Big Bad Mama* ('74)	a
Shawap, Yasin	*Hamsin* ('83)	a
Shea, John	*Backstreet Justice* ('93)	a
Shea, John	*Hussy* (B) ('80)	a
Sheen, Martin	*Apocalypse Now* ('79)	a
Sheffer, Craig	*Instant Karma* ('79)	a
Shellen, Steve	*Burglar* ('87)	a
Shellen, Steve	*Gimme an "F"* ('84)	a
Shellen, Steve	*A River Runs Through It* ('93)	a
Shellen, Steve	*Talking Walls* ('87)	a
Shepherd, Jack	*Ball Trap on the Cote Sauvage*	a

Shiiya, Kenji	*Lady Chatterley in Tokyo* (J)	a
Shipp, John Wesley	*The Dirtiest Show in Town*	a
Shirin, Moti	*The Little Drummer Girl* ('84)	a, p
Shor, Daniel	*Strange Behavior* ('83)	a
Shore, Pauly	*Phantom of the Mall—Eric's Revenge* ('88)	a
Shore, Pauly	*Son In Law* ('93)	a
Short, Martin	*Cross My Heart* ('88)	a
Show, Grant	*A Woman, Her Men and Her Futon* ('92)	a
Siani, Ryp	*Robby* ('67)	a, p
Sibbit, John	*Love Circles* (F) ('85)	a
Sicari, Joseph	*Jerker* ('91)	a, p
Sicari, Joseph	*Partners* ('82)	a, p
Siegel, David	*Private Passions* ('83)	a
Siemaszko, Casey	*Young Guns* ('88)	a
Sierchio, Tom	*Delivery Boys* ('84)	a
Sierra, Manuel	*L'Annello Matrimoniale* (I)	a
Sigsgaard, Thomas	*Friends Forever* (Da) ('86)	a
Sills, David	*Breakfast in Bed* ('90)	a
Silver, Ron	*Blue Steel* ('90)	a
Silverman, Eliott	*Wager of Love* ('90)	a
Simon, Mark	*Inside Out 4* ('92)	a, p
Simons, Alan	*Auditions* ('78)	a, p
Simpson, Robert E.	*Magnum Force* ('73)	a
Singer, Marc	*Body Chemistry* ('90)	a, p
Singer, Marc	*For Ladies Only* (European version) ('81)	a
Singleton, Andrew	*Death Merchant* ('90)	a
Singleton, Keith	*Student Bodies* ('81)	a
Sinise, Gary	*A Midnight Clear* ('91)	a
Skarsgard, Stellan	*Hip Hip Hurrah!*	a
Skarsgard, Stellan	*The Unbearable Lightness of Being* ('88)	a
Skerritt, Tom	*Big Bad Mama* ('74)	a
Skerritt, Tom	*Opposing Force* ('87)	a
Skerritt, Tom	*Poison Ivy* ('92)	a
Slater, Christian	*Mobsters* ('91)	a
Slater, Christian	*The Name of the Rose* ('86)	a, p
Slater, Christian	*True Romance* ('93)	a
Slater, Christian	*Twisted* ('85)	a
Slattery, Tony	*Peter's Friends* (B)	a
Sloane, Lance	*The Big Bet* ('85)	a
Slobodan, Negic	*Games of Desire* ('68)	a
Small, Ben	*Miss Mona*	a, p
Smeaton, Robert	*Accounts*	a
Smedley, Richard	*The Abductors* ('71)	a

Smiley, Brett	Cinderella ('77)	a
Smit, Maarten	For a Lost Soldier (D) ('93)	a
Smith, Charles Martin	Never Cry Wolf ('83)	a, p
Smith, Charles Martin	The Hazing ('78)	a
Smith, Charles Martin	The Spikes Gang ('74)	a
Smith, David Anthony	Terror in Paradise ('87)	a
Smith, Keith	Beyond Innocence (A) ('88)	a, p
Smith, Reid	Blood Mania ('69)	a
Smith, Reid	Dinah East ('70)	a
Smith, Rex	Transformations ('88)	a
Smith, Shannon Dow	Invasion of Privacy ('92)	a
Smith, Tracy Martin	Kansas ('88)	a
Smits, Jimmy	Old Gringo ('89)	a
Smits, Jimmy	Switch ('91)	a
Smothers, Tom	Get to Know Your Rabbit ('71)	a
Snyder, Don	Norma ('69)	a
So, Jebong	A Boy Named Cocoy (P)	a, p
Sochet, David	The Boys of Cellblock Q	a
Sohar, Ika	I Don't Give a Damn ('88)	a
Sola, Miguel Angel	Sur (M)	a
Soltoft, Ole	The Amorous Headmaster (Da) ('70)	a
Soltoft, Ole	Eric Soya's Seventeen (Da) ('65)	a
Soltoft, Ole	What the Swedish Butler Saw (Da)	a
Somma, Sebastiano	Voglia de Guardare (I)	a
Sommer, Robert	Auditions ('78)	a, p
Sont, Gerry	Girl Toy ('84)	a
Sorel, Jean	The Sweet Body of Deborah (I) ('68)	a, p
Sorel, Ted	From Beyond ('86)	a
Soth, Sandor	Time Stands Still (H) ('82)	p
Spade, David	Light Sleeper ('93)	a
Spader, James	Bad Influence ('90)	a
Spader, James	Dream Lover ('93)	a
Spader, James	White Palace ('91)	a
Spahn, Patrick	Steam Bath	a
Spall, Timothy	Gothic (B) ('87)	a
Spanjer, Maarten	Spetters (D) ('80)	a, p
Spano, Joe	Terminal Choice ('84)	a
Spano, Vincent	Creator ('85)	a
Speakman, Jeff	Street Knight ('92)	a, p
Spechtenhauser, Robert	Bizarre (I) ('86)	a
Spengler, Volker	Despair (G) ('79)	a
Sperandini, Gerardo	L'Imperature di Roma (I)	a
Spicer, Jeremy	Sunset Grill ('92)	a, p
Spiridakis, Tony	Queens Logic ('91)	a
Spiropoulos, Christo	Portrait of a Love Affair (Gr)	a, p
Springer, Wolf Dietric	Winkelman's Travels	a
Springfield, Rick	Hard to Hold ('84)	a

St. Angelo, John	*Young Lady Chatterley, Part II* (B) ('85)	a
St. Jacques	*Sistemo L'America e Torno*	a, p
St. John, Christopher	*Top of the Heap* ('72)	a
Stallings, Rex	*Undercovers Hero* ('75)	a
Stallone, Sylvester	*First Blood (Rambo I)* ('82)	a
Stallone, Sylvester	*The Italian Stallion* ('70)	a, p
Stallone, Sylvester	*Rambo II* ('85)	a
Stallone, Sylvester	*Rambo III* ('88)	a
Stallone, Sylvester	*Rocky V* ('90)	a
Stallone, Sylvester	*Stop! Or My Mother Will Shoot* ('92)	a
Stallone, Sylvester	*Tango & Cash* ('89)	a
Stamp, Terence	*Far from the Madding Crowd* (B) ('68)	a
Stamp, Terence	*Season in Hell*	a
Stamp, Terence	*Teorema* (I) ('68)	a, p
Stanczek, Wadeck	*Rendez-vous* (F) ('86)	a
Stanczek, Wadeck	*Scene of the Crime* (F) ('87)	a
Stanislas, Piotr	*We Were One Man* (F/G) ('79)	a, p
Stank, Don	*Evilspeak* ('81)	a
Stanton, Harry Dean	*Cisco Pike* ('72)	a
Stark, Graham	*Blind Date* ('87)	a
Starr, Emerald	*Men in Love* ('90)	a
Starr, Ringo	*That'll Be the Day* (B) ('73)	a
Starus, Todd	*Jaded*	a
Staskel, James	*Inside Out 3* ('92)	a
Stearns, Michael	*Chain Gang Women* ('71)	a
Stearns, Michael	*Keep It Up* ('71)	a, p
Stearns, Michael	*Zero in and Scream* ('71)	a
Steele, Richard	*With Six You Get Eggroll* ('68)	a
Steen, Peter	*The First Circle* (G) ('72)	a, p
Steiger, Rod	*The Illustrated Man* ('68)	a
Steiner, John	*Beyond the Door II* ('77)	a
Steiner, Peter	*Los Encantos de un Alpinista* (M)	a
Stephano, Tony	*The Reincarnation of Peter Proud* ('75)	a, p
Stephens, Robert	*The Shout* (A) ('78)	a
Stepp, Craig	*The Other Woman* ('92)	a, p
Stern, Daniel	*A Small Circle of Friends* ('80)	a
Stern, Tom	*The Clay Pigeon* ('71)	a
Stevens, Andrew	*Down the Drain* ('89)	a
Stevens, Andrew	*Massacre at Central High* ('76)	a
Stevens, Andrew	*Night Eyes* ('90)	a
Stevens, Andrew	*Night Eyes III* ('93)	a
Stevens, Fisher	*The Burning* ('81)	a
Stevenson, Doug	*Iced* ('88)	a
Stevenson, Eugene	*The Pamela Principle* ('92)	a

Stevenson, Parker	*A Separate Peace* ('73)	a
Stevenson, Parker	*Stitches* ('85)	a
Stewart, Robin	*Adventures of a Private Eye* (B) ('77)	a
Stewart, Robin	*Pacific Banana* (A) ('80)	a
Stiglitz, Hugo	*Tintorera* (B/M) ('77)	a, p
Stimely, Brett	*Cannibal Women in the Avocado Jungle of Death* ('89)	a
Sting	*Brimstone and Treacle* (B) ('82)	a
Sting	*Julia and Julia* ('87)	a
Stockwell, Dean	*Win, Place or Steal* ('72)	a
Stockwell, Guy	*Santa Sangre* ('89)	a
Stockwell, Jeremy	*Dinah East* ('70)	a, p
Stockwell, John	*City Limits* ('84)	a
Stockwell, John	*Dangerously Close* ('86)	a
Stoddard, Peter	*Naked Instinct* ('93)	a
Stokes, Barry	*Alien Prey* (B) ('83)	a, p
Stokes, Barry	*Confessions of an Odd Job Man* (B)	a, p
Stokes, Barry	*The Corruption of Chris Miller* (B) ('75)	a
Stokes, Barry	*Spaced Out* (B) ('80)	a, p
Stokes, Barry	*The Ups and Downs of a Handyman* (B) ('73)	a, p
Stoltz, Eric	*Haunted Summer* ('88)	a, p
Stoltz, Eric	*Manifesto* (Y) ('88)	a
Stoltz, Eric	*Naked in New York* ('94)	a, p
Stoltz, Eric	*The Fly II* ('88)	a
Stone, Christopher	*Grasshopper* ('69)	a
Stone, Christopher	*The Howling* ('81)	a
Stone, Christopher	*Love Me Deadly* ('72)	a
Strathairn, David	*A Dangerous Woman* ('93)	a
Strathairn, David	*Return of the Secaucus 7* ('80)	a, p
Strauss, Peter	*Man of Legend* (I/Sp) ('71)	a
Street, Elliott	*The Harrad Experiment* ('73)	a, p
Streeter, Tim	*Mala Noche* ('87)	a
Strietzel, Art	*Ready, Willing and Able* (S)	a, p
Strobye, Axel	*Topsy Turvy* ('84)	a, p
Strohmyer, Scott	*Bikini Carwash Company* ('92)	a
Strother, Bernard	*Not Quite Paradise* (B) ('86)	a
Suchon, Alain	*Man with Silver Eyes*	a
Sullivan, Billy	*Light of Day* ('87)	a, p
Sullivan, William Bell	*Diamond Run* ('88)	a
Sumpter, Donald	*Fiona*	a
Sundin, Michael	*Artists and Models* (B)	a
Sundquist, Folke	*One Summer of Happiness* (S) ('52)	a
Sundquist, Gerry	*Boarding School* (G) ('83)	a
Sust, David	*In a Glass Cage* ('85)	a
Sutherland, Donald	*Animal House* ('78)	a

Sutherland, Donald	*Don't Look Now* ('73)	a, p
Sutherland, Donald	*Eye of the Needle* ('81)	a
Sutherland, Donald	*Fellini's Casanova* (I) ('75)	a
Sutherland, Donald	*Nothing Personal* ('80)	a
Sutherland, Kiefer	*Last Light* ('93)	a
Sutherland, Kiefer	*The Promised Land* ('87)	a
Sutherland, Wayne	*The Great Northfield Minnesota Raid* ('72)	a
Sutton, Dudley	*Edward II* (B) ('92)	a, p
Swayze, Patrick	*Road House* ('89)	a
Sweet, Gary	*Indecent Obsession* (A) ('85)	a
Sylva, Joel	*Mrs. Barrington*	a
Szeibert, Frank	*The Wild Life* ('84)	a
Tabor, Eron	*I Spit on Your Grave* ('78)	a
Tabori, Kristopher	*Glass House* ('72)	a, p
Tabori, Kristopher	*Making It* ('71)	a
Tacchi, Phillipe	*Ars Amandi* (I)	a, p
Tait, Jim	*Both Sides*	a
Talamonti, Rinaldo	*Los Encantos de un Alpinista* (M)	a, p
Tamblyn, Russ	*Win, Place or Steal* ('72)	a
Tan, Edward	*Saint Jack* ('79)	a
Tankosic, Ratko	*Lolly Water*	a, p
Tanner, Clay	*Walking Tall: The Final Chapter* ('77)	a
Taylor, Henry	*Dreamwood* ('72)	a, p
Taylor, James A.	*Men in Love* ('90)	a
Taylor, Joe	*Dinah East* ('70)	a
Taylor, Michael	*Chatterbox* ('77)	a
Taylor, Noah	*Flirting* (A) ('90)	a
Taylor, Tim	*Tender Loving Care* ('73)	a
Taylor, Zack	*Group Marriage* ('71)	a
Taylor, Zack	*How to Succeed with Sex* ('70)	a, p
Teich, Aarin	*Dead of Night* ('77)	a
Tenny, James	*Fuses*	a
Teoderi, Giancarlo	*La Strana Voglia* (I)	a
Teoderi, Giancarlo	*Scent of Passion* (I)	a
Tepper, William	*Drive, He Said* ('72)	a
Tepper, William	*La Donna Giusta* (aka *Miss Right*) (I) ('87)	a
Terrell, John Canada	*Def by Temptation* ('90)	a, p
Terrell, John Canada	*She's Gotta Have It* ('87)	a, p
Terry, Nigel	*Caravaggio* (B) ('86)	a
Terry, Nigel	*Déjà Vu* (B) ('84)	a
Terry, Nigel	*Edward II* (B) ('92)	a
Testi, Fabio	*China 9, Liberty 37* ('78)	a
Testi, Fabio	*'Tis a Pity She's a Whore* (I) ('72)	a
Testi, Fabio	*L'Ultima Occasione* (I)	a
Testi, Fabio	*Un Amoure Casi Fragile, Casi Violerto* (I)	a

Tevini, Thierry	*Tendres Cousines* (F) ('81)	a
Thacker, Rusty	*The Line* (aka *Parades*) ('72)	a
Thayer, Max	*The Dolls* ('83)	a
Thiel, Peter	*Dark Side of the Moon* ('90)	a
Thomas, Dan	*Canterbury Tales* (I) ('71)	a
Thomas, Hugh	*if. . . .* (B) ('68)	a
Thomas, Jerome	*Exotica, Female Fantasies*	a
Thomas, Leonard Lee	*King of New York* ('90)	a
Thomas, Patrick	*The Weirdo* ('88)	a
Thomas, Phillip Michael	*El Hombre de Los Hongas* (M)	a
Thomas, Richard	*Last Summer* ('69)	a
Thompson, Andrew	*The Clinic* (A) ('82)	a, p
Thompson, Gordon	*Candy, the Stripper*	a
Thompson, Jack	*Jock Peterson* (A) ('74)	a, p
Thompson, Jack	*The Journalist* (A)	a
Thompson, Jack	*Sunday Too Far Away* (A) ('75)	a
Thompson, Peter	*The Other Woman* ('92)	a
Thomsen, Kevin	*Cleo/Leo* ('89)	a, p
Thor, Jon-Mikl	*Roll 'n' Rock Nightmare* ('87)	a
Thornbury, Bill	*Phantasm* ('78)	a
Thuileur, Luc	*Les Hors la Loi* (F) ('84)	a
Thuiller, Yves	*Les Branches a Saint Tropez* (F)	a
Thunder, Bjorn	*Romantic Memoirs* (S)	a
Tiernan, Andrew	*Edward II* (B) ('92)	a
Tiernay, Aidan	*Family Viewing* (C) ('87)	a
Tiler, Scott	*Once Upon a Time in America* ('84)	a
Tinti, Gabriele	*Black Cobra* (I) ('76)	a
Tinti, Gabriele	*Cut and Run* (I) ('85)	a
Tinti, Gabriele	*Emmanuelle in Bangkok* ('78)	a
Tinti, Gabriele	*Emmanuelle in the Country* (I) ('80)	a
Tinti, Gabriele	*Emmanuelle the Queen* (I) ('79)	a
Tinti, Gabriele	*Emmanuelle's Holiday* (I)	a
Tinti, Gabriele	*Love Camp* (F) ('76)	a
Tinti, Gabriele	*Sexy Moon* (I)	a
Tinti, Gabriele	*Trap Them and Kill Them* (I)	a
Tobias, Oliver	*Operation Nam* ('85)	a
Tobias, Oliver	*Romance of a Horsethief* (B) ('71)	a
Tobias, Oliver	*The Stud* (B) ('78)	a
Tobias, Oliver	*'Tis a Pity She's a Whore* (I) ('72)	a
Tobias, Oliver	*The Wicked Lady* (B) ('83)	a
Togay, Cain	*Malina*	a, p
Tognazzi, Ugo	*Don't Touch the White Woman* (I)	a
Tognazzi, Ugo	*La Grande Bouffe* (F) ('73)	a
Tolbe, Joe	*Men in Love* ('90)	a
Tomei, Paolo	*Nothing Underneath* (I) ('85)	a
Tomlinson, Ricky	*Riff-Raff* (B)	a
Topez, Dudu	*Tel Aviv—Los Angeles*	p
Torgl, Mark	*The First Turn On* ('84)	a

Torn, Rip	*Coming Apart* ('69)	a
Torn, Rip	*Jinxed* ('82)	a
Torn, Rip	*The Man Who Fell to Earth* ('76)	p
Torn, Rip	*Payday* ('72)	a
Torrentes, Luiz	*Latino* ('85)	a
Tovatt, Patrick	*Ellie* ('84)	a
Towles, Tom	*Henry: Portrait of a Serial Killer* ('90)	p
Tracy, Steve	*Beneath the Valley of the Ultravixens* ('79)	a, p
Travis, Len	*Private Parts* ('72)	a
Treviglio, Leonardo	*Sebastiane* (B) ('79)	a, p
Trevino, Marco	*Dona Herlinda and Her Son* (M) ('86)	a
Trujillo, Raoul	*The Adjuster* (C) ('91)	a
Tubb, Barry	*Valentino Returns* ('89)	a, p
Tubb, Barry	*Warm Summer Rain* ('89)	a, p
Tucker, Dewayne	*While the Cat's Away*	p
Tucker, Martin	*House of Death* ('82)	a
Turcel, Michael	*Grease* ('78)	a
Turco, Paolo	*The Lickerish Quartet* (I) ('70)	a, p
Turgeman, Boaz	*Drifting* (Is) ('82)	a, p
Turturro, John	*Men of Respect* ('90)	a
Tynel, Charles	*Evilspeak* ('81)	a
Tyson, Richard	*Two-Moon Junction* ('88)	a
Underwood, Jay	*The Invisible Kid* ('88)	a
Urena, Fabio	*The Bronx War* ('89)	a
Uric, Bronki DJ	*Games of Desire* ('68)	a
Urich, Robert	*Endangered Species* ('82)	a
Urkaneta, Orlando	*Vereno Salvaje* (M)	a
Ursini, Alderto	*Thrice a Woman* (I)	a
Vaananen, Kari	*Amazon* ('80)	a
Valdez, Christian	*The Boys of Cellblock Q*	a, p
Valdez, Daniel	*Zoot Suit* ('81)	a
Valentine, Scott	*Deadtime Stories* ('85)	a
Valentine, Scott	*Write to Kill* ('91)	p
Valjean, Paul	*Quiet Days in Clichy* (Da)	a, p
Vallone, Saverio	*Fotografando Patrizia* (I)	a, p
Valverde, Maximo	*Tasista de Senoras*	a
Valverde, Rodrigo	*Les Etades de Lulu* (F)	a
Van Bijk, Bill	*Dear Boys* (D) ('80)	a
Van Dam, Gene	*Stage Fright* ('87)	a
Van Damme, Jean-Claude	*Bloodsport* ('87)	a
Van Damme, Jean-Claude	*Double Impact* ('91)	a
Van Damme, Jean-Claude	*Kickboxer* ('89)	a

Van Damme, Jean-Claude	*Lionheart* ('90)	a
Van Damme, Jean-Claude	*Nowhere to Run* ('92)	a
Van Damme, Jean-Claude	*Universal Soldiers* ('92)	a
Van Der Vierght, Bram	*Tracks in the Snow*	a, p
Van Der Woude, Jim	*The Pointsman* (D) ('86)	a, p
Van Dyke, Burt	*Dutch Treat* ('86)	a
Van Dyke, Jerry	*Death Blow* ('87)	a
Van Hentenryck, Kevin	*Basket Case* ('81)	a, p
Van Hentenryck, Kevin	*Basket Case II* ('90)	a
Van Hoffman, Brant	*Further Adventures of Tennessee Buck* ('88)	a
Van Patten, Nels	*Mirror Images* ('91)	a
Van Peebles, Melvin	*Sweet Sweetback's Baadasssss Song* ('71)	a
Van Tongeren, Hans	*Spetters* (D) ('80)	a, p
Vandreelen, John	*Too Hot to Handle* ('76)	a
Vasquez, Yul	*Tales from the Crypt: On a Dead Man's Chest* ('92)	a, p
Vasut, Marek	*Fists in the Dark*	a
Vaughn, Robert	*The Statue* (B) ('70)	a
Vavrin, Michael	*Naked Instinct* ('93)	a
Velez, Fernando	*Bad Lieutenant* ('92)	a
Venantini, Venantino	*Emmanuelle, Joys of a Woman* (F) ('75)	p
Venantini, Venantino	*Final Justice* ('84)	a
Ventura, Clyde	*Terminal Island* ('73)	a
Verley, Renaud	*The Lonely Woman*	a
Vernon, John	*Point Blank* ('68)	a
Vesely, Lubos	*Anthony and Chance*	a, p
Vicious, Sid	*The Great Rock and Roll Swindle* ('80)	a
Victor, Tony	*Tender Loving Care* ('73)	a
Vidler, Steven	*Robbery Under Arms*	a
Vidov, Oleg	*Hagbard and Signe* (S) ('67)	a
Villar, Victor	*Rich Boy, Poor Boy* (P)	a, p
Villard, Tom	*The Trouble with Dick* ('86)	a
Vincent, Fred	*Girls Are for Loving*	a
Vincent, Jan-Michael	*Buster and Billie* ('74)	a, p
Vincent, Jan-Michael	*Going Home* ('71)	a
Vincent, Jan-Michael	*Hard Country* ('81)	a
Vint, Alan	*Macon County Line* ('74)	a
Vint, Jesse	*Black Oak Conspiracy* ('77)	a
Vocoret, Michel	*Mieux Vaux Etie Riche et Bien Portant* (F)	a
Vogel, Jack	*Presumed Guilty* ('90)	a

Vogel, Nikolas	*The Inheritors* (G) ('84)	a, p
Voight, Jon	*All-American Boy* ('73)	a, p
Voight, Jon	*Coming Home* ('69)	a
Voight, Jon	*End of the Game* ('76)	a
Voight, Jon	*Midnight Cowboy* ('69)	a
Voight, Jon	*Runaway Train* ('85)	a, p
Voita, Michel	*A Corps Perdu* (F)	a
Volonte, Gian Maria	*The Abyss* ('89)	a
Von Brucker, Klaus	*No Skin Off My Ass* (C)	a
von Sydow, Max	*The New Land* (S) ('75)	a
von Sydow, Max	*The Virgin Spring* (S) ('59)	a
Vosloo, Arnold	*The Finishing Touch* ('92)	a
Vouk, Miki	*Senza Buccia* (aka *Skin Deep*) (I)	a, p
Vu-An, Eric	*The Sheltering Sky* ('90)	a
Vuu, Richard	*The Last Emperor* ('87)	a, p
Wagner, Tom	*Jerker* ('91)	a, p
Wagner, Tom	*Love Bites* ('88)	a
Wahl, Ken	*The Wanderers* ('79)	a
Wahlgren, Hans	*Fear Has a Thousand Eyes* ('73)	a, p
Waite, Ralph	*Cool Hand Luke* ('67)	a
Walda, Louis	*Andy Warhol's Blue Movie* ('69)	a, p
Walken, Christopher	*Communion* ('89)	a
Walker Jr., Robert	*Angkor: Cambodia Express* ('81)	a
Walker Jr., Robert	*The Road to Salina* ('69)	a
Walker, Will	*Hardcore* ('79)	a
Wallace, David	*Mortuary* ('81)	a
Wallach, Eli	*Romance of a Horsethief* ('71)	a
Wallter, Sven	*Man on the Roof* (S) ('77)	a, p
Walsh, M. Emmet	*Fast-Walking* ('81)	a, p
Walsh, M. Emmet	*Straight Time* ('78)	a
Walter, Tracey	*City Slickers* ('91)	a
Waltz, Christopher	*Fire and Sword*	a, p
Warbeck, David	*Lassiter* ('84)	a
Warbeck, David	*The Sex Thief* (B) ('73)	a, p
Warburton, Patrick	*Master of Dragonard Hill* (B) ('87)	a
Ward, Fred	*Henry and June* ('90)	a
Ward, Fred	*Time Rider* ('83)	a
Ward, Jeff	*Rosemary Is Pregnant Again* ('70)	a
Ward, Kelly	*Grease* ('78)	a
Ward, Richard	*Mandingo* ('75)	a
Ward, Wally	*The Invisible Kid* ('88)	a
Warden, Jack	*Problem Child* ('90)	a
Warden, Jonathan	*Greetings* ('68)	a
Warnock, Grant	*Waterland* ('92)	a
Warren, Mike	*Drive, He Said* ('72)	a, p
Warwick, Richard	*if. . . .* (B) ('68)	a
Warwick, Richard	*Sebastiane* (B) ('79)	a, p

Washington, Denzel	*Cry Freedom* (B) ('87)	a
Washington, Denzel	*Mississippi Masala* ('92)	a
Washington, Denzel	*Ricochet* ('91)	p
Wass, Ted	*Sheena* ('84)	a
Wasson, Craig	*Ghost Story* ('81)	a, p
Wasson, Craig	*Second Thoughts* ('83)	a
Waters, John	*Summerfield* (B)	a
Waters, John	*The Adventures of Eliza Fraser* (B) ('76)	a
Waterston, Sam	*Sweet William* (B) ('80)	a
Waterston, Sam	*Three* ('69)	a
Watson, Mitch	*Rush Week* ('89)	a
Waybenga, Ronald	*Spider's Nest*	a
Wead, Tim	*Teen Mothers* ('68)	a
Weaving, Hugo	*. . . Almost* (A) ('90)	a
Weaving, Hugo	*The Right Hand Man* ('87)	a
Weaving, Hugo	*Wendy Cracked a Walnut* (A)	a
Webb, David	*The Unapproachable* ('82)	a
Webber, Stephen	*Single White Female* ('92)	a
Weber, Dewey	*Chain of Desire* ('92)	a, p
Wehe, Oliver	*Erendira* (Br) ('83)	a
Weiss, Steve	*Baring It All* ('85)	a, p
Weisser, Norbert	*Midnight Express* ('78)	a
Welker, Michael	*Drop Dead Fred* ('91)	a
Weller, Peter	*Apology* ('86)	a
Weller, Peter	*Cat Chaser* ('88)	a
Weller, Peter	*A Killing Affair* ('85)	a
Weller, Peter	*The Tunnel* (Sp/Ar) ('89)	a
Welles, George	*Oh! Calcutta* ('72)	a, p
Wells, Vernon	*The Shrimp on the Barbie* ('90)	a
Welsh, Jonathan	*It's All in Good Taste*	a
Welsh, Kenneth	*Covergirl* ('82)	a
West, Adam	*Fiona*	a
West, Adam	*The Happy Hooker Goes to Hollywood* ('80)	a
West, Timothy	*Joseph Andrews* (B) ('77)	a
Westmoreland, James	*Stacey* ('73)	a
Weston, Jack	*The Four Seasons* ('81)	a
Whancy, Luther Bud	*Toga Party* ('79)	a
Whitaker, Johnie	*Tom Sawyer* ('73)	a
White, Bo	*A Very Natural Thing* ('74)	a, p
White, Bo	*Wakefield Poole's Bible* ('74)	a
White, Michael	*Fun Down There* ('88)	a, p
Whiting, Leonard	*Romeo and Juliet* ('68)	a
Widmer, Alexander	*Triumph of Eagles*	a
Wierzjewski, Charly	*Super Market*	a, p
Wiggett, Mark	*Quadrophenia* (B) ('79)	a

Wilborn, Carlton	*Grief* ('93)	a
Wilborn, Carlton	*Truth or Dare* ('91)	a, p
Wilby, James	*Maurice* (B) ('87)	a, p
Wilby, James	*A Summer Story* (B) ('88)	a
Wild, Gary	*Cat Murkil and the Silks*	a
Wild, Gary	*Cruisin' High* ('76)	a
Wilde, Cornel	*The Naked Prey* ('66)	a
Wilder, Gene	*The Adventures of Sherlock Holmes' Smarter Brother* ('75)	a
Wilder, Gene	*The Sunday Lovers* ('80)	a
Wilder, Gene	*The Woman in Red* ('84)	a
Wilder, James	*Prey of the Chameleon* ('91)	a
Wiles, Michael	*Invasion of Privacy* ('92)	a
Wilker, Jose	*Bye, Bye Brazil* (Br) ('80)	a
Wilker, Jose	*Dona Flor and Her Two Husbands* (Br) ('78)	a
Williams, Billy Dee	*The Final Comedown* ('72)	a
Williams, Hutch	*Naked Instinct* ('93)	a
Williams, Jason	*Danger Zone II* ('88)	a
Williams, Jason	*Flesh Gordon* ('72)	a, p
Williams, Jerold	*Opposing Force* ('87)	a
Williams, Kenneth	*Carry on Behind* (B) ('75)	a
Williams, Kenneth	*Carry on Constable* (B)	a
Williams, Kenneth	*Carry on Emmanuelle* (B) ('78)	a
Williams, Robin	*The Fisher King* ('91)	a
Williams, Robin	*The Survivors* ('83)	p
Williams, Treat	*Flashpoint* ('84)	a
Williams, Treat	*Hair* ('79)	a
Williams, Treat	*Sweet Lies* (F) ('89)	a
Williams, Treat	*Third Degree Burn* ('89)	a
Williamson, Fred	*Black Caesar* ('73)	a
Williamson, Fred	*Hammer* ('72)	a
Williamson, Fred	*Hell Up in Harlem* ('73)	a
Williamson, Fred	*The Messenger* (I) ('87)	a
Willis, Bruce	*Color of Night* ('94)	a
Willis, Bruce	*Pulp Fiction* ('94)	a
Wilmer, Douglas	*Unman, Wittering and Zigo* (B) ('71)	a
Wilms, Andre	*Le Groupe*	a
Wilroy, Channing	*Pink Flamingos* ('72)	a
Wilson, Lambert	*The Belly of an Architect* (B) ('87)	a
Wilson, Lambert	*La Femme Publique* (F)	a
Wilson, Lambert	*Rendez-vous* (F) ('86)	a, p
Wilson, Lambert	*Strangers: Small Sounds and Tilting Shadows* ('92)	a
Wilson, Robert Brian	*Silent Night, Deadly Night* ('84)	a
Wilson, Roger	*Second Time Lucky* (A) ('84)	a
Wilson, Roger	*Thunder Alley* ('85)	a

Wilson, Stuart	*Jewel in the Crown* ('84)	a
Wilson, Teddy	*Bound by Honor* ('93)	a
Winchester, Jeff	*Olivia* ('83)	a
Winn, David	*My Therapist* ('83)	a
Winstone, Raymond	*Quadrophenia* (B) ('79)	a, p
Winter, Edward	*The Buddy System* ('83)	a
Winters, Nathan Forrest	*Clownhouse* ('88)	a
Wirth, Billy	*Red Shoe Diaries* ('91)	a
Wolff, Frank	*The Lickerish Quartet* (I) ('70)	p
Woltz, Randy	*Young Warriors* ('83)	a
Wood, David	*if. . . .* (B) ('68)	a
Wood, Timothy	*Love Circles* (F) ('85)	a, p
Woods, James	*Curse of the Starving Class* ('94)	a
Woods, James	*The Onion Field* ('79)	a, p
Woods, James	*Videodrome* ('83)	a
Woods, Michael	*Lady Beware* (C) ('87)	a
Woods, Michael	*Red Shoe Diary 2* ('92)	a
Woods, Robert	*I Cannoni Tuonana Ancora* (I)	a
Wright, Dorsey	*Hair* ('79)	a
Wright, Ed	*Necromancer* ('88)	a
Wright, Ken	*Opposing Force* ('87)	a
Wright, Patrick	*The Abductors* ('71)	a, p
Wright, Patrick	*Beneath the Valley of the Ultravixens* ('79)	a
Wright, Patrick	*Good Morning . . . and Good Bye!* ('67)	a
Wright, Patrick	*Hollywood High* ('77)	a
Wright, Patrick	*Young Lady Chatterley* (B) ('76)	a, p
Wyatt, B.	*History of the Parking Lot*	a, p
Wyler, Steve	*Passionate Pleasures*	a
Wyman, John	*Tuxedo Warrior* ('82)	a
Xzntos, Dionessis	*Angel* (Gr)	a
Yaari, Yosi	*Auditions* ('78)	a, p
Yallaly, Jim	*Swim Team* ('79)	a
Yam, Simon	*Tongs* ('86)	a
York, John J.	*Werewolf* ('87)	a
York, Michael	*Final Assignment* (C) ('80)	p
York, Michael	*Justine* (B) ('69)	a
York, Michael	*The Strange Affair* (B) ('68)	a
Young, Aden	*The Black Robe* (C) ('91)	a
Young, Richard	*Night Call Nurses* ('72)	a
Young-Evans, Mitchell	*Inside Out* ('92)	a
Youngs, Jim	*Out of Control* ('85)	a
Younnou, Spiros	*Shaved Heads*	a, p
Yulin, Harris	*End of the Road* ('70)	a
Yulin, Harris	*Fatal Beauty* ('85)	a
Yurasek, John	*Less Than Zero* ('87)	a

Zagarino, Frank	*The Revenger* ('90)	a
Zane, Billy	*Dead Calm* (A) ('89)	a
Zane, Billy	*Lake Consequence* ('92)	a
Zanin, Bruno	*Inganni*	a, p
Zdar, Robert	*Maniac Cop* ('88)	a
Zdar, Robert	*Maniac Cop 2* ('90)	a
Zeigler, Gunther	*I Like the Girls Who Do* (G)	a, p
Zelenovic, Srdjan	*Andy Warhol's Frankenstein* ('74)	a, p
Zelman, Gary	*Slammer Girls* ('86)	a
Zelnicker, Michael	*Pick-up Summer* (C) ('81)	a
Zidaric, Ranko	*The Whore's Holiday*	a
Znamenak, Istvan	*Time Stands Still* (H) ('82)	a
Zolty, Jacques	*Andrea* (F) ('75)	a
Zrncic, Zvonco	*Scent of Passion* (I)	a
Zurita, Humberto	*De Mujer a Mujer* (M)	a
Zurita, Humberto	*El Amor Esun Juego Ex* (M)	a
Zurita, Humberto	*El Camalla* (M)	a
Zutaut, Brad	*Nudity Required* ('89)	a

NECROLOGY

"I don't know if there is life after death, but I'm taking a change of
underwear just in case."

—Dennis Quaid, *D.O.A.*

Death has taken some of the handsomest stars of the silver screen
whom we'll always remember for their grace and beauty. Here are a
few of the departed at their prime.

Stephen Boyd	*The Oscar* ('66)
Jeff Chandler	*Broken Arrow* ('50)
Montgomery Clift	*A Place in the Sun* ('51)
James Dean	*East of Eden* ('55)
Brandon de Wilde	*Blue Denim* ('59)
Sean Flynn	*Son of Captain Blood* ('62)
Mark Frechette	*Zabriskie Point* ('70)

Rock Hudson	*Taza, Son of Cochise* ('54)
Jeffrey Hunter	*King of Kings* ('61)
Jim Hutton	*Walk, Don't Run* ('66)
Brandon Lee	*The Crow* ('94)
Bruce Lee	*Enter the Dragon* ('73)
Steve McQueen	*Baby the Rain Must Fall* ('65)
Audie Murphy	*The Red Badge of Courage* ('51)
River Phoenix	*My Own Private Idaho* ('91)
Robert Shaw	*Swashbuckler* ('76)

RESOURCES AND CONTACT LIST

VIDEOTAPES

Insider Video Club

International quality videotapes from around the world. Large selection of foreign and domestic nonpornographic films of high caliber. Insider Video Club, P.O. Box 93399, Hollywood, CA 90093. Toll-free (outside California) (800) 634-2242; California residents (213) 661-8330.

Campfire Video

Sells retail specially produced videotapes that trace the history of male nudity in films. Also issues *Movie Buff* newsletter. Campfire Video, P.O. Box 71318, Los Angeles, CA 90071.

CELEBRITY PHOTOGRAPHS AND PHOTOGRAPH SEARCHES

The Sexy Celebrity Photo Club

Sells retail photographs of clad and nude celebrities; offers photographs and magazines; will conduct searches for specific requests. Catalog and listings available for male and female celebrities. Membership required. Entertainment Enterprises, P.O. Box 323, Hamburg, NY 14075.

BIBLIOGRAPHY

Arce, Hector. *Gary Cooper: An Intimate Biography.* William Morrow, 1979.

Arce, Hector. *The Secret Life of Tyrone Power.* William Morrow, 1979.

Anger, Kenneth. *Hollywood Babylon.* Associated Press Professional Services, 1965.

Anger, Kenneth. *Hollywood Babylon: II.* E. P. Dutton, 1984.

Bacon, James. *Hollywood Is a Four-Letter Word.* Henry Regnery Co., 1976.

Bacon, James. *Made in Hollywood.* Contemporary Books, 1977.

Balio, Tino. *United Artists: The Company That Changed the Film Industry.* University of Wisconsin Press, 1987.

Bell-Metereau, Rebecca. *Hollywood Androgyny.* Columbia University Press, 1985.

Bergan, Ronald. *Sports in the Movies.* Proteus Books, 1982.

Brady, Frank. *Citizen Welles.* Charles Scribner's Sons, 1989.

Capote, Truman. *Answered Prayers: The Unfinished Novel.* Random House, 1987.

Capote, Truman. *Music for Chameleons.* Random House, 1980.

Castle, William. *Step Right Up: I'm Going to Scare the Pants Off America.* Putnam, 1976.

Crane, Cheryl. *Detour: A Hollywood Story.* William Morrow, 1988.

Clarke, Gerald. *Capote: A Biography.* Simon & Schuster, 1988.

Des Barres, Pamela. *I'm With the Band: Confessions of a Groupie.* Beech Tree Books, 1987.

Edwards, Michael. *In the Shadow of the King: Priscilla, Elvis and Me.* St. Martin's Press, 1988.

Eels, George. *Final Gig: The Man Behind the Murder.* Harcourt, Brace, Jovanovich, 1991.

Eels, George. *Robert Mitchum: A Biography.* Franklin Watts, 1984.

Elley, Derek. *The Epic Film: Myth and History.* Routledge & Kegan Paul, 1984.

Erens, Patricia. *The Jew in American Cinema.* Indiana University Press, 1984.

Gifford, Barry. *The Devil Thumbs a Ride.* Grove Press, 1988.

Goldman, Albert. *The Lives of John Lennon.* William Morrow, 1988.

Gordon, William A. *The Ultimate Hollywood Tour Book.* NorthRidge Books, 1992.

Haberman, J., and Jonathan Rosenblum. *Midnight Movies.* Harper & Row, 1973.

Hadleigh, Boze. *Conversations with My Elders.* St. Martin's Press, 1976.

Hardy, Phil, ed. *The Encyclopedia of Horror Movies.* Harper & Row, 1986.

Higham, Charles, and Roy Moseley. *Cary Grant: The Lonely Heart.* Harcourt, Brace, Jovanovich, 1989.

Higham, Charles. *Errol Flynn: The Untold Story.* Doubleday, 1980.

Higham, Charles. *Merchant of Dreams.* Donald I. Fine, Inc., 1993.

Kelly, Kitty. *His Way: The Unauthorized Biography of Frank Sinatra.* Bantam Books, 1986.

LaGuardia, Robert. *Monty: A Biography of Montgomery Clift.* Arbor House, 1977.

Lenne, Gerard. *Sex on the Screen: Eroticism in Film.* St. Martin's Press, 1975.

Maltin, L., ed. *Leonard Maltin's TV Movies and Video Guide.* NAL Penquin, 1988, 1989, 1990, 1991, 1992, 1993.

Malone, Michael. *Heroes of Eros.* E. P. Dutton, 1979.

McDonald, Boyd. *Cruising the Movies.* Gay Presses of New York, 1985.

Mellen, Joan. *Big Bad Wolves: Masculinity in the American Film.* Pantheon Books, 1977.

Monaco, James. *American Film Now.* New American Library, 1984.

Peary, Danny. *Guide for the Film Fanatic.* Simon & Schuster, 1986.

Phillips, Baxter. *Cut: The Unseen Cinema.* Bounty Books, 1975.

Pickard, Roy. *Who Played Who in the Movies.* Schocken Books, 1981.

Robertson, Patrick. *Guinness Film Facts & Feats.* Sterling Publishing Co., 1985.

Russell, Ken. *Altered States.* Bantam Books, 1982.

Russo, Vito. *The Celluloid Closet,* rev. ed. Harper & Row, 1987.

Rutledge, Leigh W. *The Gay Book of Lists.* Alyson Publications, 1987.

Sagin, Seth, and Philip Dray. *Hollywood Films of the '70s.* Harper & Row, 1984.

Sealy, Shirley. *The Celebrity Sex Register.* Simon & Schuster, 1982.

Siciliano, Enzo. *Pasolini.* Random House, 1982.

Spada, James. *Peter Lawford: The Man Who Kept the Secrets.* Bantam Books, 1991.

Speigel, Penina. *McQueen: Untold Story of a Bad Boy in Hollywood.* Doubleday & Co., 1986.

Stallings, Penny. *Flesh and Fantasy.* St. Martin's Press, 1978.

van Gelder, Peter. *That's Hollywood.* HarperCollins, 1990.

Wallace, Irving, et. al. *Intimate Sex Lives of Famous People.* Delacorte Press, 1981.

Waters, John. *Shock Value.* Dell Publishing Co., 1981.

Wayne, Jane Ellen. *Cooper's Women.* Prentice Hall Press, 1988.

Wood, Robin. *Hollywood: From Vietnam to Reagan.* Columbia University Press, 1986.

Yule, Andrew. *Picture Shows.* Prometheus Books, 1992.

THE
VOYEUR'S GUIDE
TO *W*OMEN
IN THE MOVIES

THE VOYEUR'S GUIDE TO 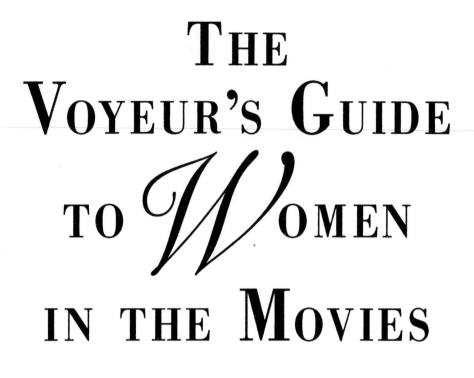OMEN IN THE MOVIES

MART MARTIN

CONTEMPORARY
BOOKS
CHICAGO

Library of Congress Cataloging-in-Publication Data

Martin, Mart.
    The voyeur's guide to men in the movies / Mart Martin.
      p.   cm.
    Title on added t.p., inverted: The voyeur's guide to women in the
movies.
    Includes bibliographical references.
    ISBN 0-8092-3642-7
    1. Motion pictures—Anecdotes.   2. Motion pictures—Humor.
3. Motion pictures—Miscellanea.   4. Men in motion pictures.
5. Women in motion pictures.   I. Title.   II. Title: Voyeur's guide
to women in the movies.
PN1994.9.M36   1994
791.43—dc20   94-35121
                                                           CIP

Published by Contemporary Books, Inc.
Two Prudential Plaza, Chicago, Illinois 60601-6790
Manufactured in the United States of America
International Standard Book Number: 0-8092-3642-7
10   9   8   7   6   5   4   3   2   1

Dedicated to
Judy Carol Martin Clifton
who is four of the finest women I know.
She is a perfect sister, a devoted mother,
a loving wife, and a shining example
to the small children she teaches each day.

CONTENTS

"Today I saw the most beautiful pair of knockers I've ever seen in my life."
—Howard Hughes, commenting on seeing his first photographs of Jane Russell

PREFACE

In assembling this book, I have purposely made no distinction between *cinema* films and *telefilms*, or those productions made for TV. Each year sees more and more of the latter appearing, with many of them also receiving a theatrical release overseas after appearing on American television.

Some avid cinemaphiles may be offended by my lack of distinction. So be it. Besides, John McCarty preceded me in doing this, when he pierced this now almost-artificial barrier in his 1985 book, *Psychos*. Keeping one of the many film review collections handily available while perusing this guide might provide some comfort to those readers so offended. Plus, those publications contain valuable information about ratings, running times, and release dates, which I have chosen to omit.

This book also makes little if no comment—except in a humorous vein—about the quality of the films mentioned. In truth, the quality varies considerably. The films noted here range from Excellent to Absolutely Excruciating for a viewer to watch. I leave such reviews to the capable likes of Leonard Maltin and the others, whose guides serve that purpose most admirably. But a cautionary note must be added. In many instances, there is a wide variance between their opinions. Astute cinema voyeurs soon learn to form their own personal opinions, naturally after having actually viewed a film.

One of the real pleasures in assembling information of this type is the friends who help with the endeavor. My sincere thanks to Joe Campbell, Scott Lee, Bob Stoll, Chuck Thompson, and Frank Wright. I appreciate the support and enthusiasm you've shown me, and hope this book meets your expectations.

The final words of thanks are for my agent and my editor. My

literary agent Mitch Rose personifies competence. That, combined with his always encouraging voice, makes any contact with him most pleasurable. As for Gene Brissie, my editor, I was fortunate in being able to work with him—for he is one of the recognized masters of his trade.

INTRODUCTION

Once upon a time I reviewed films, a perfectly respectable undertaking. Then, my attention got distracted, by, shall we say all the *nasty stuff* happening in those films. Naked butts scampered across the screen, causing me to promptly forget the plot. The most horrid creatures imaginable suddenly erupted from unsuspecting stomachs, as I slid lower in my seat, squealing over the special effects. Leading ladies vomited, and my mind drifted while I remembered how someone else devoured a cockroach with relish in another film.

Suddenly, it became impossible for me to concentrate on any particular film. All at once, I had ceased being a reviewer. I had become something else: a *voyeur*. When I watched a film, I wiggled in anticipation of what titillating thing I was going to see next. And Hollywood didn't disappoint me. Wondering if I'd missed anything important, I started viewing some of the older films again. This time what I saw in those films was enlightening. All of these *nasty* things had always been present in films. These more recent films weren't doing anything new. I merely hadn't paid close enough attention to the older films the first time around. Now, I was absolutely hooked. I had truly become a genuine cinema voyeur.

Film noir, new wave, avant-garde, psychodramas, made-for-TVers. If I wanted to read a study of the genre, or pore through a comprehensive listing of casting credits, or even peruse a critical collection of film essays, all I had to do was reach for one of the informative guides on the market. But, my addiction, you see, was for something far, far different. And no guide existed that would tell me what I wanted to know.

Ever seen a naked butt scamper across the screen of a film you were watching, and wonder where else you'd seen it? Or watched an actor gobble a cockroach—and been curious about which other actors had been brave enough to perform the same stunt? Want to see your favorite actress prance around in her black panties and bra?

Well, if so, welcome to *The Voyeur's Guide to Women in the Movies*. Forget film plots, ignore technical and performance artistry, and don't even give a thought to technique. Don't try to look for critical ratings, cast credits, or scholarly treatises in here. If that's the type of information you seek, then there are plenty of other excellent, informative references available. Exactly what will you find in this guide? Frankly put, the cheap thrills. The naughty shenanigans. The unsavory things the other guides overlooked (and your mother warned you that polite people ignored). Let's just say that this guide is full of things a true cinema voyeur looks for and relishes.

If I've made mistakes and omissions, don't curse me. Send them in, and I'll try and include them in the next edition.

One final comment about this guide. Because a voyeur's thrill comes from peeking, don't try and "read" this guide from cover to cover. It's not that kind of book. Instead, *peek at it*. Flip it open anywhere, at any page and take a peek. Go ahead; it's *gratifying*.

AFFLICTIONS

"I bet she won't live through the night. She has four fatal diseases."
—Margaret O'Brien, *Meet Me in St. Louis*

Bring me your crippled, your lame, your blind—I'll star 'em in a big Hollywood movie! Nobody loves an affliction like Tinseltown. Get out those handkerchiefs and get ready to weep profusely over these afflictions.

The Blind

Justine Bateman	*Can You Feel Me Dancing?* ('86)
Virginia Cherrill	*City Lights* ('31)
Laura Dern	*Mask* ('85)
Patty Duke	*The Miracle Worker* ('62)
Faye Dunaway	*Midnight Crossing* ('88)
Mia Farrow	*See No Evil* ('71)
Meg Foster	*Desperate Intruder* ('83)
Elizabeth Hartman	*A Patch of Blue* ('65)
Audrey Hepburn	*Wait Until Dark* ('67)
Isabelle Huppert	*Cactus* ('86)
Lynn-Holly Johnson	*Ice Castles* ('79)
Ida Lupino	*On Dangerous Ground* ('52)
Elizabeth Montgomery	*Second Sight: A Love Story* ('84)
Patricia Neal	*Psyche '59* ('64)
Maria Schell	*The Hanging Tree* ('59)
Heather Sears	*The Story of Esther Costello* ('57)

Madeleine Stowe	*Blink* ('94)
Uma Thurman	*Jennifer 8* ('92)
Jane Wyman	*Magnificent Obsession* ('54)

The Anorexics and Bulimics

Meredith Baxter Birney	*Kate's Secret* ('86)
Cynthia Gibb	*The Karen Carpenter Story* ('89)
Jane Horrocks	*Life Is Sweet* ('91)
Jennifer Jones	*Love Letters* ('45)
Jennifer Jason Leigh	*The Best Little Girl in the World* ('81)

The Crippled

Samantha Eggar	*The Walking Stick* ('70)
Marilyn Hassett	*The Other Side of the Mountain* ('75)
Rachel Levin	*Gaby—A True Story* ('87)
Donna Lai Ming Lew	*Odd Birds* ('85)
Kristy McNichol	*Just the Way You Are* ('84)
Nanette Newman	*Long Ago Tomorrow* ('70)
Eleanor Parker	*The Man with the Golden Arm* ('55)
Jean Simmons	*Dominique* ('78)
Natalie Wood	*The Affair* ('73)
Jane Wyman	*The Glass Menagerie* ('50)
Stephanie Zimbalist	*Long Journey Back* ('78)

The Deaf and Mute

Holly Hunter	*The Piano* ('93)
Amy Irving	*Voices* ('79)
Marlee Matlin	*Children of a Lesser God* ('86)
Dorothy McGuire	*The Spiral Staircase* ('46)
Susan Strasberg	*Psych-Out* ('68)
Vanessa Vaughan	*Crazy Moon* ('86)
Jane Wyman	*Johnny Belinda* ('48)
Loretta Young	*And Now Tomorrow* ('44)

The Retarded and Mentally Ill

Olivia de Havilland	*The Snake Pit* ('48)
Julie Kavner	*No Other Love* ('79)
Janet Margolin	*David and Lisa* ('63)
Yvette Mimieux	*The Light in the Piazza* ('62)
Linda Purl	*Like Normal People* ('79)
Jean Seberg	*Lilith* ('64)
Marlo Thomas	*Nobody's Child* ('86)
Natalie Wood	*The Cracker Factory* ('79)

Sufferers of an Unnamed, Mysterious, Deadly Disease

Bette Davis	*Dark Victory* ('39)
Sandy Dennis	*Sweet November* ('68)
Jodie Foster	*Echoes of a Summer* ('76)
Kay Francis	*One Way Passage* ('32)
Susan Hayward	*The Stolen Hours* ('63)
Marthe Keller	*Bobby Deerfield* ('77)
Ali MacGraw	*Love Story* ('70)
Romy Schneider	*Deathwatch* ('80)
Barbara Stanwyck	*The Other Love* ('47)

BEST MENTAL BREAKDOWNS

Kathy Bates	*At Play in the Fields of the Lord* ('91)
Bette Davis	*What Ever Happened to Baby Jane?* ('62)
Catherine Deneuve	*Repulsion* ('65)

BEST SCENE STEALER

Dorothy Malone—*Man of a Thousand Faces* ('57). Malone's a semi-frustrated singer who rushes onstage during her husband's, James Cagney's, performance and swallows acid, which severely damages her vocal cords—in addition to spoiling Cagney's act.

ANTIQUITIES

"You're better than news. You're history!"
—Stuart Erwin, *Viva Villa!*

The cinema always looks at ancient history's females with mixed results. The settings may be historical, but the language spoken is frequently so movie-star modern that it's hysterical.

SERPENTS OF THE NILE

"Queen Cleopatra is widely read, well versed in the natural sciences and mathematics. She speaks seven languages proficiently. Were she not a woman, one would consider her to be an intellectual."
—Andrew Keir, *Cleopatra*

Cleopatra and her clonish sisters: Some were rulers of Egypt, others were the Pharaohs' wives. All of them were seductive serpents of the Nile. Hooray for these honeys' hieroglyphics!

Amanda Barrie	*Carry on Cleo* ('65)
Michelle Bauer	*The Tomb* ('86)
Anne Baxter	*The Ten Commandments* ('56)
Barbara Brylska	*Pharaoh (Faroan)* ('65)
Claudette Colbert	*Cleopatra* ('34)
Joan Collins	*Land of the Pharaohs* ('55)
Jeanne Crain	*Queen of the Nile* ('62)
Linda Cristal	*Legions of the Nile* ('60)
Rhonda Fleming	*Serpent of the Nile* ('53)
Zita Johann	*The Mummy* ('32)
Vivien Leigh	*Caesar and Cleopatra* ('46)
Sophia Loren	*Two Nights with Cleopatra* ('54)
Virginia Mayo	*The Story of Mankind* ('57)
Hildegarde Neil	*Antony and Cleopatra* ('73)

Debra Paget	*Princess of the Nile* ('54), *Cleopatra's Daughter* ('60)
Elizabeth Taylor	*Cleopatra* ('63)
Gene Tierney	*The Egyptian* ('54)
Stephanie Zimbalist	*The Awakening* ('80)

THE SPLENDORS OF ROME

If all roads lead to Rome, then perhaps one might be able to see one of these beautiful Roman consorts during a cinematic journey.

Brigitte Bardot	*Nero's Big Weekend* ('56)
Gianna Maria Canale	*Theodora, Slave Empress* ('54)
Claudette Colbert	*The Sign of the Cross* ('32)
Susan Hayward	*Demetrius and the Gladiators* ('54)
Madeline Kahn	*History of the World: Part I* ('81)
Sylvia Koscina	*The Last Roman* ('68)
Patricia Laffin	*Quo Vadis* ('51)
Belinda Lee	*Messalina* ('59)
Sophia Loren	*The Fall of the Roman Empire* ('64)
Gloria Swanson	*Nero's Big Weekend* ('56)

ASS KICKERS AND BALL BUSTERS

"Don't fuck with me fellas. This ain't my first time at the rodeo."
—Faye Dunaway, *Mommie Dearest*

No sir, don't mess with these babes. They really know how to kick ass and bust balls. If you're male and cross one of these cuties, you'll be singing soprano when she's finished with you.

Tiana Alexander	*Catch the Heart* ('88)
Jeanne Bell	*T.N.T. Jackson* ('74)
Marki Bey	*Sugar Hill* ('74)
Honor Blackman	*Goldfinger* ('64)
Tamara Dobson	*Cleopatra Jones* ('73)
Farrah Fawcett	*Extremities* ('86)
Whoopi Goldberg	*Fatal Beauty* ('87)
Melanie Griffith	*Cherry 2000* ('88)
Deborra Lee-Furness	*Shame* ('88)
Kay Lenz	*Fast-Walking* ('82)
Sondra Locke	*Sudden Impact* ('83)
Amy Madigan	*Streets of Fire* ('84)
Jeanne Moreau	*The Bride Wore Black* ('68)
Brigitte Nielsen	*Red Sonja* ('85)
Jamie Rose	*Lady Blue* ('85)
Gena Rowlands	*Gloria* ('80)
Rene Russo	*Lethal Weapon III* ('92)
Carrie Snodgress	*Murphy's Law* ('86)
Connie Stevens	*Scorchy* ('76)
Sharon Stone	*Total Recall* ('90)
Sigourney Weaver	*Alien* ('79), *Aliens* ('86), *Alien³* ('92)

THE ASS BUSTER AWARD

Awarded to **Raquel Welch** for *Myra Breckenridge* ('70). As the sex-changed Myra, Raquel cons a hunky, well-built male into taking a physical examination. After tying up the stud, she jerks down his pants and dons an enormous dildo. Myra then uses her pseudosex organ to plunge the hunk's buns, giving him a taste of real ass busting, female style.

THE SEX WITH ME IS HAZARDOUS TO YOUR HEALTH AWARD

Awarded to **Jenny Runacre** of *The Last Days of Man on Earth* ('73), whose character absorbs her lovers after sex.

THE MISS CASTRATOR AWARD

Awarded to **Pam Grier**, for *Foxy Brown* ('74), in which she catches the villain, an evil white drug pusher, and deals him real female justice. She has her boys hold the dude down, unzips his pants, and castrates the baddie. His sex organ is placed in a jar, which Grier later presents to the villain's equally treacherous girlfriend.

ATHLETES

"I like a man who can run faster than I can."
—Jane Russell, *Gentlemen Prefer Blondes*

If you have a special passion for sweaty female bodies, then here's your chance to score. Following is an assorted collection of perspiring, heavy-breathing female athletes for your enjoyment.

	Aerobics
Jamie Lee Curtis	*Perfect* ('85)
Cynthia Dale	*Heavenly Bodies* ('85)
	Baseball
Robyn Barto	*Blue Skies Again* ('83)
Tatum O'Neal	*The Bad News Bears* ('76)
	Skating/Skiing
Suzy Chaffee	*Fire and Ice* ('87)
Lynn Frederick	*Schizo* ('77)
Carol Heiss	*Snow White and the Three Stooges* ('61)
Sonja Henie	*Sun Valley Serenade* ('41)
Christianne Hurt	*Blades of Courage* ('88)

Lynn-Holly Johnson	*Ice Castles* ('79)
Moira Kelly	*The Cutting Edge* ('92)
Vera Hruba Ralston	*Lake Placid Serenade* ('44)
Raquel Welch	*Kansas City Bomber* ('72)

Tennis

Carling Bassett	*Spring Fever* ('83)
Sally Forrest	*Hard, Fast and Beautiful* ('51)
Glynnis O'Connor	*Little Mo* ('78)

Track/Jogging

Susan Anton	*Goldengirl* ('79)
Patty Duke	*Billie* ('65)
Mariel Hemingway	*Personal Best* ('82)
Katharine Hepburn	*Pat and Mike* ('52)
Elke Sommer	*The Wicked Dreams of Paula Schultz* ('68)
Cicely Tyson	*Wilma* ('77)
Joanne Woodward	*See How She Runs* ('78)

Wrestling

Regina Baff	*Below the Belt* ('80)
Laura Brannigan	*Delta Pi* ('85)
Vickie Frederick	*. . . All the Marbles* ('81)
Laurene Landon	*. . . All the Marbles* ('81)

AVIA-TRIXIES

"I'm all warmed up and ready to take off . . . I fly on high octane."
—Greer Garson, *Adventure*

These are the babes of the big blue sky: pilots and flight attendants. They're a bunch of high-flying ladies—off they go into the wild blue yonder. Wanna go into a tailspin for one of these tootsies?

Ursula Andress	*Loaded Guns* ('75)
Constance Bennett	*Tail Spin* ('39)
Valerie Bertinelli	*Pancho Barnes* ('88)
Karen Black	*Airport 1975* ('74)
Honor Blackman	*Goldfinger* ('64)
Susan Clark	*Amelia Earhart* ('76)
Courtney Cox	*Till We Meet Again* ('89)
Bette Davis	*Skyward* ('80)
Doris Day	*Julie* ('56)
Marlene Dietrich	*The Ship of Lost Men (aka The Ship of Lost Souls)* ('29)
Françoise Dorleac	*The Soft Skin* ('64)
Patty Duke	*A Time to Triumph* ('80)
Alice Faye	*Tail Spin* ('39)
Sharon Gless	*The Sky's No Limit* ('84)
Julie Hagerty	*Airplane!* ('80)
Katharine Hepburn	*Christopher Strong* ('33)
Elizabeth Hurley	*Passenger 57* ('92)
Joyce Jillson	*Superchick* ('73)
Janet Leigh	*Jet Pilot* ('57)
Myrna Loy	*Petticoat Fever* ('36), *Wings in the Dark* ('35)
Yvette Mimieux	*Skyjacked* ('72)
Suzanne Pleshette	*Wings of Fire* ('67)
Stefanie Powers	*Shadow on the Sun* ('88)
Leni Riefenstahl	*SOS Iceberg* ('33)
Rosalind Russell	*Flight for Freedom* ('43)

Hanna Schygulla	*Delta Force* ('86)
Kim Stanley	*The Right Stuff* ('83)
Connie Stevens	*Way . . . Way Out* ('66)
Pamela Tiffin	*Come Fly with Me* ('63)
Lana Turner	*The Lady Takes a Flyer* ('58)
Karen Valentine	*Coffee, Tea or Me?* ('73)
Lindsay Wagner	*The Taking of Flight 847* ('88)

HIGH FLIERS

These are high fliers of another type—the trapeze and high-wire artists.

Olga Baclanova	*Freaks* ('32)
Anne Bancroft	*Gorilla at Large* ('54)
Anne Baxter	*Carnival Story* ('54)
Claudia Cardinale	*Circus World* ('64)
Pia Dagermark	*Elvira Madigan* ('67)
Marion Davies	*Polly of the Circus* ('32)
Doris Day	*Billy Rose's Jumbo* ('62)
Solveig Dommartin	*Wings of Desire* ('88)
Britt Ekland	*The Great Wallendas* ('78)
Rhonda Fleming	*The Big Circus* ('59)
Valeria Golino	*Pee-wee's Big Adventure* ('85)
Betty Hutton	*The Greatest Show on Earth* ('52)
Glynis Johns	*Encore* ('52)
Nastassja Kinski	*One from the Heart* ('82)
Gina Lollobrigida	*Trapeze* ('56)

AWARD WINNERS:
THE BEST ACTRESS ROLES

"You can always put that award where your heart ought to be."
—Bette Davis, *All About Eve*

Each of these ladies was voted by her peers in the Academy of Motion Picture Arts and Sciences as the "Best Actress" of a particular year. What is a "Best Actress"? What kinds of roles led to their victories?

Brit Babes

Greer Garson	*Mrs. Miniver* ('42)
Julie Andrews	*Mary Poppins* ('64)
Julie Christie	*Darling* ('65)
Maggie Smith	*The Prime of Miss Jean Brodie* ('69)
Glenda Jackson	*Women in Love* ('70)
Emma Thompson	*Howards End* ('92)

The Deaf and Mute

Jane Wyman	*Johnny Belinda* ('48)
Anne Bancroft	*The Miracle Worker* ('62)
Marlee Matlin	*Children of a Lesser God* ('86)
Holly Hunter	*The Piano* ('93)

Dirt Diggers

Luise Rainer	*The Good Earth* ('37)
Sally Field	*Places in the Heart* ('84)

Drama Italiano

Anna Magnani	*The Rose Tattoo* ('55)
Sophia Loren	*Two Women* ('61)
Cher	*Moonstruck* ('87)

Frumps and Flirts

Mary Pickford	*Coquette* ('28-29)
Marie Dressler	*Min and Bill* ('30-31)
Claudette Colbert	*It Happened One Night* ('34)
Shirley Booth	*Come Back, Little Sheba* ('52)
Grace Kelly	*The Country Girl* ('54)
Patricia Neal	*Hud* ('63)
Glenda Jackson	*A Touch of Class* ('73)

Girls on Their Way Up

Katharine Hepburn	*Morning Glory* ('32-33)
Ginger Rogers	*Kitty Foyle* ('40)
Loretta Young	*The Farmer's Daughter* ('47)
Barbra Streisand	*Funny Girl* ('68)
Ellen Burstyn	*Alice Doesn't Live Here Anymore* ('74)
Jodie Foster	*The Silence of the Lambs* ('91)

Got Myself a Load of Man Trouble

Janet Gaynor	*Seventh Heaven* ('27-28)
Norma Shearer	*The Divorcee* ('29-30)
Luise Rainer	*The Great Ziegfeld* ('36)
Olivia de Havilland	*The Heiress* ('49)
Simone Signoret	*Room at the Top* ('59)
Jane Fonda	*Coming Home* ('78)

Loose Morals

Elizabeth Taylor	*Butterfield 8* ('60)
Jane Fonda	*Klute* ('71)
Liza Minnelli	*Cabaret* ('72)
Jodie Foster	*The Accused* ('88)

Oddballs

Judy Holliday	*Born Yesterday* ('50)
Diane Keaton	*Annie Hall* ('77)
Kathy Bates	*Misery* ('90)

The Pains of Motherhood

Helen Hayes	*The Sin of Madelon Claudet* ('31-32)
Olivia de Havilland	*To Each His Own* ('46)
Katharine Hepburn	*Guess Who's Coming to Dinner* ('67)
Katharine Hepburn	*On Golden Pond* ('81)
Shirley MacLaine	*Terms of Endearment* ('83)

Royals

Audrey Hepburn	*Roman Holiday* ('53)
Ingrid Bergman	*Anastasia* ('56)
Katharine Hepburn	*The Lion in Winter* ('68)

Southern Stuff

Bette Davis	*Jezebel* ('38)
Vivien Leigh	*Gone with the Wind* ('39), *A Streetcar Named Desire* ('51)
Sally Field	*Norma Rae* ('79)
Sissy Spacek	*Coal Miner's Daughter* ('80)
Geraldine Page	*The Trip to Bountiful* ('85)
Jessica Tandy	*Driving Miss Daisy* ('89)

Suffering Sisters

Bette Davis	*Dangerous* ('35)
Joan Fontaine	*Suspicion* ('41)
Jennifer Jones	*The Song of Bernadette* ('43)
Ingrid Bergman	*Gaslight* ('44)
Joanne Woodward	*The Three Faces of Eve* ('57)
Meryl Streep	*Sophie's Choice* ('82)

	Tough Bitches
Joan Crawford	*Mildred Pierce* ('45)
Susan Hayward	*I Want to Live!* ('58)
Elizabeth Taylor	*Who's Afraid of Virginia Woolf?* ('66)
Louise Fletcher	*One Flew over the Cuckoo's Nest* ('75)
Faye Dunaway	*Network* ('76)

SOLO OUTINGS

Both **Miliza Korjus** (*The Great Waltz*, '38) and **Jocelyn LaGarde** (*Hawaii*, '66) each made only one film—and each was nominated as Best Supporting Actress for her solo outing.

THE BLACK NOMINEES

There have not been many Black nominees for Best Actress (BA) or Best Supporting Actress (BSA)—and only two winners, fifty-one years apart!

Hattie McDaniel	*Gone with the Wind* ('39), BSA—winner
Ethel Waters	*Pinky* ('49), BSA
Dorothy Dandridge	*Carmen Jones* ('54), BA
Juanita Moore	*Imitation of Life* ('59), BSA
Beah Richards	*Guess Who's Coming to Dinner* ('67), BSA
Diana Ross	*Lady Sings the Blues* ('72), BA
Cicely Tyson	*Sounder* ('72), BA
Diahann Carroll	*Claudine* ('74), BA
Alfre Woodard	*Cross Creek* ('83), BSA
Whoopi Goldberg	*The Color Purple* ('85), BA
Margaret Avery	*The Color Purple* ('85), BSA
Oprah Winfrey	*The Color Purple* ('85), BSA
Whoopi Goldberg	*Ghost* ('90), BSA—winner
Angela Bassett	*What's Love Got to Do with It* ('93), BA

GRAND SLAMMERS

Only four actresses have won the Grand Slam—an Oscar, an Emmy, a Tony, and a Grammy.

Helen Hayes	Rita Moreno
Liza Minnelli	Barbra Streisand

BAD, BAD, BAD, BAD GIRLS

"I'm really not a bad girl; I'm just drawn that way."
—Jessica Rabbit, *Who Framed Roger Rabbit*

Lots of adjectives could be used to describe this collection of young ladies: cute, pretty, precious, attractive, sexy. But—beware—each and every one of them is nothing but trouble. In fact, they're harmful little armfuls of trouble.

Melissa Sue Anderson	*Happy Birthday to Me* ('81)
Ann-Margret	*Kitten with a Whip* ('64)
Drew Barrymore	*Firestarter* ('84), *Poison Ivy* ('92)
Lara Flynn Boyle	*The Temp* ('93)
Catherine Deneuve	*Repulsion* ('65)
Jodie Foster	*The Little Girl Who Lives Down the Lane* ('76)
Carrie Hamilton	*Hostage* ('88)
Linda Hayden	*Baby Love* ('69)
Barbara Hershey	*Last Summer* ('69)
Isabelle Huppert	*Violette* ('78)
Sondra Locke	*A Reflection of Fear* ('73)
Patty McCormack	*The Bad Seed* ('56)
Susan Oliver	*The Green-Eyed Blonde* ('57)

Tatum O'Neal	*Paper Moon* ('73)
Winona Ryder	*Heathers* ('89)
Paula Sheppard	*Holy Terror* ('77)
Jean Simmons	*Angel Face* ('53)
Sissy Spacek	*Carrie* ('76)
Tuesday Weld	*Pretty Poison* ('68)
Carrie Wells	*The Bad Seed* ('85)

CONDOM QUEEN

In the middle '30s, all over East Asia, condoms bearing a photograph of **Sylvia Sidney**, a reigning star at Paramount, were extremely popular. The package bore a retouched photograph (slanted eyes and larger breasts) of the actress as she appeared in *Merrily We Go to Hell* ('32). Director Walter Wanger once told Sidney, "You go into any drugstore in the Far East and ask for a S.S., and you get a condom with *your* picture on it."

BATHING BEAUTIES

"Women should be kept illiterate and clean, like canaries."
—Roscoe Karns, *Woman of the Year*

Bathing beauties—glamorous ladies in luxurious marble tubs full of bubbles, frontier ladies washing in cool mountain streams, sexpots in bathtubs with their guys. Care to scrub backs with any of these bathing beauties?

Maria Conchita Alonso	*Moscow on the Hudson* ('84)
Barbara Bach	*Force 10 from Navarone* ('78)
Adrienne Barbeau	*Swamp Thing* ('82)
Jacqueline Bisset	*The Mephisto Waltz* ('71)
Linda Blair	*Savage Streets* ('84)

Martine Carol	*The Sins of the Borgias* ('52)
Claudette Colbert	*Cleopatra* ('34)
Joan Crawford	*The Women* ('39)
Doris Day	*Pillow Talk* ('59)
Faye Dunaway	*Barfly* ('87)
Diane Keaton	*Looking for Mr. Goodbar* ('77)
Hanna Schygulla	*Forever Lulu* ('87)
Cornelia Sharpe	*Serpico* ('73)
Sharon Stone	*Sliver* ('93)
Sharon Tate	*The Fearless Vampire Killers* ('67)
Elizabeth Taylor	*Cleopatra* ('63)
Sigourney Weaver	*Half Moon Street* ('86)
Debra Winger	*Mike's Murder* ('84)
Susannah York	*Brotherly Love* ('69)

SHOWER SCENES

Angie Dickinson	*Dressed to Kill* ('80)
Valerie Kaprisky	*Breathless* ('83)
Janet Leigh	*Psycho* ('60)
Caroline Munro	*Slaughter High* ('86)
Sissy Spacek	*Carrie* ('76)
JoBeth Williams	*Endangered Species* ('82)

THE I DON'T LIKE WATER AWARD

Awarded to **Claudette Colbert** for her ass's milk bath in *The Sign of the Cross* ('32).

NEW THRONES FOR NEW KINGS

Whenever **Joan** *(Queen Bee)* **Crawford** remarried—she had four husbands—she also changed the name of her Brentwood estate and installed all new toilet seats. Evidently, the Queen thought a new King deserved a new throne.

BEHIND BARS

"I always thought it was a ridiculous name for a prison, Sing Sing,
I mean. Sounds more like it should be an opera house
or something."
—Audrey Hepburn, *Breakfast at Tiffany's*

Keepers of the keys: the female wardens and prison matrons. A rough, tough package of cookies. These matrons will push you in the slammer and toss away the key to your cell. According to them, it's always lockup time for bad girls. Don't get caught and sent to a slammer where one of this crew is in charge.

Pat Ast	*Reform School Girls* ('86)
Irene Dunne	*Ann Vickers* ('33)
Shirley Jones	*Inmates: A Love Story* ('81)
Ida Lupino	*Women's Prison* ('55)
Deborah May	*Caged Fear* ('91)
Mercedes McCambridge	*99 Women* ('69)
Agnes Moorehead	*Caged* ('50)
Jill St. John	*The Concrete Jungle* ('82)
Barbara Steele	*Caged Heat* ('74)

Voyeurs can get an adequate dose of "slammer girl" thrills in the following films:

The Big Bird Cage ('72)	*Jackson County Jail* ('76)
The Big Doll House ('71)	*The Naked Cage* ('86)
Black Mama, White Mama ('72)	*Nightmare in Badham County* ('76)
Born Innocent ('74)	*99 Women* ('69)
Caged Fury ('84)	*Red Heat* ('85)
Caged in Paradise ('89)	*Reform School Girls* ('86)
Caged Women ('84)	*Slammer Girls* ('86)
Chained Heat ('83)	*Swamp Women* ('55)
Girls in Prison ('56)	

THE MISS SLAMMER GIRL AWARD

"Mama, face it: I was the slut of all time."
—Elizabeth Taylor, *Butterfield 8*

Awarded to **Linda Blair** for her appearances in *Born Innocent* ('74), *Chained Heat* ('85), *Red Heat* ('85), and several other slammer films. During her various incarcerations, Linda has been sexually assaulted by broomsticks, prison guards, depraved wardens, and even a communist lesbian. And, to make her appearances even more outstanding, nobody—but nobody—can participate in a slammer slut fight with more vigor than that possessed little devil Linda.

GLAMOUR IN THE SLAMMER

"I'll say one thing for prison. It's a better class of people."
—Humphrey Bogart, *We're No Angels*

No acting roles here: real glamour girls can run afoul of the law and find themselves tossed into the slammer, too.

Arletty, the French star, received a two-month sentence in France in 1945 for collaborating with the Germans during World War II.

Dorothy Comingore was busted for prostitution in March 1953. The charges were dismissed against Welles's *Citizen Kane* costar after she agreed to enter a clinic for alcoholism treatment.

Frances Farmer was arrested and charged with several traffic violations in 1942 but was paroled. She was rearrested shortly thereafter for parole violation, after which a series of episodes ensued that escalated into her being declared a mental incompetent and institutionalized.

Zsa Zsa Gabor, after being tried and convicted in 1989 in a Beverly Hills court, served time in jail because she did not fulfill the full conditions of her first sentence. The original charges against her stemmed from an expired driver's license, an expired automobile tag, an open container of liquor in her Rolls-Royce, and a policeman she slapped.

Sophia Loren spent thirty days in an Italian prison in 1982 for income-tax irregularities.

Jane Russell was charged with drunk driving in 1978.

Mae West, charged with writing and performing in a lewd play on Broadway, was jailed briefly in New York City in 1926.

THE BIG BUSTS

"One more success like that, and I'll sell my body to a
medical institute."
—Groucho Marx, *Cocoanuts*

Here they are: the Big Busts. They all had a chance at movie mega-
stardom and went bust.

Some were fine actresses, while many others weren't. Several
went bust quickly—after making only one or two films; others stag-
gered through endless films, their parts growing smaller, hoping
something would ignite their careers. The wiser ones gave up to
pursue other interests; Europe called still more to return home; a few
had more success onstage, in television, or as foreign film stars;
many of them still remain in films, appearing in both major and
minor roles.

What went wrong? What happened to their careers? View these
random samplings and see if you can determine the reason these
ladies went bust.

Pier Angeli	*Teresa* ('51)
Annabella	*Suez* ('38)
Diane Baker	*Krakatoa, East of Java* ('69)
Ina Balin	*The Comancheros* ('61)
Diana Barrymore	*Ladies Courageous* ('44)
Eva Bartok	*The Crimson Pirate* ('52)
Barbara Bel Geddes	*Vertigo* ('58)
Marisa Berenson	*Barry Lyndon* ('75)
Vivian Blaine	*Guys and Dolls* ('55)
Ronee Blakley	*Nashville* ('75)
Ann Blyth	*Mildred Pierce* ('45)
Shirley Booth	*The Matchmaker* ('58)
May Britt	*The Blue Angel* ('59)
Cathy Burns	*Last Summer* ('69)
Corrine Calvet	*What Price Glory?* ('52)

Capucine	*A Walk on the Wild Side* ('62)
Joan Caulfield	*Monsieur Beaucaire* ('46)
Cyd Charisse	*Singin' in the Rain* ('52)
Etchika Choreau	*Lafayette Escadrille* ('58)
Anjanette Comer	*The Loved One* ('65)
Dorothy Comingore	*Citizen Kane* ('41)
Valentina Cortesa	*The House on Telegraph Hill* ('51)
Jeanne Crain	*Cheaper by the Dozen* ('50)
Virginia Dale	*Holiday Inn* ('42)
Dorothy Dandridge	*Porgy and Bess* ('59)
Kim Darby	*True Grit* ('69)
Denise Darcel	*Flame of Calcutta* ('53)
Linda Darnell	*Forever Amber* ('47)
Bella Darvi	*Hell and High Water* ('54)
Marion Davies	*Cain and Mabel* ('36)
Sandra Dee	*Rosie!* ('67)
Gloria DeHaven	*Best Foot Forward* ('43)
Diana Dors	*King of the Roaring Twenties* ('61)
Betsy Drake	*Pretty Baby* ('50)
Joanne Dru	*She Wore a Yellow Ribbon* ('49)
Sandy Duncan	*The Star-Spangled Girl* ('71)
Britt Ekland	*The Bobo* ('67)
Taina Elg	*Watusi* ('59)
Felicia Farr	*Kiss Me Stupid* ('64)
Farrah Fawcett	*Somebody Killed Her Husband* ('78)
Susanna Foster	*The Phantom of the Opera* ('43)
Anne Francis	*Forbidden Planet* ('56)
Pamela Franklin	*The Night of the Following Day* ('69)
Rita Gam	*Sign of the Pagan* ('54)
Peggy Ann Garner	*A Tree Grows in Brooklyn* ('45)
Mitzi Gaynor	*South Pacific* ('58)

Genevieve Gilles	*Hello-Goodbye* ('70)
Gila Golan	*The Valley of Gwangi* ('69)
Gloria Grahame	*Oklahoma!* ('55)
Juliette Greco	*The Roots of Heaven* ('58)
Linda Harrison	*Planet of the Apes* ('68)
Mariette Hartley	*Ride the High Country* ('62)
Elizabeth Hartman	*You're a Big Boy Now* ('66)
Jill Haworth	*Exodus* ('60)
Tippi Hedren	*Marnie* ('64)
Florence Henderson	*Song of Norway* ('70)
Wanda Hendrix	*The Prince of Foxes* ('49)
Katherine Houghton	*Guess Who's Coming to Dinner* ('67)
Olivia Hussey	*Romeo and Juliet* ('68)
Betty Hutton	*Incendiary Blonde* ('45)
Carolyn Jones	*King Creole* ('58)
Shirley Jones	*The Music Man* ('62)
Christine Kaufmann	*Taras Bulba* ('62)
Marthe Keller	*Fedora* ('78)
Sally Kellerman	*M*A*S*H* ('70)
Nancy Kelly	*The Bad Seed* ('56)
Suzy Kendall	*The Penthouse* ('67)
Phyllis Kirk	*House of Wax* ('53)
Shirley Knight	*The Rain People* ('69)
Susan Kohner	*Imitation of Life* ('59)
Miliza Korjus	*The Great Waltz* ('38)
Veronica Lake	*So Proudly We Hail!* ('43)
Hedy Lamarr	*Algiers* ('38)
Hope Lange	*Peyton Place* ('57)
Barbara Loden	*Wanda* ('71)
Ida Lupino	*The Hard Way* ('42)
Carol Lynley	*Bunny Lake Is Missing* ('65)

Diana Lynn	*Our Hearts Were Young and Gay* ('44)
Elsa Martinelli	*Hatari!* ('62)
Ilona Massey	*Frankenstein Meets the Wolf Man* ('43)
Lois Maxwell	*That Hagen Girl* ('47)
Patty McCormack	*Kathy O'* ('58)
Maggie McNamara	*Three Coins in the Fountain* ('54)
Patricia Medina	*Phantom of the Rue Morgue* ('54)
Dina Merrill	*I'll Take Sweden* ('65)
Cleo Moore	*Strange Fascination* ('52)
Mary Tyler Moore	*Thoroughly Modern Millie* ('67)
Terry Moore	*Beneath the 12 Mile Reef* ('53)
Hildegarde Neff	*Decision Before Dawn* ('51)
Sheree North	*Living It Up* ('54)
Margaret O'Brien	*Meet Me in St. Louis* ('44)
Debra Paget	*The Ten Commandments* ('56)
Suzy Parker	*Ten North Frederick* ('58)
Barbara Parkins	*Valley of the Dolls* ('67)
Marisa Pavan	*The Rose Tattoo* ('55)
Millie Perkins	*The Diary of Anne Frank* ('59)
Jean Peters	*Captain from Castile* ('47)
Suzanne Pleshette	*Youngblood Hawke* ('64)
Rosanna Podesta	*Helen of Troy* ('55)
Mala Powers	*City That Never Sleeps* ('53)
Michelline Presle	*Under My Skin* ('50)
Dorothy Provine	*Wall of Noise* ('63)
Deborah Raffin	*Jacqueline Susann's Once Is Not Enough* ('75)
Vera Hruba Ralston	*Fair Wind to Java* ('53)
Martha Raye	*Monsieur Verdoux* ('47)
Dany Robin	*Topaz* ('69)
Katherine Ross	*Butch Cassidy and the Sundance Kid* ('69)

Eleonora Rossi Drago	*Under Ten Flags* ('60)
Dominique Sanda	*Damnation Alley* ('77)
Dany Saval	*Boeing Boeing* ('65)
Gia Scala	*I Aim at the Stars* ('60)
Maria Schell	*The Hanging Tree* ('59)
Lizabeth Scott	*The Strange Love of Martha Ivers* ('46)
Martha Scott	*Our Town* ('40)
Jean Seberg	*Saint Joan* ('57)
Dinah Shore	*Aaron Slick from Punkin Crick* ('52)
Simone Simon	*Cat People* ('42)
Carrie Snodgress	*Diary of a Mad Housewife* ('70)
Catherine Spaak	*Hotel* ('67)
Kim Stanley	*Séance on a Wet Afternoon* ('64)
Anna Sten	*Nana* ('34)
Inger Stevens	*Man on Fire* ('57)
Susan Strasberg	*Chubasco* ('68)
Leigh Taylor-Young	*I Love You, Alice B. Toklas* ('68)
Phyllis Thaxter	*Thirty Seconds over Tokyo* ('44)
Marlo Thomas	*Jenny* ('70)
Pamela Tiffin	*One, Two, Three* ('61)
Marta Toren	*Sirocco* ('51)
Audrey Totter	*The Saxon Charm* ('48)
Brenda Vaccaro	*Midnight Cowboy* ('69)
Diane Varsi	*Peyton Place* ('57)
Vera-Ellen	*On the Town* ('49)
Cara Williams	*The Defiant Ones* ('58)

THE WHY I WANTED TO BE A FILM STAR AWARD

Awarded to **Tallulah Bankhead**. When asked why she was leaving the London and New York stages to go to Hollywood in 1931 for films, Tallulah replied, "Darling, they offered me all this money, and so I thought I'd go to Hollywood and fuck that divine Gary Cooper."

BIKINI BODIES

"I hadn't seen a body put together like that since I solved the case
of the girl with the murdered legs."
—Steve Martin, *Dead Men Don't Wear Plaid*

Named for the Pacific island where the H-bomb was tested, the bikini
itself is an explosive item. It's skimpy, in a most delectable way. Need
proof? Then catch an eyeful of these gorgeous bodies parading
around in their bikinis.

Brigitte Bardot	*The Girl in the Bikini* ('52)
Barbara Bouchet	*Agent for H.A.R.M.* ('66)
Jane Fonda	*On Golden Pond* ('81)
Goldie Hawn	*Overboard* ('87)
Yvette Mimieux	*Hit Lady* ('74)
Jill St. John	*Diamonds Are Forever* ('71)
Sharon Tate	*Don't Make Waves* ('67)
Karen Valentine	*The Girl Who Came Gift-Wrapped* ('74)
Raquel Welch	*Fathom* ('67)

BEACH BUNNIES

Beach bunnies are those cute pubescent nymphs frolicking on the
beach. If adolescent females stir your passions, hop on one of these
beach bunnies.

Sandra Dee	*Gidget* ('59)
Annette Funicello	*Beach Party* ('63)
Pamela Tiffin	*For Those Who Think Young* ('64)
Deborah Walley	*Gidget Goes Hawaiian* ('61)
Lana Wood	*The Girls on the Beach* ('65)

The following films award beach-bunny watchers a surplus of thrills.

Bikini Beach ('64)

California Dreaming ('79)

Ghost in the Invisible Bikini ('66)

How to Stuff a Wild Bikini ('65)

It's a Bikini World ('67)

The Malibu Bikini Shop ('84)

Pajama Party ('64)

BIMBOS

"It took more than one man to change my name to Shanghai Lily."
—Marlene Dietrich, *Shanghai Express*

Bimbos: girls who've been around the track a couple of times. They know the score—don't try and pull any fast jazz on these tootsies. They're gold diggers, out after everything they can get.

Joan Bennett	*Scarlet Street* ('45)
Karen Black	*The Day of the Locust* ('75)
Joan Crawford	*Flamingo Road* ('49)
Beverly D'Angelo	*Aria* (Julien Temple's "Verdi" segment) ('88)
Marlene Dietrich	*The Blue Angel* ('30)
Melanie Griffith	*Body Double* ('84)
Jean Harlow	*Red Dust* ('32)
Glenda Jackson	*The Nelson Affair* ('73)
Jennifer Jones	*Ruby Gentry* ('52)
Eartha Kitt	*St. Louis Blues* ('58)
Christine Lahti	*Swing Shift* ('84)

Elizabeth McGovern	*Ragtime* ('81)
Sylvia Miles	*Midnight Cowboy* ('69)
Cathy Moriarty	*Neighbors* ('81)
Marie-France Pisier	*The Other Side of Midnight* ('77)
Jane Russell	*The Revolt of Mamie Stover* ('56)
Theresa Russell	*Bad Timing: A Sensual Obsession* ('80)
Rene Soutendijk	*Spetters* ('80)
Leigh Taylor-Young	*Soylent Green* ('73)
Lesley Ann Warren	*Victor/Victoria* ('82)
Joanne Whalley-Kilmer	*Scandal* ('89)
Joanne Woodward	*The Fugitive Kind* ('59)

THE ULTIMATE GOLD DIGGER AWARD

Awarded to **Stella Stevens**, because to inherit his estate she marries a corpse at his funeral in *Arnold* ('73).

THE BEST OLD STAR AS A FLOOZY AWARD

Awarded to **Ann Sothern** as Sadie, a trashy, over-the-hill prostitute, in *Lady in a Cage* ('64).

BITCHES

"I wouldn't wear that to watch dogs fuck."
—Whoopi Goldberg, *Burglar*

Nagging, complaining, whimpering, whining. Bitch, bitch, bitch . . . that's all a bitch does. She's not happy unless she's making everyone else miserable with her catty remarks.

Nancy Allen	*Carrie* ('76)
June Allyson	*The Shrike* ('55)
Eve Arden	*Dark at the Top of the Stairs* ('60)
Ingrid Bergman	*The Visit* ('64)
Eileen Brennan	*Private Benjamin* ('80)
Susan Cabot	*Sorority Girl* ('57)
Joan Collins	*Nutcracker* ('82)
Joan Crawford	*Harriet Craig* ('50)
Bette Davis	*The Little Foxes* ('41)
Phyllis Diller	*The Adding Machine* ('69)
Debbie Harry	*Hairspray* ('88)
Susan Hayward	*The Hairy Ape* ('44)
Mariangela Melato	*Swept Away* ('75)
Bette Midler	*Ruthless People* ('86)
Rita Moreno	*The Ritz* ('76)
Nancy Parsons	*Porky's* ('81)
Suzanne Pleshette	*Leona Helmsley: The Queen of Mean* ('90)
Charlotte Rampling	*Georgy Girl* ('66)
Mercedes Ruehl	*Married to the Mob* ('88)
Elizabeth Taylor	*The Taming of the Shrew* ('67)
Lily Tomlin	*All of Me* ('84)
Kathleen Turner	*The Man with Two Brains* ('83)
Irene Worth	*Lost in Yonkers* ('93)

HELL ON WHEELS

Here's a special kind of bitch—one that's hell on wheels. She's wheel-chair bound, but that hasn't curbed her appetite for bitchiness.

Joan Crawford	*What Ever Happened to Baby Jane?* ('62)
Olivia de Havilland	*Lady in a Cage* ('64)
Eleanor Parker	*Eye of the Cat* ('69), *The Man with the Golden Arm* ('55)

GOSSIP COLUMNISTS

"The only time a woman doesn't care to talk is when she's dead."
—William Demarest, *The Miracle of Morgan's Creek*

Snooping, digging for the dirt, spilling the beans . . . ruining some careers and promoting other careers. All the while they keep proclaiming that they're doing the public a favor by relating all the news about movie stars. The pen is *indeed* mightier than the sword, especially when used by this bunch of news hens.

Jane Alexander	*Malice in Wonderland* ('85)
Coral Browne	*The Legend of Lylah Clare* ('68)
Hedda Hopper	*The Oscar* ('66)
Deborah Kerr	*Beloved Infidel* ('59)
Louella Parsons	*Hollywood Hotel* ('37)
Elizabeth Taylor	*Malice in Wonderland* ('85)

CAT FIGHTS

"We're not quarreling! We're in complete agreement! We hate
each other!"
—Nanette Fabray, *The Band Wagon*

Sooner or later it happens, the good ole female slugfest. The audience always cheers and roots for one of the combatants more than the other. Why, well maybe she's just nicer . . . or is it because the other one is really a bitch who deserves it. Here's some hair-pulling, cat fighting that shouldn't be missed.

Lucille Ball and Maureen O'Hara	*Dance, Girl, Dance* ('40)
Raquel Welch and Martine Beswick	*One Million Years B.C.* ('66)
Oprah Winfrey and Rae Dawn Chong	*The Color Purple* ('85)
Joan Crawford and Mercedes McCambridge	*Johnny Guitar* ('54)
Rebecca De Mornay and Annabella Sciorra	*The Hand That Rocks the Cradle* ('92)

Marlene Dietrich and Una Merkel	*Destry Rides Again* ('39)
Bridget Fonda and Jennifer Jason Leigh	*Single White Female* ('92)
Melanie Griffith and Joely Richardson	*Shining Through* ('92)

WITCHES

"When my mother took me to see *Snow White*, everyone fell in
love with Snow White. I immediately fell
for the wicked queen."
—Woody Allen, *Annie Hall*

Bubbling cauldrons? Forget it. Some of these witches are so modern
it's a wonder they remember their ancient evil incantations.

Melissa Sue Anderson	*Midnight Offerings* ('81)
Elizabeth Bergner	*Cry of the Banshee* ('70)
Billie Burke	*The Wizard of Oz* ('39)
Barbara Carrera	*The Wicked Stepmother* ('89)
Cher	*The Witches of Eastwick* ('87)
Bette Davis	*The Dark Secret of Harvest Home* ('78)
Faye Dunaway	*Supergirl* ('84)
Teri Garr	*Witches' Brew* ('80)
Margaret Hamilton	*The Wizard of Oz* ('39)
Anjelica Huston	*The Witches* ('90)
Veronica Lake	*I Married a Witch* ('42)
Robyn Lively	*Teen Witch* ('89)
Bette Midler	*Hocus Pocus* ('93)
Helen Mirren	*Excalibur* ('81)
Kim Novak	*Bell, Book and Candle* ('58)
Michelle Pfeiffer	*The Witches of Eastwick* ('87)
Diana Rigg	*The Worst Witch* ('86)

Susan Sarandon	*The Witches of Eastwick* ('87)
Barbara Steele	*Black Sunday* ('61)
Shelley Winters	*Witchfire* ('86)
Estelle Winwood	*The Magic Sword* ('62)

BLUE-COLLAR BABES

"I have no curiosity about the working classes."
—Gladys Cooper, *Separate Tables*

Hot, sweaty, rough 'n' tumble blue-collar babes. Hardworking women. Making it through life by the sweat of their brows.

Jennifer Beals, welder	*Flashdance* ('83)
Stockard Channing, stuntwoman	*Silent Victory* ('79)
Lisa Eichhorn, iron-pit worker	*Wildrose* ('84)
Sally Field, textile-mill worker	*Norma Rae* ('79)
Valerie Harper, factory worker	*Fun and Games* ('80)
Goldie Hawn, aircraft worker	*Swing Shift* ('84)
Jennifer Jones, plumber	*Cluny Brown* ('46)
Cheryl Ladd, coal miner	*Kentucky Woman* ('85)
Linda Lavin, assembly-line worker	*The $5.20 an Hour Dream* ('80)
Nancy McKeon, fire fighter	*Firefighter* ('86)
Ann Sothern, aircraft worker	*Swing Shift Maisie* ('43)

MAY I SERVE YOU, PLEASE?

"With this money, I can get away from you. . . . From you and your
chickens and your pies and your kitchens and everything
that smells of grease."
"My mother . . . a waitress!"

—Ann Blyth, *Mildred Pierce*

Cup of java, Honey? Hamburger with fries? Wanna see a menu, Sweetie? How about a big, big helping of fresh Waitress? Those hash-slinging Honeys of the diners are something else. Always taking orders, joshing with the customers, and banging plates of food across the counter.

Constance Bennett	*What Price Hollywood?* ('32)
Karen Black	*Five Easy Pieces* ('70)
Ellen Burstyn	*Alice Doesn't Live Here Anymore* ('74)
Cher	*Come Back to the Five and Dime, Jimmy Dean, Jimmy Dean* ('82)
Joan Crawford	*Mildred Pierce* ('45)
Linda Darnell	*Fallen Angel* ('45)
Lolita Davidovich	*Leap of Faith* ('92)
Bette Davis	*Of Human Bondage* ('34), *The Petrified Forest* ('36)
Mia Farrow	*The Purple Rose of Cairo* ('85)
Aretha Franklin	*The Blues Brothers* ('80)
Judy Garland	*The Harvey Girls* ('46)
Teri Garr	*Waiting for the Light* ('90)
Juliette Lewis	*Romeo Is Bleeding* ('94)
Liza Minnelli	*Arthur* ('81)
Terry Moore	*Shack Out on 101* ('55)
Kim Novak	*Of Human Bondage* ('64)
Eleanor Parker	*Of Human Bondage* ('46)
Michelle Pfeiffer	*Frankie and Johnny* ('91)
Julia Roberts	*Mystic Pizza* ('88)

Susan Sarandon	*White Palace* ('90)
Jan Sterling	*Return from the Sea* ('54)
Elizabeth Taylor	*Hammersmith Is Out* ('72)
Mare Winningham	*Miracle Mile* ('89)
Shelley Winters	*A Double Life* ('47)

DIDYA HEAR THE ONE ABOUT THE FARMER'S DAUGHTER?

"Now I'll be the innocent milkmaid, and you'll be the
naughty stableboy."
—Estelle Winwood, *The Producers*

Or was it the farmer's wife? It really doesn't matter because both—
daughters and wives—are included here. Earth mothers and daughters of us all: They're comely, horny, sexy, homely.

Jean Arthur	*Shane* ('53)
Verna Bloom	*The Hired Hand* ('71)
Claudette Colbert	*The Egg and I* ('47)
Faye Dunaway	*Hurry Sundown* ('67)
Irene Dunne	*Cimarron* ('31)
Sally Field	*Places in the Heart* ('84)
Betty Grable	*The Farmer Takes a Wife* ('35)
Jessica Lange	*Country* ('84)
Amy Madigan	*Field of Dreams* ('89)
Marjorie Main	*Ma and Pa Kettle* ('49)
Lori Singer	*Summer Heat* ('87)
Sissy Spacek	*The River* ('84)
Cicely Tyson	*Sounder* ('72)
Loretta Young	*The Farmer's Daughter* ('47)

BODY DOUBLES

"Oh, we're both fakers. Isn't faking the essence of acting?"
—Katharine Hepburn, *Stage Door*

Body doubles: the people who "stand in" for actresses when they decline—or are physically unable—to perform a nude scene. Nudity—it's bare work, but somebody's body has to do it.

How can body doubles be spotted? If the camera shot does not include the actress's face with the nude portion of the anatomy being featured be leery; you just might be viewing a body double. A prime example of this trickery occurred in *Dressed to Kill* ('80).

Angie Dickinson's steamy shower scenes at the beginning of that film drew rave reviews for her less-than-young body. The public soon learned, however, that all the skin exposed wasn't Angie's. Shots of her face—and the better parts of her body—had been intercut with the more nude exposures of a much younger, better developed **Lyn Johnson**, a former *Penthouse* Pet.

Watch these nude appearances in which "body doubles" were used:

Anne Archer	*Fatal Attraction* ('87)
Jane Curtin	*How to Beat the High Cost of Living* ('80)
Catherine Deneuve	*The Hunger* ('83)
Jane Fonda	*Coming Home* ('78)
Diana Scarwid	*Psycho III* ('86)
Brooke Shields	*The Blue Lagoon* ('80)

KEEPING IT IN THE FAMILY

An elder sister replaced the then-underaged **Jodie Foster** for her nude scenes in *The Little Girl Who Lived Down the Lane* ('76) and *Taxi Driver* ('76).

THE BREAST STAND-IN

Laura Gemser in *Emanuelle on Taboo Island* ('84) has a breast stand-in. Watch her sex scene on the beach closely. Each time Gemser's male costar moves his mouth to her breast, she's replaced by another actress—who looks nothing like her.

DIFFERENT FACES, SAME VOICE

> "I *am* pretty sick and tired of the sound of her voice. Not that
> she isn't a good woman. I'm just sick and tired of the
> sound of her voice."
> —Frank Overton, *The Dark at the Top of the Stairs*

What do they do when an actress can't sing? Why, use a "voice" double, of course. Is the name **Marni Nixon** familiar? One of her rare "visual" appearances was as Sister Sophia in *The Sound of Music,* but it's her voice that's more renowned. Nixon was one of the best voice doubles and has been heard on-screen as these singing voices:

Audrey Hepburn	*My Fair Lady* ('64)
Deborah Kerr	*The King and I* ('56), *An Affair to Remember* ('57)
Natalie Wood	*West Side Story* ('61)
Peggy Wood	*The Sound of Music* ('65)

Other singing voice doubles are:

Patsy Cline for Jessica Lange in *Sweet Dreams* ('85)

Anita Ellis for Rita Hayworth in *Gilda* ('46)

Anita Gordon for Jean Seberg in *Paint Your Wagon* ('69)

Gogi Grant for Ann Blyth in *The Helen Morgan Story* ('57)

Marilyn Horne for Dorothy Dandridge in *Carmen Jones* ('54)

Carole Richards for Cyd Charisse in *Brigadoon* ('54)

Betty Wand for Leslie Caron in *Gigi* ('58)

Often more surprising than "voice doubles" are those actresses who can sing—and perform rather well—when necessary in a film. Listen to these nonsongbirds give it a try:

Sophia Loren	*Boccaccio '70* ('62)
Rosalind Russell	*Gypsy* ('62)
Jean Simmons	*Guys and Dolls* ('55)
Sissy Spacek	*Coal Miner's Daughter* ('80)
Barbara Stanwyck	*Lady of Burlesque* ('43)
Elizabeth Taylor	*A Little Night Music* ('78)

And then there are the "specialized" voice doubles. For example, cartoons and special effects:

Mary Costa provided Sleeping Beauty with a voice in *Sleeping Beauty* ('59).

Mercedes McCambridge provided the demon's raspy voice emitting from Linda Blair in *The Exorcist* ('73).

Irene Woods Shaughnessy was Cinderella in *Cinderella* ('50).

Kathleen Turner speaks, while **Amy Irving** sings, as the Jessica Rabbit character in *Who Framed Roger Rabbit* ('88).

Debra Winger provided the voice for some of the extraterrestrial's vocal squeaks and sounds in *E.T. The Extra-Terrestrial* ('82).

BONDED BEAUTIES

"Hello, gorgeous."
—Barbra Streisand, *Funny Girl*

The James Bond films have featured some of the most beautiful women in the world as "sex interests" for the super-spy. These bodies are indeed bonded and certified as exquisite.

Maud Adams	*Octopussy* ('83)
Ursula Andress	*Dr. No* ('62)
Claudine Auger	*Thunderball* ('65)
Barbara Bach	*The Spy Who Loved Me* ('77)
Kim Basinger	*Never Say Never Again* ('83)

Daniela Bianchi	*From Russia with Love* ('63)
Honor Blackman	*Goldfinger* ('64)
Carole Bouquet	*For Your Eyes Only* ('81)
Barbara Carrera	*Never Say Never Again* ('83)
Lois Chiles	*Moonraker* ('79)
Maryam D'Abo	*The Living Daylights* ('87)
Britt Ekland	*The Man with the Golden Gun* ('74)
Mie Hama	*You Only Live Twice* ('67)
Grace Jones	*A View to a Kill* ('85)
Amy Lowell	*License to Kill* ('89)
Caroline Munro	*The Spy Who Loved Me* ('77)
Luciana Paluzzi	*Thunderball* ('65)
Diana Rigg	*On Her Majesty's Secret Service* ('69)
Tanya Roberts	*A View to a Kill* ('85)
Jane Seymour	*Live and Let Die* ('73)
Jill St. John	*Diamonds Are Forever* ('71)

BROADS WITH BALLS

"Maybe we should just grow peckers and join up."
—Elizabeth Perkins, *Sweet Hearts Dance*

There's no stopping this bunch. These broads have balls; nothing gets them down. They'll tackle anybody, anywhere, anytime if it suits them and their goals. They're not always the nicest females around, but you have to admire them; they know what they want and they get it. Why? 'Cause they've got balls!

| Eileen Brennan | *Incident at Crestridge* ('81) |
| Bette Davis | *Of Human Bondage* ('34) |

Faye Dunaway	*Network* ('76)
Louise Fletcher	*One Flew over the Cuckoo's Nest* ('75)
Glenda Jackson	*Hedda* ('75)
Ida Lupino	*Women's Prison* ('55)
Sissy Spacek	*Marie* ('85)
Sigourney Weaver	*Working Girl* ('88)

THE WHY SHE HAS HER NERVE AWARD

Awarded to **Shelley Duvall** in *Brewster McCloud* ('70), in which she sees a dead body, vomits, and then grabs her boyfriend saying, "Oh, it's so terrible. Kiss me quick!"

DIESEL DOLLIES

"You never fuck me, and I always have to drive."
—Kelly Lynch, *Drugstore Cowboy*

Man, oh man, these mamas know how to put the pedal to the metal and keep on truckin'. Truckin' mama, you've already won my heart, so don't drive yo' truck over my foot, too!

Dyan Cannon	*Coast to Coast* ('80)
Joan Crawford	*They All Kissed the Bride* ('42)
Kim Darby	*Flatbed Annie & Sweetpie: Lady Truckers* ('79)
Marianne Muellerleile	*Curse II: The Bite* ('88)
Annie Potts	*Flatbed Annie & Sweetpie: Lady Truckers* ('79)
Deborah Raffin	*Willa* ('79)
Helen Shaver	*High Ballin'* ('78)

CALL ME MADAM!

"When you call me madam, smile."
—Ethel Merman, *Call Me Madam*

Madams—the female flesh peddlers. Of course, they only have their girls' best interests at heart. The cinematic Madam: she usually has a heart of gold, keeps on good terms with the big boys at City Hall, and has a boyfriend who's "understanding" about her line of work. All in all, she's nothing but a lady manager making it in a business where men are known for being on top.

Elizabeth Ashley	*Great Scout and Cathouse Thursday* ('76)
Candice Bergen	*Mayflower Madam* ('87)
Dyan Cannon	*Lady of the House* ('78)
Julie Christie	*McCabe and Mrs. Miller* ('71)
Faye Dunaway	*Beverly Hills Madam* ('86)
Lotte Lenya	*The Roman Spring of Mrs. Stone* ('61)
Melina Mercouri	*Gaily, Gaily* ('69)
Ethel Merman	*The Art of Love* ('65)
Genevieve Page	*Belle de Jour* ('67)
Dolly Parton	*The Best Little Whorehouse in Texas* ('82)
Suzanne Pleshette	*Dixie: Changing Habits* ('84)
Lynn Redgrave	*The Happy Hooker* ('75)
Ginger Rogers	*Quick, Let's Get Married* ('64)
Jean Seberg	*The Great Frenzy* ('75)
Barbara Stanwyck	*A Walk on the Wild Side* ('62)
Elizabeth Taylor	*Poker Alice* ('87)
Julie Walters	*Personal Services* ('87)
Shelley Winters	*A House Is Not a Home* ('64)

LADIES OF THE HOUSE

These ladies are in a different kind of house—the White House, a statehouse, a house of Congress. Climb on the bandwagon 'cause here come the truly political animals.

Jean Arthur	*A Foreign Affair* ('48)
Polly Bergen	*Kisses for My President* ('64)
Joan Crawford	*Goodbye, My Fancy* ('51)
Angie Dickinson	*Stillwatch* ('87)
Susan Hayward	*Ada* ('61)
Kay Lenz	*Hitler's Daughter* ('90)
Loretta Swit	*Whoops Apocalypse* ('88)
Loretta Young	*The Farmer's Daughter* ('47)

House Hens

Republican **Shirley Temple Black** began her "public-service" career in 1967, when she lost a special election for a California U.S. House seat. She then went on to serve as U.S. Ambassador to Ghana and Czechoslovakia, in addition to being U.S. Chief of Protocol during the Ford administration.

Helen Gahagan Douglas, star of *She* ('35), is the only female film star to have served in the U.S. House of Representatives. She was a Democratic representative from California, 1944-1950. Her bid for a U.S. Senate seat in 1950 was thwarted by Richard Nixon.

In Great Britain, two-time Oscar winner **Glenda Jackson**, for *Women in Love* ('69) and *A Touch of Class* ('73), was elected to a seat in the House of Commons from a suburban London seat on the Labour Party ticket.

Democrat **Nancy Kulp**, who appeared in *The Three Faces of Eve* ('57), *The Parent Trap* ('61), and *Strange Bedfellows* ('64), but was better known as Miss Hathaway in TV's *The Beverly Hillbillies,* was an unsuccessful Democratic U.S. House candidate from Pennsylvania in 1984.

In 1992, after an underwhelming film career, **Alessandra Mussolini**, granddaughter of Fascist Italy's *Il Duce* and niece of Sophia Loren, was elected to the Italian Parliament. Mussolini lost a bid to become mayor of Naples during a 1993 election.

THE JUDY GARLAND OF JAPAN

In the early '30s, **Yoshiko Yamaguchi**, whose Japanese family had settled in Manchuria, was promoted throughout Asia as a young film star. Using the names *Ri Koran* in Japan and *Li Xianglan* in China, her popularity soared as she became known as the "Judy Garland of Japan." When World War II ended, she was repatriated from China to her native Japan, where she was rapidly "found" by Hollywood talent scouts and sent off to America.

Once more given another name—**Shirley Yamaguchi**—she soon was appearing in low-budget American films such as *Japanese War Bride* ('52) and *East Is East* ('53). After her American career floundered and her first marriage dissolved in divorce, Yamaguchi returned to Japan. In 1974, she was elected to the first of her several terms in the House of Councillors, the upper body of Japan's parliament. The intriguing story of her life has been made into a musical that appeared on the Tokyo stage.

CHANGING COLORS

"I smell an Ethiopian in the fuel supply."
—W. C. Fields, *Never Give a Sucker
an Even Break*

Now, wait a minute. What's going on here? Are these white girls pretending to be Black—or Black women pretending to be white? Actually, it's a little bit of both.

Joan Collins	*Island in the Sun* ('57)
Jeanne Crain	*Pinky* ('49)
Yvonne de Carlo	*Band of Angels* ('57)
Ava Gardner	*Show Boat* ('51)
Lelia Goldoni	*Shadows* ('60)
Susan Kohner	*Imitation of Life* ('59)

Julie London	*Night of the Quarter Moon* ('59)
Yvonne Mitchell	*Sapphire* ('59)
Beatrice Pearson	*Lost Boundaries* ('49)
Flora Robson	*Saratoga Trunk* ('45)
Fredi Washington	*Imitation of Life* ('34)
Sonya Wilde	*I Passed for White* ('60)
Natalie Wood	*Kings Go Forth* ('58)

BYE, BYE LADY BLACKBIRD

Lady blackbirds: white actresses in blackface—usually to perform a musical number—were permissible in the pre-Civil Rights days. It's strictly taboo now. So sing a chorus of "Bye, Bye Blackbird" for these practitioners of merry minstrelism.

Joan Crawford	*Torch Song* ('53)
Marion Davies	*Operator 13* ('34)
Judy Garland	*Ziegfeld Girl* ('41)
Betty Grable	*The Dolly Sisters* ('45)
June Havoc	*The Dolly Sisters* ('45)
Betty Hutton	*The Perils of Pauline* ('47)
Myrna Loy	*Ham and Eggs at the Front* ('42)

TECHNICOLOR EYES

Jane Seymour has different colored eyes; her left eye is green, the right one brown. Catch her in *Live and Let Die* ('72) or *Sinbad and the Eye of the Tiger* ('75) to spot them.

DIVAS

"I hate this dress. My husband says I look as though I were going to sing in it."

—Phyllis Povah, *The Women*

Diva: from the Latin feminine of *goddess*. Diva: an operatic prima donna. Diva: possessed of a divine musical voice. Diva: notorious for temperament.

Kitty Carlisle	*A Night at the Opera* ('35)
Jill Clayburgh	*Luna* ('79)
Glenn Close	*Meeting Venus* ('91)
Dorothy Comingore	*Citizen Kane* ('41)
Linda Darnell	*Everybody Does It* ('49)
Wilhemenia Wiggins Fernandez	*Diva* ('82)
Susanna Foster	*There's Magic in Music* ('41)
Kay Francis	*I Loved a Woman* ('33)
Greta Garbo	*Romance* ('30)
Kathryn Grayson	*So This Is Love* ('53)
Charlotte Henry	*Charlie Chan at the Opera* ('36)
Elissa Landi	*Enter Madame* ('35)
Sophia Loren	*Callas* ('89)
Jeanette MacDonald	*Maytime* ('37)
Anna Moffo	*The Adventurers* ('70)
Grace Moore	*One Night of Love* ('34)
Patrice Munsel	*Melba* ('53)
Eleanor Parker	*Interrupted Melody* ('55)
Lily Pons	*I Dream Too Much* ('35)
Heather Sears	*Phantom of the Opera* ('62)
Jane Seymour	*Onassis: The Richest Man in the World* ('88)
Carmilla Sparv	*The Greek Tycoon* ('78)
Risë Stevens	*The Chocolate Soldier* ('41)
Elizabeth Taylor	*Young Toscanini* ('88)

THE CLASSY HIGH-NOTE AWARD

Awarded to **Mae West** in *Goin' to Town* ('35), in which she sings the title role in Massenet's "Samson et Delilah."

BALLERINAS

"I dance like the wind."
—Sandy Dennis, *Who's Afraid of Virginia Woolf?*

Leaping, spinning, hopping, bending, dipping, swooning . . . the ballerinas are always up on their toes for their guys . . . or for those who have a "thing" for women in tutus . . .

Maud Adams	*Laura* ('79)
Judith Anderson	*Spectre of the Rose* ('46)
Anne Bancroft	*The Turning Point* ('77)
Dasha Blahova	*Howling III* ('87)
Claire Bloom	*Limelight* ('52)
Leslie Brown	*The Turning Point* ('77)
Leslie Caron	*Gaby* ('56)
Vera Cecova	*Angel in a Taxi* ('59)
Cyd Charisse	*The Unfinished Dance* ('47)
Julie Donald	*Brain Donors* ('92)
Alessandra Ferri	*Dancers* ('87)
Margot Fonteyn	*The Little Ballerina* ('60)
Greta Garbo	*Grand Hotel* ('32)
Jamie Gertz	*Silence Like Glass* ('90)
Jessica Harper	*Suspiria* ('77)
Deanne Jeffs	*Midnight Dancer* ('87)
Julie Kent	*Dancers* ('87)
Janet Leigh	*The Red Danube* ('49)
Vivien Leigh	*Waterloo Bridge* ('40)
Helen Mirren	*White Nights* ('85)
Maureen O'Hara	*Dance, Girl, Dance* ('40)
Moira Shearer	*The Red Shoes* ('48)
Jaclyn Smith	*Déjà Vu* ('85)
Ludmila Tcherina	*The Lovers of Teruel* ('62)
Gene Tierney	*Never Let Me Go* ('53)

Leslie Wing	*The Cowboy and the Ballerina* ('84)
Teresa Wright	*The Imperfect Lady* ('47)
Loretta Young	*The Men in Her Life* ('41)
Mai Zetterling	*Dance Little Lady* ('55)
Vera Zorina	*On Your Toes* ('39)

DOUBLE-DEALING DAMES

"There is no sincerity like a woman telling a lie."
—Cecil Parker, *Indiscreet*

A double-dealing dame is something else. She'll coo sweet nothings in your ear while sharpening her knife for your back. Never, never trust one of these dames, and especially never turn your back on her.

Anne Baxter	*All About Eve* ('50)
Glenn Close	*Dangerous Liaisons* ('88)
Bette Davis	*In This Our Life* ('42)
Faye Dunaway	*The Three Musketeers* ('74), *The Four Musketeers* ('75)
Joan Fontaine	*Born to Be Bad* ('50)
Ava Gardner	*The Killers* ('46)
Jane Greer	*Out of the Past* ('47)
Rita Hayworth	*The Story on Page One* ('59)
Glenne Headly	*Dirty Rotten Scoundrels* ('88)
Dorothy Lamour	*Lulu Belle* ('48)
Frances McDormand	*Blood Simple* ('84)
Simone Signoret	*Games* ('67)
Jaclyn Smith	*Nightkill* ('80)
Jill St. John	*Sitting Target* ('72)

Rachel Ward	*After Dark, My Sweet* ('90)
Joanne Whalley-Kilmer	*Kill Me Again* ('89)

BEST INDISCRETION BY A MARRIED WOMAN

Committed by the married vamp **Jessica Rabbit**, who's secretly photographed "playing patty cakes" with her admirer Marvin Acme in *Who Framed Roger Rabbit* ('88).

TWO-HUSBAND MARRIAGES

"Your idea of fidelity is not having more than one man in bed at the same time."

—Dirk Bogarde, *Darling*

Dyan Cannon	*Having It All* ('82)
Linda Fiorentino	*The Moderns* ('88)
Miou-Miou	*My Other Husband* ('85)
Jean Seberg	*Paint Your Wagon* ('69)

DOUBLE, TRIPLE, MULTIPLE PERSONALITIES

"She keep having so many identity crises, she change her head more times than Diana Ross change costumes, which be a lot."
—Raphael Sbarge, *My Man Adam*

Who are these women? Well—it all depends on which of their personalities you meet.

Karen Black	*Trilogy of Terror* ('75)
Phyllis Calvert	*Madonna of the Seven Moons* ('46)
Mary Crosby	*Deadly Innocents* ('84)
Sally Field	*Sybil* ('76)
Margot Kidder	*Sisters* ('73)
Eleanor Parker	*Lizzie* ('57)
Phyllis Thaxter	*Bewitched* ('45)
Joanne Woodward	*The Three Faces of Eve* ('57)

DRAB, DREARY, AND MOUSY

"Dogs like us, we ain't such dogs as we think we are."
—Ernest Borgnine, *Marty*

Whenever the phrase "But she has a nice personality" is uttered, everyone knows the true meaning: plain Jane. A dog . . . a drab, dreary, mousy little thing. Well, here's a bunch of drabettes without equal.

Kathy Baker	*Jacknife* ('89)
Betsy Blair	*Marty* ('55)
Shirley Booth	*Come Back, Little Sheba* ('52)
Peggy Cass	*Auntie Mame* ('58)
Jane Connell	*Mame* ('74)
Jane Curtin	*Suspicion* ('88)
Bette Davis	*The Catered Affair* ('56), *Now, Voyager* ('42)
Patty Duke	*Me, Natalie* ('69)
Julie Harris	*The Haunting* ('63)
Katharine Hepburn	*The Rainmaker* ('56)
Deborah Kerr	*Separate Tables* ('58)
Cloris Leachman	*The Last Picture Show* ('71)
Sophia Loren	*A Special Day* ('77)
Elaine May	*A New Leaf* ('71)
Lynn Redgrave	*Georgy Girl* ('66)
Rosalind Russell	*Picnic* ('55)
Talia Shire	*Rocky* ('76)
Maggie Smith	*The Lonely Passion of Judith Hearne* ('87)
Shelley Winters	*A Place in the Sun* ('51)

MISS GLAMOUR-PUSS ADOPTS THE COMMON TOUCH

In *Witness for the Prosecution* ('57), ultrachic **Marlene Dietrich** plays the accordion, proving that she had a common side, too.

DRUGS AND LIQUOR

> "I have made a discovery: Champagne
> is more fun to drink than goat's milk."
> —Cyd Charisse, *Silk Stockings*

Looking for a highway to hell? Well, drugs are one avenue, and liquor is another one-way street. If one of these broads stumbles across your path, don't be persuaded by her entreaties—she's an addict.

	Liquor Likers
Anne Baxter	*The Late Liz* ('71)
Carol Burnett	*Life of the Party: The Story of Beatrice* ('82)
Faye Dunaway	*Barfly* ('87)
Jane Fonda	*The Morning After* ('86)
Joan Fontaine	*Something to Live For* ('52)
Susan Hayward	*I'll Cry Tomorrow* ('55)
Marsha Mason	*Only When I Laugh* ('81)
Lee Remick	*The Days of Wine and Roses* ('62)
Gena Rowlands	*The Betty Ford Story* ('87)
Meg Ryan	*When a Man Loves a Woman* ('94)
Meryl Streep	*Ironweed* ('87)
Elizabeth Taylor	*Who's Afraid of Virginia Woolf?* ('66)

	Druggies
Jacqueline Bisset	*Believe in Me* ('71)
Susan Blakely	*A Cry for Love* ('80)
Joan Chen	*The Last Emperor* ('87)
Jill Clayburgh	*I'm Dancing as Fast as I Can* ('82)
Patty Duke	*Jacqueline Susann's Valley of the Dolls* ('75)
Teri Garr	*Firstborn* ('84)
Julie Harris	*Harper* ('66)
Katharine Hepburn	*Long Day's Journey into Night* ('62)
Cheryl Ladd	*Deadly Care* ('87)
Jennifer Jason Leigh	*Rush* ('91)
Kelly Lynch	*Drugstore Cowboy* ('89)
Diana Ross	*Lady Sings the Blues* ('72)
Kitty Winn	*Panic in Needle Park* ('71)
Shelley Winters	*Let No Man Write My Epitaph* ('60)
Sean Young	*The Boost* ('88)

YES, AND SHE PROBABLY WORKED FOR PEANUTS, TOO!

Mabel Normand, silent-film queen, was a drug addict hooked on cocaine-filled peanuts.

DUMB BLONDS

"She only said 'no' once—and then
she couldn't hear the question."
—George E. Stone, *42nd Street*

The proverbial dumb blond: pale hair, high voice, inane conversation. Watch yourself around these cuties. Don't laugh in her face—no

matter how dumb she seems—she just might have a Sugar Daddy waiting to fix anybody who mocks his Sweetie Pie.

Maureen Arthur	*How to Succeed in Business Without Really Trying* ('67)
Julie Brown	*Earth Girls Are Easy* ('89)
Candy Clark	*American Graffiti* ('73)
Georgia Engel	*The Outside Man* ('73)
Mitzi Gaynor	*Surprise Package* ('60)
Judy Holliday	*Born Yesterday* ('50)
Jayne Mansfield	*Kiss Them for Me* ('57)
Marilyn Monroe	*The Seven Year Itch* ('55)
Esther Muir	*A Day at the Races* ('37)
Barbara Nichols	*Where the Boys Are* ('60)
Madeleine Sherwood	*Sweet Bird of Youth* ('62)
Lesley Ann Warren	*Victor/Victoria* ('82)
Marie Wilson	*My Friend Irma* ('49)

RULE OF THE BRUNETS

In *Prehistoric Women* ('67), a lost Amazonian civilization is discovered where brunets, led by big-breasted **Martine Beswick**, have enslaved the blonds.

SCREWBALLS, WEIRDOS, DITSIES, AND KOOKS

> "Will you serve the nuts—I mean, will you serve
> the guests the nuts?"
> —Myrna Loy, *The Thin Man*

All dummies aren't blond, and neither are screwballs. In fact, screwballs come in all shapes, sizes, and hair colors. Call them weirdos, ditsies, kooks—the moniker doesn't matter. These babes just don't seem all there.

Gracie Allen	*Six of a Kind* ('34)
Rosanna Arquette	*After Hours* ('85)
Karen Black	*Can She Bake a Cherry Pie?* ('83)

Stockard Channing	*The Fortune* ('75)
Beverly D'Angelo	*Big Trouble* ('85)
Geena Davis	*The Accidental Tourist* ('88)
Sandy Dennis	*Sweet November* ('68)
Ruth Gordon	*Harold and Maude* ('72)
Melanie Griffith	*Something Wild* ('86)
Barbara Harris	*Who Is Harry Kellerman?* ('71)
Goldie Hawn	*Butterflies Are Free* ('72)
Katharine Helmond	*Shadey* ('85)
Audrey Hepburn	*Breakfast at Tiffany's* ('61)
Katharine Hepburn	*Bringing Up Baby* ('38)
Judith Ivey	*Hello Again* ('87)
Jennifer Jason Leigh	*The Big Picture* ('89)
Carole Lombard	*Twentieth Century* ('34)
Shirley MacLaine	*Two for the Seesaw* ('62)
Liza Minnelli	*The Sterile Cuckoo* ('69)
Diana Rigg	*The Hospital* ('71)
Winona Ryder	*Welcome Home, Roxie Carmichael* ('90)
Cybill Shepherd	*Special Delivery* ('76)
Maggie Smith	*The Prime of Miss Jean Brodie* ('69)
Sissy Spacek	*Crimes of the Heart* ('86)
Barbra Streisand	*What's Up, Doc?* ('72)
Lily Tomlin	*The Late Show* ('77)
Nedra Volz	*Moving Violations* ('85)

ETH-NICETIES

"You know what you are to me? Paris. That's you . . .
a spring morning in Paris."
—Charles Boyer, *Algiers*

STRICTLY KOSHER

The Jewish female as envisioned by the cinema. She's the earth mother, concentration-camp survivor, dutiful daughter, nagging wife, sexy lover.

Rosanna Arquette	*Baby, It's You* ('83)
Kathy Bates	*Used People* ('92)
Jennie Berlin	*The Heartbreak Kid* ('72)
Ellen Burstyn	*The Cemetery Club* ('92)
Blythe Danner	*Brighton Beach Memoirs* ('86)
Maruschka Detmers	*Hanna's War* ('88)
Olympia Dukakis	*The Cemetery Club* ('92)
Ruth Gordon	*Boardwalk* ('79)
Julie Hagerty	*Goodbye, New York* ('85)
Delores Hart	*Lisa* ('62)
Anjelica Huston	*Enemies, a Love Story* ('89)
Amy Irving	*Crossing Delancy* ('88)
Ida Kaminska	*The Shop on Main Street* ('65)
Carol Kane	*Hester Street* ('75)
Lainie Kazan	*My Favorite Year* ('82)
Diane Ladd	*The Cemetery Club* ('92)
Linda Lavin	*Lena: My 100 Children* ('87)
Sophia Loren	*Judith* ('66)
Shirley MacLaine	*Used People* ('92)
Cristina Marsillach	*Every Time We Say Goodbye* ('86)
Ali MacGraw	*Goodbye, Columbus* ('69)
Joanna Pacula	*Not Quite Paradise* ('86)
Geraldine Page	*Nazi Hunter: The Beate Klarsfeld Story* ('86)
Millie Perkins	*The Diary of Anne Frank* ('59)
Vanessa Redgrave	*Playing for Time* ('80)
Debbie Reynolds	*Sadie and Son* ('87)

Rosalind Russell	*A Majority of One* ('62)
Dominique Sanda	*The Garden of the Finzi-Continis* ('71)
Susan Strasberg	*Kapo* ('60)
Meryl Streep	*Sophie's Choice* ('82)
Barbra Streisand	*Funny Girl* ('68)
Jessica Tandy	*Used People* ('92)
Renee Taylor	*Made for Each Other* ('71)
Ingrid Thulin	*Return from the Ashes* ('65)
Shelley Winters	*The Poseidon Adventure* ('72)
Natalie Wood	*Marjorie Morningstar* ('58)

MAMBO ITALIANO

Mamma mia . . . it's the Italian woman. Her smell: from olive oil to expensive perfume. Her look: peasant garb to haute couture. Her demeanor: shrieking virago to coy sex kitten.

Olympia Dukakis	*Moonstruck* ('87)
Gina Lollobrigida	*Come September* ('61)
Sophia Loren	*The Gold of Naples* ('54)
Susan Lucci	*Mafia Princess* ('86)
Anna Magnani	*The Rose Tattoo* ('55)
Rosanna Schiaffino	*Arrivederci Baby!* ('66)
Jo Van Fleet	*The Gang That Couldn't Shoot Straight* ('71)

LA FEMME FRANÇAISE

La femme française—the French woman. Stylish, sophisticated, sexy—the embodiment of la belle France. *Vive la France!*

Isabelle Adjani	*Camille Claudel* ('88)
Anouk Aimée	*A Man and a Woman* ('66)
Stéphane Audran	*Le Boucheur* ('65)
Brigitte Bardot	*Shalako* ('68)
Marie-Christine Barrault	*Cousin, Cousine* ('75)

Romaine Bohringer	*The Accompanist* ('93)
Sandrine Bonnaire	*Vagabond* ('85)
Carole Bouquet	*Too Beautiful for You* ('89)
Beatrice Dalle	*Betty Blue* ('86)
Danielle Darrieux	*La Ronde* ('50)
Mylène Demongeot	*Bonjour Tristesse* ('58)
Catherine Deneuve	*The Last Metro* ('80)
Françoise Dorleac	*Cul-de-Sac* ('66)
Isabelle Huppert	*The Bedroom Window* ('87)
Marie-France Pisier	*French Postcards* ('79)
Marina Vlady	*Nude in a White Car* ('60)

BAKLAVA BEAUTIES

The sweet—and sometimes sticky—delectable pastries of Greece.

Despo Diamantidou	*Topkapi* ('64)
Helena Kallianiotes	*Five Easy Pieces* ('70)
Melina Mercouri	*The Victors* ('63)
Irene Papas	*The Trojan Women* ('72)
Katina Paxinou	*For Whom the Bell Tolls* ('43)

TEUTONIC TOOTSIES

Brunhilde's sister brood—the Teutonic tootsies ride again . . . and again . . . and again.

Marlene Dietrich	*The Blue Angel* ('30)
Lotte Lenya	*The Threepenny Opera* ('31)
Leni Riefenstahl	*SOS Iceberg* ('33)
Marianne Sagebrecht	*Rosalie Goes Shopping* ('89)
Maria Schell	*The Brothers Karamazov* ('58)
Romy Schneider	*Good Neighbor Sam* ('64)
Hanna Schygulla	*Lili Marleen* ('81)
Barbara Sukowa	*Rosa Luxemburg* ('86)
Rosel Zech	*Veronika Voss* ('82)

RUSSKIES

Russians galore . . . Reds, Whites, serfs, peasants, spies, czarinas, freedom fighters.

Vera Alentova	*Moscow Does Not Believe in Tears* ('80)
Bibi Andersson	*The Kremlin Letter* ('70)
Anne Baxter	*The North Star* ('43)
Ingrid Bergman	*Anastasia* ('56)
Daniela Bianchi	*From Russia with Love* ('63)
Jacqueline Bisset	*Anna Karenina* ('83)
Claire Bloom	*The Brothers Karamazov* ('58)
Ann Blyth	*The World in His Arms* ('52)
Natalya Bondarchuk	*Solaris* ('72)
Geraldine Chaplin	*Doctor Zhivago* ('65)
Cyd Charisse	*Silk Stockings* ('57)
Julie Christie	*Doctor Zhivago* ('65)
Claudette Colbert	*Tovarich* ('37)
Lolita Davidovich	*The Inner Circle* ('91)
Zsa Zsa Gabor	*The Girl in the Kremlin* ('57)
Greta Garbo	*Ninotchka* ('39), *Anna Karenina* ('35)
Goldie Hawn	*The Girl from Petrovka* ('74)
Audrey Hepburn	*War and Peace* ('56)
Katharine Hepburn	*The Iron Petticoat* ('56)
Glenda Jackson	*The Music Lovers* ('71)
Caroline Kava	*Little Nikita* ('88)
Diane Keaton	*Love and Death* ('75)
Sally Kellerman	*Secret Weapons* ('85), *Boris and Natasha* ('92)
Hedy Lamarr	*Comrade X* ('40)
Janet Leigh	*Jet Pilot* ('57)
Vivien Leigh	*Anna Karenina* ('48)
Lotte Lenya	*From Russia with Love* ('63)

Ilona Massey	*Balalaika* ('39)
Natalia Negoda	*Little Vera* ('88)
Lena Olin	*Romeo Is Bleeding* ('94)
Joanna Pacula	*Gorky Park* ('83)
Susan Peters	*Song of Russia* ('43)
Michelle Pfeiffer	*The Russia House* ('90)
Vanessa Redgrave	*The Sea Gull* ('68)
Isabella Rossellini	*White Nights* ('85)
Tatyana Samoilova	*The Cranes Are Flying* ('57)
Maria Schell	*The Brothers Karamazov* ('58)
Gene Tierney	*The Iron Curtain* ('48)
Audrey Totter	*Jet Attack* ('58)
Alida Valli	*We the Living* ('42)
Jane Withers	*The North Star* ('43)

EVIL PERSONIFIED

"She is bad, bad to the bone.
If ever there was an evil woman, she is one."
—Louis Jourdan, *The Paradine Case*

Truly evil, thoroughly wicked, profoundly sinister. Each of these females shares a common trait—she is evil personified.

Katherine Borowitz	*Men of Respect* ('91)
Barbara Carrera	*The Wicked Stepmother* ('89)
Bette Davis	*The Dark Secret of Harvest Home* ('78)
Faith Domergue	*Cult of the Cobra* ('55)
Ruth Gordon	*Rosemary's Baby* ('68)

Mieko Harada	*Ran* ('85)
Shirley Knight	*Dutchman* ('66)
Beatrice Lillie	*Thoroughly Modern Millie* ('67)
Susan Lucci	*Invitation to Hell* ('84)
Elizabeth Montgomery	*Amos* ('85)
Ornella Muti	*Flash Gordon* ('80)
Joanna Pacula	*The Kiss* ('88)
Barbara Parkins	*The Mephisto Waltz* ('71)
Ruth Roman	*Joe Macbeth* ('55)
Theresa Russell	*Black Widow* ('86)

EVIL EVITA: DON'T CRY FOR HER, ARGENTINA

Running away from her impoverished Argentine rural home at age fifteen, **Eva Duarte** was determined to achieve success in Buenos Aires. By most accounts, Eva's first years in the capital city were spent as a waterfront prostitute, where her specialty was fellatio. Among her customers during this time was none other than the big Daddy O himself, Aristotle Onassis.

A change in Eva's career goals eventually pulled her up off her knees; she now aspired to become an actress. After beginning with small parts in Argentine radio dramas, where she was known as Señorita Radio, Eva soon moved on to film roles. At the same time, she also caught the eye of one Juan Perón, an Army colonel whose ambitions rivaled her own.

Just as Eva's film career was becoming successful, she secretly married Perón and retired from films to help further his political career. The couple launched themselves into politics with a fury, establishing a connubial dictatorship that lasted until Eva's death from cancer in 1952. Juan muddled on alone as president until being deposed in a 1955 coup.

It had been long thought that all of Evita's films had been destroyed to avoid embarrassing her and Perón. In the mid-'80s, a copy of *La Prodiga* (*The Prodigal Woman*) was discovered locked in an Uruguayan bank vault. The now-dated film was shown nationally in the United States during July 1990 by Univision, the Spanish-language network, affording a real-life glimpse of movie star Evita.

The true story of Eva Duarte Perón—radio-film actress turned

politician-dictator—was the basis for the musical *Evita* and the TV movie *Evita Perón*, with **Faye Dunaway** portraying the harlot turned evil ruler. *Little Mother*, a sexploitation film by Radley Metzger, is also supposedly based on her life.

Filmography (all Argentine):

> *La Carga de los Valientos* ('40)
>
> *El mas Infeliz del Pueblo* ('41)
>
> *Una Novia en Apuros* ('42)
>
> *La Cabalgata del Circo* ('45)
>
> *La Prodiga* ('45)

EXOTICS

> "I want a date with those Jersey girls.
> They wear black pointy bras and white lipstick. They do
> naughty things. Like let you smell them all over."
> —Jonathan Silverman, *Stealing Home*

Exotic beauties from around the world. Some are authentic; others are filmdom's casting into exotic roles. Frequently, the casting is successful; many times it is not.

Anouk Aimée	*Justine* ('69)
Sonia Braga	*Gabriela* ('83)
Joan Chen	*On Deadly Ground* ('94)
Dorothy Dandridge	*Tamango* ('57)
Linda Darnell	*Anna and the King of Siam* ('46)
Estrelita	*Cuban Fireball* ('44)
Greta Garbo	*Mata Hari* ('32)
Ava Gardner	*Bhowani Junction* ('56)
Audrey Hepburn	*Green Mansions* ('59)

Amy Irving	*The Far Pavilions* ('84)
Jennifer Jones	*Duel in the Sun* ('46)
Hedy Lamarr	*White Cargo* ('42)
Shirley MacLaine	*Gambit* ('66)
Maria Montez	*Cobra Woman* ('44)
Debra Paget	*Journey to the Lost City* ('59)
Jean Simmons	*Black Narcissus* ('46)
Gale Sondergaard	*The Letter* ('40)
Tarita	*Mutiny on the Bounty* ('62)
Gene Tierney	*Sundown* ('41)
Lupe Velez	*Six Lessons from Madame La Zonga* ('41)
Esther Williams	*Pagan Love Song* ('50)
Zaira Zambelli	*Bye Bye Brazil* ('80)

DAUGHTERS OF THE EASTERN DRAGON

"It's China Doll! The gal that drives men mad."
—Jean Harlow, *China Seas*

Asian ladies . . . the daughters of the Eastern Dragon. Some are true daughters, while others are—again—filmdom's version of Asian females.

Jan Gan Boyd	*Assassination* ('87)
Joan Chen	*The Last Emperor* ('87)
Laureen Chew	*Dim Sum: A Little Bit of Heart* ('84)
Tsai Chin	*The Face of Fu Manchu* ('65)
Kieu Chinh	*Operation C.I.A.* ('65)
Sigrid Gurie	*The Adventures of Marco Polo* ('38)
Mie Hama	*You Only Live Twice* ('67)
Helen Hayes	*The Son-Daughter* ('32)
Katharine Hepburn	*Dragon Seed* ('44)
Sharon Iwai	*A Great Wall* ('86)

Jennifer Jones	*Love Is a Many Splendored Thing* ('55)
Nancy Kwan	*The World of Suzie Wong* ('60)
Hiep Thi Le	*Heaven and Earth* ('93)
Thuy Thu Le	*Casualties of War* ('89)
Myrna Loy	*The Mask of Fu Manchu* ('32)
Nobu McCarthy	*Walk Like a Dragon* ('60)
Cora Miao	*The Boat People* ('83)
France Nuyen	*A Girl Named Tamiko* ('62)
Luise Rainer	*The Good Earth* ('37)
Mari Sato	*Captive Hearts* ('87)
Miiko Taka	*Sayonara* ('57)
Win Min Than	*The Purple Plain* ('54)
Tung Thanh Tran	*Good Morning, Vietnam* ('87)
Irene Tsu	*Caprice* ('67)
Miyoshi Umeki	*Flower Drum Song* ('61)
Anna May Wong	*Java Head* ('34)
Vivian Wu	*Shadow of China* ('91)
Shirley Yamaguchi	*Japanese War Bride* ('52)
Loretta Young	*The Hatchet Man* ('32)

HAREMS: WIVES, CONCUBINES, AND SLAVE GIRLS

"Prepare her for my pleasure."
—Max von Sydow, *Flash Gordon*

The word *harem* is derived from the Arabic *haram*, which means "unlawful," "protected," or "forbidden." A place where women are kept separated and cloistered, waiting for their master's sexual foraging. And how do these fair beauties please their Lord and Master? Shall he choose one of them for an evening's dalliance?

Cecile Aubry	*The Black Rose* ('50)
Candice Bergen	*The Wind and the Lion* ('75)
Ann Blyth	*Kismet* ('55)

Clorinne Clery	*The Last Harem* ('85)
Joan Davis	*Harem Girl* ('52)
Yvonne de Carlo	*Slave Girl* ('47)
Marlene Dietrich	*Kismet* ('44)
Rhonda Fleming	*Yankee Pasha* ('54)
Ava Gardner	*Harem* ('86)
Kathryn Grant (Crosby)	*The 7th Voyage of Sinbad* ('58)
Beverly Johnson	*Ashanti* ('79)
Julanne Johnston	*The Thief of Bagdad* ('24)
Nastassja Kinski	*Harem* ('85)
Dorothy Lamour	*The Road to Morocco* ('42)
Marilyn Maxwell	*Lost in a Harem* ('44)
Maria Montez	*Arabian Nights* ('42)
Rita Moreno	*The King and I* ('56)
Maureen O'Hara	*The Flame of Araby* ('51)
Jennifer O'Neill	*Caravans* ('78)
Emma Samms	*Arabian Adventure* ('79)
Nancy Travis	*Harem* ('86)

FALLEN WOMEN

"Fallen women? You mean women who've tripped?"
—Maggie Smith, *The Missionary*

Fallen woman: the dictionary defines the term as a euphemism for a prostitute, a harlot. A more accurate description could be "a good girl gone astray." Fallen women fell from grace because of something adverse in the past. Given a chance, many avow that they'd change their ways and return to the straight and narrow. Regardless of the circumstances that caused it, these tootsies are definitely fallen.

Anne Baxter	*The Late Liz* ('71)
Louise Brooks	*Diary of a Lost Girl* ('29)
Claudette Colbert	*Under Two Flags* ('36)
Arlene Dahl	*Slightly Scarlet* ('56)
Marlene Dietrich	*Shanghai Express* ('32)
Lillian Gish	*The Scarlet Letter* ('26)
Susan Hayward	*I Want to Live!* ('58)
Jennifer Jones	*Madame Bovary* ('49)
Shirley Jones	*Elmer Gantry* ('60)
Shirley MacLaine	*Some Came Running* ('58)
Lori Singer	*Summer Heat* ('87)
Shelley Winters	*South Sea Sinner* ('50)

FINGERS OF FUN

"Don't point that finger at me unless you intend to use it."
Walter Matthau, *The Odd Couple*

For lack of gentlemanly companionship, these women knew what to do. Presented for your enjoyment—the masturbators.

Maud Adams	*Tattoo* ('81)
Erika Anderson	*Zandalee* ('91)
Kim Basinger	*9½ Weeks* ('86)
Beverly D'Angelo	*The Sentinel* ('77)
Fionnula Flanagan	*James Joyce's Women* ('85)
Anne Heywood	*The Fox* ('68)
Margot Kidder	*The Reincarnation of Peter Proud* ('75)
Sylvia Kristel	*Mata Hari* ('85)

Jennifer Jason Leigh	*Single White Female* ('92)
Shirley MacLaine	*Being There* ('79)
Harlee McBride	*Young Lady Chatterley* ('77)
Sarah Miles	*The Sailor Who Fell from Grace with the Sea* ('76), *White Mischief* ('88)
Brigitte Nielsen	*Baby* ('88)
Valerie Perrine	*Lenny* ('74)
Essy Persson	*I, a Woman* ('66)
Sharon Stone	*Sliver* ('93)
Ingrid Thulin	*The Silence* ('63)
Joanne Woodward	*Rachel, Rachel* ('68)

THE WELL, WHATTA YA EXPECT, SHE WAS POSSESSED AWARD

Awarded to **Linda Blair** who uses a crucifix—instead of her fingers—in *The Exorcist* ('73).

FULL FRONTALS

"My pussy hair was bright gold in high school, until I went out and scorched it with the football team."
—Debra Sandlund, *Tough Guys Don't Dance*

No shrinking violets here—this group revealed it all for patrons of their films. They're the ladies who chose to show a full frontal nude.

Maud Adams	*Tattoo* ('81)
Isabelle Adjani	*One Deadly Summer* ('83)
Ursula Andress	*Slave of the Cannibal God* ('78)
Susan Anspach	*Montenegro* ('81)

Laura Antonelli	*The Innocent* ('76)
Ellen Barkin	*Siesta* ('87)
Kathleen Beller	*The Betsy* ('78)
Sonia Braga	*I Love You* ('81)
Barbara Carrera	*I, the Jury* ('82)
Joanna Cassidy	*Night Games* ('80)
Phoebe Cates	*Paradise* ('82)
Geraldine Chaplin	*Welcome to L.A.* ('77)
Rae Dawn Chong	*The Quest for Fire* ('81)
Candy Clark	*The Man Who Fell to Earth* ('76)
Corinne Clery	*The Story of O* ('75)
Patti D'Arbanville	*Bilitis* ('77)
Angie Dickinson	*Big Bad Mama* ('74)
Amanda Donohoe	*Castaway* ('87)
Fionnula Flanagan	*James Joyce's Women* ('85)
Lisa Raines Foster	*Fanny Hill* ('87)
Marie France-Pisier	*The Other Side of Midnight* ('77)
Suzanne Hamilton	*1984* ('84)
Daryl Hannah	*At Play in the Fields of the Lord* ('91)
Mariel Hemingway	*Personal Best* ('82)
Season Hubley	*Hardcore* ('79)
Wendy Hughes	*Jock Peterson* ('74)
Diane Hull	*The Fifth Floor* ('80)
Glenda Jackson	*The Music Lovers* ('71)
Nastassja Kinski	*Cat People* ('82)
Alice Krige	*King David* ('85)
Sylvia Kristel	*Emmanuelle* ('74)
k. d. lang	*Salmonberries* ('94)
Jennifer Jason Leigh	*Flesh + Blood* ('85)
Lisa Loring	*Iced* ('88)
Kelly Lynch	*Warm Summer Rain* ('89)

Jane March	*The Lover* ('92)
Mathilda May	*Lifeforce* ('85)
Kelly McGillis	*Cat Chaser* ('89)
Julie Montgomery	*Revenge of the Nerds* ('84)
Yoko Ono	*Imagine: John Lennon* ('88)
Anne Parillaud	*Innocent Blood* ('93)
Paula Prentiss	*Catch-22* ('70)
Charlotte Rampling	*Caravan to Vaccares* ('74)
Fiona Richmond	*Fiona* ('84)
Theresa Russell	*Eureka* ('81)
Dominique Sanda	*The Inheritance* ('76)
Susan Sarandon	*Joe* ('70)
Rainbeau Smith	*Farewell, My Lovely* ('75)
Vanity	*Tanya's Island* ('80)
Julie Walters	*She'll Be Wearing Pink Pyjamas* ('85)
Edy Williams	*Chained Heat* ('83)
Mare Winningham	*Threshold* ('81)
Mary Woronov	*Angel of H.E.A.T.* ('82)
Sean Young	*Love Crimes* ('92)

. . . YES, BUT CAN IT SING?

Talking female genitalia have made at least two appearances on the screen. The French film *Pussy Talk* features a talking vagina. In *Chatterbox* ('77), star **Candace Rialson** calls her chattering part "Virginia."

PUBIES GO PUBLIC

The first female pubic hair to go public—appear in a mainstream film for general release during modern times—debuted in Michelangelo Antonioni's *Blow-Up* ('66). David Hemmings, starring in the film as a photographer, is shown in his studio snapping shots of two young ladies—**Jane Birkin** and **Gillian Hills**—as they wrestle on the floor pulling off each other's clothes.

THE PROBLEM WITH TALLULAH'S HAIR

During the making of *Lifeboat* ('44), the cameraman reported to director Alfred Hitchcock that his star Tallulah Bankhead wasn't wearing panties. Furthermore, said fact was becoming more obvious each day as filming progressed, as Tallulah and her fellow cast members were being drenched with water in the lifeboat. A bemused Hitchcock finally replied, "Would you have me call wardrobe, makeup, or the hairdresser?"

THE GALLERY OF DELICIOUS GROTESQUES

"She just acts that way because people expect it of her."
—Cecil Kellaway, *Hush . . . Hush, Sweet Charlotte*

Over-the-top, scenery-chewing performances. Gals pulling out all the stops. Compelling, mesmerizing, stupendous . . . and often truly awful. The portraits in this gallery range from cameos to full-length appearances. Their scope runs from astoundingly bad to award-winning.

Eve Arden	*The Dark at the Top of the Stairs* ('60)
Tallulah Bankhead	*Die! Die! My Darling!* ('65)
Dyan Cannon	*Heaven Can Wait* ('78)
Peggy Cass	*Auntie Mame* ('58)
Carol Channing	*Thoroughly Modern Millie* ('67)
Joan Crawford	*Strait-Jacket* ('64)
Bette Davis	*The Anniversary* ('68)
Faye Dunaway	*Mommie Dearest* ('81)
Ruth Gordon	*Rosemary's Baby* ('68)
Margaret Hamilton	*The Wizard of Oz* ('39)

Sylvia Miles	*Midnight Cowboy* ('69)
Agnes Moorehead	*Hush . . . Hush, Sweet Charlotte* ('65)
Rita Moreno	*The Ritz* ('76)
Lee Patrick	*Auntie Mame* ('58)
Siân Phillips	*Goodbye, Mr. Chips* ('69)
Vivian Pickles	*Harold and Maude* ('72)
Vanessa Redgrave	*Isadora* ('68)
Wendy Robie	*The People Under the Stairs* ('91)
Madeline Sherwood	*Sweet Bird of Youth* ('62)
Elizabeth Taylor	*Who's Afraid of Virginia Woolf?* ('66)
Raquel Welch	*Myra Breckenridge* ('70)
Shelley Winters	*Lolita* ('62)
Joanne Woodward	*Summer Wishes, Winter Dreams* ('73)

MISSED OPPORTUNITIES

"Those movies you were in! It's a sacrilege, throwing you away on things like that. When I left that movie house, I felt some magnificent ruby had been thrown into a platter of lard."
—John Barrymore, *Twentieth Century*

A special collection of unwise choices. Sometimes they turned the part down themselves, based on the script, their costars, or in the interest of maintaining their "images." For others, the director or producer rejected them. A few weren't even considered for the parts they so desperately desired. We can only wonder about what *might have been* . . .

Julie Andrews, so the studio thought, wasn't "big" enough for the lead in *My Fair Lady* ('64).

Kim Basinger decided against doing *Boxing Helena* ('93) and saw the part go to Sherilyn Fenn. She also saw hefty legal damages for breach of contract.

Ingrid Bergman declined to use her real Swedish accent as *The Farmer's Daughter* ('47) and let Loretta Young waltz away with an Academy Award for faking hers.

Claudette Colbert hurt her back and had to withdraw from *All About Eve* ('50), permitting Bette Davis to step in and chew the scenery as Margo Channing.

Joan Crawford decided against being in *From Here to Eternity* ('53), and Deborah Kerr went surf-smooching with Burt Lancaster instead.

Bette Davis wanted to be Vera Charles in *Mame* ('74) and Sister George in *The Killing of Sister George* ('68), but neither part was offered to her.

Doris Day rejected Mrs. Robinson in *The Graduate* ('67) because of the sexual content, but Anne Bancroft didn't have such qualms about the role.

Olivia de Havilland found the role of Blanche Dubois in *A Streetcar Named Desire* ('51) a mite too unladylike for her to consider.

Marlene Dietrich nixed *Pal Joey* ('57) after disagreements about her costars.

Jodie Foster passed on the lead role in *Dead Reckoning* ('94), so the part was rewritten for Steven Seagal!

Greta Garbo objected to playing the part of a woman who might have committed murder, plus she didn't want her public to see that she had grown older, so she declined *My Cousin Rachel* ('52), which ended up as an Olivia de Havilland role.

Judy Garland got fired from *Valley of the Dolls* ('67), and Susan Hayward stepped into her shoes.

Mitzi Gaynor wiggled out of *Some Like It Hot* ('59), and Marilyn Monroe shimmied into the role of Sugar Kane.

Rita Hayworth fell in love and out of *Born Yesterday* ('50).

Shirley Jones was fired from *A Pocketful of Miracles* ('61) so that the star's girlfriend, Hope Lange, could replace her.

Angela Lansbury lost *Mame* ('74), her big Broadway hit, to Lucille Ball, who bombed with it.

Vivien Leigh rejected the part of cousin Miriam (which Joan Crawford had started, then departed) in *Hush . . . Hush, Sweet Charlotte* ('65) by throwing the telegram offering it to her into a wastebasket. Her reason for doing so: Leigh said there was no way she was prepared to face Bette Davis at 7 A.M. each day. Olivia de Havilland didn't mind facing the Great Eyeball Roller, so she accepted as Davis's costar.

Michelle Pfeiffer, the director's first choice, found the subject matter of *The Silence of the Lambs* ('91) too painful, thus enabling Jodie Foster to win her second Academy Award for the role.

Shirley Temple missed *The Wizard of Oz* ('39) because her studio wouldn't lend her out for the role.

Lana Turner got mad and decided to drop out of *Anatomy of a Murder* ('59) because of a dispute over her costumes.

Mae West was first choice for *Sunset Blvd.* ('50) but was insulted at the idea. She also declined Federico Fellini's pleas to accept roles in *Juliet of the Spirits* ('65) and *The Satyricon* ('69).

Shelley Winters was the "backup" for Mae West as Letitia Van Allen in *Myra Breckenridge* ('70), in case anything happened to West.

Sean Young was injured in a horseback riding accident, and Kim Basinger became Vicki Vale in *Batman* ('89).

GIRLS AND THEIR GORILLAS

"Why don't you stop imitating a gorilla and imitate a man?"
—Eugene Pallette, *My Man Godfrey*

What's more romantic than a girl and her fella? Why, a girl and her gorilla, of course—or orangutan, chimpanzee, and any other kind of monkey. Since Fay Wray wiggled her way into Kong's heart, cinematic simians just can't leave the ladies alone. And the audiences love it, too. So filmmakers have tried to satisfy that demand by giving the girls plenty of monkey business to keep them occupied.

Acquanetta	*Captive Wild Woman* ('43)
Karen Allen	*Animal Behavior* ('89)
Charlotte Austin	*Bride and the Beast* ('58)
Pam Austin	*Perils of Pauline* ('67)
Anne Bancroft	*Gorilla at Large* ('54)
Thora Birch	*Monkey Trouble* ('94)
Michele Carey	*In the Shadow of Kilimanjaro* ('86)
Ellen Drew	*The Monster and the Girl* ('41)
Sidney Fox	*Murders in the Rue Morgue* ('32)

Annette Funicello	*Monkey's Uncle* ('65)
Mie Hama	*King Kong Escapes* ('68)
Linda Hamilton	*King Kong Lives* ('86)
Margo Johns	*Konga* ('61)
Carol Kane	*The Mafu Cage* ('78)
Elissa Landi	*The Sign of the Cross* ('32)
Jessica Lange	*King Kong* ('76)
Julie London	*Nabonga* ('44)
Anita Louise	*The Gorilla* ('39)
Diana Lynn	*Bedtime for Bonzo* ('51)
Helen Mack	*Son of Kong* ('33)
Trudy Marshall	*Mark of the Gorilla* ('50)
Patricia Medina	*Phantom of the Rue Morgue* ('54)
Terry Moore	*Mighty Joe Young* ('49)
Maris Nixon	*White Pongo* ('45)
Melanie Parker	*Monkey Shines* ('88)
Barbara Payton	*Bride of the Gorilla* ('51)
Ginger Rogers	*Monkey Business* ('52)
Elizabeth Shue	*Link* ('86)
June Vincent	*Zamba the Gorilla* ('49)
Sigourney Weaver	*Gorillas in the Mist* ('88)
D. D. Winters	*Tanya's Island* ('80)
Fay Wray	*King Kong* ('33)

THE MISS HAIRY AWARD

Awarded to **Annie Girardot** in *The Ape Woman* ('64), who's an overly hirsute female—a sideshow freak, actually.

THE GORILLA OF YOUR DREAMS AWARD

Awarded to **Marlene Dietrich** for *Blonde Venus* ('32), in which she emerges from inside a gorilla suit to sing "Hot Voodoo."

THE GORILLA OF *HER* DREAMS AWARD

Awarded to **Charlotte Rampling** for *Max, My Love* ('86), because she's the bored wife of a British diplomat who takes a chimp as her lover.

GODDESSES

"You're the most beautiful woman I've ever seen,
which doesn't say much for you."
—Groucho Marx, *Animal Crackers*

The deities—heavenly goddesses come to life, and tempting mere mortals with their legendary beauty. Care to worship at a shrine to one of these goddesses?

Honor Blackman	*Jason and the Argonauts* ('63)
Claire Bloom	*Clash of the Titans* ('81)
Kim Cattrall	*Mannequin* ('87)
Ava Gardner	*One Touch of Venus* ('48)
Susan Hampshire	*Malpertuis* ('72)
Rita Hayworth	*Down to Earth* ('42)
Olivia Newton-John	*Xanadu* ('80)
Maggie Smith	*Clash of the Titans* ('81)
Danitra Vance	*Limit Up* ('89)
Vanna White	*Goddess of Love* ('88)
Shirley Yamaguchi	*Madam White Snake* ('60)

BEAUTY QUEENS

"I'd never met such a pretty girl, and I guess I'm just sensitive because real—real beauty makes me want to gag."
—Woody Allen, *Take the Money and Run*

Winners of beauty pageants haven't been very successful at swapping their crowns for film stardom. Despite the myriad winners each year of smaller titles—like '48's Miss Kansas, Vera Miles—who achieve some success in films, most winners simply fade after a few screen appearances.

Besides **Rosemary LaPlanche** ('41), who was a featured player in many RKO films, very few other Miss Americas have been successful in films. **Mary Ann Mobley** ('59) can be seen as Elvis's love interest in *Harum Scarum* ('65); **Lee Meriwether** ('55) appeared in several films including *The Undefeated* ('69); **Elizabeth Ward (Gracen)** appears in *Lower Level*. **Bess Myerson** ('45) also appeared in a few films, but achieved greater success on television. Some of the Miss America also-rans such as **Vera Miles** (Miss Kansas), **Cloris Leachman** (1946, Miss Chicago), and **Veronica Lake** (1937, Miss Florida—but disqualified when she was found to be under sixteen) also have been successful.

The most notorious Miss America, **Vanessa Williams**, who resigned after photographs of her frontally nude and embracing another woman appeared in *Penthouse*, later pursued a singing career. In 1989, she also branched out into films, appearing with Sam Jones (*Playgirl*'s well-endowed centerfold of June 1975) in *Under the Gun*, a detective thriller.

Of course, there's always the myriad other "beauty" queens, such as '47's Miss California Artichoke Queen, **Marilyn Monroe**, who've been infinitely more successful in film careers than any of the Miss Americas. Plus, **Lynda Carter** (Miss World USA, '73) who starred in *Bobbie Jo and the Outlaw* ('76), not to mention *Wonder Woman* on television.

Even international beauties find the transition from beauty queen to film queen a difficult one to make. The most notable examples to try (along with one of their films) are:

1936	Miss Hungary	Zsa Zsa Gabor	*Moulin Rouge* ('52)
1946	Miss Italy	Gina Lollobrigida	*Solomon and Sheba* ('59)
1950	Miss Great Britain	Anne Heywood	*The Fox* ('68)
1951	Miss Sweden	Anita Ekberg	*I'll Take Sweden* ('65)
1953	Miss France	Christine Martel	*Adam and Eve* ('60)
1959	Miss France	Claudine Auger	*Thunderball* ('65)

| 1961 | Miss Israel | Gila Golan | *Ship of Fools* ('65) |
| 1975 | Miss Venezuela | Maria Conchita Alonso | *Moscow on the Hudson* ('84) |

Several Asian beauty title winners—most notably in Thailand and the Philippines—also have pursued careers in the film industries of their home countries.

Best Collection of Beauty Queens

Yankee Pasha ('54) contains the best collection of beauty queens. It features Miss Australia, Miss Japan, Miss Norway, Miss Panama, Miss Uruguay, Miss USA, and a Miss Universe.

GRANDE DAMES

"The prettiest sight in this fine world is the privileged class
enjoying its privileges."
—James Stewart, *The Philadelphia Story*

These dames are *la crème de la crème* of dames—the grande dames. With superior looks on their faces and lorgnettes held at attention, the grande dames sashay forth to combat a world of lesser beings. Of course, some of them fit into a category more commonly referred to as "rich bitches." Those women are far, far nastier than the more common garden-variety type of bitch. Why? They're richer—in money, word, and deed.

Jane Alexander	*Blood & Orchids* ('86)
Ingrid Bergman	*The Yellow Rolls-Royce* ('65)
Coral Browne	*The Ruling Class* ('72)
Bette Davis	*Where Love Has Gone* ('64)
Marie Dressler	*The Vagabond Lover* ('29)
Margaret Dumont	*A Night at the Opera* ('35)

Edith Evans	*The Last Days of Dolwyn* ('49)
Katharine Hepburn	*Suddenly, Last Summer* ('59)
Angela Lansbury	*Something for Everyone* ('70)
Nancy Marchand	*Brain Donors* ('92)
Barbara Stanwyck	*The Thorn Birds* ('83)
Janet Suzman	*The Draughtsman's Contract* ('82)

GROSS INDIGNITIES

"How dare you say 'penis' to a dead person!"
—Lily Tomlin, *All of Me*

Some of the indignities that women suffer in the movies are unbelievably gross . . . or are they? While gross, many of them also can be downright funny, considering how they happened and who the victim was. Here's a compilation of the gross . . . and the bizarre.

The Bed-Sitting Room ('69)—Through some strange circumstance of fate, **Rita Tushingham** is seventeen months pregnant.

Deadly Blessing ('81)—Poor **Maren Jensen**. While soaking in the tub to relax after some harrowing experiences, she discovers a large snake has appeared in her bathwater.

The Entity ('83)—Supposedly based on fact, **Barbara Hershey** plays a woman who is raped repeatedly—and in front of her children—by an unseen "demonic" entity.

Evil Dead II ('87)—As one of a group of people in a cabin attacked by monsters, **Kassie Wesley** opens her mouth wide in a loud scream. As she's screaming, one monster slams a trapdoor down on the head of Kassie's friend. His eyeball pops out and soars through the air, straight across the room into Kassie's wide-open mouth.

Madhouse ('90)—Beautiful **Kirstie Alley** gets drenched by a vomiting cat—twice.

The Mad Room ('69)—A dog wanders around with one of **Shelley Winters**'s severed hands in its mouth.

Orca ('77)—**Bo Derek**'s leg is bitten off by a whale.

Tell Me That You Love Me, Junie Moon ('70)—**Liza Minnelli**'s date first takes her to a deserted cemetery at night. Once there, he makes her strip while he merely sits and watches. Then, he drives to an abandoned junkyard, where—after beating her—he pours battery acid on her face and arms.

TOSSING HER COOKIES

"Come on, give your Mommy a big sloppy kiss."
—Elizabeth Taylor, *Who's Afraid of Virginia World?*

Ladies don't sweat, they "glisten." And ladies don't vomit, they regurgitate. Here's some star-time cookie tossing to prove just how far some of the girls will go to make their acting grossly realistic.

Linda Blair	*The Exorcist* ('73)
Julie Delpy	*Voyager* ('91)
Faye Dunaway	*Barfly* ('87)
Sissy Spacek	*Hard Promises* ('91)
Meryl Streep	*Ironweed* ('87)

GUN MOLLS

"The chances are you'll get off with life. That means if you're a
good girl, you'll be out in twenty years. I'll be waiting for you. If they
hang you, I'll always remember you."
—Humphrey Bogart, *The Maltese Falcon*

Moll: a female companion to a thief or gangster. This kind of broad is one tough cookie; her arms are more adept at cradling a firearm than a baby. No sweet, soft songs for these bimbos; the sound of gunfire is the music that thrills their ears.

Judith Anderson	*Lady Scarface* ('41)
Brenda Bakke	*Gunmen* ('90)

Kim Basinger	*The Marrying Man ('91), The Getaway ('94)*
Karen Black	*Little Laura & Big John ('73)*
Susan Blakely	*Capone ('75)*
Dyan Cannon	*The Virginia Hill Story ('74)*
Lynda Carter	*Bobbie Jo and the Outlaw ('76)*
Joan Crawford	*The Damned Don't Cry ('50)*
Peggy Cummins	*Gun Crazy ('49)*
Kim Darby	*The Story of Pretty Boy Floyd ('74)*
Bette Davis	*20,000 Years in Sing Sing ('33), Bunny O'Hare ('72)*
Faith Domergue	*Spin a Dark Web ('56)*
Jodie Foster	*Bugsy Malone ('76)*
Jean Harlow	*The Public Enemy ('31)*
Brooke Hayward	*Mad Dog Coll ('61)*
Jill Ireland	*Love and Bullets ('79)*
Carolyn Jones	*Baby Face Nelson ('57)*
Adele Jurgens	*Armored Car Robbery ('50)*
Barbara Lawrence	*The Street with No Name ('48)*
Ida Lupino	*High Sierra ('41)*
Carol Lynley	*The Four Deuces ('75)*
Pamela Sue Martin	*The Lady in Red ('79)*
Vonetta McGee	*Thomasine & Bushrod ('74)*
Patricia Morison	*Persons in Hiding ('39)*
Karen Morley	*Scarface: The Shame of a Nation ('32)*
Betsy Palmer	*The True Story of Lynn Stuart ('58)*
Michelle Pfeiffer	*Scarface ('83)*
Michelle Phillips	*Dillinger ('73)*
Ginger Rogers	*Tight Spot ('55)*
Catherine Rouvel	*Borsalino ('70)*
Gena Rowlands	*Gloria ('80)*

Jean Seberg	*Breathless* ('59)
Sylvia Sidney	*You Only Live Twice* ('37)
Sally Struthers	*The Getaway* ('72)
Angel Tompkins	*Little Cigars* ('73)
Claire Trevor	*Key Largo* ('48)
Mamie Van Doren	*Guns, Girls and Gangsters* ('59)
Diane Varsi	*Killers Three* ('68)
Shelley Winters	*I Died a Thousand Times* ('55)

THE WHO'D A-THUNK IT AWARD

Awarded to **Jane Fonda**, who was Miss Army Recruitment of 1962!

MACHINE-GUN MAMAS

> "Oh, that. That's just part of my clothes. I hardly ever shoot
> anybody with it."
> —Dick Powell, *Murder, My Sweet*

The rat-a-tat-tat you hear doesn't come from the clicking of high heels
. . . these mamas make their noise another way.

Judith Anderson	*Lady Scarface* ('41)
Angie Dickinson	*Big Bad Mama* ('74)
Faye Dunaway	*Bonnie and Clyde* ('67)
Cloris Leachman	*Crazy Mama* ('75)
Tracy Needham	*Bonnie and Clyde: The True Story* ('92)
Dorothy Provine	*The Bonnie Parker Story* ('58)
Ann Sothern	*Crazy Mama* ('75)
Lurene Tuttle	*Ma Barker's Killer Brood* ('60)
Shelley Winters	*Bloody Mama* ('70)
Blanche Yurka	*Queen of the Mob* ('40)

HIT LADIES

"Oooh, NO! A bimbo with a gun!"
—Adam Kennedy, *Assault of the Killer Bimboes*

Hit ladies . . . women who murder or assassinate for a price. Deadlier than the male. They'll charm you, enchant you, then rub you out quickly.

Carroll Baker	*Andy Warhol's Bad* ('71)
Cheri Caffaro	*Too Hot to Handle* ('76)
Ahna Capri	*The Specialist* ('75)
Barbara Carrera	*Never Say Never Again* ('83)
Bridget Fonda	*Point of No Return* ('93)
Pam Grier	*The Vindicator* ('86)
Katharine Hepburn	*Grace Quigley* ('85)
Susan Hogan	*Narrow Margin* ('90)
Grace Jones	*A View to a Kill* ('85)
Lotte Lenya	*From Russia with Love* ('63)
Yvette Mimieux	*Hit Lady* ('74)
Lena Olin	*Romeo Is Bleeding* ('94)
Luciana Paluzzi	*Thunderball* ('65)
Anne Parillaud	*La Femme Nikita* ('90)
Terri Polo	*Quick* ('91)
Diana Rigg	*The Assassination Bureau* ('69)
Cornelia Sharpe	*The Next Man* ('76)
Elke Sommer	*Deadlier than the Male* ('67)
Georgina Spelvin	*Girls for Rent* ('74)
Kathleen Turner	*Prizzi's Honor* ('85)
Lynnete Walden	*The Silencer* ('90)

THE TERRORISTS

Sandahl Bergman	*Programmed to Kill* ('86)
Irina Brook	*Captive* ('87)
Judy Davis	*The Final Option* ('82)
Morgan Fairchild	*Time Bomb* ('84)
Kim Griest	*Brazil* ('85)
Diane Keaton	*The Little Drummer Girl* ('84)
Marthe Keller	*Black Sunday* ('77)
Nastassja Kinski	*Exposed* ('83)
Lisa Kreuzer	*Birgit Haas Must Be Killed* ('81)
Kim Suh Ra	*Mayumi, Virgin Terrorist* ('87)
Natasha Richardson	*Patty Hearst* ('88)
Sissy Spacek	*Katherine* ('75)

GYPSIES

"The Gypsies love kids—especially girls.
The girls are the money makers."
—Eric Roberts, *King of the Gypsies*

A popular song once offered men this advice: to be happy the rest of your life, make a Gypsy woman your wife. True perhaps, but only unless one is intoxicated by flying skirts, thumping tambourines, and crystal balls. Most of the cinema's treatments of Gypsy women have focused on these stereotypical images, with only a rare, realistic depiction emerging.

Ljubica Adzovic	*Time of the Gypsies* ('89)
Annabella	*Wings of the Morning* ('37)
Carroll Baker	*The Miracle* ('59)

Genevieve Bujold	*Alex and the Gypsy* ('76)
Jill Clayburgh	*The Art of Crime* ('74)
Dolores del Rio	*The Loves of Carmen* ('27)
Laura Del Sol	*Carmen* ('83)
Marlene Dietrich	*Golden Earrings* ('47)
Nina Foch	*Cry of the Werewolf* ('44)
Rita Hayworth	*The Loves of Carmen* ('48)
Gordana Jovanovic	*I Even Met Happy Gypsies* ('67)
Helena Kallianiotes	*Eureka* ('81)
Sara Lezana	*Los Tarantos* ('64)
Viveca Lindfors	*Gypsy Fever* ('72)
Margaret Lockwood	*Jassy* ('47)
Gina Lollobrigida	*The Hunchback of Notre Dame* ('57)
Melina Mercouri	*The Gypsy and the Gentleman* ('58)
Julia Migenes-Johnson	*Carmen* ('84)
Hayley Mills	*Gypsy Girl* ('66)
Maria Montez	*Gypsy Wildcat* ('44)
Zoe Nathenson	*The Raggedy Rawney* ('88)
Maureen O'Hara	*The Hunchback of Notre Dame* ('39)
Maria Ouspenskaya	*The Wolf Man* ('41)
Jane Russell	*Hot Blood* ('56)
Susan Sarandon	*King of the Gypsies* ('78)
Brooke Shields	*King of the Gypsies* ('78)
Thelma Todd	*The Bohemian Girl* ('36)
Elena Verdugo	*House of Frankenstein* ('44)
Shelley Winters	*King of the Gypsies* ('78), *Déjà Vu* ('85)
Katarina Witt	*Carmen on Ice* ('90)

HACKING HONEYS

"In our family, we don't divorce men—we bury them."
—Ruth Gordon, *Lord Love a Duck*

The Queens of slicing, dicing, and chopping . . . *femmes extraordinaires* in the use of knives, axes, cleavers . . . and not in their kitchens! Meet one of these hacking honeys and lose some of your body parts. Approach these women with extreme, extreme caution. In fact, don't even go near them if there's something sharp in their hands.

Jean Arless	*Homicidal* ('61)
Diane Baker	*Strait-Jacket* ('64)
Anna Chappell	*Mountaintop Motel Massacre* ('86)
Anjanette Comer	*The Baby* ('73)
Joan Crawford	*Strait-Jacket* ('64)
Catherine Deneuve	*Repulsion* ('65)
Lynn Frederick	*Schizo* ('65)
Judy Geeson	*Beserk!* ('67)
Jill Jacobson	*Nurse Sherri* ('78)
Margot Kidder	*Sisters* ('73)
Leslie Lee	*The Axe* ('74)
Elizabeth Montgomery	*The Legend of Lizzie Borden* ('75)
Betsy Palmer	*Friday the 13th* ('80)
Barbara Steele	*Silent Scream* ('80)
Jessica Walter	*Play Misty for Me* ('71)
Rachel Ward	*Night School* ('81)

BEST-ORGANIZED HACKER

Awarded to **Glynis Johns** in *Vault of Horror* ('73), as a housewife whose husband's obsession with tidiness drives her insane. She cuts her fastidious hubby into tiny pieces, which she places in neatly labeled jars.

HONEY'S BARE BUNS

"Sodomize me!"
—Mariangela Melato, *Swept Away*

If sweet rearviews excite you, then these honeys have the bare buns for your enjoyment. Feast your eyes on these delectable goodies—as seen from the rear, of course.

Jenny Agutter	*Logan's Run* ('76)
Karen Allen	*National Lampoon's Animal House* ('78)
Nancy Allen	*Dressed to Kill* ('80)
Ursula Andress	*Loaded Guns* ('75)
Ann-Margret	*Carnal Knowledge* ('71)
Laura Antonelli	*Malicious* ('73)
Rosanna Arquette	*The Executioner's Song* ('82)
Carroll Baker	*Sylvia* ('65)
Ellen Barkin	*The Big Easy* ('87)
Sandahl Bergman	*Loving Lulu* ('92)
Sandra Bernhard	*Without You I'm Nothing* ('90)
Jacqueline Bisset	*Secrets* ('71)
Karen Black	*Miss Right* ('88)
Linda Blair	*Red Heat* ('88)
Sonia Braga	*Gabriela* ('83)
Joanna Cassidy	*Night Games* ('80)
Phoebe Cates	*Paradise* ('82)
Rae Dawn Chong	*Fear City* ('84)
Joan Collins	*The Stud* ('78)
Barbara Crampton	*Fraternity Vacation* ('85)
Sally Field	*Stay Hungry* ('76)
Melanie Griffith	*Body Double* ('84)

Daryl Hannah	*Summer Lovers* ('82)
Margaux Hemingway	*Lipstick* ('76)
Barbara Hershey	*Boxcar Bertha* ('72)
Catherine Hicks	*Laguna Heat* ('87)
Isabelle Huppert	*The Bedroom Window* ('87)
Sally Kellerman	*M*A*S*H* ('70)
Nicole Kidman	*Dead Calm* ('89)
Sondra Locke	*Death Game* ('77)
Amy Madigan	*The Prince of Pennsylvania* ('88)
Virginia Madsen	*Long Gone* ('87)
Ali MacGraw	*Goodbye, Columbus* ('69)
Juliet Mills	*Avanti!* ('72)
Brigitte Nielsen	*Bye Bye Baby* ('88)
Michelle Pfeiffer	*Into the Night* ('85)
Vanessa Redgrave	*Steaming* ('85)
Greta Scacchi	*The Coca-Cola Kid* ('85)
Jane Seymour	*Lassiter* ('84)
Brooke Shields	*Pretty Baby* ('78)
Sissy Spacek	*Carrie* ('76)
Mary Steenburgen	*Melvin and Howard* ('80)
Stella Stevens	*The Ballad of Cable Hogue* ('70)
Elizabeth Taylor	*Cleopatra* ('63)
Natalie Wood	*Splendor in the Grass* ('61)
Daphne Zuniga	*Staying Together* ('89)

THE HORROR OF IT ALL

"They all start out as Juliets and end up as Lady Macbeths."
—William Holden, *The Country Girl*

It's an awful time for actresses when the only scripts arriving for their perusal are "shock thrillers." Poor ladies; advancing age is enough of a horror without this added burden. St. Joan of the Coathangers and Battling Bette led the pack into the "aging moviestar shock thriller" genre. Since their debut, plenty of others have taken their turn performing in the shock-thriller genre.

Mary Astor	*Hush . . . Hush, Sweet Charlotte* ('65)
Lauren Bacall	*The Fan* ('81)
Carroll Baker	*Paranoia* ('69)
Tallulah Bankhead	*Die! Die! My Darling!* ('65)
Joan Bennett	*House of Dark Shadows* ('70)
Karen Black	*The Pyx* ('73)
Jeanne Crain	*The Night God Screamed* ('71)
Joan Crawford	*Strait-Jacket* ('64)
Bette Davis	*The Nanny* ('65)
Yvonne de Carlo	*American Gothic* ('88)
Olivia de Havilland	*Lady in a Cage* ('64)
Catherine Deneuve	*Repulsion* ('65)
Samantha Eggar	*The Brood* ('79)
Mia Farrow	*See No Evil* ('71)
Louise Fletcher	*Exorcist II: The Heretic* ('77)
Joan Fontaine	*The Devil's Own* ('66)
Zsa Zsa Gabor	*Picture Mommy Dead* ('66)
Ava Gardner	*Tam Lin* ('72)
Ruth Gordon	*Rosemary's Baby* ('68)
Gloria Grahame	*Mansion of the Doomed* ('77)
Lee Grant	*Visiting Hours* ('82)
Audrey Hepburn	*Wait Until Dark* ('67)
Carol Kane	*When a Stranger Calls* ('79)
Deborah Kerr	*Eye of the Devil* ('67)
Veronica Lake	*Flesh Feast* ('70)

Piper Laurie	*Ruby* ('72)
Janet Leigh	*Psycho* ('60)
Gina Lollobrigida	*Plucked* ('68)
Shirley MacLaine	*The Possession of Joel Delaney* ('72)
Marlee Matlin	*Hear No Evil* ('93)
Sylvia Miles	*The Funhouse* ('81)
Terry Moore	*Hellhole* ('85)
Patricia Neal	*The Night Digger* ('71)
Kim Novak	*Satan's Triangle* ('75)
Maureen O'Sullivan	*Too Scared to Scream* ('85)
Geraldine Page	*The Beguiled* ('71)
Eleanor Parker	*Eye of the Cat* ('69)
Debbie Reynolds	*What's the Matter with Helen?* ('71)
Simone Signoret	*Games* ('67)
Alexis Smith	*The Little Girl Who Lives Down the Lane* ('76)
Elizabeth Taylor	*Night Watch* ('73)
Lana Turner	*Terror of Sheba* ('74)
Shelley Winters	*Who Slew Auntie Roo?* ('71)

SCREAMERS

Effective screaming—for a woman—can be a large part of a role in a thriller. So who's the best screamer around? Here are a few likely candidates. Tune up your ears—and give them a listen.

Evelyn Ankers	*Son of Dracula* ('43)
Marilyn Burns	*The Texas Chainsaw Massacre* ('74)
Hazel Court	*The Premature Burial* ('62)
Cheryl Lawson	*The Dead Pit* ('89)
Estelle Parsons	*Bonnie and Clyde* ('69)

HYPE!

"Is this girl terrific or *what?*"
—Arye Gross, *The Experts*

Hyperbole . . . hype. Gross overexaggerations. Exclamation points in excess! Pearls from the lips of publicity agents and caption writers. These are the words splashed across movie posters, used in ads to entice moviegoers. And guess what? It works! Try and match the hype below to the film star (and her film) being touted.

_____ 1. "HER TREACHERY STAINED EVERY STONE OF THE PYRAMIDS!"

_____ 2. "SHE'S A BOY!"

_____ 3. "_____ _____ IN 3-D . . . IT'LL KNOCK *BOTH* YOUR EYES OUT!"

_____ 4. "SHE WAS A MIDNIGHT GIRL IN A NINE O'CLOCK TOWN!"

_____ 5. "MEN, MONEY AND MOONSHINE . . . WHEN IT COMES TO VICE, MAMA KNOWS BEST"

_____ 6. "SHE CAPTURED AMERICA'S HEART AND TORE IT APART."

_____ 7. "_____ LAUGHS!"

_____ 8. "GABLE'S BACK AND _____'S GOT HIM!"

_____ 9. "THEY DON'T COME ANY BIGGER!"

_____ 10. "THEY CALL ME BAD . . . SPELLED M-E-N!"

_____ 11. "ALWAYS A MAN . . . ALMOST ANY MAN!"

_____ 12. "EVERY INCH A LADY . . . TILL YOU LOOK AT THE RECORD!"

_____ 13. "SHE MADE FRIENDS ON THE WRONG SIDE OF THE TRACKS . . . AND SHE MADE LOVE ON THE OTHER SIDE!"

_____ 14. "WOMAN OR LEOPARD? SHE WAS BOTH!"

_____ 15. "ONE TWIN LOVES . . . AND ONE TWIN LOVES . . . TO KILL!"

_____ 16. "THE THINGS SHE DOES TO MEN CAN ONLY END IN *MURDER!*"

_____ 17. "THEY CALLED HER _____, THE HEARTLESS SIREN OF THE SOUTH!"

_____ 18. "KINDA HARD . . . KINDA SOFT . . . THE KIND OF WOMAN MOST MEN WANT BUT SHOULDN'T HAVE!"

_____ 19. "I DON'T CARE WHAT WOMEN THINK OF ME AS LONG AS MEN THINK OF ME!"

_____ 20. "SHE COULDN'T COOK AND SHE COULDN'T SEW, BUT, OH HOW SHE COULD SO-AND-SO!"

a. **Joan Bennett** in *The Housekeeper's Daughter* ('39)

b. **Joan Bennett** in *Scarlet Street* ('45)

c. **Joan Collins** in *Land of the Pharaohs* ('55)

d. **Joan Crawford** in *Mildred Pierce* ('45)

e. **Joan Crawford** in *This Woman is Dangerous* ('52)

f. **Bette Davis** in *Beyond the Forest* ('49)

g. **Bette Davis** in *Jezebel* ('38)

h. **Olivia de Havilland** in *The Dark Mirror* ('46)

i. **Angie Dickinson** in *Big Bad Mama* ('74)

j. **Greta Garbo** in *Ninotchka* ('39)

k. **Greer Garson** in *Adventure* ('45)

l. **Katharine Hepburn** in *Sylvia Scarlett* ('35)

m. **Dorothy Malone** in *Too Much, Too Soon* ('58)

n. **Barbara Payton** in *Bad Blonde* ('53)

o. **Natasha Richardson** in *Patty Hearst* ('88)

p. **Jane Russell** in *The French Line* ('54)

q. **Jane Russell** in *The Tall Men* ('55)

r. **Ann Sheridan** in *Juke Girl* ('42)

s. **Ann Sheridan** in *Kings Row* ('42)

t. **Simone Simon** in *Cat People* ('42)

Answers: 1, c; 2, l; 3, p; 4, f; 5, i; 6, n; 7, j; 8, k; 9, q; 10, o; 11, m; 12, e; 13, s; 14, t; 15, h; 16, b; 17, g; 18, d; 19, r; 20, a.

PHONIES

"People will believe any lie if it is fantastic enough."
—Leo Genn, *Quo Vadis*

For some female stars creating intriguing backgrounds—or covering up their pasts—was standard procedure. This tactic was known as the "studio biography." Somehow, often years later, the truth usually emerged.

Theda Bara—*Claim:* born in the Sahara Desert, the love child of a French artist and his Egyptian mistress. *Reality:* born in Cincinnati, Ohio, the daughter of a tailor.

Anna Kashfi—*Claim:* born in Calcutta, India, to a high Brahmin family. *Reality:* born into a Welsh coal-mining family.

Merle Oberon—*Claim:* born in Tasmania, Australia, of aristocratic parents. *Reality:* born in Calcutta, India, a half-caste (British, Indian) into a poor, lower-class existence.

CRITICAL SHOTS

"Thin. Pretty. Big tits. Your basic nightmare."
—Carrie Fisher, *When Harry Met Sally*

Lucille Ball in *Mame* ('74)—"Had she made this film fifteen years ago, she would have been terrific. But she is now too old, too stringy in the legs, too basso in the voice, and too creaky in the legs."—*The New Republic*

Hazel Court in *Masque of the Red Death* ('64)—"[Hazel Court] in whose bosom you could sink the entire works of Edgar Allan Poe and a bottle of his favorite booze at the same time."—*Time*

Doris Day—"Until this spun-sugar zombie melts from our screen, there is little chance of the American film's coming of age."—John Simon

Ava Gardner in *Show Boat* ('51)—"Is subjected to such close scrutiny by the camera that her handsome face often takes on the attributes of a relief map of Yugoslavia."—*The New Yorker*

Sophia Loren in *Man of La Mancha* ('72)—"Her singing is the pathetic burbling of a titmouse drowning in a milk pitcher."—Harlan Ellison

Melina Mercouri in *A Dream of Passion* ('78)—"As one endures the spectacle of Mercouri bearing her soul, it seems one has wandered into the home movies of a demented culture maven."—*Newsweek*

Sylvia Miles in *Andy Warhol's Women in Revolt* ('73)—"The film is like an open wound, and Sylvia is a kind of cross between Lana Turner and Gloria Swanson in *Sunset Blvd.*, eating her way through the movie like an emotional barracuda and leaving everyone around her for fishbait."—Rex Reed

Diana Ross in *Mahogany* ('75)—"Ross laughs eagerly, but never with a semblance of spontaneity, weeps without sorrow and rages without passion." —Jay Cocks

Cybill Shepherd in *At Long Last Love* ('75)—"Cybill Shepherd plays a poor little girl with a notion of sophistication that is underpassed only by her acting ability. (I will not even sully my pen by making it describe her singing and dancing.) —John Simon

Elizabeth Taylor in *Cleopatra* ('63)—"Miss Taylor is overweight, overbosomed, overpaid and undertalented."—David Susskind

Elizabeth Taylor in *The Taming of the Shrew* ('67)—"Just how garish her commonplace accent, squeakily shrill voice, and the childish petulance with which she delivers her lines are, my pen is neither scratchy nor leaky enough to convey."—John Simon

Mae West in *Myra Breckenridge* ('70)—"Mae West, playing a ghastly travesty of the travesty of womanhood she once played, has a Mae West face painted on the front of her head and moves to and fro like the Imperial Hotel during the 1923 Tokyo earthquake."—Joseph Morgenstern

JAILBAIT

"She was fifteen, going to thirty-five, Doc, and she told me she was
eighteen, and she was very willing, you know what I mean."
—Jack Nicholson, *One Flew over the Cuckoo's Nest*

Jailbait . . . hot young stuff. Sweet, juicy, delectable nymphets. What's so enticing about jailbait? Well, while jailbait is young, often it's very, very experienced. Many a wise man has been known to throw caution to the wind when jailbait wiggled by in a tight skirt.

Rosanna Arquette	*The Executioner's Song* ('82)
Ewa Aulin	*Candy* ('68)

Drew Barrymore	*Far from Home* ('89)
Lisa Bonet	*Angel Heart* ('87)
Sandrine Bonnaire	*A Nos Amours* ('83)
Carrie Fisher	*Shampoo* ('75)
Jodie Foster	*Taxi Driver* ('76)
Susan George	*Lola* ('69)
Melanie Griffith	*The Drowning Pool* ('76)
Michelle Johnson	*Blame It on Rio* ('84)
Cristen Kauffman	*Betrayed by Innocence* ('86)
Nastassja Kinski	*Stay As You Are* ('78)
Emily Lloyd	*Wish You Were Here* ('87)
Sue Lyon	*Lolita* ('62)
Elizabeth McGovern	*Ragtime* ('81)
Clare Powney	*The Girl* ('87)
Molly Ringwald	*Fresh Horses* ('88)
Winona Ryder	*Great Balls of Fire!* ('89)
Brooke Shields	*Pretty Baby* ('78)
Bernice Stegers	*The Girl* ('87)
Tuesday Weld	*I Walk the Line* ('70)

THE MISS REAL-LIFE JAILBAIT AWARD

Awarded to **Beverly Aadland** of *Cuban Rebel Girls* ('59). The seventeenish Aadland was the last in a long string of the teenage "prótegées" long favored by the dissipated Errol Flynn. Along with Bev's other duties as Flynn's companion, she also appeared in his last film, the bomb mentioned previously. After her older lover's death, Aadland wisely retired from films.

HER FIRST SCREEN KISS

Lauren Bacall	*To Have and Have Not* ('44)
Petula Clark	*Don't Ever Leave Me* ('49)
Doris Day	*Romance on the High Seas* ('48)

Deanna Durbin	*First Love* ('39)
Jodie Foster	*Moi, Fleur Bleue* ('78)
Bonita Granville	*Those Were the Days* ('40)
Margaret O'Brien	*Her First Romance* ('51)
Tatum O'Neal	*International Velvet* ('78)
Mary Pickford	*My Best Girl* ('27)
Brooke Shields	*The Blue Lagoon* ('80)
Elizabeth Taylor	*Cynthia* ('47)
Shirley Temple	*Miss Annie Rooney* ('42)
Natalie Wood	*Rebel Without a Cause* ('55)

ALL TALKEE, NO KISSEE

Two leading ladies of the screen never kissed their leading men in any of their films, but for entirely different reasons.

Mae West was convinced that she exuded such powerful sexuality on the screen that any kissing by her would be overkill.

Anna Mae Wong, an American-born Chinese star of American and British films in the '20s and '30s, who was always paired with Caucasian screen lovers, was never shown kissing because of the audience's presumed negative reaction to miscegenation.

THE LADY SPEAKS HER MIND

"Oh, if ah jes' wasn't a lady, what wouldn't I tell that varmint."
—Vivien Leigh, *Gone with the Wind*

The lady speaks her mind . . . and offers some interesting insights into what the females of the cinema think—and thought—about a variety of subjects and people.

"It was wonderful to fuck the sweet afternoon away."—**Mary Astor**, describing extramarital bliss with playwright George S. Kaufman, in her infamous diary.

"I always did want to get in Marlene's pants."—**Tallulah Bank-head,** on replacing Marlene Dietrich in *A Very Different Woman.*

"There is a broad with a future behind her."—**Constance Bennett,** on Marilyn Monroe.

"Happy Birthday, dear, Joan."—**Joan Bennett**'s birthday note to Hollywood gossip columnist Hedda Hopper, enclosed with her gift—a week-old dead skunk.

"It's been 20 years since the trial that broke my heart. If it happened today, I'd still be a whore. Grace Kelly, however, will get away with having many lovers. Know why? The damn public will never believe it."—**Clara Bow,** on the lurid aspects of her sex life that emerged during a lawsuit against her secretary and ruined her movie career.

"And you tell Miss Shearer that I didn't get where I am on my ass."—**Joan Crawford,** delivering a zinger about her rival at MGM, who was married to producer Irving Thalberg.

"My daughter . . . by Calvin Coolidge."—**Marion Davies**'s frequent jest when introducing her friend Zsa Zsa Gabor.

"Dramatic art in her opinion is knowing how to fill a sweater." —**Bette Davis,** on Jayne Mansfield.

"Daddy, buy me that!"— **Marlene Dietrich,** pleading with director Tay Garnett on first spotting the young John Wayne in the Universal commissary in 1939. Dietrich and Wayne soon were costarred in *Seven Sinners* ('40), *The Spoilers* ('42), and *Pittsburgh* ('42).

"I would prefer to be forgotten."—**Deanna Durbin,** commenting on her reclusive retirement in France.

"Kissing him was like going to heaven."—**Alice Faye,** on Tyrone Power.

"I had made enough faces."—**Greta Garbo,** replying to David Niven's query about why she had chosen to leave film making.

"How could I? I've got rainbows coming out my ass!"—**Judy Garland,** snapping at an obnoxious female fan who kept imploring her to "never forget the Rainbow."

"It could be worse. Suppose I'd been nominated and lost to Cher."—**Lillian Gish,** telling costar Ann Sothern (who *was* nominated) how she felt about *not being* nominated for their film *The Whales of August.*

"Hollywood amuses me. Holier than thou for the public and unholier than the devil in reality."—**Grace Kelly**, sparring with soon lover-to-be Clark Gable on the set of *Mogambo*.

"You could put all the talent I had in your left eye, and still not suffer from impaired vision."—**Veronica Lake**, assessing herself.

"Now don't come too fast, will you?"—**Hedy Lamarr**, issuing instructions to actor Stewart Granger during an attempted sexual liaison. (*Note:* See Granger's comment regarding Lamarr under "A Man's Opinion.")

"I am an actress—a great actress. Great actresses have lovers, why not? I have a husband, and I have lovers. Like Sarah Bernhardt."—**Vivien Leigh**.

"God knows, I love Clark, but he's the worst lay in town."—**Carole Lombard**, on screen idol and husband Clark (The King) Gable.

"That's the last cock I'll have to suck."—**Marilyn Monroe**, reacting to signing her first big contract.

"Hollywood has gone from Pola to Polaroid."—**Pola Negri**.

"Say anything you like, but don't say I *like* to work. That sounds like Mary Pickford, that prissy bitch."—**Mabel Normand**, to an interviewer.

"Just imagine, I'm in bed with Jimmy Cagney!"—**Merle Oberon**, while actually having sex with Cagney during a World War II bond-selling tour. (Cagney confided to a male friend that Merle's verbalizing somewhat diminished his ardor.)

"Come on, Bob. You know you'd like to fuck me. Admit it." —**Barbara Stanwyck**, teasing costar Bob Cummings right before shooting a scene together on the set of *The Bride Wore Boots*.

"Get away, dear, I don't need you anymore."—**Norma Talmadge**, after her retirement from the screen in '30, replying to a fan's request for her autograph.

"Some of my best leading men have been horses and dogs." —**Elizabeth Taylor**.

"I stopped believing in Santa Claus at an early age. My mother took me to see him in a Hollywood department store and he asked for my autograph."—**Shirley Temple**.

"I'll have to ask my mother."—**Lana Turner**, replying when she was asked by the agent who "discovered" her if she'd like to be in the movies.

"I can't say the miniskirt made me an actress, but it sure helped make me a star."—**Raquel Welch.**

"All they ever did for me at MGM was change my leading men and the water in my pool."—**Esther Williams**, bemoaning her splashy studio career.

"Acting is like sex. You should do it and not talk about it." —**Joanne Woodward.**

A MAN'S OPINION

"You are so goddamned beautiful, you make me feel faint."—**John Barrymore** to **Mary Astor.**

"For me the sexiest woman on the screen ever was **Joan Blondell**."—**George C. Scott.**

"There is not enough money in Hollywood to lure me into making another picture with **Joan Crawford**. And I like money."—**Sterling Hayden.**

"Do you knit when you fuck?"—**Oscar Levant**, twitting **Joan Crawford** on the set of *Humoresque* about her habit of constant knitting.

"The greatest actress of all time."—**James Mason**, describing **Bette Davis.**

"Her face was so beautiful, all I could do was stand and stare." —**Ernie Pyle**, talking about **Olivia de Havilland.**

"She gets more mileage on less talent than anyone I know." —**Earl Wilson**, debunking the myth of **Marlene Dietrich.**

"She's too fat. The American public don't like fat women." —**Louis B. Mayer**, assessing **Greta Garbo.**

"When it came to kissing—**Harlow** was the greatest."—**Jimmy Stewart.**

"The worst lay in the world. She was always drunk and she never stopped eating."—**Peter Lawford**, on **Rita Hayworth.**

"Looked like she was a cold dish with a man until you got her pants down. Then she'd explode."—**Gary Cooper**, on **Grace Kelly.**

"If only she had shut up and stopped giving orders, the ordeal might have been consummated with pleasure."—**Stewart Granger**, on making love to **Hedy Lamarr**. (*Note:* See Lamarr's comment to Granger under "The Lady Speaks Her Mind.")

"She is like a delicate fawn, but crossed with a Buick."—**Jack Nicholson**, describing **Jessica Lange**.

"She should have been sculpted in chocolate truffles, so that the world could devour her."—**Noel Coward**, expressing his appreciation of **Sophia Loren**.

"Extracting a performance from her is like pulling teeth."—**Billy Wilder**, on directing **Marilyn Monroe**.

"If that child had been born in the Middle Ages, she'd have been burned as a witch."—**Lionel Barrymore**, on child star **Margaret O'Brien**.

"Don't let her fool you. Tangle with her and she'll shingle your attic."—**Bob Hope**, on messing with **Jane Russell**.

"Oh God, she looks like a chicken."—**Truman Capote**, describing **Meryl Streep**.

"Remember that there isn't anything more important than the sleep and rest of **Elizabeth Taylor**."—**Eddie Fisher**.

"She couldn't act her way out of her form-fitting cashmeres." —**Tennessee Williams**, on the original sweater girl, **Lana Turner**.

"She was just plain and simply a sweet old lady, who told me marvelous stories about her life."—**Rock Hudson**, offering a new slant on the legendary **Mae West**.

TALK, TALK, TALK

Both **Elke Sommer** and **Stefanie Powers** are fluent in seven languages.

FOUR LITTLE WORDS

Women have the dubious distinction of being the first ones to utter four profane words on the screen.

Emma Dunn (*Blessed Event*, '32)—"Damn."

Marianne Faithful (*I'll Never Forget What's 'Is Name*, '67)—"Fuck!"

Maxine Audley (*Here We Go Round the Mulberry Bush*, '68)—"Darling, you've got him pissed again."

Elizabeth Taylor (*Boom!*, '68)—"Shit!"

FEMALE GENITALIA

Female genitalia was first mentioned in *The Arrangement* ('69), where it was called "the big 'c'," and *Carnal Knowledge* ('71), when the word "cunt" was used.

The We Didn't Know It Back Then, But We Do Now Award

To *Citizen Kane* ('41), for its mysterious use of the word "*Rosebud.*" Orson Welles used the word in the film to taunt media mogul William Randolph Hearst, because it was Hearst's lovey-dovey nickname for the clitoris of Marion Davies, his film-star mistress.

LADIES

"There is no such thing as a great American lady. Great ladies
do not occur in a nation less than 200 years old."
—Lotte Lenya, *The Roman Spring of Mrs. Stone*

There's no doubt about what's in this collection. Most definitely, these are ladies—or are they?

Jean Arthur	*The Lady Takes a Chance* ('43)
Fay Bainter	*The Lady and the Mob* ('39)
Sarah Bey	*Lady Frankenstein* ('71)
Joan Blondell	*Lady for a Night* ('42)
Sonia Braga	*Lady on the Bus* ('81)
Joan Caufield	*The Lady Says No* ('51)
Tina Chen	*The Lady from Yesterday* ('85)
Ruth Chatterton	*Lady of Secrets* ('36)
Linda Darnell	*The Lady Pays Off* ('51)
Olivia de Havilland	*Lady in a Cage* ('64)
Marlene Dietrich	*The Lady Is Willing* ('42)

Irene Dunne	*Lady in a Jam* ('42)
Deanna Durbin	*Lady on a Train* ('45)
Paulette Goddard	*The Lady Has Plans* ('42)
Sally Gray	*Lady in Distress* ('39)
June Havoc	*Lady Possessed* ('52)
Rita Hayworth	*Lady from Shanghai* ('48), *The Lady in Question* ('40)
Katherine Helmond	*Lady in White* ('88)
Mary Beth Hughes	*The Lady Confesses* ('45)
Josephine Hull	*The Lady from Texas* ('51)
Ruth Hussey	*The Lady Wants Mink* ('53)
Hedy Lamarr	*Lady of the Tropics* ('39)
Abbe Lane	*Lady Doctor* ('56)
Susan Lucci	*Lady Mobster* ('88)
Pamela Sue Martin	*The Lady in Red* ('79)
Patricia Medina	*The Lady and the Bandit* ('51)
Ona Munson	*Lady from Louisiana* ('41)
Anna Neagle	*The Lady with a Lamp* ('51)
Vera Hruba Ralston	*The Lady and the Mobster* ('44)
Ginger Rogers	*Lady in the Dark* ('44)
Emma Samms	*The Lady and the Highwayman* ('89)
Barbara Stanwyck	*The Lady Gambles* ('49)
Lana Turner	*The Lady Takes a Flyer* ('58)
Anna May Wong	*Lady from Chungking* ('42)
Jane Wyman	*The Lady Takes a Sailor* ('49)
Loretta Young	*Lady from Cheyenne* ('41)

THERE IS NOTHING LIKE A DAME

"There oughta be a home for dames like me."
—Claire Trevor, *The High and the Mighty*

Dame—the honor bestowed by the British monarch. There *is* nothing like a dame—these dames in particular.

Dame Judith Anderson	*A Man Called Horse* ('70)
Dame Peggy Ashcroft	*A Passage to India* ('84)
Dame Gladys Cooper	*My Fair Lady* ('64)
Dame Cicely Courtneidge	*The Wrong Box* ('66)
Dame Judi Dench	*Luther* ('74)
Dame Edith Evans	*Fitzwilly* ('67)
Dame Gracie Fields	*Holy Matrimony* ('43)
Dame Wendy Hiller	*Separate Tables* ('58)
Dame Celia Johnson	*Brief Encounter* ('45)
Dame Anna Neagle	*Nurse Edith Cavell* ('39)
Dame Flora Robson	*The Beast in the Cellar* ('71)
Dame Margaret Rutherford	*The Mouse on the Moon* ('63)
Dame Maggie Smith	*California Suite* ('78)
Dame Sybil Thorndike	*The Prince and the Showgirl* ('57)
Dame Irene Vanbrugh	*Moonlight Sonata* ('38)
Dame Mae Whitty	*Night Must Fall* ('37)

LADIES OF LESBOS

"I have always found girls fragrant in any phase of the moon."
—Noel Coward, *Boom!*

Rumor has it that Queen Victoria declined to sign a bill outlawing homosexuality because lesbianism was included. Prim proper Vicky refused to believe ladies capable of such behavior. Well, the Queenie would have slipped her crown if she saw these lezzies perform!

June Allyson	*They Only Kill Their Masters* ('72)
Elizabeth Ashley	*Windows* ('80)
Candice Bergen	*The Group* ('66)

Claire Bloom	*The Haunting* ('63)
Cher	*Silkwood* ('83)
Patty Duke	*By Design* ('81)
Meg Foster	*A Different Story* ('78)
Lee Grant	*The Balcony* ('63)
Nastassja Kinski	*The Hotel New Hampshire* ('84)
Lotte Lenya	*From Russia with Love* ('63)
Kristy McNichol	*Two-Moon Junction* ('88)
Estelle Parsons	*Rachel, Rachel* ('68)
Beryl Reid	*The Killing of Sister George* ('68)
Meryl Streep	*Manhattan* ('79)
Liv Ullman	*Persona* ('66)

LESBIAN COUPLES

Jane Alexander, Gena Rowlands	*A Question of Love* ('78)
Linda Bassett, Linda Hunt	*Waiting for the Moon* ('87)
Coral Browne, Susannah York	*The Killing of Sister George* ('68)
Catherine Byrd, Leslie Caron	*Nicole* (aka *The Widow's Revenge*) ('80)
Capucine, Barbara Stanwyck	*A Walk on the Wild Side* ('62)
Patricia Charbonneau, Helen Shaver	*Desert Hearts* ('85)
Sammi Davis, Amanda Donohoe	*The Rainbow* ('89)
Catherine Deneuve, Susan Sarandon	*The Hunger* ('83)
Sandy Dennis, Anne Heywood	*The Fox* ('68)
Patrice Donelly, Mariel Hemingway	*Personal Best* ('82)
Sherilyn Fenn, Kelly Lynch	*Three of Hearts* ('93)

Linda Griffiths, Jane Halloren	*Lianna* ('83)
Mariette Hartley, Lynn Redgrave	*My Two Loves* ('86)
Virginia Madsen, Mathilda May	*Becoming Colette* ('92)
Melina Mercouri, Alexis Smith	*Jacqueline Susann's Once Is Not Enough* ('75)
Amanda Redman, Liv Ullman	*Richard's Things* ('80)
Elizabeth Taylor, Susannah York	*X, Y and Zee* ('72)

THE FIRST CINEMATIC LESBIANS

The first realistic on-screen treatment of a lesbian relationship occurred in *The Children's Hour* ('62), starring Audrey Hepburn and Shirley MacLaine. Based on Lillian Hellman's play, it had been filmed before (*These Three*, '36), but then the Hays Office forced the lesbian angle to be changed to a heterosexual triangle.

OR MAYBE EVEN BULGARIANS?

When Radclyffe Hall's *The Well of Loneliness* was first published, the novel's success as a best-seller lured many movie producers, who soon were dismayed to find it impossible to adapt because of its lesbian theme.

One producer, not knowing about the lesbian theme and focusing only on the high sales record, instructed his staff to acquire the film rights. "You can't make a film of it," they told him. "It's got lesbians in it."

"That's no problem," he replied, "Where they got lesbians, we use Austrians."

LARGE LOVELIES

"I like 'em fat and vicious and not too smart.
Nothing spiritual, either"
—Anthony Quinn, *Lust for Life*

Large lovelies; big mamas; tons of love. There's sure a lot to love on these Lulu La Largettes! Be careful though; get one of these big women too stirred up and you might find yourself truly crushed by the burden of love.

Pat Ast	*Heat* ('72)
Patty Duke Astin	*Before and After* ('79)
Josiane Balasko	*Too Beautiful for You* ('89)
Roseanne Barr	*She-Devil* ('89)
Kathy Bates	*At Play in the Fields of the Lord* ('91)
Divine (Glenn Milstead)	*Female Trouble* ('75)
Hope Emerson	*Cry of the City* ('48)
Ricki Lake	*Babycakes* ('89)
Genevieve Lemon	*Sweetie* ('89)
Marianne Sagebrecht	*Bagdad Cafe* ('88)
Shirley Stoler	*The Honeymoon Killers* ('70)

THE I LOVE FOOD AWARD

Awarded to **Ayllene Gibbons** in *The Loved One* ('65). The extra-extra-large Gibbons, playing Mama Joyboy—Rod Steiger's mother—squeals with orgiastic delight watching King Chicken commercials on TV and finally ends up flat on the kitchen floor with the refrigerator on top of her.

LEATHER

"Fashions in sin change. In my day it was Englishmen."
—Lucile Watson, *Watch on the Rhine*

Got a taste for the kinky? Like to see the female form in black leather?
Then here's your chance.

Honor Blackman	*Goldfinger* ('64)
Joanna Cassidy	*Blade Runner* ('82)
Stockard Channing	*Grease* ('78)
Cher	*Mask* ('85)
Barbara Crampton	*From Beyond* ('86)
Eileen Davidson	*Easy Wheels* ('89)
Marianne Faithfull	*Girl on a Motorcycle* ('68)
Deborra-Lee Furness	*Shame* ('88)
Cloris Leachman	*High Anxiety* ('77)
Edith Massey	*Female Trouble* ('75)
Diane McBain	*The Miniskirt Mob* ('68)
Mercedes McCambridge	*A Touch of Evil* ('58)
Anne Paillaud	*La Femme Nikita* ('90)
Barbara Stanwyck	*Forty Guns* ('57)
Lisa Todd	*Woman Hunt* ('72)
Rachel Ward	*Night School* ('81)
Wendy O. Williams	*Reform School Girls* ('86)

BEST-DRESSED LEATHER VILLAINESS AWARD

Awarded to **Amanda Donohoe** for her hip-length black leather boots
worn under a sheer black, see-through negligee in *The Lair of the
White Worm* ('88).

TATTOOS

"See for yourself. His rose tattooed on my chest."
—Virginia Grey, *The Rose Tattoo*

Does a female tattoo do that voodoo and excite you? If so, catch a look at the tattoos on these bodies.

Maud Adams	*Tattoo* ('81)
Marie-Christine Barrault	*Cousin, Cousine* ('75)
Kim Basinger	*No Mercy* ('86)
Divine	*Lust in the Dust* ('85)
Jodie Foster	*The Accused* ('88)
Melanie Griffith	*Fear City* ('84)
Lainie Kazan	*Lust in the Dust* ('85)
Sally Kirkland	*Revenge* ('90)
Millie Perkins	*The Witch Who Came from the Sea* ('76)
Linnea Quigley	*Hollywood Chainsaw Hookers* ('88)
Meg Ryan	*Promised Land* ('88)
Leigh Taylor-Young	*I Love You, Alice B. Toklas* ('68)
Susan Tyrell	*Forbidden Zone* ('80)
Monica Vitti	*Modesty Blaise* ('66)

LEGS AND THIGHS

"I proved once and for all the limb is mightier than the thumb."
—Claudette Colbert, *It Happened One Night*

Get a gander at the gams on these babes . . . legs, legs, legs.

Betty Grable	*Mother Wore Tights* ('47)
Ann Miller	*Kiss Me Kate* ('53)
Juliet Prowse	*Can-Can* ('60)

. . . plus a memorable pair of thighs.

Sylvana Mangano	*Bitter Rice* ('48)

FACE SHOTS

Face shots: usually a good, hearty slap across smooth, sweet female cheeks—but, they've also included everything else from hot coffee and cream pies to grapefruit.

The I've Spilled the Beans Face Shot
Suffered by **Faye Dunaway** in *Chinatown* ('74), who chants, "She's my daughter, she's my sister," in rhythm to Jack Nicholson's slapping the truth out of her.

The One Sugar, No Cream Please Face Shot
Suffered by **Gloria Grahame** in *The Big Heat* ('53), who took a face full of hot coffee from bad guy Lee Marvin.

The Slap Me Around Some More to Show You Love Me Face Shot
Suffered by **Miranda Richardson** in *Dance with a Stranger* ('85), who allows her upper-class lover to slap her, beat her, and thrash her—yet always keeps crawling back for more, more, more.

The Squirt in Your Eye Face Shot
Suffered by **Mae Clarke** in *The Public Enemy* ('31), who had a half grapefruit smashed in her face by James Cagney.

The Take That You Slut Face Shot
Suffered by **Rita Hayworth**, who got slapped around by Glenn Ford in *Gilda*, and loved it so much she let him do it again in *Affair in Trinidad* ('52).

The Thank You, Mr. President Face Shot

Suffered by **Angie Dickinson** in *The Killers* ('64), who got her face popped by future Prez Ronnie Reagan.

The Ungrateful Daughter Face Shot

Suffered by **Ann Blyth** in *Mildred Pierce* ('45), who sassed Joan Crawford (as ex-waitress turned restaurateur Mildred) and got Joan's experienced chastising hand across her face in return.

THE SLIP OF THE TONGUE AWARD

Awarded to **Demi Moore**, who confided that she sometimes slips her male costars the tongue during their kissing scenes. She said she slipped it to **Rob Lowe** (in *About Last Night . . .* , '86) and **Patrick Swayze** (in *Ghost*, '90), but not to **Chevy Chase** (in *Nothing But Trouble*, '91).

Honorable Mention: **Lupe Velez**, who has her tongue twisted with wire by Walter Huston, an impotent slave trader, in *Kongo* ('32).

LINGERIE

"Golly, to think you can put words down on paper like that and all
I can do is hem brassieres."
—Shirley MacLaine, *Some Came Running*

What could be more feminine than sexy lingerie? Absolutely nothing enhances the female form better than clinging, semitransparent undergarments. These ladies really know how to strut their stuff in lingerie, don't they?

Note: B = Bra, P = Panties, L = Lingerie (assorted types), and (b) = black

Karen Allen	*Secret Weapon* ('90)	L (b)
Nancy Allen	*Dressed to Kill* ('80)	B, P (b)

Kirstie Alley	*Madhouse* ('90)	B, L
Maria Conchita Alonso	*Vampire's Kiss* ('89)	B
Ursula Andress	*Loaded Guns* ('75)	B, P
Laura Antonelli	*Wifemistress* ('77)	L
Rosanna Arquette	*Black Rainbow* ('91)	B, P (b)
Adrienne Barbeau	*Open House* ('87)	L
Kim Basinger	*9½ Weeks* ('86)	L
Jennifer Beals	*Vampire's Kiss* ('89)	L (b)
Annette Bening	*The Grifters* ('90)	B, P
Sandahl Bergman	*Loving Lulu* ('92)	B, P
Jacqueline Bisset	*Forbidden* ('85)	B, L
Karen Black	*Five Easy Pieces* ('70)	L (b)
Linda Blair	*Red Heat* ('87)	L
Lisa Blount	*An Officer and a Gentleman* ('82)	B
Sonia Braga	*I Love You* ('81)	P
Danielle Brisbois	*Big Bad Mama II* ('87)	L
Randi Brooks	*The Man with Two Brains* ('83)	L (b)
Tia Carrere	*Intimate Strangers* ('91)	L (b)
Kim Cattrall	*Masquerade* ('88)	L
Jill Clayburgh	*An Unmarried Woman* ('78)	B, P
Joan Collins	*The Stud* ('78)	B, P (b)
Jane Curtin	*How to Beat the High Cost of Living* ('80)	B
Jamie Lee Curtis	*A Fish Called Wanda* ('88)	B (b)
Beverly D'Angelo	*First Love* ('77)	B, P
Lolita Davidovitch	*Blaze* ('89)	B, P (b)
Geena Davis	*Tootsie* ('82)	B, P
Rebecca De Mornay	*And God Created Woman* ('87)	P
Amanda Donohoe	*The Lair of the White Worm* ('88)	B, P (b)
Lesley-Anne Down	*Hanover Street* ('79)	L
Patty Duke	*Valley of the Dolls* ('67)	B, P
Britt Ekland	*Erotic Images* ('83)	B (b)

Morgan Fairchild	*The Seduction* ('82)	B, L
Lola Falana	*Liberation of L. B. Jones* ('70)	B, P, L
Sherilyn Fenn	*Crime Zone* ('88)	P, L (b)
Sally Field	*Norma Rae* ('79)	B
Bridget Fonda	*Scandal* ('89)	L
Jodie Foster	*Siesta* ('87)	L (b)
Meg Foster	*A Different Story* ('78)	B, P
Teri Garr	*Full Moon in Blue Water* ('88)	B
Pam Grier	*Coffy* ('73)	B, P (b)
Melanie Griffith	*Working Girl* ('88)	B, P, L (b)
Daryl Hannah	*Reckless* ('84)	B
Deborah Harry	*Videodrome* ('83)	B (b)
Joey Heatherton	*Bluebeard* ('72)	L (b)
Diane Keaton	*Looking for Mr. Goodbar* ('77)	B
Margot Kidder	*Some Kind of Hero* ('82)	B, L
Nastassja Kinski	*Maria's Lovers* ('84)	B (b)
Sally Kirkland	*Cold Feet* ('89)	B, P (b)
Apollonia Kotero	*Purple Rain* ('84)	L
Diane Lane	*Lady Beware* ('87)	B, L (b)
Janet Leigh	*Psycho* ('60)	B, L (b)
Jennifer Jason Leigh	*Sister, Sister* ('87)	L
Sophia Loren	*Yesterday, Today and Tomorrow* ('64)	L (b)
Kelly Lynch	*Drugstore Cowboy* ('89)	B, P (b)
Madonna	*Desperately Seeking Susan* ('85)	B (b)
Melina Mercouri	*Never on Sunday* ('60)	B, P (b)
Hayley Mills	*Deadly Strangers* ('74)	B, P (b)
Helen Mirren	*Cal* ('84)	B, L
Demi Moore	*About Last Night . . .* ('86)	B
Ornella Muti	*Love and Money* ('82)	B, P
Lena Olin	*The Unbearable Lightness of Being* ('88)	B, P (b)

Annie Potts	*Who's Harry Crumb?* ('89)	B (b)
Lynn Redgrave	*The Happy Hooker* ('75)	B, P (b)
Tanya Roberts	*Forced Entry* ('84)	B, P
Isabella Rossellini	*Blue Velvet* ('86)	B, P (b)
Theresa Russell	*Eureka* ('81)	L
Helen Shaver	*In Praise of Older Women* ('78)	B, P
Sally Struthers	*Five Easy Pieces* ('70)	B
Lea Thompson	*The Wild Life* ('84)	B, P
Meg Tilley	*The Girl in a Swing* ('89)	B
Kathleen Turner	*The Man with Two Brains* ('83)	L
Vanity	*Never Too Young to Die* ('86)	B, L
Rachel Ward	*Night School* ('81)	B, P
Susannah York	*The Killing of Sister George* ('68)	B, P (b)
Sean Young	*No Way Out* ('87)	L (b)

EVERYBODY
OUGHT TO HAVE A MAID

"I got so many maids some of the maids are taking care of maids."
—Thelma Ritter, *Titanic*

Black and white, young and old. Sassy, funny, domineering. Everybody ought to have a maid like these scurrying around the kitchen. Along with the food and clean linen, she dispenses savvy wisdom and put-downs by the score. Hired help, indeed. These are the real queens of the castle.

Jean Arthur	*If You Could Only Cook* ('35)
Louise Beavers	*Mr. Blandings Builds His Dream House* ('48)

Diahann Carroll	*Claudine* ('74)
Nell Carter	*Modern Problems* ('81)
Claudette Colbert	*Tovarich* ('37)
Joan Fontaine	*Maid's Night Out* ('38)
Paulette Goddard	*Diary of a Chambermaid* ('46)
Whoopi Goldberg	*Clara's Heart* ('88)
Jean Hill	*Desperate Living* ('77)
Gertrude Howard	*I'm No Angel* ('33)
Glenda Jackson	*The Maids* ('75)
Abbey Lincoln	*For Love of Ivy* ('68)
Hattie McDaniel	*Family Honeymoon* ('48)
Butterfly McQueen	*Mildred Pierce* ('45)
Liza Minnelli	*A Matter of Time* ('76)
Eulabelle Moore	*The Horror of Party Beach* ('64)
Agnes Moorehead	*Hush . . . Hush, Sweet Charlotte* ('65)
Jeanne Moreau	*Diary of a Chambermaid* ('64)
LaWanda Page	*Mausoleum* ('81)
Thelma Ritter	*The Mating Season* ('51)
Esther Rolle	*Driving Miss Daisy* ('89)
Irene Ryan	*Diary of a Chambermaid* ('46)
Ally Sheedy	*Maid to Order* ('87)
Penny Singleton	*Hard to Get* ('38)
Ethel Waters	*The Member of the Wedding* ('52)
Charlaine Woodard	*Twister* ('88)
Susannah York	*The Maids* ('75)

THE THAT'S WHY I HAVE SERVANTS AWARD

Awarded to **Mae West**, for *I'm No Angel* ('33), in which she orders her maid, "Beulah, peel me a grape."

THE BEST SASSY REMARK BY A MAID AWARD

Awarded to **P. J. Johnson**, in *Paper Moon* ('73). Johnson, as Imojean, a maid who delights in drolly sassing her employer, Miss Trixie Delight, played by Madeline Kahn. Her best remark occurs while Miss Trixie is rambling on about her life to her latest beau, Ryan O'Neal. From the backseat of the car in which they're riding, Johnson interrupts to squelch Miss Trixie's pretensions when she says loudly, "Tell 'm 'bout that time the man hit you in the head with a beer bottle in Tuscaloosa, Miss Trixie."

MAMMARY MADNESS

"I say, you Americans are positively obsessed with mammaries!"
—Terry-Thomas, *It's a Mad, Mad, Mad, Mad World*

Hollywood certainly seeks to satisfy the American obsession with mammaries—especially large ones. As proof of this obsession, these incidents are offered into evidence.

Deadly Weapons ('64)—Features the gargantuan-sized, aptly named "Chesty" Morgan as an assassin who suffocates her victims between her you-know-whats.

Everything You Always Wanted to Know About Sex ('72)— An enormous breast roams the countryside creating destruction and mayhem, even killing by squirting people with milk from its large nipple. It is finally trapped by being lured into a gigantic brassiere.

Mother, Jugs & Speed ('76)—A comedy starring Raquel Welch, Harvey Keitel, and Bill Cosby. Guess who's "Jugs," and why the nickname is appropriate.

The Outlaw ('43)—Howard Hughes used his aeronautical design experience to create a special "uplift and spread 'em" bra to show off Jane Russell's two largest assets. The Hays Office objected so strongly to this emphasis on Russell's breasts that it caused Hughes to delay releasing the film for several years. Meanwhile, his publicists continued to tout it—and them—using slogans such as "How'd you like to tussle with Russell?" and "What are the two big reasons for Jane Russell's rise to fame?" Celebrated wit George S. Kaufman paraphrased Dickens to mock Hughes's hoopla, calling the effort "The Sale of Two Titties."

Reflections in a Golden Eye ('67)—Several conversations in the film dwell on Julie Harris's mental problems; among other cute stunts, she cut off her nipples with garden shears.

S.O.B. ('81)—Blake Edwards's wicked satire on Hollywood, in which he describes the obsession filmdom had with getting Edwards's real-life wife—Julie Andrews—to bare her breasts in a film. As part of the film's denouement, Andrews finally did reveal her rather delectable pair.

THE VOLUPTUOUS BREADHOLDER

In *Battleground* ('49), bosomy **Denise Darcel** places one end of a long loaf of French bread between her breasts, then cuts the loaf with a knife blade downward toward her chest.

THANKS FOR THE MAMMARIES

"Look at these breasts! Aren't they beautiful?"
—Elizabeth Taylor, *Ash Wednesday*

Big knockers. Bodacious ta-tas. Ba-zooms. Call 'em what you will, these women are stacked. We're eternally grateful for having had the opportunity to appreciate them—covered and uncovered. Thanks for the mammaries!

Lindsay Bloom	*Six-Pack Annie* ('75)
Bobbie Bresee	*Mausoleum* ('81)
Sybil Danning	*The Howling II: Your Sister Is a Werewolf* ('85)
Elvira	*Elvira, Mistress of the Dark* ('88)
Sophia Loren	*Boccaccio '70* ('64)
Jayne Mansfield	*Will Success Spoil Rock Hunter?* ('57)
Kim Novak	*The Amorous Adventures of Moll Flanders* ('65)
Dolly Parton	*The Best Little Whorehouse in Texas* ('82)
Dolly Read	*Beyond the Valley of the Dolls* ('70)
Joyce Redman	*Tom Jones* ('63)
Mamie Van Doren	*Three Bolts in Search of a Nut* ('64)
Edy Williams	*Mankillers* ('87)

Big-Boobed Slut Fight

Like to watch big-boobed bimbos get into a good old-fashioned, knock-down, drag-out "slut" fight? Then watch *The Lost Empire* ('83).

Big 'Uns

"You remind me of my Daddy, y' know. Mama told me he liked
skinny women with breasts that stood up and said 'Hello'."
—Laura Dern, *Wild at Heart*

If you find large statistics impressive, look at these big 'uns, measured during their prime growth. Compare them with the two big reasons for Jane Russell's success—her pair of 38s.

Gina Lollobrigida	36-22-35
Joan Collins	38-23½-37
Sophia Loren	38-24-38
Anita Ekberg	39-23-27
Jayne Mansfield	40-18½-36
Dolly Parton	42-19-34
June Wilkinson	44-20-36
Kitten Natividad	44-25-35

And, of course, don't forget Miss Extra-Extra Large herself, **"Chesty" Morgan** of *Deadly Weapons* ('64) and her 73-inch bust.

Prime-Time Breasts

"Be on the lookout for a large female breast.
It's about a 4,000x cup."
—Woody Allen, *Everything You Always
Wanted to Know About Sex*

Sooner or later, they all start to sag . . . but once they were in their prime. Here's some prime-time breasts:

Ann-Margret	36½"
Brigitte Bardot	35"
Jacqueline Bisset	37"
Bo Derek	35"

Ava Gardner	36″
Betty Grable	36″
Rita Hayworth	36½″
Bette Midler	36½″
Marilyn Monroe	37″
Jill St. John	35″
Barbra Streisand	36″
Elizabeth Taylor	36″
Raquel Welch	36″
Shelley Winters	37″

Titty Talk

"There's nothing wrong with my tits, but I don't go around throwing them in people's faces."—**Joan Crawford**, commenting on the Monroe-Mansfield mammary assault on the media. Take a look at Crawford's tits in her last film, *Trog*—by then they had sagged so badly only midgets had to worry about her tits in their faces.

"Christ! You never know what size boobs that broad has strapped on! She must have a different set for each day of the week! She's supposed to be shriveling away, but her tits keep growing. I keep running into them, like the Hollywood Hills!"—**Bette Davis**, raging about Joan Crawford's use of monumental-sized, granite-hard falsies during the filming of *What Ever Happened to Baby Jane?*

"If I woke up to find two big boobs in bed beside me, I would *die*!"—**Bette Davis**

"We live in a tit culture."—**Bette Davis**

"Miss United Dairies, herself."—**David Niven**, on **Jayne Mansfield**

"The only gal who came near to me in the sex-appeal department was pretty little Marilyn Monroe. All the others had were big boobs."—**Mae West**

Her Cups Runneth Over
"Sheriff! I want to report an escaped tit!"
—Woody Allen, *Everything You Always
Wanted to Know About Sex*

Now these are ridiculous—why, her cups runneth over. If her bra explodes, we'll all be boobied to death!

Anita Ekberg	*La Dolce Vita* ('60)
Jayne Mansfield	*The Girl Can't Help It* ('56)
Jane Russell	*The French Line* ('54)
June Wilkinson	*Macumba Love* ('60)
Edy Williams	*Dr. Minx* ('75)

Officer, Arrest That Bra for Murder!

Two '60s films featured murderous, bullet-firing brassieres. In *The Tenth Victim* ('65), a futuristic thriller where "players" in a game track and kill victims for points, player **Ursula Andress** scores one of her wins by using her brassiere that fired a gunshot from each cup. Ursula's killer boobs bring a whole new dimension to the phrase, "She was twirling a pair of 38s."

The Ambushers ('68), a Dean Martin/James Bondish-type of film, also showcased a female with a killer bra.

Nipples of Death

In *Running Out of Luck* ('86), **Rae Dawn Chong** puts poison on her nipples, then lets a prison guard suck them. She deadly nipples the guard to death to help her lover, Mick Jagger, escape from prison.

Here She Is Folks, Miss Multiboobs!

Total Recall ('90) has a barmaid with three; *The Warrior and the Sorceress* ('84) features a dancing girl with four. But the winner of Miss Multiboobs, however, is **Lee Ann Baker** in *Necropolis* ('87); she's a 300-year-old witch with six.

. . . And Miss Nipples, Too

During a dream sequence in *Gothic* ('86), **Miriam Cyr** has eyeballs instead of nipples on her breasts.

But Sears Has Them at Retail!

At a September 1991 charity auction in Michigan, one of **Madonna**'s pink brassieres was purchased for $11,000 by a pair of restaurant owners.

THE BARE BOSOM BRIGADE

"You can't sho' yo' bosoms 'fore three o'clock!"
—Hattie McDaniel, *Gone with the Wind*

These are some of the better-known troopers in the bare bosom brigade; female warriors in the cinematic nudity wars. Each has made her contribution by exposing herself on-screen in portraying a character. The exposures that follow range from quick glimpses to lengthy full exposures. Some gave only side views, while others permitted a peep at just one boob; but some are real "double-barreled" darlings—they took aim, pointed 'em at the camera, and boldly showed the world their treasured chests!

Maud Adams	*Tattoo* ('81)
Jenny Agutter	*Equus* ('77)
Karen Allen	*Until September* ('84)
Nancy Allen	*Carrie* ('76)
Maria Conchita Alonso	*Colors* ('88)
Ursula Andress	*The Sensuous Nurse* ('76)
Julie Andrews	*S.O.B.* ('81)
Ann-Margret	*Carnal Knowledge* ('71)
Laura Antonelli	*Till Marriage Do Us Part* ('74)
Rosanna Arquette	*The Executioner's Song* ('82), *Black Rainbow* ('91)
Margaret Avery	*Hell Up in Harlem* ('73)
Carroll Baker	*My Father's Wife* ('76)
Adrienne Barbeau	*Open House* ('87)
Brigitte Bardot	*. . . And God Created Woman* ('56)
Ellen Barkin	*Siesta* ('87)
Kim Basinger	*9½ Weeks* ('86)
Kathleen Beller	*The Betsy* ('78)
Annette Bening	*The Grifters* ('90)
Barbi Benton	*Deathstalker* ('84)
Marisa Berenson	*S.O.B.* ('81)

Candice Bergen	*A Night Full of Rain* ('78)
Sandahl Bergman	*She* ('85)
Jacqueline Bisset	*Secrets* ('71)
Karen Black	*Miss Right* ('88)
Linda Blair	*Chained Heat* ('83)
Susan Blakely	*Capone* ('75)
Lisa Bonet	*Angel Heart* ('87)
Sonia Braga	*Dona Flor and Her Two Husbands* ('78)
Danielle Brisbois	*Big Bad Mama II* ('87)
Genevieve Bujold	*Monsignor* ('82)
Ellen Burstyn	*The Ambassador* ('84)
Irene Cara	*Fame* ('80)
Barbara Carrera	*I, the Jury* ('82)
Elpedia Carrillo	*Beyond the Limit* ('83)
Helena Bonham Carter	*Lady Jane* ('85)
Veronica Cartwright	*Inserts* ('76)
Joanna Cassidy	*Blade Runner* ('82)
Phoebe Cates	*Fast Times at Ridgemont High* ('82)
Kim Cattrall	*Masquerade* ('88)
Rae Dawn Chong	*Quest for Fire* ('81)
Julie Christie	*Don't Look Now* ('73)
Jill Clayburgh	*An Unmarried Woman* ('78)
Glenn Close	*The Big Chill* ('83)
Joan Collins	*The Bitch* ('79)
Jamie Lee Curtis	*Trading Places* ('83)
Maryam D'Abo	*Xtro* ('82)
Beverly D'Angelo	*National Lampoon's Vacation* ('83)
Sybil Danning	*The Loves of a French Pussycat* ('76)
Rebecca De Mornay	*And God Created Woman* ('87)
Bo Derek	*Bolero* ('84)

Susan Dey	*First Love* ('77)
Angie Dickinson	*Big Bad Mama* ('74)
Patty Duke	*By Design* ('81)
Faye Dunaway	*Chinatown* ('74)
Lisa Eichhorn	*Opposing Force* ('86)
Morgan Fairchild	*The Seduction* ('82)
Mia Farrow	*Rosemary's Baby* ('68)
Farrah Fawcett	*Saturn 3* ('80)
Sherilyn Fenn	*Two-Moon Junction* ('88)
Cristina Ferrare	*Mary, Mary, Bloody Mary* ('75)
Jane Fonda	*Klute* ('71)
Jodie Foster	*Backtrack* ('89)
Susan George	*Straw Dogs* ('71)
Pam Grier	*Coffy* ('73)
Melanie Griffith	*Something Wild* ('86)
Joan Hackett	*One-Trick Pony* ('80)
Daryl Hannah	*Reckless* ('84)
Jessica Harper	*Inserts* ('76)
Deborah Harry	*Videodrome* ('83)
Goldie Hawn	*Wildcats* ('86)
Joey Heatherton	*Bluebeard* ('72)
Mariel Hemingway	*Star 80* ('83)
Marilu Henner	*The Man Who Loved Women* ('77)
Barbara Hershey	*The Entity* ('83)
Isabelle Huppert	*Heaven's Gate* ('80)
Glenda Jackson	*Women in Love* ('69)
Diane Keaton	*Looking for Mr. Goodbar* ('77)
Sally Kellerman	*Serial* ('80)
Margot Kidder	*The Reincarnation of Peter Proud* ('75)
Nastassja Kinski	*Cat People* ('82)

Sally Kirkland	*In the Heat of Passion* ('92)
Tawny Kitaen	*The Crystal Heart* ('87)
Appollonia Kotero	*Purple Rain* ('84)
Sylvia Kristel	*Emmanuelle* ('74)
Hedy Lamarr	*Extase* ('33)
Diane Lane	*Big Town* ('87)
Jennifer Jason Leigh	*Flesh + Blood* ('85)
Kay Lenz	*Fast-Walking* ('82)
Sondra Locke	*The Outlaw—Josey Wales* ('76)
Sophia Loren	*Era Lui, Si, Si* ('57)
Ali MacGraw	*Goodbye, Columbus* ('69)
Shirley MacLaine	*Desperate Characters* ('71)
Amy Madigan	*Alamo Bay* ('85)
Madonna	*A Certain Sacrifice* ('85)
Virginia Madsen	*Creator* ('85)
Jayne Mansfield	*Promises! Promises!* ('63)
Pamela Sue Martin	*The Lady in Red* ('79)
Mathilda May	*Lifeforce* ('85)
Kelly McGillis	*Witness* ('85)
Elizabeth McGovern	*Ragtime* ('81)
Kristy McNichol	*Two-Moon Junction* ('88)
Sarah Miles	*The Sailor Who Fell from Grace with the Sea* ('76)
Juliet Mills	*Avanti!* ('72)
Helen Mirren	*Caligula* ('80)
Demi Moore	*About Last Night . . .* ('86)
Jeanne Moreau	*Chére Louise* ('72)
Ornella Muti	*Swann in Love* ('84)
Tatum O'Neal	*Circle of Two* ('80)
Carré Otis	*Wild Orchid* ('90)
Anne Parillaud	*Patricia* ('91)

Mary-Louise Parker	*Grand Canyon* ('91)
Valerie Perrine	*Slaughterhouse-Five* ('72)
Joanna Pettet	*Double Exposure* ('82)
Victoria Principal	*The Naked Ape* ('73)
Charlotte Rampling	*The Night Porter* ('74)
Vanessa Redgrave	*Isadora* ('68)
Joely Richardson	*Drowning by Numbers* ('87)
Natasha Richardson	*The Comfort of Strangers* ('91)
Tanya Roberts	*The Beastmaster* ('82)
Isabella Rossellini	*Blue Velvet* ('86)
Theresa Russell	*Whore* ('91)
Susan Sarandon	*The Hunger* ('83)
Greta Scacchi	*A Man in Love* ('87)
Maria Schneider	*Last Tango in Paris* ('73)
Cybill Shepherd	*The Last Picture Show* ('71)
Brooke Shields	*Pretty Baby* ('78)
Ione Skye	*The Rachel Papers* ('89)
Elke Sommer	*Sweet Ecstasy* ('62)
Renee Soutendijk	*The Fourth Man* ('79)
Sissy Spacek	*Welcome to L.A.* ('77)
Mary Steenburgen	*Melvin and Howard* ('80)
Sharon Stone	*Basic Instinct* ('92)
Brenda Sykes	*Mandingo* ('75)
Uma Thurman	*Dangerous Liaisons* ('88)
Kathleen Turner	*Body Heat* ('81)
Vanity	*52 Pickup* ('86)
Julie Warner	*Doc Hollywood* ('91)
Sigourney Weaver	*Half Moon Street* ('86)
JoBeth Williams	*Endangered Species* ('82)
Debra Winger	*An Officer and a Gentleman* ('82)
Mare Winningham	*One-Trick Pony* ('80)

| Sean Young | *The Boost* ('88) |
| Pia Zadora | *The Lonely Lady* ('83) |

The First Bare Ones

The first bare boobs in a modern, mainstream film occurred in *The Pawnbroker* ('64), when a black prostitute bared her upper torso to Rod Steiger. Once those knockers flopped out, the bras of Hollywood soon were unfastened and a deluge of boobies bounced across the movie screens of America.

Famous T & A

The best collection available of celebrity tits, asses, and frontals can be found on the 1982 video release **Celebrity T & A**, a compilation of celebrity nude scenes and clips.

BBB: THE SWEATER

BBB: Before Bare Boobs—the era of the sweater, and the sweater girls. Take a look at these upper torsos in sweaters.

Barbara Stanwyck	*Double Indemnity* ('44)
Lana Turner	*They Won't Forget* ('37)
Mamie Van Doren	*High School Confidential* ('58)

MANHUNTERS

"You're going to have a wedding whether you like it or not!"
—Bette Davis, *The Catered Affair*

The man-crazy, husband hunters—they've definitely got the wedding-bells blues. Their priority is finding a man first; then they'll worry about getting to the church on time.

Ann-Margret	*Carnal Knowledge* ('71)
Lauren Bacall	*How to Marry a Millionaire* ('53)
Betty Grable	*How to Marry a Millionaire* ('53)
Marilyn Monroe	*How to Marry a Millionaire* ('53)
Jean Peters	*Three Coins in the Fountain* ('54)
Beatrice Romand	*Le Beau Mariage* ('82)
Rosalind Russell	*Picnic* ('55)

ALTAR GIRLS

> "Not all the men in my sex life were artistic geniuses. Some—
> I must admit—were perfect strangers."
> —Lea Thompson, *Casual Sex?*

There are three female contenders for the title of *Most Married Female Star*: **Lana Turner** (eight times, twice to the same man), **Zsa Zsa Gabor** (eight times, no repeats), and **Elizabeth Taylor** (eight times, twice to the same man, plus three broken engagements). Their full married names are:

Lana Turner Shaw Crane Crane Topping Barker May Eaton Dante

Zsa Zsa Gabor Belge Hilton Sanders Hutner Cosden Ryan O'Hara von Anhalt

Elizabeth Taylor Hilton Wilding Todd Fisher Burton Burton Warner Fortensky.

To see why each made such a lovely "altar girl," catch their beauty at its prime in the following films: **Turner** in *Diane* ('56), **Gabor** in *Moulin Rouge* ('52), and **Taylor** in *Father of the Bride* ('50).

Short Runs, or Did She Wear a Wedding Dress or a Tracksuit?
The record for a short-run marriage is held by silent star **Dagmar Godowsky**. One of her marriages broke up immediately following the marriage oath; her new husband asked her a question that offended her so she ditched him a few hours later.

Jean Acker, another silent film actress, married Rudolph Valentino and locked him out of the bedroom later that same evening. Neither the Godowsky nor Acker marriages were ever consummated.

Some other short runs were:

Michelle Phillips's marriage to actor/director Dennis Hopper lasted eight days.

Ethel Merman's marriage to actor Ernest Borgnine lasted thirty days. When Merman wrote her autobiography, she included a chapter called "My Marriage to Ernest Borgnine," which consisted of *one blank page.*

Barbara Payton's marriage to actor Franchot Tone lasted thirty days.

CHILD BRIDES

Child brides, indeed! Their first marriages were at a *very young* and tender age.

Eva Bartok	15
Doris Day	17
Zsa Zsa Gabor	16
Jean Harlow	16
June Havoc	12
Jayne Mansfield	16
Mary Martin	16
Sheree North	15
Shirley Temple	17
Diane Varsi	15
Ethel Waters	12
Loretta Young	17

THE SHE'D DO *ANYTHING* TO GET A MAN AWARD

Awarded to **Sarah Bey** (aka Rosalba Neri) of *Lady Frankenstein* ('71). Playing the good Doctor's daughter, Bey creates a "handsome" monster for her personal sex pleasure—and promptly screws him on the operating table in her laboratory.

MEAT EATERS

"And, God as my witness, I'll never be hungry again."
—Vivien Leigh, *Gone with the Wind*

Cannibals. Female human flesh eaters. If offered an invitation to dinner by one of these voracious females, be cautious about accepting; you just might be the entrée.

Jill Banner	*Spider Baby* ('64)
Karen Black	*Auntie Lee's Meat Pies* ('92)
Devin DeVasquez	*Society* ('89)
Donna Dixon	*Lucky Stiff* ('88)
Deborah Harry	*Tales from the Darkside: The Movie* ('90)
Mary Beth Hurt	*Parents* ('89)
Mary Jackson	*Terror at Red Wolf Inn* ('72)
Sheila Keith	*Frightmare* (aka *Cover Up*) ('74)
Andrea Martin	*Cannibal Girls* ('73)
Mary Stuart Masterson	*Fried Green Tomatoes* ('91)
Mary Louise Parker	*Fried Green Tomatoes* ('91)
Nancy Parsons	*Motel Hell* ('80)
Joanna Pettet	*Welcome to Arrow Beach* ('74)
Fiona Richmond	*Eat the Rich* ('87)
Mary Woronov	*Eating Raoul* ('82)

If the above lovelies can't satisfy your appetite, then try these films:

Blood Feast ('63)

Flesh Eating Mothers ('88)

Raw Meat ('72)

2000 Maniacs ('64)

THE MUNCH-AHOLIC AWARD

Awarded to **Priscilla Alden** of *Criminally Insane* ('74) and *Crazy Fat Ethel II* ('87), who's such a compulsive eater that she slaughters anyone who gets between her and her food.

BEST TITLED CANNIBAL FILM

The winner—*Cannibal Women in the Avocado Jungle of Death* ('88).

MEAT EATERS OF ANOTHER KIND

These are strictly meat eaters of another kind—the fellators. Consumed with passion for her guy, she just had to put him into her mouth.

Nancy Allen	*Carrie* ('76, John Travolta)
Julie Christie	*Shampoo* ('75, Warren Beatty)
Lesley-Anne Down	*The Betsy* ('78, Tommy Lee Jones)
Liza Minnelli	*Charlie Bubbles* ('68, Albert Finney)
Rita Moreno	*Carnal Knowledge* ('71, Jack Nicholson)
Isabella Rossellini	*Blue Velvet* ('86, Kyle MacLachlan)
Winona Ryder	*Bram Stoker's Dracula* ('92, Gary Oldman)
Meryl Streep	*She-Devil* ('89, Ed Begley Jr.)
Daphne Zuniga	*Prey of the Chameleon* ('92, James Wilder)

Yes, but How Is She on the Real Thing?

In *Truth or Dare* ('91), the incomparable **Madonna** demonstrates her oral sex technique on a mineral water bottle.

Marilyn's Taste for Aged Meat

Joseph Schenck, seventyish and one of the founders of 20th Century Fox, was an early mentor of Marilyn Monroe. She frequently dined at his house, where after dinner he'd have her strip and perform fella-

tio—often for hours. Marilyn's views on eating at Schenck's: "All the other girls thought I had it made. Ha! But I kept going back. At least the food was good."

MERMAIDS AND ANGELS

"Well, you look about like the kind of angel I'd get. Sort of a fallen angel, aren't you? What happened to your wings?"
—James Stewart, *It's a Wonderful Life*

Mermaids . . . legends of the sea. Alluring, mysterious, half fish and half human. At the other extreme are angels: shimmering, flighty, feathered. First, decide if you're aquatically oriented or heaven-struck; then cast your hook or net for these comely creatures.

The Mermaids

Ann Blyth	*Mr. Peabody and the Mermaid* ('48)
Jeri Lynne Fraser	*Mike and the Mermaid* ('67)
Daryl Hannah	*Splash* ('84)
Glynis Johns	*Miranda* ('48)
Marta Kristen	*Beach Blanket Bingo* ('65)
Cyndi Lauper	*Off and Running* ('89)
Linda Lawson	*Night Tide* ('63)
Connie Sellecca	*The Bermuda Depths* ('78)
Diane Webber	*The Mermaids of Tiburon* ('63)
Amy Yasbeck	*Splash, Too* ('88)

The Angels

Lauren Bacall	*The Gift of Love* ('58)
Emmanuelle Beart	*Date with an Angel* ('87)

Diane Cilento	*The Angel Who Pawned Her Harp* ('54)
Audrey Hepburn	*Always* ('89)
Sally Kellerman	*Brewster McCloud* ('70)
Nastassja Kinski	*Faraway, So Close* ('93)
Jessica Lange	*All That Jazz* ('79)
Jeanette MacDonald	*I Married an Angel* ('42)
Keshia Knight Pulliam	*The Little Match Girl* ('87)
Debra Winger	*Made in Heaven* ('87)

THE MONROE DOCTRINE

"Maybe I don't have much to offer, but I've got something, and it's
something men want, and I'm willing to give it to them,
as long as they give me what I want."
—Misty Rowe, *Goodnight, Sweet Marilyn*

No, not the Monroe Doctrine on foreign intervention—it's the other
Monroe Doctrine. The one that deals with flagrant sexuality, as
espoused—visually as well as verbally—by Miss Marilyn. Here she is
. . . breathless voice, wiggling fanny, beauty mark and all. Marilyn
imitations in all varieties: funny, sexy, vulnerable, trashy.

Melody Anderson	*Marilyn and Bobby: Her Final Affair* ('93)
Constance Forslund	*This Year's Blonde* ('80)
Susan Griffiths	*Marilyn and Me* ('91)
Catherine Hicks	*Marilyn: The Untold Story* ('80)
Linda Kerridge	*Fade to Black* ('80)
Paula Lane	*Goodnight, Sweet Marilyn* ('84)
Misty Rowe	*Goodbye, Norma Jean* ('76), *Goodnight, Sweet Marilyn* ('84)

Theresa Russell	*Insignificance* ('85)
Kim Stanley	*The Goddess* ('58)
Heather Thomas	*Hoover vs. the Kennedys: The Second Civil War* ('87)

BUMP IT, MARILYN, BUMP IT!

Marilyn worked as a stripper for two weeks in September 1948 at the Mayan Theater in downtown Los Angeles. She first billed herself as Marilyn Monroe, but became worried that that could harm the movie career she hoped for. Next, she tried Marilyn Marlowe for a few days, before settling on Mona Monroe for the rest of her short "bumping and peeling" career.

MARILYN ODDS 'N' ENDS

Marilyn claimed that by age twenty-nine she had undergone thirteen abortions.

12305 Fifth Helena Drive—In the Brentwood section of Los Angeles where Marilyn's body (suicide or murder victim . . .) was discovered.

625 Pacific Palisades Beach Road (Pacific Coast Highway)—Peter Lawford's home, where she reportedly had sex with both President John F. Kennedy and Attorney General Robert Kennedy.

MOTHERS

"Well, there won't ever be no patter of little feet in my house—
unless I was to rent some mice."
—Peggy Lee, *Pete Kelly's Blues*

These are most definitely not the kind, nurturing mothers we all love. These are the mothers who breed problem kids; the mothers who make their children's lives miserable; mothers who literally drive their

offspring insane. Possessive mothers, mean mothers; these mothers are graduates of the Joan Crawford School of Child Care.

Ann-Margret	*Tommy* ('75)
Anne Bancroft	*Torch Song Trilogy* ('88)
Jeanne Bates	*Mom* ('90)
Bette Davis	*The Anniversary* ('68)
Yvonne de Carlo	*American Gothic* ('88)
Sandy Dennis	*976-EVIL* ('88)
Divine	*Polyester* ('81)
Louise Fletcher	*Flowers in the Attic* ('87)
Meg Foster	*Diplomatic Immunity* ('91)
Ava Gardner	*Regina* ('85)
Ruth Gordon	*Where's Poppa?* ('70)
Debbie Harry	*Hairspray* ('88)
Eileen Heckart	*No Way to Treat a Lady* ('68)
Katharine Hepburn	*Suddenly, Last Summer* ('59)
Sara Hunley	*Trapper County War* ('89)
Holly Hunter	*The Positively True Adventures of the Alleged Texas Cheerleader-Murdering Mom* ('93)
Anjelica Huston	*The Grifters* ('90)
Olivia Hussey	*Psycho IV: The Beginning* ('90)
Madeline Kahn	*Happy Birthday, Gemini* ('80)
Leopoldine Konstantin	*Notorious* ('46)
Diane Ladd	*Wild at Heart* ('90)
Angela Lansbury	*The Manchurian Candidate* ('62)
Shirley MacLaine	*Terms of Endearment* ('83)
Anna Magnani	*Bellissima* ('51)
Elizabeth Montgomery	*Sins of the Mother* ('91)
Mary Tyler Moore	*Ordinary People* ('80)
Geraldine Page	*You're a Big Boy Now* ('66)

Stefanie Powers	*At Mother's Request* ('87)
Mae Questal	*New York Stories* ('89)
Anne Ramsey	*Throw Momma from the Train* ('87)
Ruth Roman	*The Baby* ('73)
Rose Ross	*Mother's Day* ('80)
Zelda Rubenstein	*Anguish* ('87)
Rosalind Russell	*Oh Dad, Poor Dad, Mama's Hung You in the Closet and I'm Feeling So Sad* ('67)
Kathleen Turner	*Serial Mom* ('94)
Lana Turner	*Persecution* (aka *The Terror of Sheba*) ('74)
Billie Whitelaw	*The Krays* ('90)
Shelley Winters	*A Patch of Blue* ('65)
Joanne Woodward	*The Effect of Gamma Rays on Man-in-the-Moon Marigolds* ('72)

UNWED MAMAS

"Poor kid! Maybe this is the price you pay for sleeping together."
—Rock Hudson, *A Farewell to Arms*

The cinema looks at unmarried motherhood—and keeps abreast of changing mores. Because it does not have the social stigma it formerly did, its screen treatments also have changed.

Kirstie Alley	*Look Who's Talking* ('89)
Barbara Barrie	*Tell Me My Name* ('77)
Carol Burnett	*The Tenth Month* ('79)
Leslie Caron	*The L-Shaped Room* ('63)
Peggy Cass	*Auntie Mame* ('58)
Jane Connell	*Mame* ('74)
Bette Davis	*The Old Maid* ('39)
Geena Davis	*Angie* ('94)
Sandra Dee	*A Summer Place* ('59)

Olivia de Havilland	*To Each His Own* ('46)
Catherine Deneuve	*The Umbrellas of Cherbourg* ('64)
Sandy Dennis	*Thank You All Very Much* ('69)
Patty Duke	*My Sweet Charlie* ('70)
Joan Fontaine	*Letter from an Unknown Woman* ('48)
Judy Garland	*I Could Go on Singing* ('63)
Heather Langenkamp	*Nickel Mountain* ('84)
Carol Lynley	*Blue Denim* ('59)
Amy Madigan	*Love Child* ('82)
Molly Ringwald	*For Keeps* ('88)
Susan Sarandon	*The Buddy System* ('84)
Connie Stevens	*Susan Slade* ('61), *Parrish* ('61)
Meg Tilley	*Agnes of God* ('85)
Rita Tushingham	*A Taste of Honey* ('61)
Shelley Winters	*A Place in the Sun* ('51)
Natalie Wood	*Love with the Proper Stranger* ('63)

NANNIES AND BABY-SITTERS

"Alligators have the right idea. They eat their young."
—Eve Arden, *Mildred Pierce*

Here's a collection of nannies and baby-sitters to please the most demanding charges. Some are the kindly sweet variety—others are downright murderous.

Julie Andrews	*Mary Poppins* ('64)
Stephanie Beacham	*The Nightcomers* ('72)
Julie Christie	*Miss Mary* ('86)
Bette Davis	*The Nanny* ('65)
Rebecca De Mornay	*The Hand That Rocks the Cradle* ('92)
Susan George	*Fright* ('71)
Carol Kane	*When a Stranger Calls* ('79)

Eda Reiss Merin	*Don't Tell Mom the Babysitter's Dead* ('91)
Marilyn Monroe	*Don't Bother to Knock* ('52)
Lynn Redgrave	*Every Little Crook and Nanny* ('72)
Isabella Rossellini	*Zelly and Me* ('88)
Jennie Seagrove	*The Guardian* ('90)
Elizabeth Shue	*Adventures in Babysitting* ('87)
Billie Whitelaw	*The Omen* ('76)
Stephanie Zimbalist	*The Babysitter* ('80)

MY FATHER, MY LOVE

"I don't want a father like you. You traded me for a mule."
—Gong Li, *Red Sorghum*

Incest—the ultimate sexual taboo. Daughters and fathers, sisters and brothers, mothers and sons. Does the family that plays together stay together?

Ewa Aulin	*Candy* ('68)
Justine Bateman	*Right to Kill?* ('85)
Ariel Besse	*Beau Pere* ('81)
Julie Delpy	*Beatrice* ('88), *Voyager* ('91)
Faye Dunaway	*Chinatown* ('74)
Betty Field	*Kings Row* ('42)
Vanessa King	*Liar, Liar* ('75)
Carol Lynley	*The Last Sunset* ('61)
Linda Manz	*Out of the Blue* ('80)
Lena Olin	*After the Rehearsal* ('84)
Barbara Parkins	*The Mephisto Waltz* ('81)

Mary Regan	*Heart of the Stag* ('84)
Suzanne Snyder	*Pretty Kill* ('87)
Barbra Streisand	*Nuts* ('87)
Gene Tierney	*Leave Her to Heaven* ('45)
Roxanne Zal	*Something About Amelia* ('84)

BROTHERLY LOVE

"I'm young. I'm rich. I'm beautiful. Why shouldn't I sleep with
my brother?"
—Candy Darling, *Andy Warhol's Women in Revolt*

Tracy Arnold	*Henry: Portrait of a Serial Killer* ('90)
Meredith Baxter Birney	*Bittersweet Love* ('76)
Ann Dvorak	*Scarface: The Shame of a Nation* ('32)
Jodie Foster	*The Hotel New Hampshire* ('84)
Charlotte Gainsbourg	*The Cement Garden* ('94)
Judy Geeson	*Goodbye, Gemini* ('71)
Nastassja Kinski	*Cat People* ('82)
Mary Elizabeth Mastrantonio	*Scarface* ('83)
Helen Mirren	*Excalibur* ('81)
Lili Monori	*Forbidden Relations* ('83)
Geraldine Page	*The Beguiled* ('71)
Victoria Tennant	*Flowers in the Attic* ('87)
Susannah York	*Brotherly Love* ('69)

SON LOVERS

"A son is a poor substitute for a lover."
—Anthony Perkins, *Psycho*

Jill Clayburgh	*Luna* ('79)
Jamie Lee Curtis	*Mother's Boys* ('94)
Alice Krige	*Sleepwalkers* ('92)
Sophia Loren	*Angela* ('77)

Lea Massari	*Murmur of the Heart* ('71)
Marilia Pera	*Mixed Blood* ('85)
Theresa Russell	*Track 29* ('88)
Romy Schneider	*My Lover, My Son* ('79)
Ingrid Thulin	*The Damned* ('69)
Trish Van Devere	*The Savage Is Loose* ('74)
Alberta Watson	*Spanking the Monkey* ('93)
Shelley Winters	*Bloody Mama* ('70)
Mai Zetterling	*Night Games* ('66)

THE FAMILY TOGETHERNESS AWARD

Presented to **Giovanna Ralli** of *Deadfall* ('68), who's married to her homosexual father, Eric Portman.

THE NUDE MERMAID

"No, from now on, I am just going to swim socially."
—Janis Paige, *Silk Stockings*

Annette Kellerman, an Australian swimmer often called the "Esther Williams of silent films," was the first female lead actress to appear nude in a major U.S. film, the Fox production of *Daughter of the Gods* ('16).

Long before Annette Kellerman, female nudes had been seen in films, although mostly in minor roles or single shots, usually as prostitutes, dancing girls, or orgy participants. After Kellerman's appearance, female nudes seemed to proliferate as actresses took bath after bath on-screen. A notable example of using the bath as an excuse for female nudity is *Hula* ('27), where "the It Girl" herself, **Clara Bow,** takes a nude dip.

During this same period, foreign films also featured female

nudity. One of the most notable was *Extase*, a 1933 Czech film with the young **Hedy Lamarr**. Often cited as the first film to feature female nudity, it was instead the first to feature sexual intercourse.

With the introduction of the Hays Code in 1934, female nudity, along with lots of other things, disappeared from American films. The few nude female bodies to grace American film screens were found in small art houses, which played obscure foreign films or "naturist" (i.e., nudist) films. Often, even these were censored, or subject to outright seizure on the grounds of undermining public morals. Thirty years pass before the female nude reappeared in mainstream American films.

The pioneering nude mermaid was saluted in 1952 by a bio pic, *Million Dollar Mermaid*, starring **Esther Williams**. Annette Kellerman's celebrated nude romp was not repeated in the '52 film.

PSST . . . WANNA SEE BETTE DAVIS . . . NUDE?

. . . Then go to the Boston Museum of Fine Arts and observe the nude statue titled Young Diana. Bette Davis posed for the sculpture in 1924, when she was sixteen years old. Her secret had long been hidden, until revealed by the irrepressible Bette during a 1982 *Playboy* interview.

NUNSENSE

"I don't go to church. Kneeling bags my nylons."
—Jan Sterling, *The Big Carnival*

Get thee to a nunnery, Hollywood style. A large collection of nunsense, complete and utter nunsense.

Anne Bancroft	*Agnes of God* ('85)
Ingrid Bergman	*The Bells of St. Mary's* ('45)
Leslie Caron	*Madron* ('70)

Claudette Colbert	*Thunder on the Hill* ('51)
Joan Collins	*Sea Wife* ('57)
Whoopi Goldberg	*Sister Act* ('92)
Helen Hayes	*The White Sister* ('33)
Audrey Hepburn	*The Nun's Story* ('59)
Jennifer Jones	*The Song of Bernadette* ('43)
Deborah Kerr	*Heaven Knows, Mr. Allison* ('57)
Cloris Leachman	*Dixie: Changing Habits* ('82)
Sophia Loren	*White Sister* ('73)
Shirley MacLaine	*Two Mules for Sister Sara* ('70)
Mary Tyler Moore	*Change of Habit* ('69)
Amanda Pays	*Off Limits* ('88)
Rosalind Russell	*The Trouble with Angels* ('66)
Lilia Skala	*Lilies of the Field* ('63)
Maggie Smith	*Sister Act* ('92)
Anna Sten	*The Nun and the Sergeant* ('62)
Loretta Young	*Come to the Stable* ('49)

WOULD YOU BUY A USED CAR FROM THESE NUNS?

"Let us be crooked, but never common."
—Charles Coburn, *The Lady Eve*

Nasty Habits ('77), a wickedly humorous allegory of the 1972 Nixon-McGovern campaign and ensuing Watergate scandal, is set in a religious order headed by Nixonish **Glenda Jackson**. Jackson's assisted in her underhanded plotting to steal an election as prioress by her fellow nuns **Sandy Dennis**, as a John Dean type, and the Ehrlich-man-Haldemanish duo of **Geraldine Page** and **Anne Meara**. Throughout the shenanigans, a globe-trotting **Melina Mercouri** drops in periodically—à la Kissinger—to offer cerebral advice to Jackson.

In addition to this Watergate spoof, some other unusual behavior by nuns also can be found in *Dark Habits* ('84) and *The Devils* ('71).

ANY FRIEND OF ZORRO'S IS A FRIEND OF MINE

"I always choose my friends for their good looks . . ."
—George Sanders, *The Picture of Dorian Gray*

Remember the old joke about nuns: *Any friend of Zorro's is a friend of mine.* Be careful—these ladies really were Zorro's friends. Mess with one of them and the Big Z will be after you.

Mary Anderson	*Zorro* ('61)
Pamela Blake	*Ghost of Zorro* ('59)
Helen Christian	*Zorro Rides Again* ('37)
Linda Darnell	*The Mark of Zorro* ('40)
Lauren Hutton	*Zorro, the Gay Blade* ('81)
Ottavia Piccolo	*Zorro* ('75)

NYMPHOMANIACS

"We've got a big mob here, and I'm a little tired today.
One of these guys'll have to go."
—Mae West, *Myra Breckenridge*

Here's the girls who love too much. Way, way too much. Too many times, too many men. Well—they can't help themselves. Hot-pants Hannahs—the nymphomaniacs.

Polly Bergen	*The Caretakers* ('63)
Susan Blakely	*Secrets* ('77)
Claire Bloom	*The Chapman Report* ('62)
Sandrine Bonnaire	*A Nos Amours* ('84)
Sonia Braga	*Lady on the Bus* ('78)
Louise Brooks	*Diary of a Lost Girl* ('29)
Beatrice Dalle	*Betty Blue* ('86)

Catherine Deneuve	*Je Vous Aime* ('81)
Arielle Dombasle	*The Boss' Wife* ('86)
Faye Dunaway	*Doc* ('71)
Susan Hayward	*Demetrius and the Gladiators* ('54)
Eartha Kitt	*Anna Lucasta* ('58)
Gina Lollobrigida	*Imperial Venus* ('62)
Myrna Loy	*Love Me Tonight* ('32)
Sue Lyon	*The Night of the Iguana* ('64)
Dorothy Malone	*Written on the Wind* ('56)
Jayne Mansfield	*Female Jungle* ('56)
Melina Mercouri	*Topkapi* ('64)
Jeanne Moreau	*The Sailor from Gibraltar* ('67)
Merle Oberon	*Of Love and Desire* ('63)
Suzanne Pleshette	*A Rage to Live* ('65)
Gilda Radner	*First Family* ('80)
Lee Remick	*The Detective* ('68)
Jean Seberg	*Birds in Peru* ('68)
Maureen Stapleton	*Lonelyhearts* ('58)
Ingrid Thulin	*Games of Desire* ('64)
Lesley Ann Warren	*Choose Me* ('84)

SHORT ARMS INSPECTION

In *History of the World: Part I* ('81), the Empress Nympho (**Madeline Kahn**) inspects a large troop of naked soldiers, who have been lined up so she can select her bed partners for the evening. As she passes in front of each man, Kahn comments hilariously on his sexual assets, either by word or exaggerated facial gesture.

KILLER QUEEN BEES

"I never dreamed it would be the bees.
They've always been our friends."
—Henry Fonda, *The Swarm*

Invasion of the Bee Girls ('73) features a group of comely young women who have turned themselves into sterile but sexually driven "bees." The beautiful killers in dark glasses literally fuck their male victims to death. Naturally, the men's bodies are discovered with smiles on their faces.

OLDER WOMEN AFTER YOUNGER STUFF

"There are new lines in my face. I look like a brand-new,
steel-belted radial tire."
—Maggie Smith, *California Suite*

What older woman doesn't occasionally entertain thoughts of having a younger lover? Well, these older women made their dreams come true.

Lola Albright	*A Cold Wind in August* ('61)
Ann-Margret	*A Tiger's Tale* ('87)
Anne Bancroft	*The Graduate* ('67)
Jane Birkin	*Kung Fu Master!* ('87)
Jacqueline Bisset	*Class* ('83), *Rich and Famous* ('81)
Joan Collins	*Homework* ('82)
Beverly D'Angelo	*In the Mood* ('87)
Sybil Danning	*They're Playing with Fire* ('84)
Sandy Dennis	*That Cold Day in the Park* ('69)
Angie Dickinson	*Pretty Maids All in a Row* ('71)
Faye Dunaway	*Arizona Dream* (aka *The Arrowtooth Waltz*) ('94)
Susan Flannery	*Anatomy of a Seduction* ('79)

Annie Girardot	*To Die of Love* ('72)
Ruth Gordon	*Harold and Maude* ('72)
Barbara Hershey	*Tune in Tomorrow . . .* ('90)
Kate Jackson	*Loverboy* ('89)
Jennifer Jones	*The Idol* ('66)
Sylvia Kristel	*Private Lessons* ('81)
Carole Laure	*Get Out Your Handkerchiefs* ('78)
Piper Laurie	*Tim* ('79)
Cloris Leachman	*The Last Picture Show* ('71)
Vivien Leigh	*The Roman Spring of Mrs. Stone* ('61)
Ann Magnuson	*A Night in the Life of Jimmy Reardon* ('88)
Sylvia Miles	*Heat* ('72)
Yvette Mimieux	*Forbidden Love* ('82), *Obsessive Love* ('84)
Brigitte Mira	*Ali—Fear Eats the Soul* ('74)
Helen Mirren	*Cal* ('84)
Patricia Neal	*The Night Digger* ('71)
Merle Oberon	*Interval* ('73)
Jennifer O'Neill	*Summer of '42* ('71)
Michelline Presle	*Devil in the Flesh* ('46)
Lynn Redgrave	*Getting It Right* ('89)
Vanessa Redgrave	*Consuming Passions* ('88)
Susan Sarandon	*White Palace* ('90)
Jane Seymour	*Matters of the Heart* ('90)
Cybill Shepherd	*Chances Are* ('89)
Simone Signoret	*Room at the Top* ('59)
Jean Simmons	*Say Hello to Yesterday* ('71)
Maggie Smith	*Love and Pain and the Whole Damn Thing* ('73)
Barbra Streisand	*All Night Long* ('81)
Elizabeth Taylor	*There Must Be a Pony* ('86)

Lily Tomlin	*Moment by Moment* ('78)
Liv Ullman	*40 Carats* ('73)
Lesley Ann Warren	*A Night in Heaven* ('83)
Tuesday Weld	*Something in Common* ('86)
Mae West	*Sextette* ('78)
Jane Wyman	*All That Heaven Allows* ('55)

GLORIOUS GLORIA

In 1951, while married to director Nicholas Ray, **Gloria Grahame** made love with Tony Ray, her thirteen-year-old stepson. By 1960, Gloria and Tony—then twenty-two to her thirty-seven—were married. Tony, formerly Gloria's stepson, became her fourth husband—*and* also stepfather to his half brother, the son of Gloria and his father, Nicholas Ray.

ORGASMS

"Just once I'd like to have the type of sexual experience where you
don't go into the bathroom and cry afterwards."
—Victoria Jackson, *Casual Sex?*

Moaning, groaning, crying, panting . . . these ladies really enjoy their orgasms. Take a look at their passion. Don't you wish you were their partners?

Laura Dern	*Rambling Rose* ('91)
Faye Dunaway	*Network* ('76)
Shelley Duvall	*Brewster McCloud* ('70)
Jane Fonda	*Coming Home* ('78)
Hedy Lamarr	*Extase* ('33)

Shirley MacLaine	*Being There* ('79)
Jeanne Moreau	*Les Amants* ('58)
Meg Ryan	*When Harry Met Sally . . .* ('89)
Kathleen Turner	*The War of the Roses* ('89)

A WOMAN'S BEST FRIEND, TOO

Meryl Streep relishes the extraordinary sensual feeling she experiences early one morning in bed in *She-Devil* ('89)—that is, until she raises up to discover her pleasure is being induced by her lover's dog, who's busily licking her toes.

PAGAN SACRIFICES

"If there's two things in the world I can't abide, it's heat
and heathens."
—Maggie Smith, *Death on the Nile*

Like to see a helpless female in trouble? Enjoy a group of heathens preparing to sacrifice some comely wench to their pagan god? Don't worry, the hero usually arrives in time to save her. But, occasionally, we do get to see her clothes ripped off before he does.

Ursula Andress	*Slave of the Cannibal God* ('78)
Judi Bowker	*Clash of the Titans* ('81)
Kate Capshaw	*Indiana Jones and the Temple of Doom* ('84)
Bo Derek	*Tarzan, the Ape Man* ('81)
Jessica Lange	*King Kong* ('76)
Catherine Oxenburg	*The Lair of the White Worm* ('88)
Meg Ryan	*Joe Versus the Volcano* ('90)
Jenny Seagrove	*Nate and Hayes* ('83)

Kathy Shower	*The Further Adventures of Tennessee Buck* ('88)
Sharon Stone	*King Solomon's Mines* ('85)
Fay Wray	*King Kong* ('33)

TIED UP AND WHIPPED

> "I have this—this attraction to violence."
> —Anthony Quinn, *Lust for Life*

Another indignity used to titillate the moviegoer is to have the heroine grabbed, tied up, her clothing pulled down, and—then—whipped! Catch how this bunch stood up to their whippings.

Brigitte Bardot	*Spirits of the Dead* ('68)
Kim Basinger	*9½ Weeks* ('86)
Stephanie Beacham	*The Nightcomers* ('72)
Carita	*The Viking Queen* ('67)
Corinne Clery	*The Story of O* ('75)
Catherine Deneuve	*Belle de Jour* ('67)
Pamela Franklin	*The Night of the Following Day* ('69)
Paulette Goddard	*Unconquered* ('47)
Bonita Granville	*Hitler's Children* ('43)
Deborah Harry	*Videodrome* ('83)
Ginger Rogers	*Storm Warning* ('51)

THE DOMINATRIXES

> "I'm tired of whipping you, year after year."
> —Elizabeth Taylor, *Who's Afraid of Virginia Woolf?*

Mistress, I've been a bad, bad person. Beat me, whip me, hit me, spank me, hurt me. Make me write bad checks and do awful degrading things. Make me crawl across the floor and grovel at your feet. I

need a strong masterful woman to make me behave. Are you the one?

Victoria Abril	*Kika* ('94)
Laura Antonelli	*Venus in Furs* ('82)
Sandra Bernhard	*Track 29* ('88)
Sally Kellerman	*Moving Violations* ('85)
Gudrun Landgrebe	*A Woman in Flames* ('82)
Cloris Leachman	*High Anxiety* ('77)
Bulle Ogier	*La Maîtresse* ('75)
Kathleen Turner	*Crimes of Passion* ('84)
Raquel Welch	*The Magic Christian* ('69)
Mary Woronov	*Eating Raoul* ('82)

The Dominatrix Supreme
Dyanne Thorne, who's starred as the blond, hateful, horny dominatrix Ilsa in *Ilsa, She-Wolf of the S.S.* ('74); *Ilsa, Harem Keeper of the Oil Sheiks* ('78); *Ilsa, Tigress of Siberia* ('80), et al.

Best Female Whip Fight
The Wicked Lady ('83), between participants **Faye Dunaway** and **Marina Sirtis**. Dunaway wields her whip better and thoroughly thrashes Sirtis, tearing her bodice off.

The It Gives Me a Tingle Award
Awarded to **Myrna Loy**, in *The Mask of Fu Manchu* ('32). As Fu Manchu's evil daughter, Loy gets all sexually aroused—crying "Faster! Faster!"—when she has hunky Charles Starrett strung up and whipped.

The Revenge of the Democrats Award
Awarded to **Roberta Vasquez** in *Street Asylum* ('90). Clad in black leather, Vasquez bends the real **G. Gordon Liddy** (of Watergate fame) over a desk, and then proceeds to chastise him severely on the buttocks before finally forcing him to bark like a dog.

The Use Me, Abuse Me Award

Awarded to **Charlotte Rampling** in *The Night Porter* ('74). Ex-concentration camp inmate Rampling encounters her former torturer, with whom she soon rekindles their old kinky sadomasochistic relationship.

PEEKABOO

"With a binding like you've got, people are going to want to know what's in the book."
—Gene Kelly, *An American in Paris*

Like to play peekaboo? Prefer to get a quick look at your favorite female in a see-through blouse? Are you aroused by the sight of erect nipples pressed against wet T-shirts? If so, then catch a titillating glimpse of these girls' goodies.

Marie-Christine Barrault	*Cousin, Cousine* ('75)
Jacqueline Bisset	*The Deep* ('77)
Joan Chen	*Tai-Pan* ('86)
Olivia D'Abo	*Bullies* ('86)
Bo Derek	*Tarzan, the Ape Man* ('81)
Lisa Eichhorn	*Opposing Force* ('86)
Sophia Loren	*Boy on a Dolphin* ('57)
Ali MacGraw	*The Getaway* ('72)
Dominique Sanda	*The Garden of the Finzi-Continis* ('71)
Suzanne Somers	*Nothing Personal* ('80)

CAMEOS

"I *am* big! It's the *pictures* that got small!"
—Gloria Swanson, *Sunset Blvd.*

Cameos: the term coined to induce big stars or former stars into accepting small—but allegedly significant—parts. The true cameo isn't a small speaking part; it's a mere passing glance, one or two lines, a face glimpsed by a moving camera.

Mae Clark	*Thoroughly Modern Millie* ('67)
Marlene Dietrich	*Paris—When It Sizzles* ('64)
Billie Dove	*Diamond Head* ('62)
Ava Gardner	*The Band Wagon* ('53)
Daryl Hannah	*Crimes and Misdemeanors* ('89)
Helen Hayes	*Third Man on the Mountain* ('59)
Glenda Jackson	*The Boy Friend* ('71)
Ruby Keeler	*The Phynx* ('70)
Christine Lahti	*Miss Firecracker* ('89)
Anna Q. Nilsson	*Sunset Blvd.* ('50)
Clara Peller	*The Stuff* ('85)
Lynn Redgrave	*Tom Jones* ('63)
Vanessa Redgrave	*A Man for All Seasons* ('88)
Elizabeth Taylor	*Winter Kills* ('79)

. . . and Robert Altman's *The Player* ('92), which features a dowager's jewelry box full of innovative silent spot appearances.

PRIMITIVE PASSIONS

"If I smelled as bad as you, I wouldn't live near people."
—Kim Darby, *True Grit*

Like for your female to be of the prehistoric variety? Got a suppressed yen for bodies clad in skimpy animal fur? Want a taste of primitive passion? Want to barricade yourself in a cave with one of these primitive women?

Barbara Bach	*Caveman* ('85)
Senta Berger	*When Women Had Tails* ('70)
Martine Beswick	*Prehistoric Women* ('67)
Rae Dawn Chong	*Quest for Fire* ('81)
Julie Ege	*Creatures the World Forgot* ('71)
Dana Gillespie	*The People That Time Forgot* ('77)
Daryl Hannah	*Clan of the Cave Bear* ('86)
Carole Landis	*One Million B.C.* ('40)
Darrah Marshall	*Teenage Caveman* ('58)
Cindy Ann Thompson	*Cavegirl* ('85)
Victoria Vetri	*When Dinosaurs Ruled the Earth* ('70)
Raquel Welch	*One Million Years B.C.* ('66)

THE PRIMITIVE GLAMOUR AWARD

Awarded to **Raquel Welch** and the **entire female cast** of *One Million Years B.C.* ('66), because they were all wearing noticeably long, false eyelashes.

DAMES AND DINOS

"I arouse something in 'em. I bother 'em. It's a kind of animal thing ·
I've got. It's really quite extraordinary."
—Tom Ewell, *The Seven Year Itch*

Tyrannosaurus rex and the female *Homo sapiens* . . . dames and their dinosaurs. These women seem to have an affinity for the extinct, extra-big boys (and their cohorts) of the animal kingdom.

Acquanetta	*The Lost Continent* ('51)
Hilary Brooke	*The Lost Continent* ('68)
Arlene Dahl	*Journey to the Center of the Earth* ('59)
Laura Dern	*Jurassic Park* ('93)
Gila Golan	*The Valley of Gwangi* ('69)
Kristina Hanson	*Dinosaurus* ('60)

Carolina Munro	*At the Earth's Core* ('76)
Gigi Perreau	*Journey to the Center of Time* ('67)
Paula Raymond	*The Beast from 20,000 Fathoms* ('53)
Ann Smyrner	*Reptilicus* ('62)
Jill St. John	*The Lost World* ('60)
Joan Van Ark	*The Last Dinosaur* ('77)
Sean Young	*Baby . . . Secret of the Lost Legend* ('85)

PROTEGEES

"Get him to take you out to dinner, and work around to the play.
Good heavens, I don't have to tell you how to do these things.
How did you get all those other parts?"
—Monty Woolley, *The Man Who Came to Dinner*

Protégées . . . that most French of insinuating terms. One whose *welfare* is enhanced by the attentions of a more prominent individual. Well, some of these protégées could have made it eventually on their talent alone. For others, even their benefactors' attentions couldn't overcome their ill fortune.

Beverly Aadland	Errol Flynn (lover)
Nancy Allen	Brian de Palma (director, husband)
Ursula Andress	John Derek (director, husband)
Brigitte Bardot	Roger Vadim (director, lover)
Dorothy Comingore	Orson Welles (director)
Sofia Coppola	Francis Ford Coppola (director, father)
Bella Darvi	Darryl F. Zanuck (producer, lover)
Marion Davies	William Randolph Hearst (newspaper magnate, lover)

Bo Derek	John Derek (director, husband)
Marlene Dietrich	Josef von Sternberg (director)
Mia Farrow	Woody Allen (director, lover)
Greta Garbo	Mauritz Stiller (director)
Genevieve Gilles	Darryl F. Zanuck (producer, lover)
Lillian Gish	D. W. Griffith (director)
Juliette Greco	Darryl F. Zanuck (producer, lover)
Rita Hayworth	Harry Cohn (studio head)
Tippi Hedren	Alfred Hitchcock (director)
Anjelica Huston	John Huston (director, father)
Jennifer Jones	David O. Selznick (producer)
Anna Karina	Jean-Luc Godard (director, husband)
Nastassja Kinski	Roman Polanski (director, lover)
Sondra Locke	Clint Eastwood (director, costar, lover)
Sophia Loren	Carlo Ponti (producer, husband)
Silvana Mangano	Dino de Laurentis (producer, husband)
Giuletta Masina	Federico Fellini (director, husband)
Nobuko Miyamoto	Juzo Itami (director, husband)
Mabel Normand	Mack Sennett (director, lover)
Kim Novak	Harry Cohn (studio head)
Jane Russell	Howard Hughes (studio head, producer)
Hanna Schygulla	Rainer Werner Fassbinder (director)
Cybill Shepherd	Peter Bogdanovich (director, lover)
Anna Sten	Samuel Goldwyn (producer)
Dorothy Stratten	Peter Bogdanovich (director, lover)
Annette Stroyberg	Roger Vadim (director, lover)
Liv Ullman	Ingmar Bergman (director, lover)

RAH! RAH! RAH!

"I never dreamed any mere physical experience could be so stimulating . . . I've only known such excitement a few times before—a few times in my dear brother's sermons when the spirit was really upon him."
—Katharine Hepburn, *The African Queen*

Gimme a Y! Gimme an E! Gimme an A! Gimme an H! YEAH! It's the cheerleaders! Pom-pom girls! Short skirts! Tight sweaters! Jumping! Screaming! Tumbling! Yelling! These films are full of cheerleaders . . .

The Cheerleaders ('72)

Cheerleader's Beach Party ('82)

The Pom-Pom Girls ('76)

Pretty Maids All in a Row ('71)

Revenge of the Cheerleaders ('76)

Satan's Cheerleaders ('77)

Several film stars served stints as real-life cheerleaders:

Ann-Margret	New Trier High School, Winnetka, Illinois
Patty Hearst Shaw	Sacred Heart School, Menlo Park, California
Dinah Shore	Hume-Fogg High School, Nashville, Tennessee
Lily Tomlin	Cass Technical High School, Detroit, Michigan
Raquel Welch	La Jolla High School, La Jolla, California
Vanna White	North Myrtle Beach High School, North Myrtle Beach, South Carolina

RAPE VICTIMS

"The last time I read a book, I was raped.
So let that be a lesson to you."
—Madeline Kahn, *Yellowbeard*

The rape victim: attacked where she's most vulnerable—her sexuality.
Brutal, shocking, terrible.

Carroll Baker	*Something Wild* ('61)
Claire Bloom	*The Outrage* ('64)
Adrienne Corri	*A Clockwork Orange* ('71)
Divine	*Lust in the Dust* ('85)
Patty Duke	*The Violation of Sarah McDavid* ('81)
Lisa Eichhorn	*Opposing Force* ('86)
Linda Evans	*The Klansman* ('74)
Mia Farrow	*Rosemary's Baby* ('68)
Jodie Foster	*The Accused* ('88)
Susan George	*Straw Dogs* ('71)
Margaux Hemingway	*Lipstick* ('76)
Mariel Hemingway	*Lipstick* ('76)
Miriam Hopkins	*The Story of Temple Drake* ('33)
Madeline Kahn	*Young Frankenstein* ('74)
Christine Kaufman	*Town Without Pity* ('61)
Cheryl Ladd	*A Death in California* ('85)
Hope Lange	*Peyton Place* ('57)
Sophia Loren	*Two Women* ('61)
Madonna	*A Certain Sacrifice* ('85)
Elizabeth Montgomery	*A Case of Rape* ('74)
Jennifer O'Neill	*The Other Victim* ('81)
Lee Remick	*Anatomy of a Murder* ('59)
Diana Ross	*Lady Sings the Blues* ('72)

Talia Shire	*Windows* ('80)
Inger Stevens	*The New Interns* ('64)
Raquel Welch	*Hannie Caulder* ('72)
Shelley Winters	*A House Is Not a Home* ('64)
Jane Wyman	*Johnny Belinda* ('48)

CRUDITIES

"He pulled a knife on me. A kitchen knife.
It was still dirty from breakfast."
—George Burns, *The Sunshine Boys*

In *Demon Seed* ('77), an ultrasophisticated computer that is plotting to take over the world rapes heroine **Julie Christie.**

Pia Zadora is sexually assaulted by a male using a garden hose in *The Lonely Lady* ('83). Undoubtedly drawing on the richness of her experience, Zadora's character later becomes a leading Hollywood gossip columnist.

In *The Beast Within Me* ('82), newlywed **Bibi Besch** is raped on her honeymoon by a strange hairy "critter," which results in her giving birth nine months later to a son. As he approaches maturity, the seemingly normal son turns into a younger version of his father.

Lynn Peters, raped by a vampire in a graveyard in *Grave of the Vampire* ('72), gives birth to a vampire baby, which she nourishes on her blood—instead of milk—until she dies.

Paula Sheppard, a lesbian junkie, rapes one of her boyfriends—who's dead—in *Liquid Sky* ('83).

The Devil Made Her Do It

Raped by the devil . . .

Mia Farrow	*Rosemary's Baby* ('68)
Sandy Samuel	*Guardian of Hell* ('90)

REVENGE OF THE RAPE VICTIMS

"My nails will kill you, you cutthroat, murdering beast!
I will cut your heart out and taste your blood."
—Irene Papas, *Mohammad, Messenger of God*

The rape victims in these films may have taken their assaults lying down, but once the rapes are over the victims stood up and fought back. Their goal: revenge. Revenge by murder, revenge by castration, revenge at all costs.

> *The Animals* ('70)
>
> *Extremities* ('86)
>
> *I Spit on Your Grave* ('81)
>
> *The Ladies Club* ('86)
>
> *Lethal Woman* ('89)
>
> *Ms. 45* ('81)
>
> *Naked Vengeance* ('86)
>
> *Positive I.D.* ('87)
>
> *Rape Squad* ('74)
>
> *Sudden Death* ('86)
>
> *Sudden Impact* ('83)
>
> *Victims* ('82)

You Dirty Rat, I'll Teach You!

In the film *Fear* ('88), teenager **Geri Betzler** thwarts her rape by springing a mousetrap on her attacker's penis as he pulls it out of his pants.

RAVISHING REDHEADS

> "If I kept my hair 'natural' the way you do, I'd be bald."
> —Rosalind Russell, *Auntie Mame*

Fiery, passionate, jealous, spirited—all adjectives to describe the redheaded woman. These beauties are all ravishing redheads.

June Allyson	*The Reformer and the Redhead* ('50)
Ann-Margret	*The Cheap Detective* ('78)
Lucille Ball	*Best Foot Forward* ('43)
Arlene Dahl	*Sangaree* ('53)
Samantha Eggar	*The Collector* ('65)
Rhonda Fleming	*The Redhead and the Cowboy* ('50)
Meg Foster	*They Live* ('88)
Melanie Griffith	*Working Girl* ('88)
Page Hannah	*My Man Adam* ('85)
Jean Harlow	*Red-Headed Woman* ('32)
Susan Hayward	*Tap Roots* ('48)
Rita Hayworth	*Fire Down Below* ('57)
Miriam Hopkins	*The Lady with Red Hair* ('40)
Deborah Kerr	*Quo Vadis?* ('51)
Julie London	*The Great Man* ('56)
Shelley Long	*Troop Beverly Hills* ('89)
Shirley MacLaine	*The Trouble with Harry* ('55)
Virginia Mayo	*The Flame and the Arrow* ('50)
Anita Morris	*18 Again* ('88)
Maureen O'Hara	*The Redhead from Wyoming* ('52)
Molly Ringwald	*Sixteen Candles* ('84)
Susan Sarandon	*The January Man* ('89)
Moira Shearer	*The Man Who Loved Redheads* ('55)
Jill St. John	*Who's Been Sleeping in My Bed?* ('63)
Gwen Verdon	*Damn Yankees* ('58)
Debra Winger	*Everybody Wins* ('90)

RED-HOT SIZZLING LADIES

"It's gonna be a hot night tonight and the world goes crazy on a
hot night and maybe that's what a hot night is for."
—Burt Lancaster, *The Rainmaker*

Carrying a Torch

These dames don't want a fellow carrying a torch for them, because they're carrying one of their own. They'll set your world on fire real quick. Why, because these babes are really red-hot—they're arsonists. Yes, indeedy, do light my fire.

Arlene Dahl	*She Played with Fire* ('57)
Farrah Fawcett	*The Burning Bed* ('84)
Martha Hyer	*Pyro* ('64)

Fire Maidens

"She had visions? Who'd you fuck? Joan of Arc?"
—Bruce Martyn Payne, *Pyrates*

Is this a story absolutely made for Hollywood or what? An illiterate peasant girl who hears divine voices leads her countrymen against an enemy invader whose army she vanquishes only to be betrayed, then burned at the stake for her effort. If it weren't fact, only the cinema could have created such a fire maiden.

Ingrid Bergman	*Joan of Arc* ('48)
Sandrine Bonnaire	*Joan the Maid* ('92)
Hedy Lamarr	*The Story of Mankind* ('57)
Jean Seberg	*Saint Joan* ('57)
Alida Valli	*Miracle of the Bells* ('48)

RELIGIOSE

"I can't get with any religion that advertises in
Popular Mechanics."
—Woody Allen, *Annie Hall*

Religiose: overly religious, particularly in a conspicuous or sentimental manner. This collection spans the religious extreme from the truly religious to faith healers, zealots, kooks, and a couple of charlatans.

Carroll Baker	*Mister Moses* ('65)
Bonnie Bedelia	*Death of an Angel* ('85)
Ingrid Bergman	*The Inn of the Sixth Happiness* ('58)
Judi Bowker	*Brother Sun, Sister Moon* ('73)
Ellen Burstyn	*Resurrection* ('80)
Kim Cattrall	*Ticket to Heaven* ('81)
Lois Chiles	*Twister* ('88)
Joan Crawford	*Susan and God* ('40)
Faye Dunaway	*The Disappearance of Aimee* ('76)
Sally Eilers	*Tarnished Angel* ('38)
Ellen Greene	*Glory! Glory!* ('89)
Katharine Hepburn	*Spitfire* ('34)
Wendy Hiller	*Major Barbara* ('41)
Jennifer Jones	*The Song of Bernadette* ('43)
Elsa Lanchester	*The Beachcomber* ('38)
Madonna	*Shanghai Surprise* ('86)
Anna Magnani	*The Miracle* ('48)
Agnes Moorehead	*What's the Matter with Helen?* ('71)
Kate Mulgrew	*A Time for Miracles* ('80)
Geraldine Page	*The Day of the Locust* ('75)
Bernadette Peters	*Fall from Grace* ('90)
Silvia Piñal	*Viridiana* ('61)
Kathleen Quinlan	*The Abduction of St. Anne* ('75)
Gail Russell	*The Angel and the Badman* ('47)
Jean Simmons	*Guys and Dolls* ('55), *Elmer Gantry* ('60)
Barbara Stanwyck	*The Miracle Woman* ('31)
Mae West	*Klondike Annie* ('36)

J.C.'S MAMA

"You gentlemen aren't *really* trying to kill my son, are you?"
—Jessie Royce Landis, *North by Northwest*

Mother Mary—the magnetic icon of the automobile dashboard, and the Savior's mama.

Linda Darnell	*The Song of Bernadette* ('43)
Dorothy McGuire	*The Greatest Story Ever Story* ('65)
Siobhan McKenna	*King of Kings* ('61)
Susanna Pasolini	*The Gospel According to St. Matthew* ('66)
Myriem Roussel	*Hail Mary* ('85)
Madeline Stowe	*The Nativity* ('78)

THE I WAS A FEMALE JESUS AWARD

Awarded to **Sondra Locke**, who plays Jesus in the film within a film in *The Second Coming of Suzanne* ('73).

THE YES, BUT WE ALREADY SUSPECTED THAT AWARD

Awarded to **Marlene Dietrich**, in *The Devil Is a Woman* ('35).

ROCKERS

"Listen to them. Children of the night. What music they make."
—Bela Lugosi, *Dracula*

Wanna roll around the floor or rock around the clock with one of these? Here come the lady rockers. They're actresses in rock films, or rock stars playing rockers.

Ginger Alden	*Lady Grey* ('80)
Justine Bateman	*Satisfaction* ('88)
Susan Berman	*Smithereens* ('72)
Irene Cara	*Sparkle* ('76)
Rebecca De Mornay	*The Slugger's Wife* ('85)
Jodie Foster	*Svengali* ('83)
Ellen Greene	*Glory! Glory!* ('89)
Carrie Hamilton	*Tokyo Pop* ('88)
Marta Heflin	*A Perfect Couple* ('79)
Season Hubley	*Catch My Soul* ('74)
Joan Jett	*Light of Day* ('87)
Tawny Kitaen	*Crystal Heart* ('87)
Apollonia Kotero	*Purple Rain* ('84)
Diane Lane	*Ladies and Gentlemen, the Fabulous Stains* ('81), *Streets of Fire* ('84)
Riba Meryl	*Beyond the Doors* ('83)
Bette Midler	*The Rose* ('79)
Demi Moore	*No Small Affair* ('84)
Laraine Newman	*American Hot Wax* ('78)
Mary Catherine Stewart	*Scenes from the Goldmine* ('87)
Barbra Streisand	*A Star Is Born* ('76)
Chloe Webb	*Sid and Nancy* ('86)

ROLE REVERSALS

"I got more dick than Elvis Presley had on him."
—Billie Whitelaw, *Joyriders*

My Fair Lady's Professor Higgins wondered why a woman couldn't be more like a man. Well, these women prove they can: each one does a role reversal and plays a male, or appears in male drag. If you like your women manly, then you'll love these girlie guys.

Suzy Amis	*The Ballad of Little Jo* ('93)
Julie Andrews	*Victor/Victoria* ('82)
Annabella	*Wings of the Morning* ('37)
Jean Arless	*Homicidal* ('61)
Ann Carlisle	*Liquid Sky* ('83)
Judy Davis	*Impromptu* ('91)
Robyn Douglass	*Her Life as a Man* ('84)
Greta Garbo	*Queen Christina* ('33)
Paulette Goddard	*Pot o' Gold* ('41)
Signe Hasso	*The House on 92nd Street* ('45)
Katharine Hepburn	*Sylvia Scarlett* ('35)
Miriam Hopkins	*She Loves Me Not* ('34)
Joyce Hyser	*Just One of the Guys* ('85)
Veronica Lake	*Sullivan's Travels* ('41)
Sondra Locke	*Reflection of Fear* ('73)
Gloria Manon	*The Woman Inside* ('81)
Eva Mattes	*A Man Like Eva* ('83)
Carmen Maura	*Law of Desire* ('87)
Merle Oberon	*A Song to Remember* ('45)
Lanah Pelley	*Eat the Rich* ('87)
Mary Pickford	*Little Lord Fauntleroy* ('21)
Eleanor Powell	*Rosalie* ('37)
Vanessa Redgrave	*Second Serve* ('86)
Beryl Reid	*The Killing of Sister George* ('68)
Debbie Reynolds	*Goodbye Charlie* ('64)
Diana Rigg	*Theatre of Blood* ('73)
Julia Roberts	*Sleeping with the Enemy* ('91)

Theresa Russell	*Aria* ('88)
Pamela Segall	*Something Special* ('86)
Barbra Streisand	*Yentl* ('83)
Gloria Swanson	*Sunset Blvd.* ('50)
Tilda Swinton	*Orlando* ('93), *Man to Man* ('92)
Ingrid Thulin	*The Magician* ('58)
Liv Ullman	*Pope Joan* ('72)
Mavis Washington	*Fast Break* ('79)
Debra Winger	*Made in Heaven* ('87)
Susannah York	*The Killing of Sister George* ('68)

SEX-CHANGE OPERATIONS

"She cut off her nipples with garden shears. You call that normal."
—Elizabeth Taylor, *Reflections in a Golden Eye*

Uncommon women these characters are . . . before their sex-change operations they were men.

Victoria Abril	*I Want to Be a Woman* ('85)
Karen Black	*Come Back to the Five and Dime, Jimmy Dean, Jimmy Dean* ('82)
Anne Heywood	*I Want What I Want* ('72)
Gloria Manon	*The Woman Inside* ('81)
Vanessa Redgrave	*Second Serve* ('86)
Raquel Welch	*Myra Breckenridge* ('70)

Where's the Rest of Me?

Horrifying? Yes, it was to these ladies . . . I mean, gents. Well, they used to be men, but somehow they got changed into women against their will. Where's the rest of me? I'm missing some of my body parts!

Ellen Barkin	*Switch* ('91)
Veronica Hart	*Cleo/Leo* ('89)
Debbie Reynolds	*Goodbye Charlie* ('64)

Won for Playing a Him
"Boy, with knockers like that, I could go for this guy myself."
—John Ventantonio, *Private Parts*

Linda Hunt won the 1983 Academy Award for Best Supporting Actress for her role as Billy Kwan, a diminutive half-Chinese photographer/assistant to journalist Mel Gibson, in *The Year of Living Dangerously*. In addition to being the only person to have ever won for playing someone of the opposite sex, Hunt—four feet, nine inches—is also the shortest winner.

THE SECOND TIME AROUND

"How could this happen? I was so careful. I picked the wrong play,
the wrong director, the wrong cast. Where did I go right?"
—Zero Mostel, *The Producers*

Love may be lovelier the second time around, but do films improve their second time around when they're remade? Usually not, but there are rare exceptions. Both hits and misses are included in this sampling.

Mary Astor	*The Prisoner of Zenda* ('37)
Jane Greer	*The Prisoner of Zenda* ('52)
Marie-Christine Barrault	*Cousin, Cousine* ('75)
Isabella Rossellini	*Cousins* ('89)
Nathalie Baye	*The Return of Martin Guerre* ('82)
Jodie Foster	*Sommersby* ('93)
Edna Best	*The Man Who Knew Too Much* ('34)
Doris Day	*The Man Who Knew Too Much* ('56)

Joan Blondell, Ina Claire, Madge Evans	*The Greeks Had a Word for Them* ('32)
Marilyn Monroe, Betty Grable, Lauren Bacall	*How to Marry a Millionaire* ('53)
Shirley Booth	*The Matchmaker* ('58)
Barbra Streisand	*Hello, Dolly!* ('69)
Ruth Chatterton	*Madame X* ('29)
Gladys George	*Madame X* ('37)
Lana Turner	*Madame X* ('66)
Tuesday Weld	*Madame X* ('81)
Claudette Colbert	*Cleopatra* ('34)
Elizabeth Taylor	*Cleopatra* ('63)
Claudette Colbert	*It Happened One Night* ('34)
June Allyson	*You Can't Run Away from It* ('56)
Joan Crawford, Norma Shearer, Rosalind Russell	*The Women* ('39)
Joan Collins, June Allyson, Dolores Grey	*The Opposite Sex* ('56)
Bette Davis	*Dark Victory* ('39)
Susan Hayward	*Stolen Hours* ('63)
Bette Davis	*Of Human Bondage* ('34)
Kim Novak	*Of Human Bondage* ('64)
Delores Del Rio	*Bird of Paradise* ('32)
Debra Paget	*Bird of Paradise* ('51)
Marlene Dietrich	*The Blue Angel* ('30)
May Britt	*The Blue Angel* ('59)

Marlene Dietrich	*The Devil Is a Woman* ('35)
Brigitte Bardot	*The Devil Is a Woman* ('58)
Irene Dunne	*Anna and the King of Siam* ('46)
Deborah Kerr	*The King and I* ('56)
Irene Dunne	*Back Street* ('32)
Susan Hayward	*Back Street* ('61)
Irene Dunne	*Love Affair* ('39)
Deborah Kerr	*An Affair to Remember* ('57)
Irene Dunne	*Magnificent Obsession* ('35)
Jane Wyman	*Magnificent Obsession* ('54)
Irene Dunne	*My Favorite Wife* ('40)
Doris Day	*Move Over, Darling* ('63)
Betty Field	*The Great Gatsby* ('49)
Mia Farrow	*The Great Gatsby* ('74)
Susannah Foster	*The Phantom of the Opera* ('43)
Heather Sears	*The Phantom of the Opera* ('62)
Greta Garbo	*Ninotchka* ('39)
Cyd Charisse	*Silk Stockings* ('57)
Janet Gaynor	*A Star Is Born* ('37)
Judy Garland	*A Star Is Born* ('54)
Barbra Streisand	*A Star Is Born* ('76)
Jean Harlow	*Red Dust* ('32)
Ava Gardner	*Mogambo* ('53)

Katharine Hepburn	*The Philadelphia Story* ('40)
Grace Kelly	*High Society* ('56)
Wendy Hiller	*Pygmalion* ('38)
Audrey Hepburn	*My Fair Lady* ('64)
Judy Holliday	*Born Yesterday* ('50)
Melanie Griffith	*Born Yesterday* ('93)
Gertrude Lawrence	*The Glass Menagerie* ('50)
Katharine Hepburn	*The Glass Menagerie* ('73)
Joanne Woodward	*The Glass Menagerie* ('87)
Margaret Lockwood	*The Lady Vanishes* ('39)
Cybill Shepherd	*The Lady Vanishes* ('79)
Carole Lombard	*My Man Godfrey* ('36)
June Allyson	*My Man Godfrey* ('57)
Carole Lombard	*To Be or Not to Be* ('42)
Anne Bancroft	*To Be or Not to Be* ('83)
Jeanette MacDonald	*Rose Marie* ('36)
Ann Blyth	*Rose Marie* ('54)
Geraldine Page	*Sweet Bird of Youth* ('62)
Elizabeth Taylor	*Sweet Bird of Youth* ('89)
Anne Parillaud	*La Femme Nikita* ('90)
Bridget Fonda	*Point of No Return* ('93)
Ginger Rogers	*Bachelor Mother* ('39)
Debbie Reynolds	*Bundle of Joy* ('56)

Norma Shearer	*The Barretts of Wimpole Street* ('34)
Jennifer Jones	*The Barretts of Wimpole Street* ('57)
Norma Shearer	*Romeo and Juliet* ('36)
Olivia Hussey	*Romeo and Juliet* ('68)
Barbara Stanwyck	*Sorry, Wrong Number* ('48)
Loni Anderson	*Sorry, Wrong Number* ('89)
Barbara Stanwyck	*Stella Dallas* ('37)
Bette Midler	*Stella* ('90)
Elizabeth Taylor	*Cat on a Hot Tin Roof* ('58)
Jessica Lange	*Cat on a Hot Tin Roof* ('84)
Fay Wray	*King Kong* ('33)
Jessica Lange	*King Kong* ('76)

SEXPOTS

"Look at that! Look how she moves! That's like Jell-O on springs."
—Jack Lemmon, *Some Like It Hot*

Sexpots come in all sizes and colors—but they're always shapely. They're characterized by extratight, fanny-hugging skirts and sensuous mouths with pouty lips.

Loni Anderson	*The Jayne Mansfield Story* ('80)
Ursula Andress	*The Sensuous Nurse* ('76)
Carroll Baker	*Station Six–Sahara* ('64)
Brigitte Bardot	*. . . And God Created Woman* ('56)

Bo Derek	*Bolero* ('84)
Diana Dors	*I Married a Woman* ('58)
Cristina Ferrare	*The Impossible Years* ('68)
Hedy Lamarr	*White Cargo* ('42)
Kelly LeBrock	*Weird Science* ('85)
Tina Louise	*God's Little Acre* ('58)
Jayne Mansfield	*Will Success Spoil Rock Hunter?* ('57)
Sandra Milo	*Juliet of the Spirits* ('65)
Marilyn Monroe	*The Seven Year Itch* ('55)
Anita Morris	*18 Again* ('88)
Julie Newmar	*The Marriage-Go-Round* ('60)
Sheree North	*How to Be Very, Very Popular* ('55)
Kim Novak	*Kiss Me, Stupid* ('64)
Valerie Perrine	*Slaughterhouse-Five* ('72)
Jessica Rabbit	*Who Framed Roger Rabbit* ('88)
Jane Russell	*The French Line* ('54)
Elke Sommer	*Sweet Ecstasy* ('62)
Mamie Van Doren	*Sex Kittens Go to College* ('60)
Mae West	*Sextette* ('78)

BEST-NAMED SEXPOTS

Appassionata Von Climax, General Bullmoose's secretarial mistress, and **Stupifyin' Jones**, Daisy Mae's rival in *Li'l Abner* ('59).

Pussy Galore, Auric Goldfinger's leather-suited, pseudo-Lesbian avia-trixie, played by **Honor Blackman** in the third James Bond film, *Goldfinger* ('64).

MISS RED-HOT AWARD

Awarded to **Linda Darnell**, the sultry, sexy temptress of the late '40s. In April 1965, while visiting a friend, Darnell burned to death when the friend's house caught fire. At the time of the fire, Darnell had just completed watching a TV rerun of *Star Dust* ('46), one of her old films.

SHADY LADIES

"Remember, you're fighting for this woman's honor,
which is probably more than she ever did."
—Groucho Marx, *Duck Soup*

What's a "shady lady"? She's the type who appears normal on the surface—but dig deeper, if you dare. There's a secret hidden deep within her. If shady ladies aren't plotting something for the present, then they're hiding something from the past. Maybe it's a crime committed long ago, a mysteriously dead loved one, an illegitimate child stashed out of sight, a past she'd rather forget. Be wary; things are never quite what they appear with Shady Ladies.

Mary Astor	*The Maltese Falcon* ('41)
Stephane Audran	*Babette's Feast* ('87)
Carroll Baker	*Sylvia* ('65)
Tallulah Bankhead	*Tarnished Lady* ('31)
Genevieve Bujold	*Obsession* ('76)
Bette Davis	*That Certain Woman* ('37)
Faye Dunaway	*Chinatown* ('74)
Ava Gardner	*My Forbidden Past* ('51)
Whoopi Goldberg	*Clara's Heart* ('88)
Rita Hayworth	*They Came to Cordura* ('59)
Tippi Hedren	*Marnie* ('64)
Beatrice Lillie	*Thoroughly Modern Millie* ('67)
Sophia Loren	*Arabesque* ('66)
Marilyn Monroe	*Niagara* ('53)
Kim Novak	*The Notorious Landlady* ('62)
Merle Oberon	*Temptation* ('46)
Charlotte Rampling	*D.O.A.* ('88)
Lee Remick	*Telefon* ('77)
Isabella Rossellini	*Blue Velvet* ('86)

Theresa Russell	*Black Widow* ('86)
Sylvia Sidney	*Pick-up* ('33)
Jean Simmons	*Hilda Crane* ('56)
Maggie Smith	*Travels with My Aunt* ('72)
Renee Soutendijk	*The Fourth Man* ('79)
Gene Tierney	*Rings on Her Fingers* ('42)
Constance Towers	*The Naked Kiss* ('64)
Kathleen Turner	*Body Heat* ('81)
Jo Van Fleet	*East of Eden* ('55)
Arnetta Walker	*Scenes from the Class Struggle in Beverly Hills* ('89)
Marie Windsor	*The Narrow Margin* ('52)
Shelley Winters	*Ellie* ('84)

PLAYING WITH PORNO

"She tried to sit on my lap while I was standing up."
—Humphrey Bogart, *The Big Sleep*

It takes real guts to play a stag movie star, telephone-sex playmate, or sex-emporium employee . . . even if you don't have to take your clothes off.

Victoria Abril	*Tie Me Up! Tie Me Down!* ('90)
Jennie Berlin	*In the Spirit* ('90)
Karen Black	*Hostage* ('87), *Out of the Dark* ('88)
Veronica Cartwright	*Inserts* ('76)
Ilah Davis	*Hardcore* ('79)
Melanie Griffith	*Body Double* ('84)
Jessica Harper	*Inserts* ('76)
Deborah Harry	*Intimate Stranger* ('91)
Season Hubley	*Hardcore* ('79)
Jennifer Jones	*Angel, Angel, Down We Go* ('70)
Sally Kellerman	*Meatballs III* ('87)

Nastassja Kinski	*Paris, Texas* ('84)
Jonna Lee	*Shattered Innocence* ('88)
Jennifer Jason Leigh	*Heart of Midnight* ('88)
Darian Mathias	*Blue Movies* ('88)
Barbra Streisand	*The Owl and the Pussycat* ('70)
Zoe Tamerlis	*Special Effects* ('84)

Mommie Dearest's Blue Period

Before she broke into the silents in the late '20s, **Joan Crawford** had already experienced an earlier "blue" period in films. Her appearances in stag films such as *Velvet Lips*, *The Plumber*, and *The Casting Couch* have long been a loosely guarded Hollywood secret. Once famous, Crawford spent large sums attempting to buy all the copies of her blue movies, so they could be destroyed to protect her career. Obviously, she didn't manage to get all of them, for at least two books have included sexually graphic photos of Crawford that probably are stills from those porn films.

Porno Queen Makes Good

Ilona Staller, an Italian stripper who performed under the name **Cicciolina** and also starred in the Italian soft-porn film *Inhibition* ('83), was elected to the lower house of Italy's Parliament in 1987 on an independent ticket.

Best Porno Satires

The First Nudie Musical ('76)

Rented Lips ('87)

Judy . . . Judy . . . Judy . . . How Could You!

Hollywood maven and writer Adela Rogers St. John claimed that an unnamed MGM Studio exec used to make MGM contract starlet **Judy Garland** and a studio publicity girl put on private lesbian displays for him.

SEX SCENES

"Some people have flat feet. Some people have dandruff.
I have this appalling imagination."
—Tom Ewell, *The Seven Year Itch*

Whenever a torrid sex scene appears in a film, everyone's imagination runs rampant and rumors soon surface about its "reality." Did the actor and actress get carried away and go all the way for their roles? The rumor mill worked overtime on these examples, plus some of the partners involved kept dropping their own "hints" to fuel the speculation.

Maud Adams	*Tattoo* ('81)	(with Bruce Dern)
Kim Basinger	*The Getaway* ('94)	(with Alec Baldwin)
Julie Christie	*Don't Look Now* ('73)	(with Donald Sutherland)
Beatrice Dalle	*Betty Blue* ('86)	(with Jean-Hugues Anglade)
Bridget Fonda	*Bodies, Rest & Motion* ('93)	(with Eric Stoltz)
Jessica Lange	*The Postman Always Rings Twice* ('81)	(with Jack Nicholson)
Jane March	*L'Amant* ('92)	(with Tony Leung)
Miou-Miou	*Les Valseuses* ('74)	(with Gerard Depardieu)
Carre Otis	*Wild Orchids* ('90)	(with Mickey Rourke)
Anita Pallenberg	*Performance* ('70)	(with Mick Jagger)

Did They? Boy! Did They!

Mick Jagger really does fuck **Anita Pallenberg** and **Michele Breton** on-screen in the film *Performance* ('70). According to a recent bio of Jagger, the scenes were toned down in (or cut out of) the theatrical release, but surfaced later and were shown at a pornographic film festival in Amsterdam.

Gobble, Gobble, Gobble

Watch Dutch actress **Maruschka Detmers** in the Italian-French film *Devil in the Flesh* ('86). Detmers's role called for her to perform fellatio on costar Federico Pitzalis, which she appears to do with gusto. She apparently didn't fake her performance—it looks as if she really did fellate Pitzalis. If so, that would make this the first mainstream film in which a respected actress actually performed an explicit sex scene on-screen.

Dinner's Ready! Come and Get It!

Dinner's served! Come and get it! If using the kitchen table for sex sounds arousing, look at these meals.

Kim Basinger	*9½ Weeks* ('86)
Sonia Braga	*Gabriela* ('83)
Jessica Lange	*The Postman Always Rings Twice* ('81)
Susan Sarandon	*Bull Durham* ('88)
Mary Steenburgen	*What's Eating Gilbert Grape?* ('93)

SHE CAME FROM OUTER SPACE

"It's got tits and a ray gun!"
—Cameron Dye, *Stranded*

Aliens. Space travelers. Things from another world. The females from outer space. Some good, some evil, some human-like, some not so human. Their one shared trait is that they're definitely from outer space.

Francesca Annis	*Dune* ('84)
Candace Azzara	*Doin' Time on Planet Earth* ('88)
Jane Badler	*V* ('83)
Kim Basinger	*My Stepmother Is an Alien* ('88)

Belinda Bauer	*Starcrossed* ('85)
Leslie Bevins	*Alien Nation* ('88)
Hazel Court	*The Girl from Mars* ('66)
Carrie Fisher	*Star Wars* ('77)
Zsa Zsa Gabor	*The Queen of Outer Space* ('58)
Kim Hunter	*Escape from the Planet of the Apes* ('71)
Madeline Kahn	*Slapstick of Another Kind* ('84)
Persis Khambatta	*Star Trek—The Motion Picture* ('79)
Leigh Lombardi	*Moontrap* ('89)
Meredith MacRae	*Earthbound* ('81)
Ornella Muti	*Flash Gordon* ('80)
Priscilla Pointer	*Mysterious Two* ('82)
Molly Ringwald	*Spacehunter: Adventures in the Forbidden Zone* ('83)
Diana Scarwid	*Strange Invaders* ('83)
Tisha Sterling	*Night Slaves* ('70)
Tahnee Welch	*Cocoon* ('85)
Marie Windsor	*Cat Women of the Moon* ('54)
Pia Zadora	*Santa Claus Conquers the Martians* ('64)

MECHANICAL DOLLS

"I'm not sure she's capable of any real feeling.
She's television generation."
—William Holden, *Network*

Mechanical dolls—androids, replicants, robots, artificial females.

Barbara Carrera	*Embryo* ('76)
Pamela Gridley	*Cherry 2000* ('88)
Dayle Haddon	*Cyborg* ('89)
Daryl Hannah	*Blade Runner* ('82)
Anna Karina	*Alphaville* ('65)

Kendra Kirchner	*Android* ('82)
Elsa Lanchester	*The Bride of Frankenstein* ('35)
Kelly LeBrock	*Weird Science* ('85)
Bernadette Peters	*Heartbeeps* ('81)
Patricia Roc	*Perfect Woman* ('49)
Katherine Ross	*The Stepford Wives* ('75)
Renee Soutendijk	*Eve of Destruction* ('91)
Mary Catherine Stewart	*Annihilator* ('86)
Dorothy Stratten	*Galaxina* ('80)
Kristy Swanson	*Deadly Friend* ('86)
Clare Wren	*Steel and Lace* ('91)
Sean Young	*Blade Runner* ('82)

FANCIES FROM THE FUTURE

"Don't you know the future is already obsolete?"
—Gene Kelly, *Inherit the Wind*

It's back to the future forever, and what lovely company we'll keep after meeting up with one of these new friends.

Maria Conchita Alonso	*The Running Man* ('87)
Kathleen Beller	*Time Trackers* ('89)
Susanne Benton	*A Boy and His Dog* ('75)
Rosalind Cash	*The Omega Man* ('71)
Julie Christie	*Fahrenheit 451* ('67)
Suzanna Hamilton	*1984* ('84)
Brigette Helm	*Metropolis* ('26)
Virginia Hey	*The Road Warrior* ('81)
Lauren Hutton	*Timestalkers* ('87)
Anna Karina	*Alphaville* ('65)
Diane Keaton	*Sleeper* ('73)
Cheryl Ladd	*Millennium* ('89)
Maggie McOmie	*THX-1138* ('71)

Yvette Mimieux	*The Time Machine* ('60)
Nichelle Nichols	*Star Trek III: The Search for Spock* ('84)
Charlotte Rampling	*Zardoz* ('74)
Jan Sterling	*1984* ('56)
Sharon Stone	*Total Recall* ('90)
Rachel Ticotin	*Total Recall* ('90)
Mary Woronov	*Death Race 2000* ('75)

Stuck in Space

Living on another world . . . inhabiting rotating space stations . . . conducting experiments . . . they're stuck in space.

Farrah Fawcett	*Saturn 3* ('80)
Anne Francis	*Forbidden Planet* ('56)
Frances Sternhagen	*Outland* ('81)

Best Space Bimbo Title

The winner: *Revenge of the Teenage Vixens from Outer Space* ('85).

SHE'S GOT A STAPLE IN HER NAVEL!

"I had no idea the latest magazines had things like this in them!"
—Arnold Schwarzenegger, *Twins*

Who are these foxes with staples in their navels? Why, the "centerfold" cuties, of course. Those daring young lovelies who've bared all their charms posing as the centerfold in a magazine. Most noteworthy—and probably the most attractive—are the centerfolds from *Playboy* magazine. In addition to appearing in that magazine with all

their charms exposed—so to speak—these sweeties also have appeared in the following motion pictures or videotapes.

12/53	Marilyn Monroe	*Bus Stop* ('56)
2/55	Jayne Mansfield	*The Girl Can't Help It* ('57)
10/58	Mara Corday	*The Giant Claw* ('57)
11/58	Joan Staley	*The Ghost and Mr. Chicken* ('66)
7/59	Yvette Vickers	*Attack of the 50-Foot Woman* ('57)
9/59	Marianne Gaba	*The Choppers* ('61)
1/60	Stella Stevens	*The Ballad of Cable Hogue* ('70)
5/61	Susan Kelly	*Wild Harvest* ('61)
6/62	Marissa Mathes	*Blood Bath* ('66)
6/63	Connie Mason	*Blood Feast* ('63)
12/63	Donna Michelle	*Agent for H.A.R.M.* ('66)
4/64	Ashley Martin	*Blood Feast* ('63)
8/64	China Lee	*Good Times* ('67)
5/66	Dolly Read	*Beyond the Valley of the Dolls* ('70)
8/66	Susan Denberg	*Frankenstein Created Woman* ('67)
12/66	Sue Bernard	*Faster Pussycat! Kill! Kill!* ('66)
5/67	Anne Randall	*Stacey!* ('73)
9/67	Victoria Vetri (Angela Dorian)	*When Dinosaurs Ruled the Earth* ('70)
12/68	Cynthia Myers	*Beyond the Valley of the Dolls* ('70)
10/69	Jeanne Bell	*T.N.T. Jackson* ('75)
11/69	Claudia Jennings	*Gator Bait* ('73)
8/70	Sharon Clark	*Lifeguard* ('75)
10/70	Madeleine and Mary Collinson	*Twins of Evil* ('71)
1/71	Liv Lindeland	*Picasso Trigger* ('89)
9/71	Crystal Smith	*Hot Dog . . . The Movie* ('84)
2/73	Cyndi Wood	*Van Nuys Blvd.* ('79)
3/73	Bonnie Large	*The Happy Hooker Goes to Washington* ('77)

5/73	Anulka Dziubinska	*Vampyres* ('74)
6/73	Ruthy Ross	*The Centerfold Girls* ('74)
7/73	Martha Smith	*National Lampoon's Animal House* ('78)
3/74	Pamela Zinszer	*The Happy Hooker Goes to Washington* ('77)
6/74	Sandy Johnson	*Halloween* ('78)
8/74	Jean Manson	*Dirty O'Neill* ('74)
2/75	Laura Misch Owens	*French Quarter* ('77)
6/75	Azizi Johari	*Body and Soul* ('81)
8/75	Lillian Müller	*Casanova and Co.* ('79)
8/76	Linda Beatty (Carpenter)	*A Different Story* ('79)
1/77	Susan Lynn Kiger	*H.O.T.S.* ('79)
7/77	Sondra Theodore	*Wet and Wild* ('89)
9/77	Debra Jo Fondren	*Playmates in Paradise* ('92)
12/77	Ashley Cox	*Night Shift* ('82)
4/78	Pamela Jean Bryant	*H.O.T.S.* ('79)
9/78	Rosanne Katon	*Body and Soul* ('81)
10/78	Marcy Hanson	*10* ('79)
11/78	Monique St. Pierre	*Motel Hell* ('80)
1/79	Candy Loving	*Dorothy Stratten: The Untold Story* ('85)
4/79	Missy Cleveland	*Blow Out* ('81)
5/79	Michele Drake	*History of the World, Part I* ('81)
8/79	Dorothy Stratten	*They All Laughed* ('81)
10/79	Ursula Buchfellner	*Popcorn and Ice Cream* ('78)
12/79	Candace Collins	*Class* ('83)
4/80	Liz Glazowski	*The Happy Hooker Goes to Hollywood* ('80)
6/80	Ola Ray	*10 to Midnight* ('83)
8/80	Victoria Cooke	*Playboy Video Magazine, Vol. 2* ('83)

9/80	Lisa Welch	*Revenge of the Nerds* ('84)
11/80	Jeana Tomasina	*10 to Midnight* ('83)
12/80	Terri Welles	*Looker* ('81)
1/81	Karen Price	*Swamp Thing* ('81)
2/81	Vicki Lasseter	*Playboy's Playmate Review* ('82)
3/81	Kymberly Herrin	*Romancing the Stone* ('84)
4/81	Lorraine Michaels	*Malibu Express* ('84)
7/81	Heidi Sorenson	*Fright Night* ('85)
10/81	Kelly Tough	*Playmates at Play* ('90)
11/81	Shannon Tweed	*The Surrogate* ('84)
12/81	Patty Farinelli	*Playboy's Playmate Review* ('82)
1/82	Kimberly McArthur	*Malibu Express* ('84)
3/82	Karen Witter	*Dangerously Close* ('86)
4/82	Linda Rhys Vaughn	*Playmates at Play* ('90)
5/82	Kym Malin	*Joysticks* ('83)
6/82	Lourdes Estores	*Playboy's Playmate Review* ('82)
7/82	Lynda Wiesmeier	*Malibu Express* ('84)
8/82	Cathy St. George	*Star 80* ('83)
9/82	Connie Brighton	*Playboy's Playmate Review 3* ('85)
10/82	Marianne Gravatte	*Playboy Video Magazine, Vol. 5* ('83)
11/82	Marlene Janssen	*School Spirit* ('85)
12/82	Charlotte (Helmcamp) Kemp	*Frankenhooker* ('90)
1/83	Lonnie Chin	*Star 80* ('83)
2/83	Melinda Mays	*Playboy Video Magazine, Vol. 5* ('83)
3/83	Alana Soares	*Beverly Hills Cop II* ('87)
5/83	Susie Scott	*Student Confidential* ('87)
8/83	Carina Persson	*Playmates at Play* ('90)
9/83	Barbara Edwards	*Malibu Express* ('84)
10/83	Tracy Vaccaro	*The Man Who Loved Women* ('83)
11/83	Veronica Gamba	*A Night in Heaven* ('83)
1/84	Penny Baker	*The Men's Club* ('86)

3/84	Dona Spier	*Hard Ticket to Hawaii* ('87)
4/84	Lesa Pedirana	*Playmates at Play* ('90)
5/84	Patty Duffek	*Picasso Trigger* ('89)
7/84	Liz Stewart	*Wet and Wild* ('89)
9/84	Kim Evenson	*Kandyland* ('87)
10/84	Deborah Nicholle Johnson	*Playmates at Play* ('90)
11/84	Roberta Vasquez	*Picasso Trigger* ('89)
12/84	Karen Valez	*Wet and Wild* ('89)
2/85	Cherie Witter	*Playboy Video Calendar 1987* ('86)
3/85	Donna Smith	*Playboy Video Calendar 1987* ('86)
4/85	Cindy Brooks	*It Takes Two* ('88)
5/85	Kathy Shower	*Further Adventures of Tennessee Buck* ('87)
6/85	Devin De Vasquez	*Can't Buy Me Love* ('87)
7/85	Hope Marie Carlton	*Hard Ticket to Hawaii* ('87)
8/85	Cher Butler	*Wet and Wild* ('89)
9/85	Venice Kong	*Beverly Hills Cop II* ('87)
10/85	Cynthia Brimhall	*Hard Ticket to Hawaii* ('87)
11/85	Pamela Saunders	*Alien Warrior* ('85)
12/85	Carol Ficatier	*Playmates at Play* ('90)
2/86	Julie McCullough	*Big Bad Mama II* ('87)
3/86	Kim Morris	*Wet and Wild* ('89)
4/86	Teri Weigel	*Cheerleader Camp* ('87)
5/86	Christine Richters	*Playmates at Play* ('90)
6/86	Rebecca Ferrati	*Silent Assassins* ('88)
7/86	Lynne Austin	*Playboy Video Calendar 1989* ('88)
8/86	Ava Fabian	*To Die For* ('88)
9/86	Rebekka Armstrong	*Immortalizer* ('90)
10/86	Katherine Hushaw	*Wet and Wild* ('89)
12/86	Laurie Ann Carr	*Mortuary Academy* ('88)
1/87	Luann Lee	*Terminal Exposure* ('88)

2/87	Julie Peterson	*Playboy Video Calendar 1988* ('87)
3/87	Marina Baker	*Wet and Wild* ('89)
4/87	Anna Clark	*Wet and Wild* ('89)
5/87	Kym Paige	*Mortuary Academy* ('88)
6/87	Sandy Greenberg	*Playmates at Play* ('90)
7/87	Carmen Berg	*Wet and Wild* ('89)
8/87	Sharry Konopski	*Playboy Video Calendar 1989* ('88)
9/87	Gwendolyn Hajek	*Traxx* ('88)
10/87	Brandi Brandt	*Wedding Band* ('89)
11/87	Pamela J. Stein	*Playboy Video Calendar 1989* ('88)
1/88	Kimberley Conrad	*Playboy Video Calendar 1989* ('88)
2/88	Kari Kennell	*Playboy Playmates in Paradise* ('92)
3/88	Susie Owens	*They Bite* ('91)
4/88	Eloise Broady	*Dangerous Love* ('88)
5/88	Diana Lee-Hsu	*License to Kill* ('89)
6/88	Emily Arth	*Playboy Video Calendar 1990* ('89)
7/88	Terri Lynn Doss	*Lethal Weapon* ('87)
8/88	Helle Michaelsen	*Playboy Video Calendar 1991* ('90)
9/88	Laura Richmond	*Sexy Lingerie* ('88)
10/88	Shannon Long	*Playboy Video Calendar 1990* ('89)
12/88	Kata Kârkkâinen	*Sexy Lingerie* ('88)
1/89	Fawna MacLaren	*Dragonfight* ('90)
2/89	Simone Eden	*Playboy Video Calendar 1990* ('89)
3/89	Laurie Wood	*Playboy Video Calendar 1990* ('89)
4/89	Jennifer Lyn Jackson	*Playboy Video Calendar 1990* ('89)
5/89	Monique Noel	*Bert Rigby, You're a Fool* ('89)
6/89	Tawnni Cable	*Marilyn and Bobby: Her Final Affair* ('93)
7/89	Erika Eleniak	*The Blob* ('88)
8/89	Gianna Ardmore	*Screwball Hotel* ('90)
9/89	Karin and Miryam van Breeschooten	*Playboy Video Calendar 1990* ('89)

10/89	Karen Foster	*Wet and Wild II* ('90)
11/89	Renée Tenison	*Shout* ('91)
12/89	Petra Verkaik	*Pyrates* ('91)
1/90	Peggy McIntaggart	*Rock Video Girls 2* ('92)
3/90	Deborah Driggs	*Total Exposure* ('91)
4/90	Lisa Matthews	*Sexy Lingerie II* ('90)
5/90	Tina Bockrath	*Totally Exposed* ('91)
6/90	Bonnie Marino	*Playboy Video Calendar 1991* ('90)
7/90	Jacqueline Sheen	*Playboy Video Calendar 1991* ('90)
8/90	Melissa Evridge	*Playboy Video Calendar 1992* ('91)
9/90	Kerri Kendall	*Wet and Wild II* ('90)
10/90	Brittany York	*I Posed for Playboy* ('91)
11/90	Lorraine Olivia	*Playboy Video Calendar 1992* ('91)
12/90	Morgan Fox	*Flesh Gordon 2* ('90)
1/91	Stacy Arthur	*Playboy Video Calendar 1992* ('91)
2/91	Cristy Thom	*Playboy Video Calendar 1992* ('91)
3/91	Julie Clarke	*Playmates in Paradise* ('92)
4/91	Christina Leardini	*Playboy Video Calendar 1992* ('91)
5/91	Carrie Jean Yazel	*Death Becomes Her* ('92)
6/91	Saskia Linssen	*Playboy Playmate Review 1992* ('91)
7/91	Wendy Kaye Lawrence	*Wet and Wild III* ('90)
8/91	Corinna Harney	*Wet and Wild IV* ('92)
9/91	Samantha Dormen	*Playmates in Paradise* ('92)
10/91	Cheryl Bachman	*Playboy Video Calendar 1992* ('91)
11/91	Tonja Christensen	*Playboy Video Calendar 1993* ('92)
12/91	Wendy Hamilton	*Playboy Video Calendar 1993* ('92)
1/92	Suzi Simpson	*Playboy Video Calendar 1993* ('92)
2/92	Tanya Beyer	*Wet and Wild IV* ('92)
3/92	Tylyn John	*Playboy Video Calendar 1993* ('92)
4/92	Cady Cantrell	*Wet and Wild IV* ('92)
5/92	Angela Nicole Smith (Vickie Smith)	*Playboy Video Calendar 1993* ('92)

6/92	Angela Melini	*Wet and Wild IV* ('92)
7/92	Amanda Hope	*Wet and Wild IV* ('92)
8/92	Ashley Allen	*Playboy Video Calendar 1994* ('93)
10/92	Tiffany Sloan	*Sexy Lingerie V* ('92)
11/92	Stephanie Adams	*Playboy Video Calendar 1994* ('93)
12/92	Barbara Moore	*Sexy Lingerie V* ('92)
1/93	Echo Johnson	*Sexy Lingerie V* ('92)
3/93	Kimberly Donley	*Playboy Video Calendar 1994* ('93)
4/93	Nicole Wood	*Playboy Video Calendar 1994* ('93)
6/93	Alesha Oreskovich	*Playboy Video Calendar 1994* ('93)

Other cinematic Playmates (for whom dates are unavailable) include:

Barbi Benton	*Deathstalker* ('84)
Connie Kreski	*Hieronymus Merkin* ('69)
Connie Knudson	*Orgy at Lil's Place*
Delores Wells	*Beach Party* ('63)

The following films provide an opportunity for the voyeur to ogle multiple Playmates:

Casanova and Company ('79)

How to Stuff a Wild Bikini ('65)

Looker ('81)

Old Dracula ('74)

Picasso Trigger ('89)

Savage Beach ('90)

Sergeant Deadhead ('65)

MY PET, MY CINEMATIC PET

Not to be outdone by the competition, these centerfold "Pets" of *Penthouse* magazine also have made film or video appearances:

9/73	Anneka di Lorenzo	*The Centerfold Girls* ('77)
3/76	Priscilla Barnes (Joann Whitty)	*Seniors* ('78)

8/76	Victoria Lynn Johnson	*Dressed to Kill* ('80, Angie Dickinson's body double)
12/77	Cheryl Rixon	*Used Cars* ('80)
4/78	Mariwin Roberts	*Cinderella* ('77)
6/78, 8/81	Corinne Alphen	*New York Nights* ('81)
5/80	Monika Kaelin	*S.A.S. San Salvador* ('82)
1/81	Sue Francis Pai	*Jakarta* ('88)
5/81	Cody Carmack	*Affairs of the Heart* ('92)
7/81	Michelle Bauer	*Beverly Hills Vamp* ('89)
12/81	Sheila Kennedy	*Ellie* ('84)
12/82	Monique Gabrielle	*Chained Heat* ('83)
5/83	Linda Kenton	*Hot Resort* ('84)
8/83	Shana Ross	*Penthouse Love Stories* ('86)
9/84	Traci Lords	*Not of This Earth* ('88)
8/85	Angela Nicholas	*Wildest Dreams* ('87)
9/85	Christine Dupree	*Armed and Dangerous* ('86)
11/85	Carina Ragnarsson	*Beauty School* ('93)
2/86	Susan Napoli	*Frankenhooker* ('90)
4/86	Dominique St. Croix	*Recruits* ('86)
7/86	Krista Pflanzer	*Cheerleader Camp* ('87)
8/86	Patty Mullen	*Doom Asylum* ('87)
9/86	Ginger Miller	*Boxing Babes* ('91)
5/87	Melissa Leigh	*Affairs of the Heart* ('92)
6/87	Connie Gauthier	*18 Again!* ('88)
8/87	Andi Bruce	*Summer's Games* ('87)
10/87	Teri Lynn Peake	*Boy's Night Out* ('87)
11/87, 8/88	Lisa Alton-Bradford	*Screwball Hotel* ('90)
12/87	Janine Lindemulder	*Spring Fever USA* ('88)
5/88	Kelley Wild	*The Best of Mermaids* ('92)
4/88	Delia Sheppard	*Witchcraft II* ('89)

12/88	Kimberly Taylor	*Frankenhooker* ('90)
9/89	Lynn Johnson	*Penthouse Fast Cars/Fantasy Women* ('92)
10/90	Kelly Jackson	*Passport to Paradise* ('91)
1/91	Mahalia Maria	*Satin and Lace* ('92)
3/91	Sandi Korn	*Penthouse Passport to Paradise/ Hawaii* ('91)
4/91	Theresa Kelly	*The Great Pet Hunt—Part II* ('91)
6/91	Julie Strain	*Double Impact* ('91)
1/92	Stevie Jean	*Satin and Lace* ('92)
1/93	Natalie Lennox	*The All-Pet Workout* ('93)
2/93	Julie Smith	*Penthouse Ready to Ride* ('92)

Best Centerfold Award

Awarded to **Roxanne Kernohan** in *Critters 2: The Main Course* ('88), as the faceless, shapeless alien who transforms herself into a live *Playboy* centerfold—complete with a staple in the navel.

CANDIDLY UNCOVERED

"You're pretty enough for all normal purposes."
—Beulah Bondi, *Our Town*

Many stars have found themselves candidly uncovered by magazines such as *Playboy, High Society, Hustler,* and specialty issues such as *Celebrity Skin* or *Celebrity Sleuth.* Their uncoverings encompass stills from a particular film scene, a layout in which they posed especially for the publication, "hidden" camera shots, and even some "authorized" nude photographs. Especially noteworthy are *Playboy*'s annual pictorials "Sex in the Cinema" and "Sex Stars." Here is a brief—but certainly not complete—listing of where to gaze at some candidly uncovered stars.

Legend: *HS = High Society, PB = Playboy, PH = Penthouse*

Maud Adams	*PB* 10/81
Ursula Andress	*PB* 11/73, 4/76
Ann-Margret	*PB* 10/66

Laura Antonelli	*HS* 2/80, 11/80
Rosanna Arquette	*PB* 9/90
Barbara Bach	*HS* 8/81; *PB* 1/81
Adrienne Barbeau	*HS* 7/80
Brigitte Bardot	*HS* 11/76; *PB* 1/75
Kim Basinger	*PB* 2/83, 1/88
Sandahl Bergman	*PB* 3/80
Jacqueline Bisset	*HS* 12/78
Linda Blair	*HS* 8/83; *PB* 12/83
Lisa Bonet	*HS* 10/88
Sonia Braga	*PB* 5/79, 10/84
Dyan Cannon	*HS* 6/80
Barbara Carrera	*HS* 9/81; PB 7/77, 3/82
Phoebe Cates	*HS* 10/84
Cher	*HS* 5/81
Jill Clayburgh	*HS* 3/81
Joan Collins	*HS* 4/83; *PB* 12/83, 12/84
Teri Copley	*PB* 11/90
Joan Crawford	*HS* 6/82
Jamie Lee Curtis	*HS* 12/83, 7/84
Maryam D'Abo	*PB* 9/87
Patti D'Arbanville	*PB* 5/77
Bo Derek	*PB* 3/80, 8/80, 9/81, 7/84, 9/89
Angie Dickinson	*HS* 3/79, 11/80
Faye Dunaway	*HS* 6/82
Britt Ekland	*HS* 4/81
Linda Evans	*PB* 12/81, 1/89
Morgan Fairchild	*HS* 6/81, 7/88
Lola Falana	*PB* 6/70
Farrah Fawcett	*HS* 1/81
Sally Field	*HS* 10/81

Jodie Foster	*HS* 3/82, 1/83; *PB* 11/83
Susan George	*PB* 12/72
Pam Grier	*HS* 6/80; *PB* 11/72, 11/73
Melanie Griffith	*PB* 10/76, 1/86
Daryl Hannah	*HS* 12/84
Goldie Hawn	*HS* 12/81
Margaux Hemingway	*PB* 5/90
Mariel Hemingway	*HS* 8/82; *PB* 4/82, 1/89
Barbara Hershey	*PB* 12/72
Lauren Hutton	*PH* 9/86
Grace Jones	*PB* 7/85
Diane Keaton	*HS* 9/80
Paula Kelly	*PB* 8/69, 7/72
Margot Kidder	*HS* 1/80; *PB* 3/75
Nastassja Kinski	*HS* 7/81, 8/82; *PB* 5/83
Kay Lenz	*HS* 4/80; *PB* 11/82
Sophia Loren	*PB* 1/89
Carol Lynley	*HS* 12/79
Ali MacGraw	*HS* 12/80
Madonna	*HS* 10/85; *PB* 9/85
Jayne Mansfield	*HS* 8/80
Pamela Sue Martin	*PB* 7/78
Barbara McNair	*PB* 10/68
Sarah Miles	*PB* 7/76, 12/76
Marilyn Monroe	*PB* 12/53, 1/79
Brigitte Nielsen	*PB* 8/86, 12/87
Kim Novak	*HS* 7/87
Tatum O'Neal	*PB* 11/82
Valerie Perrine	*PB* 5/72, 8/81
Paulina Porizkova	*HS* 8/86

Tanya Roberts	*PB* 10/82
Misty Rowe	*PB* 11/76
Dominique Sanda	*PB* 3/72
Susan Sarandon	*PB* 3/78
Cybill Shepherd	*HS* 10/87; *PB* 11/72
Elke Sommer	*PB* 9/70, 1/79
Sissy Spacek	*HS* 7/81, 2/82
Connie Stevens	*HS* 10/79
Stella Stevens	*PB* 1/60
Meryl Streep	*HS* 09/84
Barbra Streisand	*HS* 11/79
Elizabeth Taylor	*HS* 5/81
Lea Thompson	*HS* 2/86
Angel Tompkins	*PB* 2/72, 12/72
Kathleen Turner	*HS* 8/86
Vanity	*PB* 4/88
Rachel Ward	*HS* 10/84; *PB* 3/84
Sigourney Weaver	*HS* 3/88
Vanna White	*PB* 5/87, 12/87
Vanessa Williams	*PH* 9/84, 11/84
Debra Winger	*HS* 1/87
Pia Zadora	*PB* 3/82, 11/83

In addition to the above offerings, several issues of *Celebrity Sleuth* each year are especially recommended for star gazers:

> "The Anatomy Awards"
>
> "The 25 Most Beautiful Women in the World"
>
> "The Women of Fantasy"

SISTER, SISTER

"We're high-tempered. We fight amongst ourselves,
but let trouble come from outside and we stick together."
—Agnes Moorehead, *Johnny Belinda*

Sisters of the true blood: real-life sisters. Might we detect the occasional glimmer of thespian jealousy between any of them?

Pier Angel and Marisa Pavan

Patricia Arquette and Rosanna Arquette

Brigitte Bardot and Mijanou Bardot

Constance Bennett and Joan Bennett

Sally Blane and Loretta Young

Olivia de Havilland and Joan Fontaine

Catherine Deneuve and Françoise Dorleac

Mia Farrow and Tisa Farrow

Dorothy Gish and Lillian Gish

Melanie Griffith and Tracy Griffith

Daryl Hannah and Page Hannah

June Havoc and Gypsy Rose Lee

Margaux Hemingway and Mariel Hemingway

Hayley Mills and Juliet Mills

Deedee Pfeiffer and Michelle Pfeiffer

Lynn Redgrave and Vanessa Redgrave

Jennifer Tilley and Meg Tilley

Quick Quiz

Real-life sisters (and film actresses) Loretta Young, Sally Blane, Polly Ann Young, and Georgianna Young appear as sisters in what film?

The answer is *The Story of Alexander Graham Bell* ('39).

SOAPY BEGINNINGS AND ENDINGS

"Without that job and those lines to say, an actress is just like any
ordinary girl, trying not to look as scared as she feels."
—Andrea Leeds, *Stage Door*

Where do some actresses learn their craft? Many have served a tour
of duty on that staple of daytime television—the soap opera. The
soaps also have offered some refuge to aging actresses when the
silver screen no longer called their names.

Joan Bennett	"Dark Shadows"
Ellen Burstyn	"The Doctors" ('65)
Kate Capshaw	"The Edge of Night" ('81)
Jill Clayburgh	"Search For Tomorrow" ('69-70)
Sandy Dennis	"The Guiding Light" ('56)
Olympia Dukakis	"Search for Tomorrow" ('83)
Patty Duke	"The Brighter Day"
Morgan Fairchild	"Search for Tomorrow"
Lee Grant	"Search For Tomorrow" ('53-54)
Tippi Hedren	"The Bold and the Beautiful" ('90)
Kate Jackson	"Dark Shadows"
Louise Lasser	"The Doctors"
Marsha Mason	"Dark Shadows" ('69), "Love of Life" ('72)
Dorothy McGuire	"The Young and the Restless" ('85)
Gena Rowlands	"The Way of the World"
Meg Ryan	"As the World Turns" ('82-84)
Eva Marie Saint	"The Edge of Night"
Susan Sarandon	"A World Apart" ('70-71), "Search for Tomorrow" ('72)
Kathleen Turner	"The Doctors" ('78-79)
Cicely Tyson	"Guiding Light" ('66)
Sigourney Weaver	"Somerset" ('76)

SOUTHERN BELLES

"Ah'd love to kiss ya, but ah jes' washed mah hair."
—Bette Davis, *The Cabin in the Cotton*

Southern belles: virginal white hoop skirts; a large mammy hovering protectively nearby; a girlish woman, her fan poised for coy flirtations. She's an enigmatic figure; one magnified by our imagination of what constitutes Southern womanhood. Is our perception all wrong? Remember, it was a Briton—not a Southerner, not even an American—who brought life to those two cinematic embodiments of Southern womanhood: Scarlett O'Hara and Blanche Dubois. The old Southern belles of yesteryear are gone, but their descendants are alive—and have transformed themselves into today's spunky version of their ancestors.

Antebellum Beauties

Delta Burke	*Charleston* ('79)
Arlene Dahl	*Sangaree* ('53)
Bette Davis	*Jezebel* ('38)
Yvonne de Carlo	*Band of Angels* ('57)
Olivia de Havilland	*Gone with the Wind* ('39)
Catherine Deneuve	*Mississippi Mermaid* ('69)
Ava Gardner	*Show Boat* ('51)
Susan George	*Mandingo* ('75)
Lillian Gish	*Birth of a Nation* ('15)
Susan Hayward	*Tap Roots* ('48)
Margot Kidder	*Louisiana* ('84)
Dorothy Lamour	*Dixie* ('43)
Vivien Leigh	*Gone with the Wind* ('39)
Maureen O'Hara	*The Foxes of Harrow* ('47)
Jennifer O'Neill	*Love's Savage Fury* ('79)
Debra Paget	*The Gambler from Natchez* ('54)

Gail Patrick	*Mississippi* ('35)
Margaret Sullavan	*So Red the Rose* ('35)
Elizabeth Taylor	*Raintree County* ('57)

Postwar Women

Ingrid Bergman	*Saratoga Trunk* ('45)
Ann Blyth	*Another Part of the Forest* ('48)
Bette Davis	*The Little Foxes* ('41)
Paulette Goddard	*Reap the Wild Wind* ('42)
Jane Wyman	*The Yearling* ('46)

Modern Sweets

Mary Badham	*To Kill a Mockingbird* ('62)
Kim Basinger	*No Mercy* ('86)
Kathy Bates	*Fried Green Tomatoes* ('91)
Phoebe Cates	*Shag* ('89)
Joan Crawford	*Queen Bee* ('55)
Sally Field	*Steel Magnolias* ('89)
Holly Hunter	*Miss Firecracker* ('89)
Shirley MacLaine	*Steel Magnolias* ('89)
Frances McDormand	*Mississippi Burning* ('88)
Geraldine Page	*Toys in the Attic* ('63)
Sissy Spacek	*Crimes of the Heart* ('86), *The Long Walk Home* ('90)
Jessica Tandy	*Driving Miss Daisy* ('89)

STARS!

"Aiiee! Caramba! Now that's the kind of woman that'll make a man
write a bad check."

—Jorge Lopez, *Easy Wheels*

The stars aren't in the heavens, they're up on the movie screens. Real
film stars portraying fictitious film stars, Broadway stars, other real-
life film stars, and those two dreads of all film stars—stars on the
skids and stars with obsessive fans.

	Fictitious Stars
Julie Andrews	*S.O.B.* ('81)
Patti Astor	*Underground U.S.A.* ('80)
Carroll Baker	*The Carpetbaggers* ('64)
Brigitte Bardot	*A Very Private Affair* ('62)
Constance Bennett	*What Price Hollywood?* ('32)
Karen Black	*The Day of the Locust* ('75)
Bette Davis	*Dangerous* ('35)
Judy Garland	*A Star Is Born* ('54)
Whoopi Goldberg	*The Telephone* ('88)
Jean Harlow	*Bombshell* ('33)
Ida Lupino	*The Big Knife* ('55)
Kim Novak	*The Legend of Lylah Clare* ('68)
Mia Sara	*Queenie* ('87)
Elizabeth Taylor	*There Must Be a Pony* ('86)
Lana Turner	*The Bad and the Beautiful* ('52)
Raquel Welch	*The Wild Party* ('75)
Mae West	*Go West, Young Man* ('36)
Natalie Wood	*Inside Daisy Clover* ('65)

Stage Stars

Carol Burnett	*Noises Off* ('92)
Joan Crawford	*Torch Song* ('53)
Bette Davis	*All About Eve* ('50)
Glenda Jackson	*The Incredible Sarah* ('76)

Film Star Biographies

Loni Anderson	*The Jayne Mansfield Story* ('80), *White Hot: The Mysterious Murder of Thelma Todd* ('91)
Julie Andrews	*Star!* ('68)
Carroll Baker	*Harlow* ('65)
Angela Bassett	*What's Love Got to Do with It* ('93)
Lynda Carter	*Rita Hayworth: The Love Goddess* ('83)
Jill Clayburgh	*Gable and Lombard* ('76), *Reason for Living: The Jill Ireland Story* ('91)
Doris Day	*Love Me or Leave Me* ('55)
Patty Duke	*Call Me Anna* ('90)
Faye Dunaway	*Mommie Dearest* ('81)
Frances Fisher	*Lucy and Desi: Before the Laughter* ('91)
Kathryn Grayson	*So This Is Love* ('53)
Kathryn Harrold	*Bogie* ('80)
Susan Hayward	*I'll Cry Tomorrow* ('55)
Betty Hutton	*The Perils of Pauline* ('47)
Glenda Jackson	*The Patricia Neal Story* ('81)
Ann Jillian	*Mae West* ('82)
Cheryl Ladd	*Grace Kelly* ('83)
Jessica Lange	*Frances* ('82)
Sophia Loren	*Sophia Loren: Her Own Story* ('80)
Carol Lynley	*Harlow* ('65)
Shirley MacLaine	*Out on a Limb* ('87)

Virginia Madsen	*The Hearst and Davies Affair* ('85)
Dorothy Malone	*Too Much, Too Soon* ('58)
Mel Martin	*Darlings of the Gods* ('90)
Andrea McArdle	*Rainbow* ('78)
Kim Novak	*Jeanne Eagels* ('57)
Jean Simmons	*The Actress* ('53)
Barbra Streisand	*Funny Girl* ('68), *Funny Lady* ('75)
Kinuyo Tanaka	*Actress* ('47)
Kristina Wayborn	*Movieola: The Silent Lovers* ('84)
Lynn Whitfield	*The Josephine Baker Story* ('91)
Esther Williams	*Million Dollar Mermaid* ('52)
Natalie Wood	*Gypsy* ('62)

Stars on the Skids

Karen Black	*Hostage* ('87)
Bette Davis	*The Star* ('52), *What Ever Happened to Baby Jane?* ('62), *Dangerous* ('35)
Joan Crawford	*What Ever Happened to Baby Jane?* ('62)
Jane Fonda	*The Morning After* ('86)
Marthe Keller	*Fedora* ('78)
Sally Kirkland	*Double Threat* ('92)
Vivien Leigh	*The Roman Spring of Mrs. Stone* ('61)
Geraldine Page	*Sweet Bird of Youth* ('62)
Kim Stanley	*The Goddess* ('58)
Gloria Swanson	*Sunset Blvd.* ('50)
Lana Turner	*The Bad and the Beautiful* ('52)
Rosel Zech	*Veronika Voss* ('82)

Stalked Stars

Lauren Bacall	*The Fan* ('81)
Morgan Fairchild	*The Seduction* ('82)

Anne Heywood	*Scenes from a Murder* ('72)
Catherine Oxenberg	*Overexposed* ('90)
Theresa Saldana	*Victims for Victims: The Theresa Saldana Story* ('84)

THE MISS STARSTRUCK AWARD

Awarded to **Maureen Arthur**, for her role as **Ethel Evans**, who's nicknamed *The Star Fucker*, in *The Love Machine* ('71). Dear, dear Ethel . . . she only does it with stars . . . the bigger the better.

THE STRIPPERS

"And when she started to do the Naked Dance of Love,
I knew right then that I was—for a fact—in love."
—Wayne Rankin, *The Underachievers*

Bump it! Grind it! Toss those hips! Twirl those tassels! Rotate your pelvis! Bounce up and down that runway! Show all the customers a good time as you peel your clothing off piece, by piece, by piece.

Lola Albright	*A Cold Wind in August* ('61)
Sandahl Bergman	*Kandyland* ('87)
Rae Dawn Chong	*Fear City* ('84)
Julie Christie	*Crooks Anonymous* ('62)
Joan Collins	*Fearless* ('78)
Lolita Davidovich	*Blaze* ('89)
Judy Davis	*High Tide* ('87)
Anita Ekberg	*Screaming Mimi* ('58)
Britt Ekland	*The Night They Raided Minsky's* ('68)
Melanie Griffith	*Fear City* ('84)
Goldie Hawn	*Crisscross* ('92)

Rita Hayworth	*Pal Joey* ('57)
Marilu Henner	*Saturday Night Fever* ('77)
Grace Jones	*Vamp* ('86)
Anna Karina	*A Woman Is a Woman* ('60)
Paula Kelly	*Jo Jo Dancer, Your Life Is Calling* ('86)
Margot Kidder	*Little Treasure* ('85)
Diane Lane	*The Big Town* ('87)
Kay Lenz	*Stripped to Kill* ('87)
Jayne Mansfield	*Too Hot to Handle* ('60)
Rita Moreno	*Marlowe* ('69)
Valerie Perrine	*Lenny* ('74)
Paula Prentiss	*What's New, Pussycat?* ('65)
Lesley Ann Warren	*Portrait of a Stripper* ('79)
Gwen Welles	*Nashville* ('75)
Natalie Wood	*Gypsy* ('62)
Joanne Woodward	*The Stripper* ('63)

THE GO-GOS

Jennifer Beals	*Flashdance* ('83)
Anita Morris	*A Sinful Life* ('89)
Mary Steenburgen	*Melvin and Howard* ('80)
Raquel Welch	*Flareup* ('69)

THE BURLY-QUE QUEENS

"That's it, baby! When you got it, flaunt it! Flaunt it!"
—Zero Mostel, *The Producers*

Lucille Ball	*Dance, Girl, Dance* ('40)
Vivian Blaine	*Doll Face* ('45)
Joan Crawford	*Dancing Lady* ('33)
Yvonne De Carlo	*Salome, Where She Danced* ('45)

Virginia Mayo	*She's Working Her Way Through College* ('52)
Marilyn Monroe	*Ladies of the Chorus* ('49)
Helen Morgan	*Applause* ('29)
Ginger Rogers	*Once upon a Honeymoon* ('42)
Barbara Stanwyck	*Ball of Fire* ('41), *Lady of Burlesque* ('43)

THE SPECIALIZED DANCERS

"You said you wanted to dance with me the worst way, and I must
say you've kept your word. This is the worst way I've ever seen."
—Marjorie Weaver, *Young Mr. Lincoln*

Britt Ekland	*The Wicker Man* ('73)
Rhonda Fleming	*Little Egypt* ('51)
Jennifer Grey	*Dirty Dancing* ('87)
Zizi Jeanmaire	*Black Tights* ('60)
Shirley MacLaine	*Can-Can* ('60)
Vanessa Redgrave	*Isadora* ('68)

DANCING WITH FRED

"You make it with some of these chicks,
they think you gotta dance with them."
—John Travolta, *Saturday Night Fever*

The elegant ladies who made Fred's dancing feet seem so fancy.

Leslie Caron	*Daddy Long Legs* ('55)
Cyd Charisse	*The Band Wagon* ('53), *Silk Stockings* ('57)
Petula Clark	*Finian's Rainbow* ('68)
Joan Crawford	*Dancing Lady* ('33)
Judy Garland	*Easter Parade* ('48)
Rita Hayworth	*You'll Never Get Rich* ('41), *You Were Never Lovelier* ('42)
Audrey Hepburn	*Funny Face* ('57)

Betty Hutton	*Let's Dance* ('50)
Joan Leslie	*The Sky's the Limit* ('43)
Ann Miller	*Easter Parade* ('48)
Eleanor Powell	*Broadway Melody of 1940* ('40)
Jane Powell	*Royal Wedding* ('51)
Ginger Rogers	*Flying Down to Rio* ('33), *The Gay Divorcee* ('34), *Roberta* ('35), *Top Hat* ('35), *Follow the Fleet* ('36), *Swing Time* ('36), *Shall We Dance* ('37), *Carefree* ('38), *The Story of Irene and Vernon Castle* ('39), *The Barkleys of Broadway* ('49)
Vera-Ellen	*Three Little Words* ('50), *The Belle of New York* ('52)

Quick Quiz

What British prime minister's daughter once danced with Fred, and in which film?

The answer is **Sarah Churchill**, Sir Winston's daughter, in *Royal Wedding* ('51), which used the wedding of the then-Princess Elizabeth as the background against which the plot is laid.

SUICIDAL

"Maybe I could just disappear somewhere or—just kill myself."
—Carol Lynley, *Blue Denim*

They couldn't stand it anymore—and thought suicide was the only way to solve their problems.

The Cinematic Suicides

Anne Bancroft	*The Slender Thread* ('65)
Danielle Darrieux	*Mayerling* ('36)
Melinda Dillon	*Absence of Malice* ('81)
Jodie Foster	*Stealing Home* ('88)
Ruth Gordon	*Harold and Maude* ('72)
Olivia Hussey	*Romeo and Juliet* ('68)
Paula Prentiss	*What's New, Pussycat?* ('65)
Cristina Raines	*The Sentinel* ('77)
Sissy Spacek	*'Night, Mother* ('86)
Natalie Wood	*Inside Daisy Clover* ('65)

LUPE VELEZ—SUICIDE BY TOILET BOWL

Lupe Velez, better known as "the Mexican Spitfire," committed suicide on December 15, 1944. Pregnant and unable to marry, Velez's Catholicism eliminated abortion or an illegitimate birth but was not strong enough to deter her from seeing suicide as the solution to her dilemma.

To prepare for her suicide, she placed mounds of flowers and candles around her bedroom, had her hair done, dressed in a fancy new gown, and feasted on a spicy Mexican meal. At the end of her final repast, Velez downed seventy-five Seconals with a brandy chaser and climbed into bed to await the end. Several hours later, the fiery Mexican dinner upset her stomach and Velez rambled into the bathroom, regurgitating violently. In her dazed state, she managed somehow to drown herself in the toilet bowl, now filled with her vomit.

The police speculated that had Velez been sick in her own bed—instead of going to the bathroom—she probably would have survived, as she disgorged the Seconals with her dinner. If you want to see what Lupe looked like before her toilet-bowl dunking, then catch *Mexican Spitfire* ('39).

THE HOORAY FOR HOLLYWOOD AWARD

Awarded to **Peg Entwhistle**. After completing a small part in *Thirteen Women* ('32), the depressed Entwhistle climbed atop the fifty-foot H in the famed Hollywood sign and jumped to her death.

DEATH IS COLDER THAN LOVE

Caress me, stroke me, paint me, touch my cold dead body, make me look alive and beautiful again. In death, you are the restorer of my beauty . . . for thou art my lovely cosmetologist, my favorite mortician's assistant . . .

Anjanette Comer	*The Loved One* ('65)
Marianne Sagebrecht	*Sugarbaby* ('85)
Ally Sheedy	*Only the Lonely* ('91)

SWAN SONGS

"There is no place to return to when you retire from the movies."
—Geraldine Page, *Sweet Bird of Youth*

The swan song, the last legendary appearance or performance. Death caused some of these swan songs; voluntary (or involuntary) retirement was responsible for others. Because only the death-induced swan song is permanent, the possibility exists that we might see another performance. Comeback? No—as Norma Desmond phrased it, "a return, a return to the millions of fans who've never forgiven me for deserting them."

Gracie Allen	*Two Girls and a Sailor* ('44)
The Andrews Sisters	*The Road to Rio* ('47)
Annabella	*Don Juan* ('50)
Jean Arthur	*Shane* ('53)
Mary Astor	*Hush . . . Hush, Sweet Charlotte* ('65)
Pearl Bailey	*Peter Gunn* ('89)
Fay Bainter	*The Children's Hour* ('62)
Lucille Ball	*The Stone Pillow* ('85)
Tallulah Bankhead	*Die! Die! My Darling!* ('65)

Brigitte Bardot	*Ms. Don Juan* ('73)
Lynn Bari	*The Young Runaways* ('68)
Binnie Barnes	*40 Carats* ('73)
Ethel Barrymore	*Johnny Trouble* ('57)
Constance Bennett	*Madame X* ('66)
Joan Bennett	*Suspiria* ('77)
Ingrid Bergman	*A Woman Called Golda* ('82)
Betsy Blair	*A Delicate Balance* ('73)
Amanda Blake	*The Boost* ('88)
Sally Blane	*A Bullet for Joey* ('55)
Ann Blyth	*The Helen Morgan Story* ('57)
Beulah Bondi	*Tammy and the Doctor* ('63)
Shirley Booth	*Hot Spell* ('58)
Clara Bow	*Hoopla* ('33)
Alice Brady	*Young Mr. Lincoln* ('39)
Fanny Brice	*Ziegfield Follies* ('46)
Louise Brooks	*Overland Stage Raiders* ('38)
Virginia Bruce	*Strangers When We Meet* ('60)
Billie Burke	*Sergeant Rutledge* ('60)
Spring Byington	*Please Don't Eat the Daisies* ('60)
Mrs. Patrick Campbell	*Crime and Punishment* ('35)
Judy Canova	*Cannonball* ('76)
Diahann Carroll	*Claudine* ('74)
Madeleine Carroll	*The Fan* ('49)
Joan Caufield	*Pony Express Rider* ('76)
Carol Channing	*Skidoo* ('68)
Ina Claire	*Claudia* ('43)
Petula Clark	*Never Never Land* ('80)
Rosemary Clooney	*Deep in My Heart* ('54)
Claudette Colbert	*Parrish* ('61)
Joan Crawford	*Trog* ('70)

Laura Hope Crews	*The Man Who Came to Dinner* ('41)
Dorothy Dandridge	*Malaga* ('60)
Bebe Daniels	*The Lyons in Paris* ('55)
Denise Darcel	*Seven Women from Hell* ('61)
Linda Darnell	*Black Spurs* ('65)
Jane Darwell	*Mary Poppins* ('64)
Marion Davies	*Ever Since Eve* ('37)
Bette Davis	*The Wicked Stepmother* ('89)
Doris Day	*With Six You Get Eggroll* ('68)
Laraine Day	*The House of Dracula's Daughter* ('72)
Sandra Dee	*Ad Est di Marsa Matruh* ('71)
Dolores del Rio	*The Children of Sanchez* ('78)
Marlene Dietrich	*Just a Gigolo* ('79)
Marie Dressler	*Christopher Bean* ('33)
Joanne Dru	*Supersnooper* ('81)
Margaret Dumont	*What a Way to Go!* ('64)
Irene Dunne	*It Grows on Trees* ('52)
Deanna Durbin	*For the Love of Mary* ('48)
Ann Dvorak	*The Secret of Convict Lake* ('51)
Florence Eldridge	*Inherit the Wind* ('60)
Dale Evans	*Pals of the Golden West* ('51)
Edith Evans	*The Slipper and the Rose* ('76)
Frances Farmer	*The Party Crashers* ('58)
Glenda Farrell	*Tiger by the Tail* ('68)
Alice Faye	*The Magic of Lassie* ('78)
Gracie Fields	*Paris Underground* ('45)
Rhonda Fleming	*The Nude Bomb* ('80)
Joan Fontaine	*The Devil's Own* ('66)
Kay Francis	*Wife Wanted* ('46)
Greta Garbo	*Two-Faced Woman* ('41)

Ava Gardner	*Harem* ('86)
Judy Garland	*I Could Go on Singing* ('63)
Greer Garson	*The Happiest Millionaire* ('67)
Janet Gaynor	*Bernadine* ('57)
Mitzi Gaynor	*For the First Time* ('69)
Hermione Gingold	*A Little Night Music* ('78)
Lillian Gish	*The Whales of August* ('87)
Paulette Goddard	*Time of Indifference* ('64)
Ruth Gordon	*Mugsy's Girls* ('85)
Betty Grable	*How to Be Very, Very Popular* ('55)
Bonita Granville	*The Magic of Lassie* ('78)
Kathryn Grayson	*The Vagabond King* ('56)
Margaret Hamilton	*The Anderson Tapes* ('72)
Jean Harlow	*Saratoga* ('37)
Helen Hayes	*Murder with Mirrors* ('84)
Susan Hayward	*The Revengers* ('72)
Rita Hayworth	*The Wrath of God* ('72)
Sonja Henie	*Hello London* ('58)
Audrey Hepburn	*Always* ('89)
Judy Holliday	*Bells Are Ringing* ('60)
Miriam Hopkins	*The Chase* ('66)
Lena Horne	*The Wiz* ('78)
Betty Hutton	*Spring Reunion* ('57)
Gloria Jean	*The Madcaps* ('63)
Celia Johnson	*The Hostage Tower* ('80)
Ruby Keeler	*The Phynx* ('70)
Grace Kelly	*High Society* ('56)
Kay Kendall	*Once More, with Feeling* ('60)
Veronica Lake	*Flesh Feast* ('70)
Hedy Lamarr	*The Female Animal* ('58)
Dorothy Lamour	*Creepshow 2* ('87)

Elsa Lanchester	*Die Laughing* ('80)
Elissa Landi	*Corregidor* ('43)
Carole Landis	*The Noose* ('48)
Peggy Lee	*Pete Kelly's Blues* ('55)
Eva LeGallienne	*Resurrection* ('80)
Margaret Leighton	*Great Expectations* ('74)
Bea Lillie	*Thoroughly Modern Millie* ('67)
Gina Lollobrigida	*La Romana* ('88)
Carole Lombard	*To Be or Not to Be* ('42)
Myrna Loy	*Summer Solstice* ('81)
Ida Lupino	*Food of the Gods* ('76)
Diana Lynn	*The Protectors* ('70)
Jeanette MacDonald	*The Sun Comes Up* ('49)
Marjorie Main	*Friendly Persuasion* ('56)
Mae Marsh	*Donovan's Reef* ('63)
Mary Martin	*Main Street to Broadway* ('53)
Jessie Matthews	*tom thumb* ('58)
Virginia Mayo	*French Quarter* ('77)
Hattie McDaniel	*The Big Wheel* ('49)
Melina Mercouri	*A Dream of Passion* ('78)
Ann Miller	*The Great American Pastime* ('56)
Carmen Miranda	*Scared Stiff* ('53)
Marilyn Monroe	*The Misfits* ('61)
Maria Montez	*The Pirate's Revenge* ('51)
Agnes Moorehead	*Dear Dead Delilah* ('72)
Pola Negri	*The Moon-Spinners* ('64)
Merle Oberon	*Interval* ('73)
Margaret O'Brien	*Amy* ('81)
Geraldine Page	*Native Son* ('86)
Eleanor Parker	*Sunburn* ('79)
Jean Peters	*A Man Called Peter* ('55)

Mary Pickford	*Secrets* ('33)
ZaSu Pitts	*It's A Mad Mad Mad Mad World* ('63)
Eleanor Powell	*The Duchess of Idaho* ('50)
Jane Powell	*Enchanted Island* ('58)
Luise Rainer	*Hostages* ('43)
Donna Reed	*The Yellow-Headed Summer* ('74)
Thelma Ritter	*What's So Bad About Feeling Good?* ('68)
Ginger Rogers	*Harlow* ('65)
Gail Russell	*The Silent Call* ('61)
Rosalind Russell	*Mrs. Pollifax—Spy* ('71)
Ann Rutherford	*They Only Kill Their Masters* ('72)
Lizabeth Scott	*Pulp* ('72)
Norma Shearer	*Her Cardboard Lover* ('42)
Ann Sheridan	*Woman and the Hunter* ('57)
Jean Simmons	*Dominique* ('78)
Barbara Stanwyck	*The Night Walker* ('64)
Inger Stevens	*A Dream of Kings* ('69)
Gale Storm	*Woman of the North Country* ('52)
Margaret Sullavan	*No Sad Songs for Me* ('50)
Gloria Swanson	*Airport 1975* ('74)
Norma Talmadge	*DuBarry, Woman of Passion* ('30)
Shirley Temple	*A Kiss for Corliss* ('49)
Sybil Thorndike	*Uncle Vanya* ('63)
Gene Tierney	*The Pleasure Seekers* ('64)
Thelma Todd	*The Bohemian Girl* ('36)
Claire Trevor	*Kiss Me Goodbye* ('82)
Sophie Tucker	*Follow the Boys* ('44)
Lana Turner	*Bittersweet Love* ('76)
Lupe Velez	*Nana* ('44)
Ethel Waters	*The Sound and the Fury* ('59)

Mae West	*Sextette* ('78)
Esther Williams	*The Magic Fountain* ('61)
Marie Wilson	*Mr. Hobbs Takes a Vacation* ('62)
Jane Withers	*Captain Newman, M.D.* ('63)
Anna May Wong	*Portrait in Black* ('60)
Peggy Wood	*The Sound of Music* ('65)
Teresa Wright	*Somewhere in Time* ('80)
Jane Wyman	*How to Commit Marriage* ('69)
Loretta Young	*It Happens Every Thursday* ('53)

THE FORTY-FOUR-YEAR COMEBACK

Lillian Roth, whose life was portrayed by Susan Hayward in *I'll Cry Tomorrow* ('55), made a film called *Ladies They Talk About* in 1933. After that appearance, and because of personal problems with alcohol and eight unsuccessful marriages, Roth was off the screen for forty-four years, until 1977 when she returned with a small part in *Communion* ('77).

Mae West holds the Hollywood record for a major star, however. There was a thirty-five-year hiatus between her film *The Heat's On* ('43) and her next appearance in *Myra Breckenridge* ('70).

REAL DEATH SCENES

Suite 121 (bedroom), St. Francis Hotel, San Francisco—starlet **Virginia Rappe** attacked and mauled by fat Fatty Arbuckle on September 5, 1921. She died of her injuries several days later.

730 North Bedford Drive, Los Angeles—minor gangster Johnny Stompanato killed by teenaged Cheryl Crane, daughter of **Lana Turner**.

1436 South Beatty Avenue, Los Angeles—**Gail Russell** found sprawled on the living room floor, dead from alcohol abuse and liver disease.

1465 Capri Drive, Pacific Palisades—**Carole Landis** found dead in the bathroom from an overdose of Seconal and alcohol.

7944 Woodrow Wilson Drive, Hollywood Hills—**Gia Scala** found dead in her second-floor bedroom, with several bottles of medication and empty liquor bottles cluttering the room.

8000 Woodrow Wilson Drive, Hollywood Hills—**Inger Stevens** found face down on the kitchen floor, a suicide by Tedral washed down with alcohol.

8787 Shoreham Drive, Shoreham Towers, Los Angeles—Aspiring starlet **Diane Linkletter**, daughter of TV's Art Linkletter, jumps to her death, depressed over her drug and alcohol problems. The circumstances of her death have been lampooned in a most wickedly humorous short film, *The Diane Linkletter Story*, directed by John Waters and starring Divine.

10050 Cielo Drive, Beverly Hills—**Sharon Tate** and friends murdered by members of the Charles Manson family.

17531 Posetano Road, Pacific Palisades—Actress and restaurant owner **Thelma Todd** found dead under mysterious circumstances in her garage.

TEMPTRESSES

"Kiss me, my fool!"
—Theda Bara, *A Fool There Was*

The temptress entices her male victims to commit an unwise or immoral act for her benefit by promising them a reward. Naturally, the reward promised is usually the temptress herself. Could one of these tempt you into something foolish?

Louise Brooks	*Pandora's Box* ('28)
Martine Carol	*Lola Montes* ('55)
Joan Collins	*Land of the Pharaohs* ('55)
Joan Crawford	*The Women* ('39)
Jamie Lee Curtis	*A Fish Called Wanda* ('88)
Linda Darnell	*Summer Storm* ('44)
Bella Darvi	*The Egyptian* ('54)
Greta Garbo	*Mata Hari* ('32)
Paulette Goddard	*Sins of Jezebel* ('53)
Susan Hayward	*David and Bathsheba* ('51)
Rita Hayworth	*Salome* ('53)
Mariel Hemingway	*Steal the Sky* ('88)

Hedy Lamarr	*Samson and Delilah* ('49)
Jessica Lange	*The Postman Always Rings Twice* ('81)
Gina Lollobrigida	*Solomon and Sheba* ('59)
Sylvana Mangano	*Ulysses* ('55)
Melina Mercouri	*Topkapi* ('64)
Rosanna Podesta	*Helen of Troy* ('55)
Barbara Stanwyck	*Double Indemnity* ('44)
Elizabeth Taylor	*Cleopatra* ('63)
Nadja Tiller	*Portrait of a Sinner* ('59)
Lana Turner	*The Postman Always Rings Twice* ('46), *The Prodigal* ('55)
Gwen Verdon	*Damn Yankees* ('58)
Tuesday Weld	*Pretty Poison* ('68)

MOST APTLY NAMED TEMPTRESS

Jezebel Desire (**Ann-Margret**) is the ravishing voluptuous temptress in *The Cheap Detective* ('78).

BUT WERE THEY CLEAN?

In *The Blue Angel* ('30), cabaret singer-temptress **Marlene Dietrich** tosses her underpants to Emil Jannings, who first sniffs them and then sticks them in his pocket.

THE TRAGIC TEMPTRESS

Bella Darvi, whose best known role was Nefer, the Babylonian prostitute in *The Egyptian* ('54) was Polish-born Bayla Wegier. She had been incarcerated in a German concentration camp at age twelve, and attracted the attention in 1951 of cinema mogul Darryl Zanuck while he was in Paris.

Smitten with Bayla's charms, Zanuck whisked her back to Hollywood, where she was installed under the same roof as his wife. As Zanuck's protégée, Darvi—her assumed name is a combination of Darryl and his wife, Virginia—soon appeared in three films for him where her attempts at acting were widely scorned. Amid scandalous

rumors that she was sexually involved with both Zanucks, she was driven from their home and, when her 20th Century Fox contract was canceled, fled back to Europe to pursue her lust for gambling.

After her three earlier suicide attempts failed, Bella's 1971 effort succeeded. Alone and burdened with heavy gambling debts, Bella Darvi was found asphyxiated in her meager Monte Carlo apartment. Police speculated that she had been dead a week, having opened the gas jets on her stove. Ironically, Darvi's character in *The Egyptian* meets a similarly tragic fate, after a lifetime of tempting men.

Filmography:

> *Hell and High Water* ('54)
>
> *The Egyptian* ('54)
>
> *Je Suis un Sentimental* ('55)
>
> *The Racers* ('55)
>
> *Sinners of Paris* ('59)
>
> *Lipstick* ('65)

THREE OF A KIND

"Obviously, a hardened criminal. I can tell by the Kewpie-bow lips."
—Clint Eastwood, *Pink Cadillac*

Not all pirates had eye patches and peg legs; all highwaymen weren't men; and a woman can "sling" a gun as fast as a man. Want proof? Then observe any of these three types in action.

	Pirates
Glenn Close	*Hook* ('91)
Jean Peters	*Anne of the Indies* ('51)
Marie Windsor	*Hurricane Island* ('51)

Brigands

Faye Dunaway	*The Wicked Lady* ('83)
Joan Fontaine	*Frenchman's Creek* ('44)
Margaret Lockwood	*The Wicked Lady* ('45)

Gunslingers

Merry Anders	*Young Jesse James* ('60), *The Dalton Girls* ('57)
Jean Arthur	*The Plainsman* ('36)
Drew Barrymore	*Bad Girls* ('93)
Geraldine Chaplin	*Buffalo Bill and the Indians* ('76)
Lisa Davis	*The Dalton Girls* ('57)
Doris Day	*Calamity Jane* ('53)
Frances Farmer	*Badlands of Dakota* ('41)
Betty Hutton	*Annie Get Your Gun* ('50)
Isabel Jewell	*Badman's Territory* ('46)
Elizabeth Montgomery	*Belle Starr* ('80)
Jane Russell	*Montana Belle* ('52)
Barbara Stanwyck	*Annie Oakley* ('35)
Gene Tierney	*Belle Starr* ('41)
Audrey Totter	*The Woman They Almost Lynched* ('53)
Raquel Welch	*Hannie Caulder* ('72)

TRASH, PURE AND SIMPLE TRASH

"All she ever thinks about is getting honey on her muffin."
—Lorie Griffin, *Cheerleader Camp*

There's not but one way to describe this collection: trash, pure and simple trash. So low class, they can't even be called bimbos.

Michelle Bauer	*Sorority Babes in the Slimeball Bowl-O-Rama* ('88)
Sybil Danning	*They're Playing with Fire* ('84)
Claudia Jennings	*Truck Stop Women* ('74)
Jennifer Jones	*Ruby Gentry* ('52)
Diane McBain	*Claudelle Inglish* ('61)
Terry Moore	*Peyton Place* ('57)
Linnea Quigley	*Hollywood Chainsaw Hookers* ('88)
Gloria Talbot	*Taming Sutton's Gal* ('57)
Mamie Van Doren	*Girls Town* ('59)

THE I WAS REALLY HORNY AWARD

Awarded to **Jane Fonda** in *Hurry Sundown* ('67), for simulating fellatio on hubby Michael Caine's saxophone.

TWINS

"She's a phony, but she's a *real* phony. Know what I mean, kid?"
—Martin Balsam, *Breakfast at Tiffany's*

No, you're not seeing double. Twins: brought to you through the magic of trick cinematography and clever special effects. For the viewer, it's the opportunity to see two performances—from one actress—for the price of one.

Bette Davis	*Dead Ringer* ('64), *A Stolen Life* ('46)
Olivia de Havilland	*The Dark Mirror* ('46)
Zsa Zsa Gabor	*The Girl in the Kremlin* ('57)
Greta Garbo	*Two-Faced Woman* ('41)
Bonita Granville	*The Guilty* ('47)
Ann Jillian	*Killer in the Mirror* ('86)

Margot Kidder	*Sisters* ('73)
Stefanie Kramer	*Twin Sisters* ('74)
Bette Midler	*Big Business* ('88)
Hayley Mills	*The Parent Trap* ('61)
Maria Montez	*Cobra Woman* ('44)
Stefanie Powers	*Deceptions* ('85)
Martha Raye	*Keep 'Em Flying* ('41)
Rosanna Schiaffino	*The Minotaur* ('61)
Jane Seymour	*Dark Mirror* ('84)
Delia Sheppard	*Mirror Images* ('91)
Lily Tomlin	*Big Business* ('88)
Nancy Valen	*Final Embrace* ('92)
Sean Young	*A Kiss Before Dying* ('91)

THE DIONNES

Darryl F. Zanuck, 20th Century Fox studio mogul, was seized by a brilliant idea, or so he thought. Because Fox's little money-making moppet Shirley Temple was generating so much income, Zanuck believed the filmgoing public would go crazy over five identical little moppets. The two-year-old Canadian **Dionne quintuplets**—the world's first surviving quints—were screen-tested and insured for millions of dollars. They soon appeared, but only during the last ten minutes, in *The Country Doctor* ('35), which told the story of the doctor who delivered them. After two further appearances in *Reunion* ('36) and *Five of a Kind* ('37) failed to generate the box-office bonanzas Zanuck envisioned, the Dionnes' film career quietly evaporated.

The quints never left their home in Canada to make their films. All footage of them was shot there in their nursery. Their footprints even resided for a while with those of other, more famous film stars in the courtyard of Graumann's Chinese Theatre in Hollywood before being removed. How did their prints get placed in the concrete? Simple, their shoes were sent from Canada.

SEXIEST TWINS

Lee Anne and **Lynette Harris** are the gorgeous—and nude—sex surrogates in *I, the Jury* ('82).

VAMPIRES

"It's like any other business, only here the blood shows."
—Kirk Douglas, *Champion*

Lady vampires, the female bloodsuckers. Exotic, alluring, thoroughly evil. Their parted red lips carry a very special kind of kiss. Approach them at your own risk.

Jennifer Beals	*Vampire's Kiss* ('89)
Julie Carmen	*Fright Night II* ('89)
Marilyn Chambers	*Rabid* ('77)
Chantel Contouri	*Thirst* ('79)
Maryam D'Abo	*Nightlife* ('89)
Geena Davis	*Transylvania 6-5000* ('85)
Catherine Deneuve	*The Hunger* ('83)
Britt Ekland	*Beverly Hills Vamp* ('89)
Louise Fletcher	*Mamma Dracula* ('88)
Lesley Gilb	*Lady Dracula* ('73)
Mariette Hartley	*The Return of Count Yorga* ('71)
Gloria Holden	*Dracula's Daughter* ('36)
Lauren Hutton	*Once Bitten* ('85)
Grace Jones	*Vamp* ('86)
Sylvia Kristel	*Dracula's Widow* ('89)
Mathilda May	*Lifeforce* ('85)
Anne Parillaud	*Innocent Blood* ('93)
Paloma Picasso	*Immoral Tales* ('90)
Ingrid Pitt	*Countess Dracula* ('72)
Cheryl Pollack	*My Best Friend Is a Vampire* ('88)
Delphine Seyrig	*Daughters of Darkness* ('71)
Barbara Stock	*I, Desire* ('82)
Lori Sutton	*A Polish Vampire in Burbank* ('85)

Annette Vadim	*Blood and Roses* ('61)
Jenny Wright	*Near Dark* ('87)
Celeste Yarnall	*The Velvet Vampire* ('71)

VAMPIRE TWINS

Madeleine and **Mary Collins** in *Twins of Evil* ('72), who were also *Playboy*'s first twin centerfold playmates.

I LOST MY LOVE TO A VAMPIRE

In the '70s French film *The Bare-Breasted Countess* (aka *Les Avaleuses*), vampire **Lina Romay** fellates her male lovers to death. During one such sexually gory session, she bites off the penis of costar Jack Taylor.

VIRGINS AND SEMIVIRGINS

"Men are usually so bored with virgins. I'm so glad you're not."
—Maggie McNamara, *The Moon Is Blue*

Pure as snow . . . that's a virgin for you. What's a semivirgin? Why, that's a girl who tried it once or twice and didn't like it.

The Virgins	
Bibi Andersson	*The Devil's Eye* ('60)
Stockard Channing	*The Cheap Detective* ('78)
Doris Day	*Pillow Talk* ('59)
Jane Fonda	*Sunday in New York* ('63)
Nastassja Kinski	*Cat People* ('82)
Shirley MacLaine	*Ask Any Girl* ('59)
Maggie McNamara	*The Moon Is Blue* ('53)

Kristy McNichol	*Little Darlings* ('80)
Geraldine Page	*Summer and Smoke* ('61)
Sarah Patterson	*The Company of Wolves* ('84)
Mary Steenburgen	*Goin' South* ('78)
Rita Tushingham	*The Knack, and How to Get It* ('65)
Natalie Wood	*Splendor in the Grass* ('61)
Joanne Woodward	*Rachel, Rachel* ('68)

The Semivirgins

| Paula Prentiss | *What's New, Pussycat?* ('65) |
| Joanne Woodward | *A New Kind of Love* ('63) |

THE TIGHTEST CROSSED LEGS AWARD

Awarded to **Carroll Baker** in *Baby Doll* ('56), who refuses to have sex with husband Karl Malden until she turns 20, and he replaces the "five complete sets of furniture" he had bought her as part of their marriage agreement, which have been repossessed by the Ideal Pay-As-You-Go Furniture Company. The virginal Baby Doll eventually does hubby Karl out of his marital right by bestowing her charms on his business rival, Eli Wallach—who doesn't even give Baby Doll one set of furniture for her virgin's cherry.

WHORES GALORE

"OK, Johnny, you give me fifteen dollar, you get nice filthy time."
—Tsai Chin *The Virgin Soldiers*

Whores galore. The world's oldest profession . . . the female sex peddlers. Gone-wrong girls looking for a good time, as long as they're paid for it. You no pay, you no play with these chippies.

Nancy Allen	*Dressed to Kill* ('80)
Loni Anderson	*My Mother's Secret Life* ('84)
Jacqueline Bisset	*The Grasshopper* ('70)
Debbie Boone	*Sins of the Past* ('84)
Susan Clark	*Porky's* ('81)
Jill Clayburgh	*Hustling* ('75)
Joan Crawford	*Rain* ('32)
Rebecca De Mornay	*Risky Business* ('83)
Catherine Deneuve	*Belle de Jour* ('67)
Farrah Fawcett	*The Red-Light Sting* ('84)
Sally Field	*Back Roads* ('81)
Jane Fonda	*Klute* ('71)
Jodie Foster	*Taxi Driver* ('76)
Anne Francis	*Girl of the Night* ('60)
Veronica Hamel	*Sessions* ('83)
Helen Hayes	*The Sin of Madelyn Claudet* ('31)
Season Hubley	*Prettykill* ('87)
Martha Hyer	*The Carpetbaggers* ('64)
Madeline Kahn	*Paper Moon* ('73)
Nancy Kwan	*The World of Suzie Wong* ('60)
Gina Lollobrigida	*Go Naked in the World* ('61)
Shirley MacLaine	*Irma la Douce* ('63)
Jayne Mansfield	*Single Room Furnished* ('68)
Giulietta Masina	*Nights of Cabiria* ('57)
Marsha Mason	*Cinderella Liberty* ('73)
Melina Mercouri	*Never on Sunday* ('60)
Liza Minnelli	*Rent-a-Cop* ('88)
Marilyn Monroe	*O. Henry's Full House* ('52)
Kim Novak	*Kiss Me, Stupid* ('64)
Annie Potts	*Corvette Summer* ('78)
Julia Roberts	*Pretty Woman* ('90)

Theresa Russell	*Whore* ('91)
Susan Sarandon	*Pretty Baby* ('78)
Brooke Shields	*Pretty Baby* ('78)
Simone Signoret	*Madame Rosa* ('77)
Gloria Swanson	*Sadie Thompson* ('28)
Elizabeth Taylor	*Butterfield 8* ('60)
Kathleen Turner	*Crimes of Passion* ('84)
Cathy Tyson	*Mona Lisa* ('86)
Sigourney Weaver	*Half Moon Street* ('86)
Debra Winger	*Everybody Wins* ('90)
Shelley Winters	*A Patch of Blue* ('65)

WHOREHOUSE DOCUMENTARIES

What's life really like in a whorehouse? Here's some accurate depictions:

Chicken Ranch ('83)

Working Girls ('86)

YOU *CAN* LEAD A WHORE TO CULTURE

Once when challenged to use the word *horticulture* in a sentence, the tart-tongued Dorothy Parker replied, "You can lead a whore to culture, but you can't make her think." **Melina Mercouri**, best known to American audiences for her role as Illya, the light-hearted whore, in husband Jules Dassin's '60 film *Never on Sunday*, proved Parker's observation wrong. When the Socialist government came to power in her native Greece in '81, Mercouri was appointed Greece's Minister of Culture, and she served until '89. In '90, she narrowly lost a bid to become mayor of Athens.

THE BEST BLACK KILLER HO' AWARD

Awarded to **Pam Grier** for *Fort Apache, the Bronx* ('81), as a Black killer ho' who dispatches her victims with a razor blade hidden in her mouth.

THE WOMEN OF TENNESSEE

"How extravagant you are, throwing women away like that.
Someday they may be scarce."
—Claude Rains, *Casablanca*

Nobody wrote roles for women like playwright Tennessee Williams.
Fortunate were the women who translated those roles onto the
screen.

Karen Allen	*The Glass Menagerie* ('87)
Judith Anderson	*Cat on a Hot Tin Roof* ('58)
Ann-Margret	*A Streetcar Named Desire* ('84)
Mary Badham	*This Property Is Condemned* ('66)
Carroll Baker	*Baby Doll* ('56)
Beverly D'Angelo	*A Streetcar Named Desire* ('84)
Mildred Dunnock	*Baby Doll* ('56)
Jane Fonda	*Period of Adjustment* ('62)
Ava Gardner	*The Night of the Iguana* ('64)
Grayson Hall	*The Night of the Iguana* ('64)
Katharine Hepburn	*The Glass Menagerie* ('73), *Suddenly, Last Summer* ('59)
Kim Hunter	*A Streetcar Named Desire* ('51)
Deborah Kerr	*The Night of the Iguana* ('64)
Shirley Knight	*Sweet Bird of Youth* ('62)
Gertrude Lawrence	*The Glass Menagerie* ('50)
Vivien Leigh	*The Roman Spring of Mrs. Stone* ('61), *A Streetcar Named Desire* ('51)
Lotte Lenya	*The Roman Spring of Mrs. Stone* ('61)
Sue Lyon	*The Night of the Iguana* ('64)
Anna Magnani	*The Fugitive Kind* ('59), *The Rose Tattoo* ('55)
Joanna Miles	*The Glass Menagerie* ('73)

Rita Moreno	*Summer and Smoke* ('61)
Geraldine Page	*Summer and Smoke* ('61), *Sweet Bird of Youth* ('62)
Lynn Redgrave	*Last of the Mobile Hot-Shots* ('70)
Madeline Sherwood	*Cat on a Hot Tin Roof* ('58), *Sweet Bird of Youth* ('62)
Joanna Shimus	*Boom!* ('68)
Elizabeth Taylor	*Boom!* ('68), *Cat on a Hot Tin Roof* ('58), *Suddenly, Last Summer* ('59), *Sweet Bird of Youth* ('89)
Natalie Wood	*This Property Is Condemned* ('66)
Joanne Woodward	*The Fugitive Kind* ('59), *The Glass Menagerie* ('87)
Jane Wyman	*The Glass Menagerie* ('50)

YOU NEVER WERE LOVELIER

"Your eyes! Your eyes! They shine like
the pants of a blue serge suit."
—Groucho Marx, *Cocoanuts*

Shining eyes, radiant hair, enticing smile, flawless skin, trim body. Beauty is . . . beauty does. Beauty comes . . . beauty goes. Timeless beauties, one and all; truly, you never were lovelier.

Ursula Andress	*What's New, Pussycat?* ('65)
Lucille Ball	*Best Foot Forward* ('43)
Ingrid Bergman	*Notorious* ('46)
Jacqueline Bisset	*High Season* ('87)
Clara Bow	*Call Her Savage* ('32)
Capucine	*The Pink Panther* ('64)

Julie Christie	*Doctor Zhivago* ('65)
Linda Darnell	*Forever Amber* ('47)
Danielle Darrieux	*The Rage of Paris* ('38)
Bette Davis	*All About Eve* ('50)
Ava Gardner	*Mogambo* ('53)
Jean Harlow	*Red-Headed Woman* ('32)
Rita Hayworth	*Gilda* ('46)
Audrey Hepburn	*Roman Holiday* ('53)
Grace Kelly	*To Catch a Thief* ('55)
Sophia Loren	*Arabesque* ('66)
Melina Mercouri	*Topkapi* ('64)
Marilyn Monroe	*Gentlemen Prefer Blondes* ('53)
Greta Scacchi	*White Mischief* ('88)
Elke Sommer	*A Shot in the Dark* ('64)
Gene Tierney	*Leave Her to Heaven* ('45)

YES, VOYEURS, THERE IS A RULA LENSKA

In the early '80s, television commercials for a popular beauty lotion cited it "as the choice of beautiful women around the world, like International Film Star Rula Lenska." While baffled viewers tried to figure out exactly who Lenska was, catty tabloids claimed that she had no film credits to her name and was merely a figment of some ad agent's imagination. Wrong, wrong, wrong. Yes, viewers, there is a real **Rula Lenska**! She appears as the evil sorceress Morgwyn of Ravenscar in *Robin Hood: The Swords of Wayland* ('86), a BBC production available as a videotape movie, and in *Oh, Alfie!* ('75), the limp sequel to *Alfie*.

BIBLIOGRAPHY

Arce, Hector. *Gary Cooper: An Intimate Biography.* William Morrow, 1979.

Arce, Hector. *The Secret Life of Tyrone Power.* William Morrow, 1979.

Anger, Kenneth. *Hollywood Babylon.* Associated Press Professional Services, 1965.

Anger, Kenneth. *Hollywood Babylon: II.* E. P. Dutton, 1984.

Bacon, James. *Hollywood Is a Four-Letter Word.* Henry Regnery Co., 1976.

Bacon, James. *Made in Hollywood.* Contemporary Books, 1977.

Balio, Tino. *United Artists: The Company That Changed the Film Industry.* University of Wisconsin Press, 1987.

Bell-Metereau, Rebecca. *Hollywood Androgyny.* Columbia University Press, 1985.

Bergan, Ronald. *Sports in the Movies.* Proteus Books, 1982.

Brady, Frank. *Citizen Welles.* Charles Scribner's Sons, 1989.

Capote, Truman. *Answered Prayers: The Unfinished Novel.* Random House, 1987.

Capote, Truman. *Music for Chameleons.* Random House, 1980.

Castle, William. *Step Right Up: I'm Going to Scare the Pants Off America.* Putnam, 1976.

Crane, Cheryl. *Detour: A Hollywood Story.* William Morrow, 1988.

Clarke, Gerald. *Capote: A Biography.* Simon & Schuster, 1988.

Des Barres, Pamela. *I'm With the Band: Confessions of a Groupie.* Beech Tree Books, 1987.

Edwards, Michael. *In the Shadow of the King: Priscilla, Elvis and Me.* St. Martin's Press, 1988.

Eels, George. *Final Gig: The Man Behind the Murder.* Harcourt, Brace, Jovanovich, 1991.

Eels, George. *Robert Mitchum: A Biography.* Franklin Watts, 1984.

Elley, Derek. *The Epic Film: Myth and History.* Routledge & Kegan Paul, 1984.

Erens, Patricia. *The Jew in American Cinema.* Indiana University Press, 1984.

Gifford, Barry. *The Devil Thumbs a Ride.* Grove Press, 1988.

Goldman, Albert. *The Lives of John Lennon.* William Morrow, 1988.

Gordon, William A. *The Ultimate Hollywood Tour Book.* NorthRidge Books, 1992.

Haberman, J., and Jonathan Rosenblum. *Midnight Movies.* Harper & Row, 1973.

Hadleigh, Boze. *Conversations with My Elders.* St. Martin's Press, 1976.

Hardy, Phil, ed. *The Encyclopedia of Horror Movies.* Harper & Row, 1986.

Higham, Charles, and Roy Moseley. *Cary Grant: The Lonely Heart.* Harcourt, Brace, Jovanovich, 1989.

Higham, Charles. *Errol Flynn: The Untold Story.* Doubleday, 1980.

Higham, Charles. *Merchant of Dreams.* Donald I. Fine, Inc., 1993.

Kelly, Kitty. *His Way: The Unauthorized Biography of Frank Sinatra.* Bantam Books, 1986.

LaGuardia, Robert. *Monty: A Biography of Montgomery Clift.* Arbor House, 1977.

Lenne, Gerard. *Sex on the Screen: Eroticism in Film.* St. Martin's Press, 1975.

Maltin, L., ed. *Leonard Maltin's TV Movies and Video Guide.* NAL Penquin, 1988, 1989, 1990, 1991, 1992, 1993.

Malone, Michael. *Heroes of Eros.* E. P. Dutton, 1979.

McDonald, Boyd. *Cruising the Movies.* Gay Presses of New York, 1985.

Mellen, Joan. *Big Bad Wolves: Masculinity in the American Film.* Pantheon Books, 1977.

Monaco, James. *American Film Now.* New American Library, 1984.

Peary, Danny. *Guide for the Film Fanatic.* Simon & Schuster, 1986.

Phillips, Baxter. *Cut: The Unseen Cinema.* Bounty Books, 1975.

Pickard, Roy. *Who Played Who in the Movies.* Schocken Books, 1981.

Robertson, Patrick. *Guinness Film Facts & Feats.* Sterling Publishing Co., 1985.

Russell, Ken. *Altered States.* Bantam Books, 1982.

Russo, Vito. *The Celluloid Closet,* rev. ed. Harper & Row, 1987.

Rutledge, Leigh W. *The Gay Book of Lists.* Alyson Publications, 1987.

Sagin, Seth, and Philip Dray. *Hollywood Films of the '70s.* Harper & Row, 1984.

Sealy, Shirley. *The Celebrity Sex Register.* Simon & Schuster, 1982.

Siciliano, Enzo. *Pasolini.* Random House, 1982.

Spada, James. *Peter Lawford: The Man Who Kept the Secrets.* Bantam Books, 1991.

Speigel, Penina. *McQueen: Untold Story of a Bad Boy in Hollywood.* Doubleday & Co., 1986.

Stallings, Penny. *Flesh and Fantasy.* St. Martin's Press, 1978.

van Gelder, Peter. *That's Hollywood.* HarperCollins, 1990.

Wallace, Irving, et. al. *Intimate Sex Lives of Famous People.* Delacorte Press, 1981.

Waters, John. *Shock Value.* Dell Publishing Co., 1981.

Wayne, Jane Ellen. *Cooper's Women.* Prentice Hall Press, 1988.

Wood, Robin. *Hollywood: From Vietnam to Reagan.* Columbia University Press, 1986.

Yule, Andrew. *Picture Shows.* Prometheus Books, 1992.